YOU WILL PAY

Center Point
Large Print

Books are produced in the United States using U.S.-based materials

Books are printed using a revolutionary new process called THINKtech™ that lowers energy usage by 70% and increases overall quality

Books are durable and flexible because of smythe-sewing

Paper is sourced using environmentally responsible foresting methods and the paper is acid-free

Also by Lisa Jackson and available from Center Point Large Print:

Expecting to Die
Deserves to Die
Wicked Ways
Never Die Alone
After She's Gone

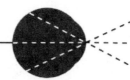

This Large Print Book carries the Seal of Approval of N.A.V.H.

YOU WILL PAY

Lisa Jackson

CENTER POINT LARGE PRINT
THORNDIKE, MAINE

This Center Point Large Print edition is published
in the year 2017 by arrangement with
Kensington Publishing Corp.

The text of this Large Print edition is unabridged.
In other aspects, this book may vary
from the original edition.
Printed in the United States of America
on permanent paper.
Set in 16-point Times New Roman type.

ISBN: 978-1-68324-432-5

Library of Congress Cataloging-in-Publication Data

Names: Jackson, Lisa, author.
Title: You will pay / Lisa Jackson.
Description: Center Point Large Print edition. | Thorndike, Maine :
Center Point Large Print, 2017.
Identifiers: LCCN 2017016519 | ISBN 9781683244325
     (hardcover : alk. paper)
Subjects: LCSH: Large type books. | GSAFD: Suspense fiction.
Classification: LCC PS3560.A223 Y684 2017 | DDC 813/.54—dc23
LC record available at https://lccn.loc.gov/2017016519

YOU WILL
PAY

Chapter 1

Cape Horseshoe
Then
Elle

So this was the end.

Her life over. At nineteen.

Elle's chin trembled. She told herself to be brave, but her courage failed her.

"God help me," she whispered, though no one could hear. Her words were lost with the rush of the wind and roar of the surf raging twenty feet below. She stood on the precipice, her bare toes curling over the edge of the rock, her heart in her throat, her pale hair whipping over her face. A storm was brewing, whitecaps frothy on the dark water, rain threatening, the air sharp and bracing.

She didn't care, barely noticed as she gathered her courage and touched her belly through the thin cotton of her nightgown.

Jump! Now! It's the only answer. You know it. It's best for you. It's best for Lucas. It's best for the baby. . . . Or was it? A new life. As yet unborn? A headache blasted behind her eyes, and doubts assailed her even as she told herself this was for the best.

Tears drizzled down her cheeks. She knew that

7

what she contemplated was madness. Yet she had no other options, no place to go, no one to trust. She closed her eyes for a second, took a deep breath of salty sea air, thought of all the might-have-beens that now were only lost dreams. Here, at this pathetic little camp on the Oregon coast, a place that was to have been an oasis, an Eden, but a place that had crumbled into the very pit of Hades.

She'd come here on the verge of summer, filled with eager anticipation, knowing she could work with children, spread the Lord's word, make that final step before college in the fall. Instead . . . Oh, God. She'd found hatred and pain, known love and rejection, discovered treachery so deep it curdled one's soul.

And she'd sinned.

Oh, Lucas. She swallowed at the thought of him. Tall, blond, with muscular shoulders, a strong jaw, and a wicked sense of humor.

She blinked against the tears and the rain, miserable and alone.

Could she do it?

Just let go and leap into the frigid, swirling waters of the Pacific? Really, was this the only answer? She teetered with the buffeting wind. Her eyes flew open and she caught her balance. She blinked but couldn't see the horizon in the darkness, felt the first drops of rain drizzle from the midnight sky.

Do it! Do it now! You have nothing to live for. Nothing!

But that wasn't true, there was—

Scritttccch!!

Though the roar of the sea was nearly deafening, she thought she heard a scraping sound, like a jagged piece of metal screaming against solid rock. The hairs on the back of her neck lifted, a warning.

She wasn't the only one here?

No way. No one in his right mind would be out here at midnight in the middle of a storm.

She hazarded a quick look over her shoulder, inland toward the rocky hillside broken only by a few contorted pines. Beyond this stony ridge, the forest of old-growth firs loomed dark and foreboding. But she was alone tonight. Right? Of course! Who besides a crazy girl with nothing to live for would be out in the woods on a slippery ledge jutting over the ocean in the middle of a storm?

Not a soul.

You're imagining things.

Rain started to pelt in earnest, splashing against the rocky escarpment, soaking through the thin fabric of her nightdress, distorting the night. She swallowed back her fear. She was alone and she would do this. She had to.

Another deep breath.

Thoughts of family and friends, scattered

pictures sliding through her mind, no memory strong enough to dissuade her, nothing permanent or secure enough to force her to grab on and find a little shred of hope.

She was lost.

Just be calm. It will all be over soon. You'll be at peace . . . you and the baby. Guilt ripped through her and she placed a comforting hand over her flat abdomen. "It's all right," she murmured to her unborn child, her voice inaudible over the keen of the wind. "We'll be fine."

Liar! You're contemplating taking your own life, as well as that of your baby. It's not fine, Elle. It's murder! She could almost hear her mother's warning, her high-pitched voice accusing and brittle on the wind. "Do this, Elle, and you'll spend eternity burning in hell. Is that what you want?"

But her mother wasn't here. She was alone. The voice she heard was only her own fear keeping her from taking that fateful, final step.

Scritttccch! She started. Turned. Wobbled. Caught her balance.

Oh, Jesus, what was that? Definitely metal, scratching hard against stone. Definitely something that shouldn't be here.

She swallowed hard.

Straining to listen, she heard nothing more. She squinted into the woods, dark and jagged, a tree line barely visible in the night. A gust of wind pressed hard against the back of her legs.

Surely there was no one, nothing, no—then she saw it, a glimmer that was out of place, a movement that went beyond the dance of branches in the storm.

Oh. God.

Her heart stilled and everything around her—the rain, the sea, the black of night—faded as she concentrated on that one area.

It's your damned imagination. Nothing more. Don't freak out. Deep breath and—Oh, crap! A dark figure appeared from the shadows, slowly advancing through the curtain of rain.

Her heart leapt to her throat.

Oh, my Lord, was that a knife? In one curled fist, something? A blade?

"No."

Fear clawed deep into her soul.

Then she recognized her tormentor! Gasped.

No. No. No.

Shaking her head involuntarily, her gaze glued on the advancing attacker, she held one hand out as if to fend off a blow. The other covered her abdomen, a protection of her unborn child. Involuntarily, she shrank backward, her heel sliding off the wet shelf.

Wait!

She wobbled, her hands flailing wildly, the bitter-cold wind swirling and pushing.

At that second, lightning flashed. In front of

her, the figure eased onto the ledge, the knife visible, a wicked, satisfied smile showing just the hint of teeth, eyes hidden in dark sockets.

Another harsh blast from the sea as she rocked crazily, the cold air whipping the hem of her sodden nightgown, slapping at the back of her head, causing wet strands of her hair to whip over her eyes. She caught herself. Balanced precariously, her feet half-on, half-off the ledge.

Suddenly she didn't want to die!

Nor did she want to snuff out the life of her baby.

No way.

Her toes tightened on the stone and she threw her weight forward. *If I go—if we go—*we're taking this fucking monster with us. But it was too late. She landed wrong, sliding on the slippery escarpment. Her gaze locked with one of pure evil. *Come on,* she thought, readying herself, *come the hell on.*

As thunder cracked, booming across the water, her assailant lunged, springing agilely, a dark demon pouncing.

Elle shifted to avoid the attack, but her feet slipped again. She slid backward. She started to tumble, tried to right herself, feet scrambling. A gloved hand grabbed hold of her just before she fell, steely fingers clenching around her wrist, preventing the fall.

What? This was her savior?

For a second her heart soared with hope, but then she felt the fingers release. She slid just a fraction, before a hand pushed her backward, propelling her over the edge, and this time there was no quick-reflex attempt to save her.

She fell, tumbling backward through the darkness, the salty sea air surrounding her as she plummeted into the sea. Just as she hit the icy water she saw the figure on the ledge, leaning over, watching vigilantly to make sure she fell to her—and her baby's—death.

Chapter 2

Camp Horseshoe
Then
Monica

She'd made a mistake.

A big mistake . . . no, make that a *colossal* mistake.

One she might not be able to fix.

Damn it all to hell, Monica thought, lying fully dressed on the cot in the cabin where she, barely nineteen herself, was in charge of eight eleven-year-olds. She had a semiprivate room, a tiny space with an open window to a larger area where the girls slept in sleeping bags tossed over canvas and wood cots straight out of the fifties. Everything about this stupid camp was beyond retro, all due to the domineering rule of Jeremiah Dalton, the preacher who owned and ran this crap hole of a summer camp. Dalton was little more than a dictator, a man who claimed to be a strict follower of Christ, but he was one of the least Christian men Monica had ever met. A tall, imposing figure with sharp eyes and strong features, Dalton had a doctorate in theology, and was so proud of it he expected everyone to call him Doctor or Reverend. Even his wife and kids. How sick was that?

Not that she could think about him now.

She had bigger, more personal problems to deal with, she thought bitterly as she stared upward to the exposed rafters that supported the pitched ceiling. Through the open windows she heard the lonesome hoot of an owl over the ever-present sound of the surf pounding the cliffs not a quarter of a mile away.

She checked her watch. Nearly midnight.

The other girls would be gathering at the cove, waiting for her. They were counselors at Camp Horseshoe as well, and bitches, every damned one of them. She hated them all and wondered why she'd even drawn any of them into her confidence, especially Bernadette. What had she been thinking? Yeah, Bernadette Alsace could keep a secret, or at least Monica hoped so, but still, she should never have confided in the athletic girl with the sharp wit and even sharper tongue. Then there was Bernadette's younger sister, Annette. How in the world had that wimpy little tattletale gotten a job here? Barely older than the campers, Annette slunk around the cabins and rec hall, her tiny ears open, listening for gossip. Truth to tell, Annette with her wide eyes and not-so-innocent smile kinda freaked Monica out.

Another freakoid bitch.

Oh, bloody hell, she had to quit thinking and get going!

She felt something inside her shift, but she could do nothing about it.

She'd been pregnant, had even given Tyler the news that, like it or not, he was going to be a father. Had secretly hoped that he would change with learning the knowledge, that he would love her and marry her. She swallowed hard. That had been two weeks ago. Now everything had changed. She'd been spotting and cramping and . . . a deep sadness yawned within her. She hadn't planned on getting pregnant.

No! Oh, God, no. Never!

But it had happened. And though she hadn't thought she'd wanted a baby—for fuck's sake, she was much too young to raise a child—she'd been disappointed at the thought of a miscarriage, her silly, romantic fantasies about a life with Tyler destroyed. He was so handsome, with his

15

thick brown hair, square jaw, and eyes the color of steel.

Virile, athletic, ready for any challenge, he was everything she'd ever wanted, she'd thought, and then the baby and then no baby and . . . Tears flooded her eyes, but she told herself it was for the best. Now, they both could go on to college and . . . and Tyler was free to marry Jo-Beth, the girl to whom he was nearly engaged. No, make that the *bitch* to whom he was almost engaged.

At that thought, Monica winced.

Cautiously she raised up and peered over the windowsill into the main area of the cabin. The bigger room was dark, faintly illuminated by one night-light. All of the cots were occupied, the girls dead asleep after a rigorous day of tending to the horses, swimming in the lake, Bible classes, and kitchen or latrine duty before an outdoor sing-along and prayer meeting.

Lights out at ten and after nearly a half hour of whispered gossip between her charges, they'd all fallen asleep. Even scaredy-cat Bonnie Branson, who was smaller than the other girls and had long blond curls that had never seen a pair of scissors, was out. She slept each night clutching a ratty, one-eyed teddy bear. The stuffed animal was forbidden, of course, no camper was to have brought any toys from home, according to camp rules per Dr. Dalton, but Monica had allowed the girl to have her stupid pink bear. If it kept the crying kid quiet and allowed her to get some sleep, who cared? Well, the other girls did, especially Kinley Marsh, who eagerly pointed out the violation and wanted to report it. Monica had warned that if any one of her charges mentioned a word of it, she wouldn't do the snake perimeter check each night and all of the girls would have to worry about timber rattlers slithering into the cabin. That was an idle threat; there were no rattlers here, near the sea, but fortunately even incredibly bookish and bright Kinley Marsh hadn't known or mentioned it. Though Kinley had seemed ready to bolt to the reverend's office, she hadn't, and the others had fallen in line, especially after Monica had promised them chocolate each night if they'd held their tongues. She'd then stolen the chocolate from the kitchen, bars meant for s'mores, and the girls had sworn to keep the secret of one-eyed teddy.

It was all such bullshit.

She did a quick head count, found all campers still sleeping, then rolled out of bed, slipped into her shoes, tied them quickly, and then with a final look over her shoulder, snagged her hoodie from a peg and shouldered open the swinging door outside to the cool of the night.

The smell of the ocean was ever present but tinged by the scent of the dying campfire, still smoldering in the pit at the center of the cabins, the few embers glowing red and casting weird shadows. For a second Monica imagined she saw someone sitting on a bench, a dark figure crouching, his head turned to stare straight at her.

Her heart leapt to her throat and she gasped, taking a step back. Squinting, she realized it was just a shovel someone had left propped against one of the seats that ringed the stone fire pit.

Jesus, Mary, and Joseph! she thought, her mother's old form of cursing running quickly through her mind. How had she mistaken a damned shovel for a person? She inched backward and cursed her wild imagination. No one knew her plans. Her own guilt was causing her to see things.

Letting out her breath, she scanned the area. Eight cabins, including the one that was her responsibility, ringed the center area of the fire pit. All were as dark as hers, no flashlight beams disturbing the umbra, no movement in the shadows, just the reddish glow from the few remaining embers. She slipped between two of the small structures to the backside of the cabins and to a path that ringed this area, where the female portion of the campers and counselors resided. Once she was past a short spur leading to the outhouses, she paused, making certain she was alone, then she broke into a jog, heading behind the last cabin and taking a path that wound through the forest and away from the barracks. Her route was circuitous, just in case she met any of the other counselors, the girls she'd agreed to meet and intended to ditch.

For now, though, she had to meet Tyler, at least one last time and tell him—

She heard voices. Whispers.

Crap! She couldn't be seen. Not by anyone.

From the sound of their voices, they were getting nearer. Monica caught sight of the thin beam of a flashlight. *Oh, shit!*

She slipped off the path, stepped on a twig that snapped loudly, then bolted to the far side of a fir tree, where she pressed her back against the rough bole and silently prayed she wouldn't be discovered.

"What was that?" a voice that she recognized as belonging to Reva Mercado whispered.

Monica's heart sank. Reva Mercado was tough and smart and blessed with a mercurial temper that Monica had witnessed more than once. Monica didn't trust her, and she sure as hell didn't like her. The flashlight beam quit bobbing, remaining steady. Footsteps halted. The thin stream of illumination swept the surrounding area as whoever was holding it attempted to find the source of the noise.

Monica tried to meld into the rough bark of the tree, to disappear. She couldn't risk the chance of them finding her when she intended to leave them all stranded. Her mind raced. What would she say if they found her hiding in the woods?

That she had to pee? Or that she'd heard them coming, seen their flashlight, and hidden because she'd thought maybe Reverend Dalton or one of his sons was on patrol?

"What?" The voice that answered belonged to Jo-Beth Chancellor.

Great. Just fucking great. Jo-Beth was a piece of work, a willowy redhead who planned to attend some fancy Ivy League school in the fall. She came from money and smelled of it; the only reason she'd agreed to be a counselor here at Camp Horseshoe was because she was in love with Tyler Quade, who'd come for the adventure of it all, to get away from his smothering parents, to taste a little freedom before he headed to Colorado State. Of course he hadn't anticipated running into the iron-fisted rule of Reverend Dalton.

Monica swallowed hard when she thought of Jo-Beth and what Monica had done behind her back.

Reva said, "Didn't you hear it?"

"Hear what?"

"I don't know. Like a cracking sound. Someone stepping on a branch, maybe?" Reva said nervously. "I think someone is out here."

Oh, God, no. No, no, no.

"We're all out here," Jo-Beth reminded her. "Because of Elle. Remember?"

"I know, but—"

"For *Elle*. That's the reason we're meeting the others," she said in an undertone that was nearly a threat, as if Reva might not have their mission clear in her head, which was odd because, if nothing else, Reva was a schemer, knew how to cover her ass.

Not so ethereal, head-in-the-clouds Elle Brady, the missing camp counselor who had been in charge of cabin 5. No one knew what had happened to her, or so they said, but everyone had a reason to lie about it. If she wasn't found soon . . .

"Don't remind me. Elle's a whackjob." Dark-eyed Reva, with her sly smile and wide eyes, had never been one to keep her opinions to herself. "I wouldn't be surprised if she jumped off Suicide Ledge in some kind of sick romantic gesture."

"Oh, God, why would she do that?"

"Because Lucas dumped her. For that bitch Bernadette." Reva seemed sure of her theory and, in truth, it sounded good. One the police might buy. Lucas was the first-born son of Reverend Dalton and the handyman of the camp. "Elle's unstable. Everyone knows it. She should never have even been considered to be a counselor."

That much was true. And Bernadette, one of the two Alsace sisters who were counselors at Camp Horseshoe, was a whole lot saner than Elle ever thought of being.

Jo-Beth didn't answer for a second and Monica

could almost hear the gears whirling in the brainiac's mind. "That sounds good," she said.

"Good? What are you talking about? What do you mean?"

"The story about her flinging herself off the ledge into the sea. We can run with it."

"In what way?" Reva asked suspiciously.

"Oh, come on. You know. We need a story, right? So that the cops won't think we had anything to do with it."

"I know, but—"

"All of us need one. Even you," Jo-Beth snapped. "The cops are coming to investigate tomorrow."

"Shit."

"So we all need to get our stories straight. And I mean everyone who's meeting us at the grotto, okay? They're coming, right?"

"Right. Jayla said she'd be there for sure."

Jayla Williams was the African-American counselor who hailed from Portland. She was supposed to have a boyfriend up there, practically engaged, apparently, but she'd obviously had a wandering eye. Monica had seen her looking over some of the male counselors and some of the workers, too.

"The klepto?"

"Yeah," Reva said.

If rumors were true, Jayla had a bad case of sticky fingers.

"And Sosi? She's not gonna bail, right?"

"She said she'd be there and I made her swear to it," Reva assured Jo-Beth.

Sosi Gavin, the pixie-like religious gymnast, had her hopes pinned on a scholarship.

"And the sisters?"

Reva snorted. "Bernadette and Annette both said they'd be there. But Nell's supposed to be staying back at the camp. She doesn't know about our plans."

"I don't care about her. Just the others."

"I worry about the sisters," Reva admitted. "Bernadette's . . . I don't know. Too much of a goody-goody, and her sister's weird, always listening in at conversations, though she pretends not to. Kind of gives me the creeps."

"Doesn't matter. We just need everyone on board!"

"Including Monica?" Reva asked with a sneer in her voice.

"Riigghht." Jo-Beth let the word linger in the air over a long pause as Monica's heartbeat soared into triple-time. "None of us are innocent now, are we?"

"But if we can help the police find Elle—"

"The police with their manpower and computers and everything. They don't need help, trust me." Jo-Beth's voice was withering.

"But if we withhold evidence—"

"We're not! Did I say that? Did I so much as suggest that we try to cover up something or . . .

or whatever? No. What I said is we just propose a theory, tell everyone how sad she was, like morose, and maybe she didn't want to go on living. And that's the truth, isn't it?"

Reva was silent. Only the sigh of the wind and the distant roar of the sea and the pounding of Monica's frantic heart disturbing the quietude of the forest.

"Isn't it?" Jo-Beth repeated as a breeze rustled through the branches overhead. God, she could be such a pushy bitch.

"I guess."

"You *know!*"

Monica imagined Jo-Beth pointing a long finger at the shorter girl's chest.

"Right?" Jo-Beth said.

"Okay. Fine. Right." Reva could hold her own. Even against Jo-Beth at her most aggressive. Reva had grown up in East LA, had only moved to Oregon to the small town of Woodburn a couple of years earlier. Wily and street-smart, Reva was beautiful, bold, and didn't back down easily.

"Good." Jo-Beth sounded satisfied. "Now. Where's the knife?" A pause.

The knife? What was she talking about?

"I forgot it."

"You what?"

"I'm sorry. I stashed it beneath a rock. I'll go get it. It's not far from here."

"Fuck!" Jo-Beth exploded.

"I said I'd get it. Hold on to your damned horses. It's just . . . wait, okay?"

"We don't have much time!"

And then there were footsteps. Reva was running away to go and get a knife? Why the hell? Monica held her breath, wished she could just sneak away. But she couldn't risk it. Not with Jo-Beth out there. The wind crept through the branches overhead, rustling the leaves, and she waited, feeling time slip away, wondering if Tyler would wait for her or give up.

"Come on, come on," Jo-Beth muttered under her breath, and for once Monica agreed with the bitch. God, she hated her.

She checked her watch. Reva had been gone for at least ten minutes, and Monica was actually considering trying to slip past Jo-Beth, who was blocking the path, risk taking off through the trees, but without a flashlight . . .

No, for now, she had to wait.

Jo-Beth was seething. Burning. Wanting to spit. To scream. But she didn't. Instead, she waited for Reva at the split in the trail near the old chapel. Jesus, where was she? If she didn't show up soon, this would all be a huge waste. How could she have forgotten the damned knife?

For this plan to come off without a hitch, the knife was critical. Reva knew that and she'd failed. *Shit!*

"Come on, come on," she said, antsy as hell, her nerves strung tight as bowstrings as she waited in the dark. Ears straining, she considered lighting a cigarette but couldn't risk it. She had so much to do and so little time.

And then there was talk of an escaped prisoner? A murderer, no less? Isn't that what Doctor Dalton or Reverend Dalton, or whatever you wanted to call the director of this camp, had said? He hadn't issued a warning, had intended to soothe any of the campers' or counselors' jittery nerves, but for Jo-Beth at least, his confirmation of the rumor that had been spreading like a wildfire stoked with gasoline had produced the opposite reaction. Now, she was more stressed than ever, paranoid even. But that was probably because of her own sick situation with her cheating boyfriend.

"Ridiculous," she muttered quietly between clenched teeth.

She didn't know who to be more pissed at, Tyler or Monica, but she decided to go with Monica because the girl was such a conniving, fake bitch. But who would have guessed that she would have crossed the line and flirted, then kissed, then made out with, then fucked Tyler? No, it was all Monica's fault. Guys were just so stupid and horny they never thought straight, so . . . she deserved everything she was going to get.

But was she really pregnant?

Tyler, that dick, had come to Jo-Beth two days earlier, before that head case Elle had disappeared. He'd pulled her aside after the flag ceremony and the final benediction of the evening, when the stars were just beginning to show and a fuchsia glow had glimmered through the trees, the remains of a brilliant sunset over the Pacific. She'd thrilled at the touch of his hand, and when he'd pulled her behind a hedge of salal and other brush, she'd actually thought he was coming to apologize, to tell her he'd made a big mistake, that he loved her and only her, and that Monica was just a slut who had turned his head, but that he was back.

Not so.

He'd been sweating and nervous and running his hands through his hair and, damn it, near tears.

"What?" she'd demanded.

Blinking hard, he'd rasped, "She's knocked up."

The knell of doom. And it echoed in her heart. "What?" she'd whispered, pretending not to comprehend as her insides turned to ice. "Who?" But before he could answer, she knew; oh, dear God in heaven, she knew. The panicked look in his eyes was more than enough to convince her, and she saw remorse on his shadowed features, but more than that he was scared to death. She'd forced out the words, "Oh, God, Tyler, what have you done?"

Sniffing and sniveling, he'd wiped his nose with the back of his hand and glanced away for a second, toward the fading sunlight. The muscles in his face worked as he tried to speak. "I . . . Jesus . . . I, oh shit, you *know* what I did. I mean, it was stupid and dumb and . . . oh, I am *so* fucked." He'd dropped into a squatting position and held his hands over his head as if he thought his brain might explode. "So fucked." With an obvious effort, he'd looked up at her, tilting his face toward the darkening sky, his big eyes shining with tears, and squeaked out, "What the fuck am I supposed to do?"

Like *she* should know. But then, hadn't it always been that way? He'd fuck up and she'd clean up? They'd been together, dating exclusively, at least on her part, since homecoming of their sophomore year and she'd always fixed things. For herself. For him. For both of them. He was, after all, the catch of the class: tall, athletic, handsome as well, and came from some money.

"This is your baby," she'd spat out. "You god-damn fix it."

"Jo, please. Help me."

The muscles in her back had tightened. "Your baby. Your problem. Take care of it!"

"I can't! Not without you."

She'd tried to walk away, to find a place to hide and bawl her eyes out, but he'd gotten to his feet, caught her wrist, and stood, drawing her to him. "You have to help me, Jo. It's you and me. It's always been you and me. You know that." In the moonlight he looked so sincere, tears causing his eyes to shimmer. "And . . . and I know I mess up. Shit, all the time. I'm so, so sorry. But it's always been us, babe." He'd brushed her hair away from her face, so damned tenderly that her heart had nearly broken. Except that it was already in pieces, shattered at the magnitude of his betrayal.

"Then how the hell did *she* get pregnant? Huh? If it's 'you and me,' why is another girl having your baby?"

"Jo—"

Smack! She'd slapped him then, so hard that her hand stung and his fists balled reflectively. "It's over, Ty. Fix your own damned problem. A *baby?* You're going to be a father? To *her* kid?" She stared at him with wide eyes and felt tears of shame and pure fury pool in her eyes. "You're on your own this time. Good luck, Daddy! You're gonna need it with that one!" She'd meant to leave, but he still held on to her wrist. His grip had been hot and like steel clamped over her arm.

"I love you," he'd whispered rawly. He'd sounded tortured, as if in physical pain.

"Then why?"

"I don't know. Jo, please . . ." Letting go of her wrist, he'd wrapped his arms around her. "Believe me. I love you. Just you."

"You prick!" Furious, she'd started hitting him then, her hands curled into fists as she pummeled his chest, wildly, her anger and embarrassment exploding. "You dumbass prick! What's wrong with you? Why did you have to fuck her? To get her pregnant? I hate you, you fucker. I *hate* you." She pounded away, intent on killing him, but as he held her, not flinching, taking blow after blow as if it were some kind of penance, she couldn't keep up the fight and collapsed against him.

"Are . . . are you sure it's yours?"

A beat. If possible, she'd crumbled even more inside. Then he'd said, "I . . . I don't know."

"You don't?"

"She told me it was mine, but . . . I don't know." He'd seemed excited, as if the cretin had never considered the possibility that someone else could have slept with the bitch and gotten her pregnant. "She does . . . she does hang out with David and Ryan, and she told me she thought Ryan was hot."

The Tremaine brothers. Sister Naomi's boys, stepsons of Dr. Dalton.

"Do . . . do you even know she's pregnant, for sure?"

Another beat. "Nooo . . . ." His breath whispered across her crown and his arms tightened around her. "But why would she say it if . . ."

Could he really be so dumb? "It happens all the

time. A girl says she's pregnant, marries the guy, and then oops, no baby."

"What? Like in a miscarriage?"

"Like in a lie, you idiot!" She'd whispered so harshly that some creature, a bird or rabbit or squirrel or who-knew-what, rustled quickly away through the undergrowth.

"You know, maybe she did lie, set me up." There was a change in his voice, an excitement, new hope. "I wouldn't put it past her."

Me neither, Jo Beth had thought, but that wasn't exactly the point. The true problem was Tyler had cheated on her.

To think that Tyler would step out on her? Jo-Beth Chancellor? She knew she was beautiful, hadn't she been asked to model? You don't get to do that unless you're slim, and beyond attractive, and she had a 4.0 plus GPA, was destined to go to Yale, and . . . and she was a goddamned genius. Make that a gorgeous, rich, sexy as hell genius, and Monica O'Neal was what? Little more than trailer trash. Oh, okay, she was kind of pretty in a slutty kind of way with big lips and big boobs, the way guys liked, but she was a nothing. A zero. Lower than a zero.

And now, the slut thought she was pregnant. Fury had burned through Jo-Beth and she'd wanted to hit, to kick, to scream at the injustice of it all. "Pull yourself together," she'd said as she'd stepped away from him and had started thinking clearly again, trying to come up with a solution to the problem. His. Not hers. And yet to let that cheap, sleazy whore fuck with Tyler's life, with Jo-Beth's life? An idiot skank who was so stupid she couldn't bother to get herself on the damned pill? No, that wouldn't do. Monica needed to be taught a lesson, or at least have the crap scared out of her but good.

"Look, baby, I'll come up with something. We'll handle it."

"You'll help?"

"Don't I always?"

Deep in her heart she knew she was a fool where he was concerned, but at that time it hadn't mattered; she just wanted to get even. Jo-Beth had never backed down from a fight and she certainly wasn't going to start now. Already a plan was forming deep in her vengeful soul. What she'd like to do, what she'd told Reva, was to wrap her fingers around that horrid bitch's throat and squeeze until Monica's eyes popped out of her pathetic little skull, but she couldn't. Smart as she was, incensed as she was, *betrayed* as she was, Jo-Beth Chancellor was into self-preservation. Already she had her mind set on law school, and no dirty little whore was going to stop her. She couldn't murder the bitch, much as she'd like to. She'd end up in jail. So, she'd figured she had to come up with something that wouldn't kill Monica, just scare the bejesus out of her. That was all.

"I knew you'd understand," Tyler had said, a bit too smugly.

"Oh, no, I do *not* understand," she'd flashed, and the loving touches to his cheek had stopped. Instead she'd scratched him. Hard. Drawing blood beneath the stubble on his cheek.

"Ouch! Stop it! *Crap,* that hurts! What's wrong with you?"

"What's wrong with me?" She'd almost laughed, but was too damned mad. "I will never understand why, when you could have me, you chose her. What the fuck is wrong with you?"

"I didn't—"

"Shut up, Tyler! Just shut the fuck up. And you'd better never do this again. Do you get it? Because, I swear to God, if you ever slam your dick into some other slut's vagi, I'll make what we're going to do to Monica look like child's play. You get it. Obviously you didn't wear a condom, right? So you could catch whatever that whore has and pass it on to me. Jesus, you're so damned stupid!"

"I just—"

"No excuses, Tyler. Either you are with me and you keep your damned cock in your pants except with me, or we're through, and I won't help you with your little 'problem.' Got it?"

His jaw had tightened and she'd seen a flare of rebellion in his eyes. Dumb as he was, he didn't like to be told what to do. But in a glimmer of self-preservation, all he'd said was, "God, I love you, babe," and she'd let most of her anger go . . . well, no, *some* of her anger, the part that had been aimed with razor-sharp intensity at Tyler. And finally, when he'd admitted his love, she'd stroked his cheek, feeling the drying blood from the scratch she'd inflicted, and seen how sexy he was. Then, trusting that he really did love her, that he'd just been a horny guy out for a good time with a whore who offered to spread her legs, Jo-Beth had refocused and all of her white-hot rage, all of her pent-up fury had been zeroed in on Monica O'Neal, the true villain here.

The Jezebel.

The seductress.

That bitch was gonna pay.

So now, here Jo-Beth was, hiding behind an old-growth Douglas fir in the middle of the night, trying to remain calm as she waited for Reva and could finally set their plans into motion.

To what end?

Revenge?

Because what you're planning is not *going to assure you of Tyler Quade's undying love and fidelity?*

Uh-huh.

Once a cheater, always a cheater.

That aggravating voice in her head was only saying what she knew to be true, much as she'd wanted to believe him. The simple truth was:

Tyler couldn't be trusted. He was a risk-taker, an extreme sports fanatic, and a daredevil; he got a rush out of pushing things to the extreme, even in sex. She'd already known that and she feared that when he sailed off to college in Colorado this coming fall, he was likely to screw a broad swath through all those supple, lean, mountain-climbing, outdoorsy, and willing coeds attending the university. It made Jo-Beth's blood boil to think about it. Stupidly she'd believed he wouldn't fuck around on her at this Christian camp, with her here, but obviously she'd been wrong, an idea she hated. She'd only come here and been a counselor because of him and the fact it would look good on her damned résumé, for God's sake.

What the hell was he thinking?

Man, she needed to light up, but she'd left her cigarettes hidden in a backpack at the cabin.

She heard the sound of approaching footsteps, saw a bobbing light through the trees, and then slipped back against a big evergreen for cover, her back pressed to the rough bark of the fir's trunk, just in case whoever was approaching wasn't Reva. The footsteps slowed and she heard heavy breathing.

"Jo-Beth?" Reva whispered raggedly.

Finally! "I'm here." Stepping from behind the tree, she found Reva, leaning down, hands on her knees as she gulped air, as if she'd run a damned

35

marathon instead of less than a quarter mile. She straightened. "We don't have much time. Sosi saw this." Straightening, she held up the knife.

Jo-Beth could have kissed her. They needed the knife, and Reva was the only person who could have swiped it from beneath Cookie's nose. That was good news. She didn't like the fact that Sosi, that wimp, had a glimmer as to what was going on. "Jesus, Reva. Why did you let her see it?"

"I didn't mean to. I literally stumbled into her in a major make-out session with Nell."

"Nell? You mean—?"

"I don't know what it was all about, and it doesn't matter, but they were into it. So, anyway, Nell took off. I don't think she saw the knife. And Sosi, blubbering and all upset that they'd been caught, was a mess, but I insisted she meet the others. That's when she saw the knife. Couldn't be avoided."

"Of course it could have been avoided. Are you a moron?"

"Hey! Don't go there. I stuck my neck out for you, remember? All because your cheating boy-friend can't keep it in his pants. So don't get on me, okay. I did what I had to and if I don't leave right away, this whole thing is going to blow up in your face." She took a menacing step forward. That was the problem with her. The girl's temper was mercurial. Calm wasn't in her vocabulary. She actually held up the knife and waggled the tip under Jo-Beth's nose.

"Oh, just calm down," Jo-Beth snapped, not worried that Reva might attack. Still, you never knew. "You just shouldn't have let her—"

"This is your party, Jo-Beth. You're the one who's supposed to be so damned smart," Reva said. "You figure it out, okay? I stuck my neck out for you, so you fix the problem. This was all your idea." She held the knife up and the blade caught in a bit of moonlight. "Handle it."

"Fine. Go back. Tell them I was delayed. I was sick. In the latrine. No, no, my period, that's it. Cramps. But . . . but . . . I'll be there about five, maybe ten minutes after you."

"And if you're not back right away?"

"Wait for me."

"How long?"

Good question. God, please let nothing go wrong. "Half an hour tops."

"And then?"

"Go with the plan. You tell everyone what they're supposed to say about Elle."

Reva said, "They'll ask about Monica."

"Shit, figure it out!" She had to get going. Couldn't *any*one in this camp do anything without her?

"The tide is going to start to come in."

"I know!"

"I just need to know what to do. You know,

alternate plan B in case you don't show up."

"I told you and don't worry about it, okay. I'll be there! I have more at stake here than anyone. If . . . if I'm not there in half an hour, then something went very, very wrong." She didn't want to think what that might be.

Reva's eyes glinted. "Then let's not let that happen, okay?" She brandished the knife as if she'd done it a thousand times, then handed the weapon to Jo-Beth. "I need that back. Tonight. So I can put it back. Otherwise Cookie's going to be all over me."

"I know, I know." Jo-Beth checked her watch. Shit! She was running late.

"Let's do this," Reva said.

Chapter 3

Camp Horseshoe
Then
Monica

Just leave. Sweating nervously despite the cool night breeze, Monica felt the seconds of the night ticking away.

Jo-Beth seemed to answer her prayers. "Okay, let's go. We've all got to work together to pull this off! We're running out of time."

"Yeah, yeah, okay." Reva didn't sound convinced, but went along, their footsteps fading, the flashlight's beam becoming fainter.

Monica let out the breath she'd been holding and sagged against the tree. *Pull* what *off?* Not that it mattered. Not tonight, anyway. Thank God they were more interested in putting together their stories about what they all were doing when Elle disappeared than investigating the noise they'd heard on the path. Good.

For a split second Monica wondered about Elle, what had really happened to the girl, but she put that thought quickly out of her mind. She would probably turn up. The police would find her . . . right?

Now, Monica felt the pressure of time. She had her own problems and already she was late. But she waited. Caught her breath, had to make sure they were completely gone. She was really late. Tyler might not even wait for her. Quietly, every nerve strung tight, she slipped onto the path again, then took off at a dead run.

She couldn't help thinking of the other counselors, her peers. But they weren't her friends. Never her friends. Monica saw the counselors more like convicts forced to be together and interact in a prison, the warden being Reverend Dalton. There were nine female counselors in all, if you counted the missing Elle, and, except for herself, Monica despised each and every one of them.

As she jogged through the forest, the rush of

the ocean in her ears, the smell of the sea permeating the darkened landscape, the moon offering a weak stream of light, acid curled through her stomach. Her feet pounding along the ever-rising path, she set her jaw and ignored the guilt that had become her ever-present companion.

The plan that Reva and Jo-Beth had discussed was that the female counselors had agreed to sneak out and meet at the cavern to discuss what had happened to Elle, the ninth "Sister," as Reverend Dalton had referred to them. Not as "Miss" or even "Ms.," but as "Sister." Even his tiny little wife, Naomi, referred to them all as Sister Whatever. She was Sister Monica, like some old nun or something. It was weird. Demeaning. Monica hated it.

Just a few more days—less than a week, then you'll be out of here.

That thought was bittersweet.

Because of Tyler.

Her heart cracked a little when she thought of him. And what Jo-Beth would do to her if she ever guessed. She couldn't think of that now, because it didn't matter anymore. She loved Tyler, she did. She didn't just flirt and hook up with him to get back at that horrid, snooty, rich bitch Jo-Beth.

Or did she?

No! No way!

Still, it sure would have been better if Jo-Beth had been the girl who'd gone missing instead of that waiflike weirdo Elle. Better yet if Jo-Beth would just keel over and die. What a snobby bitch. All because she'd been born with money, the same as Tyler. It just wasn't fair.

And why the hell did she need a knife tonight? For the meeting? It didn't make sense, and it worried Monica. Jo-Beth just wasn't that stable. What was it they said about the super-smart ones? The geniuses? That they were just a few degrees off of being crazy. Well, that made sense. In Monica's estimation Jo-Beth was as close to a psychopath as she'd ever want to meet.

Don't think about her now. Just get there!

Monica pushed herself, taking a more circuitous path to avoid anyone else, as all the female counselors except for Nell, as she was too young, were supposed to meet. She couldn't chance another encounter. She paused once to get her bearings, thought she heard someone on the trail behind her and, more on edge than ever, looked over her shoulder, but saw nothing. Just her damned nerves again. As she crested a hill she noticed the trees gave way to open headland. Here, the path split, one fork doubling back a bit to angle down the hillside to the sea and the cavern where the others, Jo-Beth and her "bestie" Reva and the rest of them, were waiting. Running, Monica considered them all: Bernadette and her wimp of a sister, Annette, along with doe-eyed, know-it-all Sosi, as well as Jayla, a girl from Portland whom she didn't really know other than that Jayla was originally from Southern California, now lived in Portland somewhere, and was heading to some Christian college on a scholarship . . . and might be a kleptomaniac, if rumors could be believed. But she was friends with the others, so Monica didn't trust her.

Jo-Beth, of course, was the worst of the sorry lot, a girl Monica would never have chosen as a friend, but now, now . . .

Her mouth went dry and her stomach twisted at the thought that she and the others were not just a group of teens who'd been tossed together as camp counselors anymore. Now they were so much more, inextricably bound together, and she was with these bitches, all of whom had so much more in life than she did. Because of what they had done, what they *all* had done, the lie they'd spun.

You're as guilty as the others.

Elle is missing and it's your fault.

And, admit it, deep in your heart, you know she's dead.

For all of a nanosecond she thought about the girl, Elle, waifish and ethereal in life and now . . . possibly, no, probably no longer living, a spirit . . .

Stop it! You can't bring her back now,

42

can you? Can't undo what you so willingly did.

"Oh, shut up!" she hissed, her voice drowned by the surf as she noticed the fog rolling steadily inland, wispy fingers crawling along the underbrush.

Monica bit her lip, didn't want to think of the horrid deed that ensured for the rest of her life she was inextricably chained to the girls she despised. Their secrets and lies would bind them until the end of time.

"Shit," she whispered, and continued along the ridge of a wind-sculpted dune to an area where the trail wound slightly downward in a ragged loop toward the camp. "Shit, shit, shit!" One foot slipped a little and she caught herself, then forced herself to jog more carefully as her eyes scoured the gloom. Around a wide curve in the path she spied a boulder protruding from the ground, its massive form marking a spur in the trail, where another pathway, now overgrown, once used and now nearly forgotten, had wound toward the ridge.

She turned and followed the path as it turned inland.

Here, the beach grass grew heavy between the twisted trunks while native salal rose in towering clumps, encroaching on the trail. Brambles and berry vines clutched at her bare legs, scratching and scraping the skin, while, as she ran, small, dry pinecones crunched beneath the soles of her running shoes. To ensure that she was on the right path, she pulled a small flashlight from her pocket, risked shining the beam on the uneven ground, then snapped it off and tucked it away.

Inside her mind a clock was ticking away. She would be late. The others—the bitches—were probably even now wondering if she was going to show, if something had happened to her, or if she was just standing them up.

Too bad. She had something she had to do, something important. Something . . . life-changing. She just had to—

Her foot caught on a root and she tumbled forward. Her arms flew out as she hit the ground, half catching herself but twisting an ankle and going down on all fours, scraping her knees. "Nooo," she cried. "Oh, ow! Damn it!" She sucked in her breath through her teeth with the pain.

Rolling onto her back, she held her knees to her chest and winced as she tested her ankle, rotating it gingerly and feeling as if God, or the Fates, or whatever the hell supreme being was supposed to be watching, had just turned His, Her, or Its back on her.

You're on your own, Monica, but then you always have been. You can't rely on anyone. Not your parents, with your wacko mother and drunk of a father who can't hold a job. Certainly not Tyler, and certainly not God.

Pain throbbed, but she rolled onto her rear, dug out the flashlight, and shined its tiny beam over her lower legs. Tiny droplets of blood showed on her knees where raspberries bloomed, but she'd live.

Wincing, she tried moving her ankle again, decided it wasn't broken or severely sprained, just tweaked, so she gingerly climbed to her feet and turned off the flashlight. She didn't have time for any distractions or delays. Starting out again, she was more careful, still half jogging, half limping, but cognizant of the rocks and roots that could trip her.

Tyler.

Would he be waiting?

She let out her breath in a heavy sigh. She'd fallen for him. So hard. So fast. With such wild abandon that she'd been mad with lust for him and hadn't cared about the fact that he wasn't exactly available.

Oh, fuck it. That was all in the past.

Right?

After the last time they'd met, when she'd given him the news and he'd been stunned, she now half expected that he wouldn't show. Absently she rubbed her flat abdomen and thought about what lay within, beneath the layers of skin and muscle. Tears threatened her eyes, but she steadfastly pushed them back as the grass tickled her calves and she nearly tripped again, this time over a fallen log, but somehow managed to leap across it and land softly on the far side.

She'd been a fool. A silly, lovesick fool. For a heartbeat she thought again of a new deception, of not telling him the truth, of hoping to continue seeing him and getting pregnant all over again. So what if the baby just happened to be born a few months later than originally planned? By that time, Ty wouldn't care and . . . Or better yet, she wouldn't admit it. She could elope with Ty, and later, once they were married, lose the baby. She cringed inwardly at the thought, but she certainly wouldn't be the first one to trick a guy into marriage. And then . . . and then . . . he would fall so far into love with her that he'd never want to leave her. This marriage to Ty was her ticket to a better life, one like all the other bitches took for granted. They didn't understand or couldn't. And she hadn't told them, never admitted that her mother was a waitress trying to make ends meet while her father, a hard-drinking Irishman, was as busy chasing skirts as he was construction jobs. No, she'd never say as much. And she'd thought she wouldn't have to because of the baby. For a few short weeks she'd dreamed that she'd transform from poor-as-dirt Monica O'Neal to become Mrs. Tyler Quade and—

Oh, who was she kidding?

It was too late. The camp was closing for the summer, the closure sped up by the disappearance of pain-in-the-ass Elle.

Setting her jaw, she kept forging ahead. She

rounded a final corner and spied a clearing, or what once had been a clearing. Now, the grassy area was choked with weeds and brush, branches and drying leaves visible in the moonlight. Beyond the clearing, where once there had been a flagpole, was the sole building, a dilapidated structure that had once been a chapel, but now . . . now had become their trysting spot, the place where she'd meet Tyler.

Trysting spot? Seriously? Are you that deluded? You mean fucking place, don't you? Because that's what it is, a nearly decrepit building that's rotting away, a hideout where you can screw Tyler's brains out, all behind his bitch of a fiancée's back. You came to this place with the intent of fucking him, and possibly or maybe even probably you figured you might get pregnant, even secretly hoped that it would be so. Right? In the back of your mind, you knew this might happen. Trysting spot? Oh, my God. Get a grip, Monica. Quit romanticizing it. What's wrong with you? Call it what it is, for crying out loud!

She turned away from the nagging voice and stepped around the clearing to what had once been a wide porch but now listed, the floorboards rotting, the gutters falling away.

Would he be inside?

Waiting?

Thump!

She jumped at the sound and whipped her head around.

What the hell was that?

Her heart started jackhammering.

Was someone out here? Some*thing?* Some kind of wild animal? What? Deer? Elk? Cougar? Maybe just a skunk or rabbit or . . .

Ears straining over her drumming heart, she held her breath but heard nothing more over the rush of the wind and the dull roaring of the surf. She stared into the surrounding forest, where wind-twisted trunks and spreading branches ringed the clearing in front of the abandoned chapel. Half a century ago, before the newer structure had been built closer to the other buildings of the campground, this had been the designated place of worship, the chapel in the woods.

She saw no one.

No dark figure moving stealthily in the shadows.

No wild creature prowling through the trees.

Not one thing.

Whatever had made the noise was either gone, skulking off into the woods, or . . . silently watching and waiting.

Waiting for what? You're letting your paranoia and your guilt get to you.

It's nothing. Just your ridiculous imagination. Now, get on with it.

Despite her rationalization, Monica's skin was

still prickling as she skirted the open area, keeping close to the edge of the woods as if unseen eyes were tracking her. Then, telling herself she was an idiot, she sprinted across a stretch of silvery dry dune grass and onto the sagging porch.

Her shoes scraped against the sandy boards as she reached the double doors and tried one of the handles. The door fell open, squeaking as if in protest, but luring her into the even darker interior.

"Tyler?" she whispered, crossing the threshold and hearing the whistle of the wind through the rotting roof. The interior smelled of moist earth, rot, and mold, the floor soft. "Ty?"

No response.

She yanked the door shut behind her.

Swallowed hard.

As her eyes adjusted to the darkness, she focused on the wall behind the altar, where a tall stained-glass window rose to the ceiling. The curved top of the panes were tucked high under the rafters, but the window itself stretched nearly to the floor. A few of the panes were missing or cracked, but for the most part, the window was intact. Tonight moonlight slanted through the colored panes of a weeping Mother Mary.

Monica couldn't make out the Madonna's features in the gloom, but she remembered them from the lazy afternoons or early twilight hours when she and Tyler had sneaked to this quiet, nearly forgotten church.

"Ty?" she called again, moving slowly through the broken pews, toward the crumbling altar. "Are you here?"

What a stupid question. Obviously, if he were here, he would answer.

Nothing but the whistle of the wind.

He'd stood her up? Or had he been the noise in the woods? Was he playing with her? Hiding in the shadows? Ready to leap out at her and scare the living hell out of her?

"If this is a game, it isn't funny," she said. She listened hard and *felt* as if she wasn't alone. She couldn't see anyone, didn't smell or hear anything that would suggest someone was nearby, but she *sensed* a presence. "Ty?" she whispered, his name sounding tremulous. She licked her lips. Nerves tight as bowstrings, she rotated slightly, peering into the umbra. From the corner of her eye she caught a glimpse of a shadow, a fleeting darkness skittering across the colored panes of the window.

Oh, Jesus.

Her heart nearly stopped. "Ty?" she whispered again, and licked her lips. She was suddenly sweating, and she could barely breathe as she made her way up the aisle between the pews. Like a damned bride on the way to the altar, ready to pledge her life, her love to her groom. For a split second she envisioned it all, a real wedding, complete with Tyler standing at the altar near the preacher. Wearing a tux and his trademark cocky grin, he would watch her entrance and tears of joy would fill his eyes.

But now, in this moldering chapel, her fantasy withered and died just as had the fragile little life she'd so recently carried. Her throat grew thick with tears, but she shrugged off the case of the blues over what might have been.

"I'm not kidding," she said to the still air. "If you're here, Ty, we really need to talk. I have to tell you that—"

The toe of her running shoe hit something hard that protruded into the walkway. She nearly stumbled, only catching herself by grabbing the back of a rotting pew. "What the—?" The rest of the aisle had been clear, but . . . She peered down at her feet but couldn't make out the obstruction, then found her flashlight again and flicked it on, shining the beam on the floor.

She was looking at a bare foot. A scream erupted from her throat as she quickly shone the light up the tanned, bare leg past the man's limp dick and upward across a naked torso and neck to Ty's face, his eyes fixed as if staring at the rotting ceiling over the Madonna.

"Noooo!" she shrieked, dropping the flashlight, her stomach lurching. "No, no . . . Oh, God, no!" Hyperventilating, her gaze fastened to the still form, she backed up, her rubbery legs threatening to buckle.

Get ahold of yourself. He may not be dead. You have to check! Don't be a coward.

But he was gone, she knew it, her fears confirmed by the dark red stain spreading beneath him. Oh, God, oh, God, *oh, God!*

Shaking, she forced herself forward, inching toward his beautiful body. "Ty," she whispered. "Ty . . ." She fell to the uneven floorboards and eased between the pews where his body was wedged. His flesh was still warm.

This wasn't happening! No way! Not to Ty. It had to be a dream—a fucking nightmare. That was it. Shaking, she touched his chest, springy hair beneath her fingertips. "Oh, God, Ty, please, please . . . don't be . . . don't let this . . ." Her voice broke and she pushed her head closer to his, resting her ear to next to his nose, silently praying for any indication of breath. Was there just a whisper of air coming through his nostrils? She squeezed her eyes shut, her scraped knee wet with his blood.

Surely there was just the hint of a rasp, just a bit of air flowing? *Please, God . . . please!*

"Ty," she said next to his lips, but there was no response. Nothing. And the air she'd thought she'd heard escaping from his lungs ceased to exist. "Come on. Come on." The blood was flowing slowly, so surely his heart was still pumping.

Right? Wasn't that what she'd been taught at that first-aid course? Or was it running because of gravity? Sliding on the listing floor. "Ty, it's me, Monica!" She placed her fingers at his neck, searching for any sign of pulse, but he lay still. Unmoving. And she couldn't find a damned pulse.

No! No, no, no!

He was gone . . . Dead. Never knowing that he wasn't going to be a father.

The knife. Jo-Beth. Oh. God. No.

Fear coiled within her. She thought she might throw up. *Ty! Oh, Ty!* She had to go, to get help, maybe an ambulance, though she knew deep in her heart it was too late.

"I'm so, so sorry," she murmured, and tears welled in her eyes.

How had this happened? Why?

You know why. Jo-Beth found out. She came here with the damned knife and killed him. Oh, dear Christ . . .

Should she roll him over? Try to staunch the blood, or just leave and tell someone that—

Scraaaape!

Her head whipped up.

What the hell was that?

The noise sounded close. *Inside.*

Her heart flew to her throat.

Fear spurted through her blood.

Friend or foe?

Hands on the back of the pew, she pulled herself to her feet. "Who's there?" she demanded anxiously, ready to sprint out of this place.

"Monica," a voice whispered from the shadows, from somewhere at the back of the chapel. Her skin crawled. Was there a smile, a sound of satisfaction in the low rumble? "I knew you'd come."

Chapter 4

Cape Horseshoe
Now
Lucas

Caleb Carter didn't believe in rules. In fact, he considered anyone who followed a damned rule to be a gutless pansy-ass. And that went double for laws about huntin' and fishin' and livin' off the damned land. The Federal government? Bunch of city-slicker, bureaucratic know-nothings in Washington, D.C., most of whom had never set foot in the goddamned wild, never lifted a .22 to a shoulder, never hoisted a crab pot over the side of a bridge, and damned well had never taken down a bull elk, much less dressed it and hauled it out of the woods.

Pansy-asses.

Damned politicians knew nothin'. Not about

his life. Not about livin' off the grid. Not about the West, for Christ's sake. Pissed him off. And the fact that the little town he'd grown up in, Averille, had grown to the point that it had a goddamned McDonald's, as well as the damned sheriff's department, really chapped his hide. Of course there had always been the law, being the county seat and all, but hell, the department, as well as the town, had grown over the course of his lifetime too much. Too damned much. How many real-estate offices, insurance companies, and goddamned coffee shops did one town need? Fuckin' yuppies with their fancy flavored lattes and the like? Sheeit, it burned his butt. He never figured the town for a boom, it bein' inland from the ocean about five miles, but when all the sawmills and logging operations took off again, not only the millers and the loggers returned, guys who pulled green chains and set chokers, but their fancy-ass counterparts, engineers and lawyers and accountants and such, came right along with 'em, growing the damned town and the county.

Worse yet, folks were markin' their property and fencin' it off, so as no one could hunt or fish on it. Who the hell did they think they were? God made this earth filled with plenty to be harvested, and Caleb got down on his knees every night, his rifle on the bed, as he prayed and thanked the Good Lord for all of the bounty.

Despite those who would want to take it from him.

Wasn't the U. S. of A. supposed to be for the men who were citizens? Isn't that what all the great forefathers had planned for? Sure it was, and no one was gonna take away Caleb's way of life, not with any stupid sign bought at the local lumber yard and posted on a damned tree trunk.

No siree.

Angrily, he spat on the ground, sent a great spurt of tobacco juice into the nettles and berry vines that lined the path down to the cove, a secret spot where he harvested clams, in season or out of season, paying no attention to taking a "limit." Sheeit, no.

Along with his shovel and backpack, he carried his .30-06, complete with scope, just in case he saw a blacktail on his way through the forest to the beach and the sandy strip leading to the cove. This time in the morning, no tellin' what you might find. So, yeah, you weren't allowed to kill a doe and it wasn't quite elk season yet, but who would be the wiser? And dates and seasons, made by some asshole in the wildlife department in Salem, meant nothing to him. And some law about not being able to hunt between the coast highway and the sea—was that even a thing? Who cared?

Along the sandy path, hearing the echoing roar of the sea, he hiked downward and saw no game, nothing that would fill the freezer for the winter as the forest gave way to a tangle of driftwood lying fifteen feet thick at the base of the hill. He crossed it quickly, glanced out at the ocean on this, a foggy October morning just before dawn. He felt the spray of the sea, smelled the salt in the water, and felt energized. This here was God's country. No doubt about it. And it was pretty much his own private hunting grounds, what with all the ridiculous legal restrictions and the rumors that the area was haunted by some gal who took a dive off of Suicide Ledge twenty years ago and died. Some people claimed her ghost still walked on this stretch of beach, never leaving foot-prints, mind you. She was, after all, a ghost.

Bunch of hooey. Same with that damned story about a prisoner who got loose a couple of decades ago, a murderer no less, and was said to have been spotted in the woods. Around here. Sometimes carrying a bloody butcher knife, other times a machete—there was even a variation where he was hauling a severed and bloody head.

Caleb snorted at the thought.

Damned teenagers, drunk or high, makin' shit up. But the scary stories worked.

Saved the hunting grounds for him.

Caleb figured he was just lucky to have been born around here, coming into the world in a tiny hospital thirty miles to the north. Or unlucky, whichever way you saw it. Caleb preferred to think that it was a blessing to have grown up in an area where game and freedom were for those who took it, but the downside had always been his father, a binge drinker who, when sober, was a fine, upstanding Christian man, but when drunk let his fists do his talking. Caleb had learned "respect" the hard way.

But he didn't think about his daddy now. The old man had died of liver cancer over a decade earlier, gone home to see if Saint Peter would let him through the pearly gates or if, as Caleb believed, Satan had received the son of a bitch in hell. Either way, it didn't matter.

Dawn was just beginning to erupt over the steep hillside, the sky lightening, small wisps of fog drifting in from the ocean to crawl across the sandy stretch of secluded beach leading to the cove. His were the first footprints breaking the smooth sand, maybe the only footsteps all day.

He made his way to the water's edge, spied a clam hole, slung his rifle over his back, and began to dig, quickly, the blade edge of his shovel honed sharp. Around the hole he worked furiously, then dropped to his knees just as the tide raced inland and an icy inch of water splashed around him.

He felt the clam's shell, pinched it with his fingers, and dragged the bivalve out of the sand. The foot was still digging, a white protrusion moving in and out of the golden shell. "Gotcha," he said, and, still clamping the clam with both fingers, washed it in the receding tide, then tossed it into his pack. He climbed to his feet and spied another hole, dropped to his knees again, and repeated the process. This area, known only to a few—hell, maybe only to him—on private land was his own personal clam bed, and he could almost taste the fried razor clams as he pulled one long-necked bivalve after another from the sand, the sucking noise of the vacuum left by the clam as he yanked it from the shore music to his ears.

By the time the sun chased away the fog as it crested over the ridge, he'd harvested fifteen of the buggers and had inched his way to the cavern at the far end of the cove. Here the sea raced inward, rushing and roaring through this deep niche that time and the surf had carved into the rock. He saw another clam hole beneath the ledge protruding over this protected space, and he grabbed his shovel one last time, forcing the blade into the sand, digging a ring, and then falling to his knees just as the surf returned. Inside the cavern the noise was deafening as he reached his hand and arm deep into the hole he'd created, felt the edge of the shell, and grabbed hold. He pulled and nothing happened, then tried harder, gritting his teeth and wondering just how big the damned thing was. He yanked hard as the frigid water swirled around him, pulled with all his strength until with a great *whoosh* the shell wrenched free. He nearly fell back on his ass as he hauled the thing to the surface and surveyed his prize, only to drop it as if it had burned him.

He'd found no clam beneath the surface.

No siree.

And he felt his heart stutter as he bent over to look at it more closely.

Sure enough, what he'd dragged from its hiding place was a jawbone, bleached white, free of flesh. And not of some marine creature, no way, he decided, examining the teeth and spying a silver filling visible in a back molar.

No doubt about it: This bone was part of a human skull.

A skitter of fear crawled up the back of his neck on spidery legs. He'd heard stories, of course, of dead men and ghosts that had inhabited this area of the cape, but he'd discounted them as the stuff of boyhood tales meant to scare the piss out of friends, but now, as the sea roared around him, echoing through the cave, he stared at the jawbone of a very dead human and wondered. He backed up, dropped the bone, and made fast tracks up along the hillside.

"Goddamn . . ."

Hell, he'd probably have to tell someone, but first he'd climb up to the ridge and have himself a smoke. Didn't want to appear a pantywaist. Not even to that dick Lucas Dalton, well, especially not to him, but he was the law around these parts and they'd known each other for years.

"Shit," he said as he made his way up to the ridge and found a fallen log to drop onto. He'd have to stash the clams, of course. Maybe take them back to his house first. His fingers shook as he pulled a Winston from a crumpled pack and lit up. Taking a huge lungful of smoke deep into his lungs, he felt a little better, calmer as the nicotine began to make its way into his blood-stream.

No reason to hurry. Not now. Not with the tide turning soon. The cove would soon be under-water again, the damned jawbone hauled out to sea. He could keep his mouth shut and no one would be the wiser.

Another long drag and as he expelled a geyser of smoke toward the heavens, he thought of his mama, the damned church organist who never missed a Sunday service or a Wednesday Bible study meeting. She was dead now, of course, but he could still hear her shrill, tinny voice, just as loudly as if she were still standing at the kitchen stove, her back to him as she turned the fish in the pan, the hot oil sizzling in the tiny room, amping up the already soaring temperature another five or ten degrees. She'd been a tall woman. Rangy. With angular features and hair, until the cancer treatments, a deep red color in stark contrast to her knowing blue eyes.

"God sees all, Caleb," she'd said, forking the trout in the frying pan. Oil bubbled noisily and

61

the fish's scales glittered as the flesh seared. "And he forgives most, the little things, y'know? He don't care when your pa bags a deer out of season or takes down an elk to feed the family. No siree. That's not the good Lord's concern. But when you lie, or you cheat, or you break one of the commandments?" She would turn her head just a bit, to glance over her shoulder, the short curls that had escaped the pins holding her hair onto her head wet with sweat. "Then He gets interested. Real interested." He could see her lift her fork and shake it. "And He don't forget. So mind yerself. Do what's right in yer heart and you'll be okay." As the fish fried, she would pick up the cigarette that had been burning in the ashtray on the counter and suck hard on her Pall Mall 100. "He's watchin', Caleb. He's always watchin', so you do what's right. Y'hear?"

And he had. Okay, so he'd bent a few rules here and there, and maybe hadn't been on the straight and narrow with *all* of the commandments *all* of the time, but today, he figured, he'd better not mess around. Do the right thing.

Even though he hated Lucas fuckin' Dalton.

Twelve hours?

The son of a bitch had waited *twelve hours* before reporting that he'd found the remains of a human at the cove? *If* that's what Caleb had actually stumbled across. Who knew?

Lucas Dalton's fingers curled around the steering wheel of his Jeep Renegade in a death grip, his knuckles showing white, his mind spinning faster than the blur of landscape flying by as he trod on the accelerator. There was more at stake here than what met the eye. If Caleb wasn't lying, if he'd actually found human remains down at the cove, then life for Lucas was about to take a sharp turn and veer off his carefully planned path.

Was it possible? Had that damned poacher actually discovered a well-hidden secret, one the sea had kept to itself for twenty years? He glanced at his reflection in the rearview mirror of his county-owned vehicle.

Accusing hazel eyes glared back at him.

You knew this day was coming, Dalton, didn't you? The day of reckoning? The intricate fabrication that you planned and created about to be destroyed? But you just didn't expect it would come in the form of some bad cell phone connection from a moron like Carter, right? You should have been prepared, should have realized that God is known to have a wicked sense of humor.

His jaw tightened and he turned his attention to the strip of asphalt that was the county road, then eased up on the accelerator as he realized how fast he was traveling, how quickly the faded and broken center line was blurring past, the wet leaves and standing water flying from beneath his tires. No reason to panic.

At least not yet.

Not until he knew exactly what Carter had found, if he'd found anything. More times than he could count he'd walked into the local jailhouse and found Carter sleeping it off in the drunk tank with reports from the officer on duty that the man had tied a fierce one on, so much so that he'd been talking nonsense. Ranting and raving and completely out of it.

Maybe . . . but nah, the phone call from Caleb had been indistinct and broken, but from what Dalton could tell, he'd sounded sober. And scared.

"Hell," Dalton muttered, slowing the Renegade, his gaze focused on the familiar terrain as he discovered the barely visible lane that cut from the county road to the campground situated near the cape. A real-estate sign marked the entrance, a reminder that his father was selling the place, which was odd, Lucas reflected. He remembered how once, a long time ago, when Jeremiah had first married Naomi, how excited he'd been. Finally, the reverend had told his son, he would be able to rebuild this old camp into a new, vibrant source of worship for the Lord, a refuge for the lost, a school for those who wanted to be educated in the ways of Jesus, a place where Jeremiah and Naomi could nestle in with their blended family and be a beacon for those in need.

And now, years later, after an ugly divorce, the place was up for sale.

Lucas turned into the old lane and pushed aside thoughts of the past to concentrate on the here and now and Caleb Carter's story. Even sober, Carter wasn't exactly reliable. Lucas had known the man since the second grade when Caleb, who'd had ten pounds and five inches on Lucas, had clocked Lucas with a hardball at recess. Knocked him out. Laughed at Lucas's stunned expression as he'd come to on the hardpan of the school's baseball field, which at that time had been little more than a dusty, diamond-shaped track cut out of the dry, weed-choked grass. Lucas hadn't liked him at seven, and over the past thirty years that feeling hadn't altered much.

Still, he had to check it out.

For a lot of reasons. Some of them very personal.

Shifting down, he nosed his Jeep down the twin ruts of this long-forgotten roadway that cut through stands of old-growth timber. Shafts of weak sunlight pierced the canopy of fir boughs to dapple the forest floor and a curious doe, neck stretched around the bole of a tree, ears flickering, stared at him with wide eyes.

How many times had he walked or run along this twisted lane? As a child and into his teenage years, he'd spent most of his summers on these acres strung along the sea. A familiar sign still nailed to the rough bark of an ancient Douglas fir tree greeted him. Once gleaming white, the background was now gray and the bright blue letters had faded, though he could still read:

WELCOME TO CAMP HORSESHOE
ESTABLISHED 1947

And then tacked on many years later, when his father had begun his own, ill-fated religious camp:

J. B. DALTON, TH.D., PASTOR

Jeremiah Bernard Dalton. No, wait. *Dr.* Jeremiah Bernard Dalton. His old man. Dedicated man of God and a colossal dick. At least in Lucas's opinion. Even though he and the Good Lord were at odds often enough, this time Lucas figured God just might agree.

And yet another sign, newer and nailed beneath the first, was a warning in bold orange letters cast upon a black background:

NO TRESPASSING
TRESPASSERS WILL BE PROSECUTED

Prosecuted? Oh, sure. By whom? And what about prospective buyers and their real-estate agents? He snorted.

Ignoring the warning, he drove another three hundred yards through the woods to a wide clearing rimmed by several log buildings where a dented pickup was taking up space. He glanced at Columbia Hall, the largest of the structures, its windows boarded, the long porch surrounding it covered with sand and fir needles.

Here, in this building, the campers and counselors had gathered for meals, or crafts or games, the loft above used for private counseling and classes. He remembered his father preaching so fervently, tears running from his eyes as he clasped the Bible in his large hands. He also recalled how easily his old man had lied, with the elegance and shamelessness of a silver-tongued orator. A captivating speaker, Jeremiah Dalton could enthrall as he stood at the pulpit, his tie loosened, sweat beading in his jet-black hair, his body lean and athletic, his eyes turned heaven-ward. Through his devotion to Jesus, the love and power of the Lord seemed to course through his veins, and he could make everyone in the congregation believe it, everyone but his son.

Because Lucas knew the truth about his old man.

What was the verse? From 1 John 2:4? *"Whoever says 'I know him,' but does not do what he commands is a liar, and the truth is not in that person."* Yeah, something like that. Close enough.

Jeremiah Dalton sermonized about the Good Lord as if he truly believed, yet lied with the silver tongue of a snake oil salesman.

In his mind's eye Lucas could see Jeremiah

standing in Columbia Hall, the campers gathered around him on the floor or the built-in benches of the large, recessed area that had been a cross between a college lecture hall and a conversation pit. His father reigned in the center, a striking man, his voice grim, his gaze touching each and every camper in turn. Naomi had been at his side, her makeup perfect, her red hair caught behind her nape with a clip, her eyes, too, searching those of the campers and staff and lingering just a second too long on Lucas.

"We've had some unsettling news," Reverend Dalton was saying, his eyes dark, his jaw set, his expression grim. All in black, his clerical collar visible, a Bible, as ever, in one hand, he'd been nodding. "You may have heard that a prisoner has escaped. He was being transported from one prison to another."

A murmur had slithered through the campers, but Naomi had started shaking her head and Dr. Dalton had raised his free hand.

"Now, now," he'd said, "there's no cause for concern. To the contrary, I want to assure you all that we are safe. As to the man who was incarcerated, his name is Waldo Grimes and he's been convicted of the heinous crime of slaying his girlfriend."

More concerned whispers had erupted and Naomi had held a finger to her lips and given off a sharp, "Shhh!"

As the hall had quieted again the reverend had offered a serious smile, meant to assure everyone that he and the Good Lord were very much in control. "This all happened almost twenty miles from here and I believe we are safe, but I wanted to squelch any rumors that he is in the immediate area. His escape was three days ago and as yet, despite a manhunt by the authorities, he hasn't been found, but we all must have faith that God, in His divine benevolence, will keep us safe. It's extremely unlikely that he would end up anywhere near Camp Horseshoe. Of course there have been calls from your parents, but I've assured them, as I've assured you, that we are all fine."

That much of the talk was a lie. Lucas had seen the newspaper before Naomi had scooped it up and burned it. The escape had happened less than two miles to the south, not twenty, and his father had been in contact with the police, who were providing extra patrols on the nearby county road. The prisoner was still on the loose, though, and the working theory was that he was headed to meet friends north of the camp in Astoria, where he would hop a boat and slip through the mouth of the Columbia to the open sea and disappear.

The story his father had been spinning to the campers was pure fabrication. Meanwhile the reverend's grin had broadened and Naomi, as if taking her cue, had let the corners of her mouth curve into a smile as well. Lucas hadn't let his gaze land on her too long, nor think about what that mouth could do.

The reverend had added, "We need to ask for His guidance and safety, as well as pray for the souls of all who are involved in this tragedy."

Before any questions could be asked, he'd lowered his head and begun, "Dear Lord, we come humbly before you . . ."

Now, glancing at the old hall, Lucas felt a sour taste in the back of his throat. His father was such a prick, then and now, despite the clerical collar he hid behind. Running his hand around the back of his neck, he noticed an old bench beneath the sagging boughs of a fir, a spot where he'd sat for long hours as the sky had turned dark and summer stars had peeked from behind a thin shroud of clouds. He'd heard frogs and crickets, and felt the warmth of a summer breeze caress his bare skin. There had been good times here, as well as some very bad.

A twinge of nostalgia crept through him, but he quickly tamped it down. In his youth he'd spent his summers here, and there were fleeting memories he savored: skinny-dipping in the cove, the foul taste of his first cigarette, the warmth of his first kiss during a junior-high game of spin the bottle. He remembered the taste of a shot of Jack Daniels and the starry night he'd lost his virginity. Again, down at the cove.

Images of innocence. Images of guilt. Of purity and treachery, of courage and cowardice.

He drew a breath. He wouldn't go there. Not now, though it seemed he would have to face the past sooner than he'd hoped.

Stepping out of his Renegade and onto the sparse gravel, he threw open the back of the SUV and pulled out a shovel and a spade.

How long had it been since he'd set foot in this place? Fifteen years? Eighteen? Half his lifetime?

It still felt as if he'd come back too soon.

"Carter?" he yelled, and the man appeared, rounding the corner of the hall and adjusting his zipper, as if he'd just taken a leak. Great. Dressed head-to-foot in camo, Carter hitched his chin toward the path on the north side of the clearing, the one that angled down to the private stretch of beach that butted up to the cape.

"This way."

Dalton fell into step with his old nemesis and together they worked their way through the shadowy forest, branches of firs green with moss, the cloudy sky nearly blocked from the boughs. As they crossed a ridge to the sea, the sound of the ocean became a roar and the trees grew more sparse. The path narrowed and began switching crookedly back and forth down the side of the cliff to the stretch of sand that curved from one rocky tor of the point of the cape to the cavern beneath it. No footsteps were visible in the sand as the tide had washed in and was now out again.

The sun was hanging low on the horizon, seeming to rest above a bank of clouds that stretched as far as the eye could see.

"Explain to me again why you didn't call this in earlier," Lucas suggested.

"No reason. The tide was coming in."

"And you were here, why?"

"Just pokin' around. Beach combin'," Carter said, but they both knew it was a lie. The man was a known poacher and a petty thief.

"And that's when you found the jawbone."

"Yeah, right in here." As they reached the cavern, he ducked slightly, as did Lucas, then made their way deeper into the darkened recess. A small stream split the smooth, unbroken sand, starfish visible in the tide pool, a rock jutting from the cold water. No bones. "It was . . . just about here," he said, and pointed to an area in the middle of the cavern. "I thought I saw somethin', reached down, and pulled it out. Turned out to be a jawbone." He looked around then, as if he were telling a lie and expected God to strike him down.

"And you just left it here?" Dalton eyed the floor of the cavern. Nothing.

"Yeah, didn't want to mess with the scene or whatever. I seen those crime shows on TV."

"But the tide could have washed it away

and if, as you said, there was dental work on the teeth, then that might be our only way of ID'ing the body. If there is one."

"Hey." Carter lifted both hands up, as if surrendering. "I did what I thought I should. I wasn't under any obligation to let you know."

"Yeah, I think you were. If you found a body." He glanced at his watch. The tide would be turning soon, refilling this grotto, making excavation impossible. "Show me where."

"Around there," Carter said, indicating a spot not far from the creek.

"You sure?"

A lift of one massive shoulder.

Dalton cast the spade aside and pushed in the blade of his shovel, digging deep, tossing out a pile of wet sand, then sifting through it with the shovel. Nothing. Water began to fill the hole. He dug another scoopful, and another. Still nothing. He widened the area while the sound of the sea crashed and echoed through the cavern. Still nothing. Whatever Carter had discovered was gone, washed away. Or never existed. Though why the big man now smoking a cigarette would want to mess with him, Dalton didn't understand.

He slammed his shovel into the sand again as the tide, in foamy fingers, began to trickle into the shadowed space. Not much time left. Another shovelful of wet sand, then another.

He glanced up at Carter.

"I'm tellin' ya, it was here!" Between his lips Carter's cigarette bobbed.

"Well, it's not any longer."

"That jaw came from a body!" He took a long drag. "Or at least a head." Smoke curled from his nostrils.

A head. Great. He forced the blade of his shovel deep into the soft, soupy sand. Would finding one part of a body be any worse than—

Clunk! The tip of the blade struck something hard. It could be anything, he told himself. A buried rock, or shell or whatever, but he dug more furiously in the hole, tossing back globs of sand as saltwater refilled it. *Damn it.*

"Told ya," Carter said. While he looked on, Dalton worked up a sweat, clearing the sand away and seeing a bit of white, then another piece, until as the frigid tide started swirling at his feet, he found himself staring at the upturned face of a very human skull.

"Oh, shit," he said under his breath.

All hell had just broken loose.

Chapter 5

Camp Horseshoe
Then
Bernadette

"I'm pregnant," Monica had admitted to Bernadette a week earlier. They'd been alone, the two counselors who'd been given the task of banking the campfire. All of the other counselors and the campers had returned to their cabins.

"What?" Bernadette gasped, thinking she hadn't heard right. She hadn't even known that Monica had a boyfriend.

"You heard me." Monica, who had been leaning over the stone-lined pit, stood and dusted the ash from her gloves. Around five seven or so, she was thin but curvy, and there wasn't the tiniest hint of a baby bump showing beneath her jacket. Monica's abdomen was perfectly flat. "About six weeks, I think, maybe more like eight. I'm not sure exactly." She was blinking, biting her lip, and looking past the ring of cabins to the trees beyond. Without makeup, her hair scraped back into a curly ponytail, her face illuminated by the reddish coals, Monica had looked younger than her nineteen years. Pregnant? Really? It seemed wrong to think she might soon be a mother.

"Maybe it's a false alarm. Maybe you're just late."

Monica rolled her eyes expressively. "I'm like clockwork, okay? My cycle is twenty-seven days on the dot. Usually starts in the morning. So, yeah, I'm sure, but if you mean have I taken a pregnancy test? Then, no. It's not like I can walk into the infirmary and ask Mrs. Dalton for one, can I?"

Mrs. Dalton, "Mother Naomi," was the reverend's wife, a pretty woman whose interpretation of the camp's rules and her Christian duty usually pinched her otherwise even features.

"No, guess not."

"Since we're trapped here in this"—she'd glanced around the area again, then leaned her head back as if to observe the stars winking high in the heavens—"this *place* I haven't been able to get to a pharmacy, but it doesn't matter. I know."

The fire forgotten, Bernadette stood up and stuffed her work gloves into the back pocket of her jeans. If Monica was only as far along as she claimed, obviously she'd gotten pregnant at the camp. They'd all arrived on the first of June and now it was mid-August. "So what happened?"

"You mean how did I get pregnant?"

"Yeah."

"One-night stand. I was stupid and careless."

"And the father?"

"He, um, I told him."

76

"And?"

"He's not exactly into being a daddy, if you know what I mean."

"So who is he?"

She'd opened her mouth, as if to tell Bernadette everything, then had thought better of it. "Doesn't matter." Bernadette's mind flashed through the faces of the males around the camp—eight counselors and various workmen who kept the place running, Lucas Dalton and his two step-brothers, David and Ryan Tremaine, along with a few others including Tyler Quade and Demarco Lewis.

Monica sank onto one of the benches sur-rounding the fire. "What am I going to do?" Her voice was a whisper. She dropped her face into her hands. "My dad will kill me."

"I thought your parents were divorced," Bernadette said.

She shook her head. "Separated. Some of the time. She gets mad, throws him out, and he comes crawling back with candy and flowers and good intentions or whatever. Breaks her down and then for a while they're all lovey-dovey, like thirteen-year-olds all giggly and sweet. They even go out on dates until he weasels his way back into the house. It's sickening. Maybe worse than when they're fighting. Oh, I don't know. But they're together right now. Or at least they were when I left, so, trust me, he's gonna hit the roof when he finds out." She shook her head, ponytail swinging, as she thought of the upcoming scene.

"But you're nineteen."

"Big deal. It doesn't matter. His roof, his rules." She kicked at the soft dirt in front of one of the benches. "Look, I shouldn't have said anything. Don't worry about it, okay? I-I'll figure it out." Then, as if regretting she'd confided in Bernadette, she'd added, "Don't tell anyone, okay? No one."

"I won't," Bernadette had promised.

"Not even your sister." Her voice had been a warning.

"No, no, of course not." But Bernadette had glanced over her shoulder to make certain Annette wasn't lurking nearby, hiding in the shadows, eavesdropping.

"Good." Monica had then taken off at a jog toward her cabin, leaving Bernadette to deal with the remains of the damned fire.

Now, Bernadette replayed the scene in her mind. Since that confession, Monica had avoided her. Bernadette needed to talk to her, tell her that her secret was safe, that she hadn't told a soul and wouldn't. Maybe tonight she'd get a chance to talk to Monica alone.

Glancing at her watch, she knew she was late, was supposed to meet the others at the cove, but they would have to wait. For how long, she didn't know, but time was running out here at the camp, summer nearly over and soon she'd leave, not just Cape Horseshoe and this camp, but also Lucas Dalton.

At that thought, she flung herself back onto her bed. It was crazy. She knew it. She had a boyfriend back in Seattle, but this summer, away from the city, trapped with a bunch of kids she'd never met before, something had changed.

And of course she'd met Lucas.

The minister's son.

You'll leave on Saturday and never think of him again, her mind insisted, but her heart just didn't believe it. How could she forget the boy, well, almost a man, at eighteen, with wheat-blond hair, sharp features, and hazel eyes that seemed to pierce into hers and see her soul?

She knew it was a romantic fantasy. The feelings her mother had called "puppy love" or a "teenage crush" or whatever. Didn't matter. Bernadette felt it. The pain of knowing she might never see Lucas again, never stare into those knowing eyes, never see his crooked, irreverent smile again, never feel his hands skimming down her skin and causing her to heat from the inside out, was enough to kill her. It was nuts. And stupid. And . . . And she ached inside at the thought of it.

You'll get over him. You have to.

"Hey! Come on!" A whisper pierced the darkness and she recognized her sister's voice. "Are you coming or what?"

"Shh!" she hissed back, and rolled off the bed. Snatching her sweatshirt from its hook, she carried her shoes to the doorway and stepped quickly outside. The girls she was supposed to be watching were sleeping; she'd made sure of it. Even Therese McAllister, whose bladder had to be no bigger than a pea, had returned from her eleven-thirty run to the latrine. Therese had shuffled past, probably blushed as she'd said a quick word of explanation to Bernadette, "Gotta go," before she'd hurried outside and returned within three minutes—fastest tinkler known to man or woman. Now, she was out cold in dreamland and would be until her bladder alerted her to wake up again, probably around 4:30 or 5:00.

"This is crazy," she told her sister as she leaned over and pulled on her Nike running shoes.

"I know."

Bernadette wasn't finished tying the laces when Annette took off at a jog, toward the back of the cabins, away from the glow of the dying campfire to the woods beyond. "Hold up!" Bernadette warned under her breath, but, of course, mule-headed Annette wasn't listening. Bernadette didn't dare shout, not with the windows of each of the cabins open. With a final knot of her laces, Bernadette got to her feet and started hurrying after her sister down the trail that was littered with fir needles and rocks. She caught Annette just as she reached a final rise. Here, where the trees gave way to the headland, the path turned, angling steeply downward in a series of sharp switchbacks that led across the cliff face to the sea. Annette was already starting the descent.

"Wait!" Bernadette caught her sister's arm. "I don't know about this. Jo-Beth is going to try to get us to all say that Elle is suicidal, but I'm not sure."

"Well, join the party. I'm not sure about anything." Annette yanked her arm away and threw her sister a wounded look. "I don't know what this is all about—just that we were supposed to meet down at the cove, so okay, I'm in. But what the hell is going on with Elle?" she demanded. "All I know is that she's missing and the girls in her cabin have been doled out to everyone else." Her little chin jutted forward. "No one tells me anything."

There was a reason for that, of course. Annette wasn't known to keep secrets.

"Why are we meeting at the cavern at midnight? It's like we're witches in a coven. It's stupid. What we should be doing is organizing a search party or something. I mean, she's been gone a whole day, right? So why haven't the cops been called? This 'camp' is a joke."

That much was right. At least in Bernadette's opinion.

"Okay, take it down a notch. We're not, like,

witches, for God's sake. And I don't know about the cops. Maybe it's the twenty-four-hour thing? Who knows? But we've all got to get our story straight."

"Maybe we should all just tell the truth," Annette argued.

"You want to do that?"

Annette, no matter how she liked to think of herself, was no innocent. None of them were. That was the problem.

"I don't know. Yeah, maybe. Oh, crap. Come on!" She pulled away, started descending. The ocean's roar grew louder, the air smelling of brine. More cautiously, they picked their way down the steep hillside, their feet sliding a bit on the narrow, sandy trail. They didn't bother with flashlights as moon glow offered a weak, silvery illumination and the path was familiar.

At the bottom of the steep hill where they came across a band of stumps and branches, driftwood bleached white, Annette started in again. "We didn't do anything wrong," she said, as if trying to convince herself. She climbed over the snags and headed to the far end of the crescent-shaped strand that led to the cape, a spiny ridge that curled like a dragon's tail into the sea. Beneath that long arm of rock and wind-blasted pines was a cavern where all the counselors had agreed to meet.

"Some of us . . . make that most of us, you

included, haven't been staying in our bunks," Bernadette admitted as she caught up with her sister, "and so it looks bad, like maybe we had something to do with Elle's disappearance."

"With Elle's disapp—are you kidding? That's crazy! I say we just tell the truth and, you know, let whatever happens happen."

"It's not that simple. Everyone, you included, has broken camp rules, right? And Reverend Dalton won't take that lightly. If there's any whiff of scandal or impropriety, he'll nail our collective hides to the wall, tell our parents, make a stink that might get in the papers, let potential employers know if they get requests for recommendations, and even bring in the police. Who knows?" She grabbed hold of Annette's elbow and spun her around, saw her dark hair flying around her face as she twirled. "So, let's just hear what the others have to say, okay. Then we'll figure out what we're going to do."

Annette hesitated, and no doubt the wheels were turning frantically in her scheming little mind. And it wasn't as if Bernadette could argue with her. It was true enough that all of the counselors, Annette included, had been breaking all kinds of camp rules that could get them in trouble, not just here at the camp, but also could cause bigger repercussions when they got home. Legal repercussions, the kind that might cause people to lose scholarships or admissions to college or mess up résumés for jobs or, in her case, cost her a boyfriend.

Which might be okay.

Or not.

Chapter 6

Averille, Oregon
Now
Lucas

His phone jangled just as Lucas wheeled his Renegade into the parking lot of the sheriff's department. Wet leaves littered the asphalt, and the storm drain in the center of the crumbling asphalt was clogged, water standing in an ever-growing puddle. His partner's name appeared on the small screen and he picked up, then cut the engine.

"Hey, Mags," he said, staring through the rain-dappled windshield to the concrete block exterior wall. Gray paint was beginning to peel. "I'm here."

"About time."

"I'm only a coupla minutes late . . . well, maybe ten." He climbed out of the Jeep, phone pressed to his ear.

"Or twenty. Anyway, brace yourself. She's on the warpath today."

She being Sheriff Nina Locklear, his boss.

"When isn't she?" he asked, hitting the remote lock on his key chain and hearing the responding chirp from his vehicle. "And I don't think 'warpath' is politically correct."

"She's less than a quarter Native American. Anyway, I'm telling you, she's on a rampage. Mad as hell," Maggie warned.

"About?"

"About the fact that no more bones have been found, and the skull that you and Caleb discovered can't yet be ID'ed. The lab can't even decidedly say whether it's male or female. Too much degradation."

"It hasn't even been twenty-four hours." Ducking around a gutter that was overflowing, he said, "The lab will figure it out."

"Eventually, yeah. But that's not good enough. Not fast enough. She's already pulled all the computer data and physical files of people who've gone missing in the last century."

He cut through a couple of cars in the lot and headed toward the front steps. "Yeah."

"And for some reason, she's zeroed in on about twenty years ago."

His stomach clutched, though he'd been expecting just that news. "That so?"

"Look, I've got another call, but I thought you should know what was up."

"Thanks." He hung up, took the steps two at a time, and opened the front door of the sheriff's department, then waited while an older woman using a walker made her way outside.

Winifred Olsen, the local town crier and a parishioner who had sat front and center in the first pew of the First Christian Church for all the years Lucas had attended services, gave him the once-over.

Her eyes narrowed behind oversize glasses straight out of the eighties. "You're the preacher's boy," she accused as a bit of summer wind swept over the porch.

"Guilty as charged, Winny."

Her thin lips, colored with bright bubble-gum pink lipstick, pursed. "You always were a smart aleck. It's the mark of the devil, y'know, that snarly sarcasm of yours. I hate to say it, but as wild as you were, I'm surprised you turned out at all."

No love lost there. "Ah, c'mon, Winny, you don't 'hate to say it' at all. In fact, you get off reminding me that I don't quite measure up to your standards." He offered her a lazy smile that was met with a look of pure venom.

Moving past, she muttered, "You and your lot should go straight to hell."

"Afraid I'm already there, Winny," he said truthfully, and walked inside to be greeted with the sounds of clicking keyboards, a wheezing air-conditioning unit, and muted conversation. He waited for Dottie at the front desk to buzz him through the interior door leading to the back offices. Behind a huge bulletproof glass window, she heard the alarm indicating the front doors had opened, slid him a look, and simultaneously hit a button that tripped a lock.

All of which was a pain in the ass, but installed a year or so back when a nutcase named Stubby Hanson, who had a grudge with his neighbor that the department hadn't resolved, had taken matters into his own hands. One October morning, Stubby had burst through the front doors, chainsaw in hand. Then, hyped up on adrenaline and fueled by Jack Daniel's, revved up his weapon. With the saw spewing exhaust and roaring loudly, he attacked the office, beginning by taking big gouges out of the front counter. Oak cabinetry topped with ancient Formica had splintered. The glass fronts of the cabinets had shattered, shards spewing into the room, and Dottie had screamed bloody murder as she'd taken refuge behind her secretary's desk. All the while Stubby continued taking his frustrations out on the department's furnishings.

No one had been able to talk him down. Three deputies, one using a Taser, had finally been able to subdue him, though in so doing, his hands had flailed and he'd dropped the still-running saw. The spinning blade had cut through his jeans and taken a piece of flesh out of his thigh, spraying blood before landing on the floor and chopping off the front legs of a nearby chair. One deputy managed to grab the saw and turn it off while the other two wrestled Stubby into cuffs. An EMT had seen to his wound and he'd been hauled off to the nearest hospital.

All because a neighbor wouldn't move his tractor six inches.

Surveying the damage to the reception area afterward, the sheriff had decided that things could have been much worse had Stubby arrived armed with a rifle or sawed-off shotgun rather than the chainsaw. Extra security in the form of the heavy bulletproof glass partition and a locked inner door had been added. After a week's absence, Dottie Jenkins had decided against quitting the department as she'd threatened and returned to her desk and her drill-sergeant persona.

"Mornin'," Lucas said as he filed past what everyone in the station referred to as "Command Central."

"Detective." Dottie didn't look away from her computer screen, her nose pressed near the monitor as she was too vain to wear glasses, all of which tended to give her a birdlike posture. Her hair was nearly white and poofed up, cut in layers, and clipped at her neckline. Neat. Tidy. And sharp as a tack. "The sheriff wants to see you." No inflection—just an order. "She's in her office."

Not good news.

Lucas braced himself, then walked down the short hallway to Sheriff Nina Locklear's office. As Dottie had said, the sheriff was seated behind a clean, spacious faux-wood desk. Slim and athletic, a hint of her Native American heritage visible in the height of her cheekbones and the sheen of her black hair, she was around five foot eight and all business. Lucas figured had she not had an all-consuming passion for law enforcement, she might have been a model.

This morning she wasn't alone.

One of the visitor's chairs was occupied by Ryan Tremaine.

His stepbrother. Well, once-upon-a-time stepbrother. Since Naomi and Jeremiah Dalton had divorced, the whole stepbrother thing had disintegrated. Their only connection, these days, was Leah, the one remaining connection between Naomi and Jeremiah. Everything had been split—except, of course, Leah.

What a mess.

And now Lucas got to deal with Ryan.

Great.

Tremaine, a year younger than Lucas, currently worked for the DA's office. With the build of a baseball player, he was tall and lanky, his short hair dark and trimmed to match his goatee. His eyes, always unreadable, met Lucas's and he gave a curt nod. Didn't bother to smile. But then he never did. Not around Lucas when they'd been stepbrothers. Now, they were just two men who lived in the same small town and didn't much like each other.

Lucas said to the sheriff, "Dottie said you wanted to see me."

"That's right," Locklear said. "It's about the skull found out at the cape."

Which is what Maggie had told him. Was Ryan here in an official capacity with the District Attorney's office, or for a personal reason?

"Sit down," Locklear suggested, and Lucas slid into the vacant chair. She frowned, her eyebrows pulling together as she glanced at a file on her desk. The manila backing had yellowed, the newspaper articles within also showing signs of age.

"I've had the records pulled for the last fifty years, just to give me an overview of how many people have gone missing in that time." She slid the file across to him. "Most everything is on the computer now, but I wanted to see some of the original records. As you can see, it's not a big file, the missing persons who've never turned up in all of Neahkahnie County.

"There are several men still unaccounted for, a fisherman from 1986, a hunter in 2001, and a nineteen-year-old hitchhiker in 2012. Then there's the group who went missing all around the same time, just about twenty years ago." She looked from one of the ex-stepbrothers to the other. "First up: Waldo Grimes."

Lucas felt the muscles in his back tighten. *Here it comes.*

Locklear continued. "Grimes escaped while being transported from a prison near Salem. Big accident. In the hubbub, Grimes got away and was seen by a witness heading west and was supposedly lost somewhere in the mountains, but some people think he made it all the way to the coast." She pointed to the file. "A woman reported seeing Grimes on a boat in the marina in Astoria, but if it was him, he slipped away. No boats reported missing." She paused. "But you know all of this, don't you? Both of you?"

Before either could even nod, she went on. "The other missing person was what everyone assumed was a runaway, a kid who worked part-time at the camp here that summer: Dustin Peters. Never returned from his workday at Camp Horseshoe. Picked up his check and never came home."

Lucas remembered Dusty. At seventeen, he had a way with horses and dogs, probably all animals, and had been in charge of taking care of the small herd kept at the camp. With long hair and an easy smile, he was a calm kid, kind of a loner.

"Then we come to the females," Locklear went on. "A total of four missing in the same time frame that I went through, a housewife in the seventies, a grandmother with Alzheimer's in the nineties. Both too old to be our Jane Doe, we think, on first examination of the few teeth that were still in the skull. The ones who interest me are Eleanor Brady and Monica O'Neal, both of whom were counselors at Camp Horseshoe about twenty years ago." She paused for effect, then said, "Which just happens to be the exact same time period when Waldo Grimes was on the loose. And Dustin Peters vanished." She leaned back in her chair, and her eyes narrowed. "It's also the time both of you worked as counselors at the camp."

Lucas nodded. "We were there. And you're right, two girls did go missing that summer." He remembered all too vividly the fear, the panic of realizing both Elle and Monica had disappeared.

Beside him, Ryan looked out the single window as if finding the cloud cover suddenly fascinating.

"The presumptive theory at the time was that they had both been kidnapped by Grimes," Locklear continued, "and when they or their bodies never were found, the case went cold. But now it looks like we may have found at least one of the bodies."

"Too soon to tell," Ryan pointed out, the first words he'd spoken. He swung his gaze back onto the sheriff.

"You're right, but I thought I would point out

what was happening to both of you. If it turns out that we find any evidence to suggest that the bones belong to someone associated with the camp, then each of you will have to be taken off the case. Conflict of interest."

Ryan snorted. "You're not my boss."

"I'm sure the DA will be on board with this."

"Maybe." Ryan stood. "Until then, if you'll excuse me, I've got work to do." Then without waiting for a response, he marched swiftly out of the room.

"Friendly guy," Locklear observed, arching an eyebrow.

"You should meet his brother."

"David. Already had the pleasure." She hesitated. "He's your brother, too."

"Was. Stepbrother," he clarified.

She nodded. "My problem isn't with David," she said, mentioning Ryan's brother. "At least not today." David Tremaine had more than his share of run-ins with the local authorities. While Ryan had, after a few false starts, finished college and gone on to law school, his younger brother had never left Averille and still worked on a ranch outside of town. They had a sister as well. Little Leah. Well, she wasn't so little any longer, not at thirty. Leah was the one and only good thing to come out of his father's marriage to Naomi Tremaine. Even if Leah still held a grudge and barely returned his calls. After all this time. His stomach soured a little as he considered his family and his damned guilt.

Sheriff Locklear continued. "You work for the department, and even though Ryan doesn't think I'm his boss, I know the DA would agree that if the remains that we found belong to any of the people missing during the time you all worked at the camp, that would be a decided conflict of interest."

"And?"

"And if it's decided there was foul play involved and we find enough evidence to take a case to trial, you'll be reassigned, as will he." She pushed the thick file toward him. "This is all on the computer, I think. It happened about the time the department was converting to digital records, but in its very early stages, so we'll double-check what's in the system"—she motioned to her monitor—"against that. But before we start, is there anything you want to tell me?"

"No," he said, picking up the old papers in their worn manila cover.

"Think about it."

He stood and made his way to the door.

"Detective?" she called, and he looked over his shoulder. "You should know that a reporter from Astoria is asking questions."

"A reporter?"

"With the Astoria *NewzZone*. Ever hear of it?"

"Don't think so."

"Small, online, kind of out-there news Web

94

site, not affiliated with any newspaper. I think it's pretty much just the reporter who serves as editor. It's mostly a very popular blog. The reporter, Kinley Marsh, does in-depth stories germane to the area."

"Kinley Marsh?"

"Ring some bells?"

He nodded slowly, but couldn't quite call it up. "I've heard the name before."

"She was a camper at Camp Horseshoe when the girls went missing and Waldo Grimes was on the loose, so she has a personal and unique interest in the case."

"If there is a case," he said, forcing himself to remember the girl who would now be around thirty. She'd been a gawky kid, her hair in a wild red tangle, her eyes always covered with glasses or clip-on shades, one of those pushy campers with a million questions.

"She thinks there is. Check it out. Online."

"I will." File in hand, he walked to the office he shared with Maggie. Their desks were pushed together, one facing the other in a room that was just large enough to accommodate them.

Maggie, coffee cup near her keyboard, was typing rapidly, her eyes on the screen. The rest of the fake walnut of the desktop was clear, aside from her phone and the computer monitor at which she was staring. "You don't seem permanently damaged," she said without looking up.

"Nope."

"I thought she might tear you a new one." Her fingers clicked with the rapid-fire accuracy of someone who had once been a court reporter.

"She must've calmed down. I'm still intact."

Spinning in her chair, she retrieved some papers from the credenza stretched behind her and slid them across the expanse of their shared desktops.

He scooped up the papers before they dropped to the floor. "What's this?"

"A list of everyone who was at Camp Horseshoe the year that Eleanor Brady, Monica O'Neal, and Dustin Peters went missing. Their names are on it as well, along with the counselors and people hired by your father to run the place. Everyone from the building maintenance people to the cooks, janitors, and ranch hands. I've compiled a list of the campers, too, and I'm trying to find out what, if any, company serviced the camp. Maybe you could help me out there."

As he picked up the papers, she quit typing and looked up at him over the edge of her monitor. She was staring at him over the tops of her half-glasses, the ones she wore while on the computer. Her hair was a tousled mess of unruly brown curls, her eyes gold and keen with intelligence. A smattering of light freckles showed upon a face devoid of makeup, and her lips were thin and, often as not, tightly pursed as she was forever working out a knotty problem, just as they were now.

"How did you gather all this?" He held up the pages she'd sent him.

One side of that mouth curved up smugly. "Got my ways."

It was true. She was a wizard on the computer and could gather information quickly, but this seemed impossible.

"You hacked into the camp's files."

She smiled, showing a dimple. "Dalton, you're giving me far too much credit." Gold eyes twinkled. "This isn't the first time our department has looked into the case, right? It might be cold, but it hasn't vanished. So I pulled up what we already had, updated the info I could, and voilà."

"Good work."

"I still need to find some more addresses and phone numbers. In twenty years, people have a tendency to move, marry, divorce, change their names, or whatever. But it's a start."

He scanned the computer printout, his gaze sliding down the list to pause at a familiar name. Instead of Bernadette Alsace, he found Bernadette Alsace Warden. So she was married. Of course. "A helluva start."

"I'm hoping you might be able to fill in a few blanks."

"Yeah?" he said, though deep inside he balked.

The last thing he wanted to do was dredge it all up again. Now, it seemed, he didn't have much of a choice.

As he sat down, Maggie said, "Before we go into the whole list thing, why don't you tell me what you know."

"I think it's all in here." He slapped the file that he'd received from Sheriff Locklear onto the desk. "I think you've probably already seen this."

"Scanned it this morning."

"As I said, you've been busy." He couldn't help the trace of acrimony in his words.

Folding her arms over her desk, she leaned forward. "I don't want to reread a twenty-year-old statement from a scared kid who was probably hell-bent on covering his own ass or protecting his girlfriend or whatever. I want to hear it from you, as an adult. Now." She raised her eyebrows, encouraging him. "What do you remember?"

He glanced at the names on the list, his gaze dropping to Monica O'Neal's. *Too much and not enough,* he thought grimly. *That's what I remember.*

Chapter 7

Camp Horseshoe
Then
Monica

RUN!!!

Terror chasing her, Monica flew through the open door of the old chapel. She stumbled down the rotting porch, took off racing across the clearing, and dove into the woods.

Oh, God. Oh, God. Oh. God! Tyler was dead! *Dead!* Someone had killed him, stabbed him in the back and left him to die alone between the rotting pews!

Why—oh, dear God, why?

And who?

Don't think about that now! Just keep moving. Faster. Faster! Her brain urged her onward through the forest. She didn't dare use her flashlight to light the way because she could hear whoever had killed Tyler racing through the darkness behind her.

Over the thundering beat of her heart, she could discern the heavy footsteps, the deep breathing . . . or were they her own footfalls, her own uneven, gasping breaths?

It doesn't matter, just get away from him. Find

help! There's a chance Tyler's still alive. Maybe you were mistaken. He was warm, wasn't he? And the blood pooling around him, it was still flowing, wasn't it?

She didn't know, couldn't think. She just had to keep moving, find a way to escape the monster who was chasing her. She heard branches snapping behind her and she sped forward, sweating, her legs beginning to burn, the darkness of the night swallowing her.

Arms stretched forward to avoid running into trees, Monica blindly hurtled her way through the forest. Branches slapped at her face, cobwebs clung to her hair, and she kept tripping on roots and rocks and sticks on her path.

Run, run, run!

Don't stop. Don't ever stop.

Sheer panic forced her legs to keep driving forward even though she heard him, his footsteps pounding faster and harder, chasing her to the ground.

Move, Monica. Keep moving!

For a split second she considered racing to the cove, heading toward the roar of the sea to try to locate the path leading down to the cavern and the other girls, but she discarded the idea immediately. No, she'd be trapped there. A better, saner idea would be to run to the heart of the camp, wake Dr. and Mrs. Dalton, call the police. There were rifles at the ranch, she'd seen the reverend and his sons toting the weapons on occasion, at the threat of a coyote or bear, she thought. It didn't matter. Not now. Monica just had to get to the camp headquarters where the director and his wife lived in a suite of rooms above the main office.

But was she heading in the right direction? How could she tell?

Slow down. Find a place to hide. Where you can catch your breath and get your bearings. If you don't, you could be running in circles and find yourself trapped at the cliffs or even running into the maniac who's chasing you.

Searching frantically, she nearly ran into a snag, a tree that had been snapped off in a storm and had left a huge, ragged stump that she sank gratefully behind. The tree itself was rotting as it lay on the forest floor. Shaking, she strained to listen. Where was he? Had he given up?

She held her breath, tried to still her racing heart. Did she hear footfalls? Or was that her imagination? A breeze was rustling the leaves and needles overhead, the branches moving slightly. The ocean was to the west and she'd definitely been running away from it. Good. Closer to the camp.

What had happened to Tyler? Who would want to kill him? Or her? What kind of monster was on the loose? She pressed her hands over her face, shaking. She'd heard rumors that a

101

murderer had broken out of prison, that he'd been spotted heading west, that he might have found his way to this part of the coast; but why would he be here and why would he *kill Tyler?* She realized there was dirt or . . . oh, God, *blood,* on her sticky fingers. Tyler's blood.

She almost screamed but bit it back.

Who would have thought she would experience this horror at a church camp? The very camp her father, when he hadn't been smoking dope or drinking beer, had helped build as he'd been part of a framing crew that was responsible for the new church, not the old chapel where she and Tyler met, but the larger church and rec center. In fact, she'd been told her parents had met here one summer, that she'd been conceived here . . . how ironic was that given the fact that she had been so recently pregnant.

Tears filled her eyes and began to run down her face. The baby. Tyler. All gone. Her fanciful dreams of marriage, turned to dust. *Tyler . . .*

Brushing her tears away with the back of her hand, she searched the darkness, her gaze scouring the forest. Who knew how many ghosts haunted these sprawling acres now owned by the Dalton family and the church?

She heard no one.

Saw no movement.

Tentatively, she got to her feet. Her right ankle throbbed, but supported her. Noiselessly she pushed herself over the fallen log and edged past a thicket. If the sea was to her left, then . . . She bore right and found a path, a gap between the stands of fir and cedar, around clumps of salal.

The ocean was behind her, so surely she was heading toward camp. She began to jog through the trees, a pinprick of light winking in the distance as she ran. Her heart soared and she increased her pace, veering as the path forked, altering her route, her feet finding the dusty path again.

Thank God!

Go! Go! Go!

She surged forward, her throbbing ankle and burning lungs forgotten. Now, finally, she could get help. Save herself. Save Tyler. *Oh, please, please!*

The light loomed brighter—a security lamp mounted high over the stable.

Yes! Less than a quarter mile away.

You can do this, Monica. You can!

She pushed herself, running faster, her lungs on fire, her heart feeling as if it might burst.

Oh, God, she was going to make it!

Tears of relief flooded her eyes as she forced herself onward, staring at the light, glowing ever brighter, seeing it as her salvation. A sob tore from her throat and . . . and the light disappeared.

The forest was suddenly black again.

What?

"No!" she cried aloud, as she blinked away the sheen of drops in her eyes and realized some illumination still existed, like an aura surrounding a huge, dark figure standing in the path in front of her.

She skidded to a stop, stumbling, falling to the ground. Her vision cleared and she spied a knife, held high, its wicked blade glinting in the security light's glow. Frantic, she tried to scramble way, to backpedal into the darkness.

Her attacker leapt forward. On her in an instant. A gloved hand covered her mouth, pinching her nostrils, cutting off her scream.

No, no, no! This can't be happening!

Flailing, she fought. Biting, swinging her fists, kicking. She writhed and flung her entire body, trying to wrest free.

Help me. Please, oh, please somebody help me.

But none of her blows had any impact on her attacker and her silent pleas went unheeded.

Slowly she was dragged away from the path, into the jet black woods, ever closer to the roar of the sea.

Chapter 8

Lucas flipped on the wipers as he drove steadily south, Maggie in the passenger seat. He'd put her off for the time being. Didn't really feel like getting into what he remembered and what he didn't. He'd told what he knew twenty years earlier and it was in the report.

They were heading to Cape Horseshoe and the forgotten camp that sprawled on its southern face. Though the actual cape was part of a state park and could be reached by the parklands to the north, the southern side was still owned by his father.

Well, that wasn't quite true.

Legally in Oregon, no one owned the actual beachfront property, it all belonged to the state, but the acres abutting the wet sand area that were indicated as state lands could be private, including Camp Horseshoe. So the beach wasn't part of the camp, but the property leading up to it, on the south side, was.

The law had always bothered his father. Jeremiah didn't like the fact that hikers and sightseers were legally allowed to approach the camp from the north. Even with Reverend Jeremiah Bernard Dalton's close relationship with the Almighty, there had been nothing he could do about the state law, aside from erecting fences around the camp's perimeter.

"It's a darned shame," the reverend had told his family. "Nature's beauty should be honored and cherished by God-fearing folks, those who will take care of it." He'd shaken his head, his black hair gleaming nearly blue as he'd stood on the cliff and surveyed the moonlight casting a shimmering ribbon on the dark Pacific.

"I thought the law was there to ensure everyone could enjoy the beach," Lucas had ventured.

His father had frowned but never broken his gaze from the frothy waves rolling into the shore. "Well, see, that's the problem, son. What gives the nonbelievers the right? I mean, of course there are plenty of those who would look at the wonders of the Lord and take in its beauty without doing it harm. Sure. But then there are those who are heathens and troublemakers and, well, criminals, who litter and spray graffiti, vandals, you know. Criminals really. They spoil it for everyone, so it's best to keep these pristine lands for those of us who are good shepherds, who will preserve it and take care of it."

The lecture that Lucas had thought was sure

to come did not, fortunately. Nor did his father ask him to recite verses to make his point.

All the same, Lucas had spent too many hours to count working with his stepmother's sons from her first marriage, repairing the seemingly endless miles of fence line surrounding the camp.

It had been the one and probably only thing that he, Ryan, and David had agreed upon; they'd all hated the constant job of making and fixing the damned fence.

"You think I'm putting the cart before the horse," Maggie observed now, not looking up from her cell phone as Lucas took one of the ess curves south of the town of Cannon Beach, where the road curved twice, offering wide-angled views of the ocean. Whitecapped swells rolled beneath a gray canopy of clouds, and the horizon was blurred, no definitive line visible in the drizzle.

Lucas answered, "We're not certain about the identity of the skull, nor have we found any more bones to go with it, so it could have become detached from the body in the surf. We don't know if the bones are male or female, or how old they are. The damage is significant, but it doesn't take long to decompose or deteriorate in the sea."

Leaning a shoulder against the passenger window, she said, "So you think we might be on a wild goose chase. That just because the majority of missing persons and unsolved cases happened near or in Camp Horseshoe and the bones were discovered only feet from the camp's borders, that we're wasting our time."

"Guess we'll find out."

"So what did you tell the sheriff when she asked you what you knew about everything that happened twenty years ago?"

"Same as I told you. My statement hasn't changed."

"And she didn't pressure you for more?"

"There isn't much more to tell, and back then it was all fresh. Newer. Seared in my mind. Over time, memories get fuzzy and you can twist them to suit your needs."

"And she just let you go?"

"Yep."

Actually, her phone had rung, an important call, and as she picked up, Locklear said she'd get back to him. Her actual words had been, "This isn't the end of this, Dalton. You're not off the hook. I'll read over the file, but you and I?" Her dark gaze had been determined. "We're gonna have ourselves a little chat. This is my department and I won't have it compromised. Find everyone who knew Monica O'Neal, Dustin Peters, and Eleanor Brady. Get them to come in for a statement. I don't care how far they live, I want to see them, face-to-face." She'd picked up the phone then and Lucas had gotten the message. He'd already started making calls.

Now, reaching the familiar turnoff, he drove

through the forest and into the center of the camp to park near an array of vehicles belonging to the county and state. Wedged between two county marked SUVs was the crime lab van, and nearer to the old rec center stood a pickup with its tailgate open, coffee urns and cups available. Two deputies stood near the truck, each with a steaming paper cup, the older guy smoking a cigarette as Maggie and Lucas walked past. They hiked through the woods and down the switch-backed trail to the shore. A team of searchers was scouring the bleached driftwood and the rocks that separated the cliff from the sand. More searchers were sifting through the sand near and in the cavern. Lucas and Maggie avoided the searchers' grid, stepping past the ropes marking off an area that would probably be eroded away when the tide turned and washed closer to the shore.

"How's it going?" Lucas asked a woman who was busy looking through the smooth rocks surrounding a tide pool.

"Slow. Haven't found any more bones that we think are human. Just the remains of a sea lion and a couple of birds, possibly California gulls, and a lot of junk." She was ruddy-faced, her short hair tethered by a hat, and she was dressed in rain gear and wearing gloves. She had to speak loudly over the wind and tide so that she could be heard. Indicating a bag of what appeared to be trash, pieces of paper and plastic and fishing line that had washed ashore as debris from the sea, she said, "Who knows what treasures we'll find?"

"Good luck," Lucas said, and turned up the collar of his jacket as he and Dobbs headed toward the cavern where just yesterday he'd met with Caleb Carter. "Anything new?" he asked Gina Leonetti, a raw-boned woman wearing thick, horn-rimmed glasses. Tufts of short graying hair poked from beneath the wide brim of her hat, and lines feathered from the corners of her eyes and around her mouth. She was working with a heavy-set man, both wearing rain slickers, pants, boots, and gloves.

"Not yet," she said. She paused to clean her glasses with a bit of cloth she pulled from a pocket. As she wiped the wet lenses, she added, "I sure hope this isn't all for nothing. I can't tell you how often I've been called out to the middle of no-goddamned-where, only to be told, 'Oh, sorry. Guess we were mistaken.' " Sharp brown eyes narrowed as she stared at Lucas, slipping the specs onto her face again. "I detest wasting time."

"Me too," her companion said, his voice echoing in the vaulted grotto. He yanked off his hat and rubbed the stubble that apparently wasn't allowed to grow into a full head of hair.

"Found some candles, though. Buried here, in the dry sand. All white tapers. All burned down to about an inch. Five of 'em."

"Is that significant?" Lucas asked.

Gina shrugged. "Maybe. Maybe not."

The man near her said, "Could be like points in a pentagram. You know, witchcraft."

Gina rolled her eyes. "That's a leap, Howard."

"I know. I'm just saying."

She flashed what Luke supposed was intended to be a tirelessly patient smile. "I guess not, then." She was turning back to the area in the cave they were excavating when they heard a man shout.

"Hey! Over here!"

Lucas and Maggie moved outside to where one of the searchers was working on an area covered with driftwood, snags, and limbs. As they approached, Gina Leonetti on their heels, the searcher shined a light between a short piece of charred wood that had probably been used for a campfire at one time and a snarl of roots from what had been a stump.

"Whatcha got?" Gina demanded, and shot past Lucas to reach the mass of twisted logs and peer into a hole lit by the shaft of the searcher's flashlight. "Dear Jesus," she said, glancing over her shoulder to Lucas. "Looks like we just hit the mother lode."

Lucas peered over her shoulder and sure enough spied a scattering of twisted bones, which appeared, at first glance, to be human.

"How about that? If these bones are a match to the skull, we should be able to figure out pretty quickly if we've got a male or female, and maybe how long they've been down here," Gina said.

"Or you might end up with more than one body if they don't match. We have two or more cases," Maggie pointed out.

"Possibly." Gina was clearly pleased their work had amounted to something. "Let's get to it," she said with renewed energy. "I think I might need a bigger crew."

As the ocean pounded the shore, salt spray blowing up against the cape jutting into the sea, Lucas realized that life as he knew it would be no more. Maybe that was for the best.

While the crew excavated the area, extracting the bones and anything that might be of interest in the area—tissue or clothing or personal belongings, anything that might help identify the body or bodies—Maggie and Luke headed back to the Renegade. "Looks like we got lucky," Maggie said, climbing the steep path leading to the old camp.

"Lucky."

"I wonder if we'll find more than one body along that stretch of beach." She sounded eager, the thought of solving cold cases energizing. "It just feels that way, y'know?"

"Yeah." Lucas couldn't speculate. Didn't want to. He thought of Elle Brady, the first missing girl. According to local legend and ghost stories, her spirit still haunted this stretch of coastline.

Over the years, several reports had been made, though, of course, never substantiated.

She was a myth, a local legend.

He couldn't help wonder if now, at last, they'd discovered her grave.

Turning his collar to the wind, he held his thoughts to himself and kept hiking. As they made their way along the wet trails, the rising mist thickening, Maggie called into the station and asked for more deputies to secure the scene. "Partial skeleton so far . . . don't know if it's part of the skull that was discovered . . . yeah, that should do it." She killed the connection just as they reached the boarded-over rec center.

The two cops they'd passed on the way down were no longer hanging out at the coffee urn, but as Lucas reached his Renegade, he heard the rumble of an engine and turned to spy a Cadillac SUV tearing down the lane. Water and leaves flew from beneath the silver vehicle's tires and behind the wheel, glaring through the wind-shield, was the reverend himself. Good old Dad.

Praise be.

The Caddy had barely stopped when Jeremiah Dalton, his face a color close to crimson, burst from behind the driver's side. "What in heaven's name is going on here, Lucas?" he demanded. His hair, once raven black but now definitely more salt than pepper, was clipped and neat, but catching raindrops as they fell.

"Looks like they found a body, or partial body, or more than one body down on the beach," Lucas answered.

"And so the sheriff's department thinks they have the right to set up here?" he demanded. "This is private property!"

"With access to a potential crime scene."

"So you gave them permission?"

"No one asked."

"Exactly." Jeremiah was livid as he strode up to Lucas. Two inches taller than his son, Jeremiah had the advantage of staring down at him.

Lucas was used to it. Didn't give an inch as the passenger door of the Caddy opened and David Tremaine, a year younger than his brother, Ryan, appeared. David was about five ten and built more solidly than his brother, his hair almost blond, his eyes as blue as his mother's, his attitude evident in the set of his jaw. He squared a baseball cap on his head and approached the small group.

"David," Lucas said with a curt nod, and made hasty introductions. "Detective Margaret Dobbs. My father, Jeremiah, and . . . what the hell are you to me, David? My ex-stepbrother?"

The corners of David's mouth tightened within his three days' growth of beard. "Acquaintance."

"That'll do," Lucas agreed. He didn't understand why Naomi's sons were still hanging around Jeremiah but suspected it had something to do with this very camp and the smell of money. With an upswing in the economy, developers were eyeing the camp for some kind of resort the last Lucas had heard, not that he paid that much attention. However, he couldn't miss the scuttlebutt as it swept through the small cafés, shops, and coffee shops in town.

"You tell that sheriff that she can't just come onto private land or she'll hear from my attorney!" Jeremiah fumed.

"Why don't you tell her yourself?" Lucas said, and the old man actually sputtered.

"You always were an upstart."

Lucas nodded. "So I've heard. And worse. Just this morning, in fact."

"Why I try to reason with you, I don't know. The Good Lord has tested me with one son, and I should have paid more attention to Proverbs 23:13: *'Withhold not correction from the child: for if thou beatest him with the rod, he shall not die.'* "

"I know the verse," Lucas gritted, feeling the decades-old outrage and fury burning through him. "You always brought it up about the same time you undid your belt and then proceeded to beat the shit out of me."

His father's jaw slid to one side and Lucas smelled a fight, saw the flare of anger in the older man's eyes.

"Go ahead," Lucas goaded, and from the corner

of his eye, he saw the edges of David's mouth twitch. The last time his father had taken the belt to him, Lucas had been eighteen and had grabbed that vicious strap of leather, wrapping the slim whip around his own fist before his old man could jerk it away. The belt had cut deep, blood had oozed from between Lucas's fingers, but he'd held fast, and when he and his father were nose to nose, Jeremiah, teeth gritted, cords standing out on his neck, muscles bunched in hatred, had taken a swing at him. Lucas had ducked and swung hard in return, smashing his free fist into his father's chest and cracking two of the older man's ribs.

That had been the last of Jeremiah's attempts to physically rein in his son. Once Lucas's jab had connected, the old man had dropped his belt and, holding on to his rib cage, had kicked Lucas out.

Naomi had protested, but that was it. From that point on in his life, Lucas Dalton had been on his own. And he'd made good, in spite of his old man.

Lucas said, "What about this one? Ephesians 6:4? *'Fathers, do not provoke your children to anger, but bring them up in the discipline and instruction of the Lord.'* We could probably stand here all day and spout Bible verses at each other to no end. I got your message and I'll pass it along."

Jeremiah scowled and glanced at the path leading toward the beach.

"Off-limits," Maggie said, as if sensing that he might want to make his way down to the beach. "You can take the path down to the strand, but the area where the tide reaches is now considered a crime scene."

Jeremiah's head swung around to stare at Lucas's partner.

Maggie didn't flinch as she added, "We're posting deputies to ensure that no one can compromise or contaminate the scene. Once we're finished, the beach and cavern will be able to be accessed again."

"The cavern? What the heck did you find down there?"

"Human remains. Yesterday a skull, and today, possibly, more bones."

His lips blade-thin, Jeremiah rubbed his chin. "Okay, I understand. I don't like it, but I understand." He threw his son a look. "I want the camp off-limits to anyone but the authorities, all right? No press. No gawkers or lookie-loos coming out here. As I said before, 'This is private property.'"

"We can do that," Maggie assured him.

"You agree?" Jeremiah asked Lucas.

"Yup."

Jeremiah hesitated long enough to witness a county cruiser pull into the drive and park next to his SUV.

"The cavalry," Maggie explained to Jeremiah as

117

two deputies emerged from the vehicle. "They're here to make sure no one unwanted shows up."

"Good enough?" Lucas asked his father.

Jeremiah said grudgingly, "Guess it'll have to do." With a hitch of his chin to David, the preacher climbed into his silver rig and once they were both inside, switched on the ignition, reversed, and swung wide, then drove off, the taillights of the Caddy disappearing into the tendrils of mist floating through the craggy-barked firs.

The heavier deputy who had been riding shot-gun grinned as he saw Lucas and Maggie. "Such a pleasure working with detectives Dalton and Dobbs, the Double Ds." His idea of a joke. Frank Allen's sense of humor hadn't evolved since the fifth grade.

"Can it, Allen," Maggie said, cutting him off. "We've got work to do."

The leering smile fell from his face as his partner climbed out of the cruiser.

Lucas said, "Let's get to it."

After a few minutes of discussion with the deputies, Lucas and Maggie slid into the cool interior of his Jeep. Lucas was behind the wheel and reversed to the steps of the building that had housed the office and was connected with the infirmary, where all of the counselors had originally reported for duty. He remembered seeing Bernadette for the first time as she'd

118

climbed up the dusty steps twenty years earlier. Wearing white shorts and a loose T-shirt, her auburn hair wound to the top of her head in what these days would be called a messy bun, she, with her younger sister in tow, had approached the counter and smiled confidently at his stepmother.

Lucas had been striding in through the back door of the reception area. Sweaty from spending the morning mucking out the stable and grooming the horses, he'd needed the keys to the pickup and had retrieved them from a peg behind the reception counter.

"Bernadette Alsace," she was saying to Naomi, her voice low, eyebrows pulled together in concentration. "And my sister, here, Annette Alsace. Our paperwork was sent by e-mail, but I've got a copy of it with me." Their mother was hovering over them, and Lucas caught a glimpse of an older model Volvo parked outside.

"No, no. It's fine. Everything's in order," Naomi had assured them, and the clouds of worry in Bernadette's eyes had disappeared. "We're glad you made it." Naomi had rained her most benevolent, if false, smile on them. "Just give me a sec and I'll get it. Would you like to come with me to see that everything's in order?" she'd added to the mother, a tall woman whose lined face suggested she smiled often.

"Oh, yes. Sure." Carrying a huge bag, the mother hurried after Naomi, who had turned away and stepped into the adjoining room where the records had been kept, leaving Lucas alone with the two newcomers.

"Hi," he'd said, slipping the keys off the hook. "I'm Lucas Dalton."

"Dalton? So you're her"—Bernadette's eyes had followed Naomi's wake—"her son?"

"Stepson," he'd corrected. Naomi was nearly fifteen years older than he but didn't look her age. Though she had two boys from her previous marriage, they were younger than Lucas.

"Oh, then the reverend is your father."

"Yes." He'd wanted to say more but held his tongue. For once.

"I'm Bernadette," she'd introduced, sticking out her hand. He'd taken it even though he felt dirty and grimy. Worse yet, he'd held it a second too long.

Her green gaze had lingered on his, and he was reminded of the forest at daylight. "I'll take your bags to your cabin."

Clearing her throat, she'd said, "Great. Oh, and this is my sister, Annette." The younger, shyer girl hadn't offered a hand, but stared at him with worried eyes. A couple of inches shorter than Bernadette, she was pretty enough, her eyes and hair a shade lighter than her older sibling's, but her confidence, it had seemed, was in short supply. Annette had clutched her purse to her chest and eyed him as if she suspected him to be the devil incarnate. Which, he decided now, he had been.

Maggie said now, breaking into his thoughts, "So, no love lost between you and your father."

"Not much."

"And your stepbrothers?"

"Even less."

"What about your stepmother?"

He felt the muscles in the back of his neck clench. "She and the old man are divorced."

"I know. You don't see her?"

"Nope."

"But her sons hang out with Jeremiah."

"I guess." He didn't like talking about his family or ex-family or anything personal for that matter, but of course, that was all about to change.

Maggie fell silent until they rounded the curve that swept around Neahkahnie Mountain, a headland where a viewpoint had been constructed and offered sweeping views of the Pacific.

She eyed the vast stretch of gray water and said, "No matter how you cut this, Lucas, it looks like we've got ourselves a couple of dead bodies."

He didn't argue, just turned north on the county road.

"Once we establish identity or at least the age of the victims and the approximate time they've been dead, we might well have a homicide or two on our hands."

"Yeah."

121

"So how do you want to handle this?" she asked. "If it turns out that the bones belong to one of the people who was at the camp twenty years ago, the sheriff will take you off the case."

He nodded. They'd already gone over this ground.

"But I think we need you. I think you might be able to persuade some of your friends to come to us, rather than the other way around. It would be easier to interview them in person, here, rather than wherever they've scattered to."

"No one will agree to that."

"No?" She was looking out the side window now, gathering her thoughts, constructing her argument as she stared at the forest and cliffs that rimmed the highway on the passenger side. "You could be wrong there. If the choice to those we want to talk to is to discuss it with the local authorities and risk people they know—family, friends, and clients—learning that they could be part of a murder investigation, they might decide a quick trip to Cape Horseshoe might be a better idea."

"You're assuming the bones that were found belong to someone who went missing from the camp, and that people care what happened two decades ago, and that they might want to cover it up."

"I'm just suggesting you, as a counselor at the time and son of the owner and now a detective with the sheriff's department, might get more insight, more evidence than a rookie cop at some Podunk jurisdiction in Timbuktu."

"That's where you're dead wrong."

"Am I?" She turned to face him, intelligent eyes sparking with a challenge. "Then let's see, shall we?"

He grappled with the decision, his fingers tightening over the wheel as he drove. "If we know definitively that the body is from that time frame, I'll do what I can, okay? As long as the sheriff lets me."

She nodded. "That's fair enough. But what do you want to tell Kinley Marsh?"

"Oh, right. The reporter."

"And ex-camper. She's been calling." Maggie made a big show of checking her phone's menu of recent calls. "Three times already this morning."

"I'll think of something to put her off. No press. Not even an online blog, until we know what we're dealing with."

Chapter 9

Seattle, Washington
Now
Bernadette

Bernadette had just scooped up her keys from the kitchen counter, slipped her arms through her raincoat, and started out the door when her cell phone started to ring. Probably Annette. "I'm coming already," she said crossly, though she was alone in her townhouse. Annette had the worst timing. She called when Bernadette was just stepping into the shower, in the middle of her yoga routine, or often, like now, when she was almost out the door.

Slipping the phone from her pocket, she checked the screen while stepping into the garage. Annette's face and number didn't appear. Instead the small display read, *Private Caller.* Maybe a telemarketer? Swell. She almost hung up, then placed the phone to her ear and, intending to tell the person on the other end to get a life, barked out an impatient, "Hello?"

"Is this Bernadette Alsace? Or Bernadette Warden?" a female voice asked.

"Both," she said, slapping at the button to open the garage door. "Who's this?" For a second she wondered if it was one of Jake's girlfriend's besties, calling to gloat or titter or get their jollies by somehow taunting his ex-wife. It had happened before, when it mattered. Now she really didn't care so . . . *fine. Bring it on.*

The garage door started rolling up noisily, exposing a curtain of rain splattering against the short concrete drive of her recently purchased townhouse.

"My name is Kinley Marsh," the voice said, striking some faraway chord of remembrance in Bernadette's brain.

She opened the door and slipped behind the wheel of her Honda. "Kinley?" Why did that name ring bells? Tossing her purse onto the passenger seat and noting that her umbrella—the one she never used—was tucked into the side pocket of the passenger door, she jabbed her key into the ignition.

"You don't remember me?"

Did she? "I don't think so." With a twist of her wrist, the Honda's engine sparked to life.

"I was a camper in your cabin at Camp Horseshoe twenty years ago."

Ah, yes. Bernadette now remembered the nosy little girl with the long red pigtails and gaps in her teeth. She'd been a pain in the backside then, always asking a million questions and puppy-dogging around after the counselors.

"I'm a reporter now." A pause. "I've got my own blog and I write for an online newspaper, the *NewzZone*. The paper is based out of Astoria, and so we keep up with everything happening up and down the coast. Oregon mainly, but sometimes we print stories that are from California or Washington. Not just local news."

"Okay." Bernadette slid the gearshift into reverse.

"You may not have heard, but it looks like at least one body's been found on the beach near Cape Horseshoe."

"What?" Bernadette said, her attention suddenly riveted to the call. "A body?"

"Well, from what I understand it's not so much a body but bits of human remains, part of a skeleton and a skull."

"Dear God." Bernadette cut the engine. Sat frozen. She'd known this would happen. Expected it, really. But with the passage of time, that long-ago summer had faded, the worry easing. Now, it was back. And hitting hard.

"Exactly." Kinley's voice was smug, as if she were finally satisfied that she'd gotten all of the attention she deserved, the attention Bernadette needed to give her. "The local police are trying to identify the bones and connect them to anyone who went missing in the area."

"Has anyone been reported missing?" she forced out.

"Recently, no. But from what I understand the sheriff of Neahkahnie County, Sheriff Locklear, is concentrating on the people who went missing twenty years ago. You remember."

Like it was yesterday.

"But . . . But they don't know who it is?"

"Not yet. The state crime lab is trying to make that determination."

All of her insides seemed to shrink. "But why . . . I mean, there have been other people who've disappeared along the coast. . . ."

"Of course, but not so many in a concentrated time period. You have to admit, three people, well, I guess four if you count the fugitive who was supposed to be in the area at the time, all vanishing in the space of less than a week? That's odd."

"But the disappearances were investigated." The story had been big news, the investigation intense, the reporters and police crawling all over the campgrounds and surrounding parks and forest area, and small, nearby coastal towns were searched. None of the missing people had been found, no bodies discovered, the case never closed. The circus event mentality of it had waned, the curious moving on to other mysteries to solve, the police concentrating on more active and solvable cases.

"The case was never closed, of course, but shelved, I guess you'd say. The investigation wound down. Apart from Monica O'Neal's mother, Meredith O'Neal, pressing for answers, no one else has pushed for a resolution. Meredith keeps in touch with the sheriff's department and now, with a relatively new sheriff and a body being discovered, trust me, the case is warming up. Twenty years is a long time, technologically speaking. Now, there are all kinds of advances in DNA technology, computers, cameras, digital enhancement, you name it. So, I'm pretty sure all the missing persons cases will be dusted off and pored over again."

Bernadette glanced into the rearview mirror, saw her own eyes staring back at her, and behind them the opening of the garage and the rain falling from the leaden sky. "So why are you calling me?"

"I'd like to interview you," Kinley said. "Get your take on what happened back then, find out what you think might have happened to those who vanished into thin air. You were there."

"I don't know what happened."

"A lot of it would be conjecture, sure, but that's okay. I've got a blog and our newspaper is edgy. We don't exactly write news stories, or at least not exclusively. It's looser, I guess you'd say." She was warming to her subject. "So, being there when it all happened, I have my perspective, but I thought it would be great to do a series, you know? What I saw and heard, and then the same from the other people at the camp, especially the counselors who knew Eleanor Brady and Monica O'Neal, and anyone who was close to Dusty Peters."

"What . . . What about Grimes?" Bernadette asked, stalling for time. "You mentioned him."

"I've got a line on his sister and his cell mate. They've agreed to be part of the story."

"I don't think there's anything I can add," Bernadette said. "I gave a statement to the police at the time and since then, aside from Annette, I haven't kept in touch with anyone who was at the camp."

"Oh. Really? No e-mail? Letters? Phone calls?

No online site where old friends can catch up? Christmas cards?"

So the reporter was baiting her. "We were counselors. Not friends."

"But weren't you, like . . . involved with Lucas Dalton, the son of the camp's owner."

"He . . . He was going with Elle . . . Eleanor Brady."

"I know," Kinley said slowly, as if thinking hard. "But I was there and I'm pretty sure I saw the two of you—you and Lucas—together."

"Well, I knew him. Of course." Bernadette felt a flush climb up the back of her neck, which was just ridiculous. She licked her lips.

"You two would sneak off to that old church on the edge of the campground. Alone."

Bernadette's heart was thundering. No one knew about that. No one! Except, it seemed, Kinley Marsh. "Who told you that?"

"As I said, I was there."

"Look, Kinley, I don't really know where you're going with all of this and I think you're jumping the gun on thinking that a body, if there is one, has anything to do with anything that happened twenty years ago at Camp Horseshoe. I don't have anything more to say."

"Well, think about it. Sheriff Locklear is up for reelection and she's looking for something to make her shine. Solving a cold case of this magnitude, the biggest story to hit the coast in nearly two decades, that wouldn't hurt her and she knows it. She'd be a local hero, and Meredith O'Neal would have justice for her daughter."

"But no one knows what happened to Monica."

"Yet. But I'm thinking this whole thing is going to blow up, big-time. You might want to tell me your side of the thing before that happens. Put your spin on it."

"There is no 'my side,' no 'spin,'" she said tautly. "I've got nothing more to say." She killed the connection, then clicked the phone off, dropped the cell onto the passenger seat, and slammed her fist on the steering wheel.

"Damn, damn, damn!" Just when she was getting her life back together, just when she was starting to feel good about herself, when being single was a badge of honor rather than a disappointment, just when she'd thought she could take on the world again despite losing her baby, as well as her husband and the life they'd led . . . and now this? The door to the past that hadn't quite closed. It was ajar, about to be banged open.

"Get over yourself," she said. She hit the gas and tore out fast, only to stand on the brakes as a bicyclist shot by, zipping down the hill and glaring at her before flipping her off and speeding away.

"Pull yourself together," she warned herself tightly, her heart pounding with a surge of adrenaline. *For the love of God, you could have hit the biker, killed him. Or a mother pushing a jogging stroller down the street. Get a grip, Bernadette. It was only a damned phone call. That's all. Kinley was just poking around. Fishing. Nothing may come of this.*

She drew in a deep breath, held it, and slowly exhaled.

That's it. Calm down. Focus. Find your safe place.

Nothing was going to happen. What had occurred twenty years ago was long dead and buried.

Surely, *surely* she wouldn't have to live through the horror of it again.

She sure as hell hoped not.

She looked back at her townhouse, a new retreat, the place she'd settled on once the divorce was final, her new little nest. Eleven hundred square feet belonging just to her: Ms. Bernadette Alsace, as she was in the process of taking her maiden name again and destroying any remnant of having been Jake Warden's wife. Why keep a name that had proved so false? It wasn't as if she had children with whom to share it. She felt an emptiness at that particular thought, a sadness that comes only at the promise of a child that is shattered by miscarriage, a worse pain than knowledge of the betrayal: Jake's betrayal.

Maybe he just couldn't cope with a wife so

131

caught up in her own grief that she couldn't find happiness anywhere.

"It doesn't matter," she said, and surprised herself with her own words. She hadn't intended to speak them; aloud. Losing the baby, at eighteen weeks, had been heartbreaking, losing her husband after five years of marriage had probably been inevitable. Child or no child.

She blinked, found her eyes were wet, and got angry all over again. She'd thought she'd found a way to bury her grief, to tamp down her pain, to finally move forward again. Wasn't this new home in the Queen Anne District proof enough of that?

But now . . . now, all this old trouble reared its head.

It was a phone call. One lousy phone call. Nothing more. Heart still beating rapidly, but no longer in the stratosphere, she took in a final breath and checked her mirrors once more. She eased out of the driveway and instead of driving to her yoga class, headed straight to Annette's apartment located two blocks off the waterfront and which, from the eighth story, had a pigeon-hole view of Elliott Bay.

Traffic was thick, the going slow, but she managed to snag one of the visitor parking slots for the building and by the time she'd made her way inside, up the elevator and along a short hallway to her sister's apartment, she was calmer.

She knocked and the door opened almost immediately.

"Thank God you're here!" Annette said, her face white, her eyes rounded. In pink sweats, her hair falling all around her face in lank strands, she was upset and not bothering to hide it. "I just got a call from Jo-Beth Chancellor . . . I mean, her name's Leroy now . . . Jo-Beth Leroy. She's a junior partner at some law firm in Portland now."

"I know who you mean." Bernadette stepped into the apartment, a modern one-bedroom unit. The living room was furnished with sleek, modern pieces, decorated in grays with splashes of orange and yellow in the cabinetry, lamp bases, and pillows. Soft jazz was playing from speakers hidden in the walls and ceiling. A yoga mat was stretched out in front of the sliding door leading to a narrow balcony.

Opposite the couch a wall with floating shelves held a flat-screen, a picture of their parents on their wedding day, and all kinds of computer equipment necessary for a one-woman office. Annette, a travel agent, had created an app for bed-and-breakfast inns around the world and, as such, had made a small fortune when she'd sold the app to a larger company. She still consulted and got some kind of fees off the app, and Bernadette thought she was financially set. At least for a while. Who would have guessed that her dreamer of a sister would become techno-savvy in her twenties?

Right now, though, her computer wiz of a sister was as freaked out as Bernadette. Maybe more so.

Annette locked the door behind her and then walked to the kitchen, where a teapot was beginning to whistle.

"What did Jo-Beth want?" Bernadette asked.

"For us to return to the scene of the crime, if you can believe that." She started to pick up the shrieking kettle and then dropped it so fast it clattered back onto the stove. "Ouch! Shit. What's wrong with me?" Finding a pot holder in a nearby drawer, she picked up the kettle again and poured hot water over a tea bag into a cup decorated with her app. "You want some?"

"I'm okay." Well, on a broader scale that was a lie. She wasn't okay at all, her insides were still feeling watery after Kinley's call. Walking to the window, she stared through the glass and past a slit between two high-rises to the "view" of the water, where a white ferry boat was chugging across the sound and seagulls wheeled over its hull. "Jo-Beth wants us to go back to Camp Horseshoe?"

"I don't think it's even a camp anymore, not a working one, but yeah, she thought we should all go down there. She talked to Reva and Sosi and tried to call you, but she couldn't get through. She hasn't connected with Jayla yet, something

134

about losing her number and e-mail, so she's trying Facebook or Twitter, or something, but she wants all of us who were counselors at the time to meet down there."

"And repeat the same old story?"

Annette was nodding as she turned on the kitchen faucet and ran cold water over her scalded hand.

"Ice works better," Bernadette said.

"Does it? Okay. Good. God, this hurts." She turned off the water, found a plastic baggie in a drawer, then crossed to the side-by-side refrigerator and opened the slim freezer door. As she filled the bag with the cubes, she said, "I don't know if I can do it. I mean, essentially lie all over again."

"Did we really lie?" Bernadette asked, guilt gnawing at her.

"Hell, yeah, we lied. And don't say, 'Oh, we stretched the truth,' or 'It was just a little white lie,' because we both know better. And we knew it then. If we go back there, we have to make things right. No matter what happens." She plunged her hand into the baggie of ice, then sharply drew in a breath, air hissing through her teeth. "Ssss! Man, that's cold!"

"That would be the idea of the ice."

"I know, I know. Wow." She turned her attention from her injured hand for a second. "Jo-Beth said she wanted to set the record straight. Can you believe that? 'Straight'? As if our stories were the truth." Wiggling her fingers within the bag of melting ice, she said, "The thing is, I'm not sure I even know what the truth is now. We've been telling the same old story for so long, it's like it really happened. Y'know?"

"Mmm-hmm." Bernadette did know, unfortunately. In dealing with Jake, during the last months of the marriage when she was desperately trying hold them together, Jake would lie to her about what he did, about where he was, and the weird thing about it was that he believed his own words. When she would hit him with the truth, he'd seem stunned, as shocked as Annette had been when she'd plunged her hand into the ice, as if he'd told himself his own version of reality so long that he actually believed it. She definitely understood how lies could be twisted into one's perception of the truth.

"This is too damned cold! How can anyone stand it?" Tossing the ice bag into the sink, Annette picked up her cup and began dunking the soggy tea bag up and down, and staring into the amber depths of her cup.

"*Namaste.*"

Annette frowned at her. "What? Oh, you're trying to be funny."

"A little."

She shook her head. "I can't believe this is happening. Why now?"

"Because of the bones they found."

"But according to Jo-Beth, they don't even know whose they are. I mean, it's crazy to assume it's about when we were there."

"Is it? Just this morning, before I came over here, I got a call from Kinley Marsh. She upset me so badly that I hung up on her and turned the phone off. That's probably why Jo-Beth couldn't reach me."

"Kinley who? Oh, God. She was one of the campers, wasn't she? Yeah, yeah. Now I remember. I think she was in Monica's cabin," she added soberly.

"Right."

"She was the one who always hung around and looked like she needed braces. Had a close friend in my—our—cabin. Mine and Nell's. That girl's name was . . . God, what was it. Real common, I think." Annette's eyebrows drew together as she thought. "Smith—no, Jones. Sarah Jones. That was it. A real pain in the butt, always poking through everyone's stuff, including mine."

"Sounds like you."

"Hah. She really pissed Nell off, though. Nell was always having to corral her, get her to stop." Annette discarded her tea bag into the sink and took a sip from her cup. "What did Kinley want?"

"Essentially the same thing Jo-Beth does. To

talk to me. Us. All of us, I'd guess. She's a reporter now, looking for a story. A big one. She thinks this is it. She didn't say as much, but I could hear it in her voice." Bernadette then explained about her phone call from Kinley, and Annette fell silent. Listening. Drinking her tea. The wheels turning in her head.

"You think we should go down there, to the camp? Talk to the reporter and the police?" Annette asked when Bernadette finished.

"I don't want to, but I think if we don't go down and straighten this out, the reporters and police will come to us." Bernadette didn't want that. She'd moved, gotten on with her life since the divorce and the embarrassment of Jake's affair and quickie marriage to his pregnant girlfriend. Her jaw clenched at that thought. Such a betrayal! God, the man had no decency.

"I'm trying to get a full-time teaching position, not just subbing. I don't need any negative publicity right now, or ever, for that matter."

"So you don't want to return to the scene of the crime?" Annette asked.

"There was no crime."

"Keep repeating that and maybe you'll believe it. You're good at it."

Their gazes clashed and Bernadette knew what her sister was thinking. To that dark time in their own family life. She was talking about Mom. They both knew it, but Bernadette couldn't think about their mother's death, the pain that had destroyed her, how she'd suffered in the end . . . not now. She glanced at a picture on the wall, one of their mother as a young woman, standing and squinting in the sun, each hand holding one of her children's, Bernadette to the left of her, Annette to the right. That's how Bernadette wanted to always remember her.

"If we don't go, I suppose we'll look guilty," Bernadette muttered reluctantly.

"So now there really was a crime? Otherwise no guilt, right?"

Bernadette dragged her gaze from the photograph and glared at her sister. Geez, Annette could be such a bitch sometimes.

And so can you, Bernadette. . . .

She closed her mind to that horrid, nagging voice that always brought up her shortcomings. She didn't have time for it now. No recriminations. No letting her past cloud her judgment. She had to think. To get through this. And she needed Annette's help.

But arguing with her sister never did work. Annette was too analytical. "So, can you get away?"

Annette shrugged, her silent accusations seeming to have evaporated. For the moment. Bernadette knew all too well that they would return. "I consult now," Annette said, "which means I make my own hours and can work from my mobile devices, phone and iPad. I'm just not sure I want to dredge up all that old stuff again."

"Me neither, but . . ."

"Yeah." She tossed the dregs of tea into the sink and dropped her cup in an ever-growing pile of dirty dishes. "Maybe it'll be a good thing, kind of like a spiritual cleanse, you know?" She paused. *"Namaste."*

Bernadette smiled thinly. Withdrawing her phone from her pocket, she saw that she had three messages. All from Jo-Beth. Great. She glanced up at her sister and held up the phone for her to see. "I don't think either Kinley or Jo-Beth are just going to fade away."

"Nope."

"So I guess we'd better start packing."

Annette pulled a sour face. "Let's do this thing, then."

"Okay. You've got her number. Let's call Jo-Beth." The more Bernadette thought about it, the more she wanted to return to Oregon. What had happened twenty years ago at the camp, how the counselors had handled it, had never set well with her. They'd all been young and scared and stupid. And they hadn't been sure what had happened to either Elle or Monica. They'd merely comforted themselves with the thought that they would both show up sooner or later. At least she had . . . and she'd been wrong. It was time to make things right, no matter what.

Annette headed toward her bedroom, but

paused, hand on the doorframe, and glanced over her shoulder. "Your capitulation . . . it happened pretty fast. Doesn't have anything to do with Lucas Dalton, does it?"

"No," she denied quickly. Too quickly.

Annette's eyes narrowed, accusing her of the lie.

"Really. I don't even know where he is."

"I know about you two, at the camp."

"So you've said." Bernadette didn't add that she suspected Annette had experienced a major crush on Luke at the time. It was old news, too.

"And I figure your feelings for him might have been part of the reason Jake and you, well . . . you didn't make it."

"I haven't seen Lucas Dalton since the day we left Camp Horseshoe. I have no idea what he's doing."

"Oh, right. You haven't talked to Jo-Beth yet. She said he's the law down there now, a deputy or detective or something."

Her heart squeezed painfully. "It doesn't matter," she lied.

Annette regarded her knowingly, then she walked into the bedroom. Bernadette was left to try to tamp down the sudden rapid beat of her heart. Yes, she'd fancied herself in love with Lucas twenty years earlier, and yes, she'd never truly forgotten him, but she'd buried him, along with as many memories of that time in Oregon as she

141

could. Buried them all way down deep as she tried like hell to get over the emotional detritus of that summer. But now it was all rising up again, the sins of the past about to reveal themselves and Lucas Dalton was there, front and center.

God help her.

Chapter 10

Camp Horseshoe
Then
Reva

"Whatcha doin'?" Kinley asked. She was carrying a stack of dirty trays from the cafeteria as she sauntered into the camp's kitchen.

Reva, butcher knife in hand, looked over her shoulder quickly and spied the girl's sharp eyes staring back at her. Damn it. Reva had thought she'd been alone. Cookie was out for a smoke on the back porch despite the No Tobacco rule at Camp Horseshoe, and the girls on mess duty were supposed to be wiping down tables in the cafeteria. But the nosy Marsh girl, along with her little friend Bonnie Branson, who was either crying from some emotional trauma, sniffing due to her allergies, or pouting because she didn't get her way, was with her. Reva didn't like either girl, but she pasted a smile on her face and said, "Cleaning up."

"With that?" Kinley asked, staring at the long butcher knife Reva had quickly returned to the magnetic rack bolted onto the wall above the ancient stove, where a huge pot with a quart of leftover spaghetti sauce was congealing, the odors of garlic and tomato sauce hanging in the air.

"It was dirty."

Bonnie scowled. "It didn't look dirty."

"That's because I just washed it," Reva said, lying easily. She picked up the huge pot and poured the contents into a Tupperware container. Avoiding the truth had become a nasty habit, but one, she knew, she wouldn't break anytime soon, not with that ghost of a girl missing since the night before. She slid on the plastic lid and burped the container.

One eyebrow cocked suspiciously, Kinley snagged an apron from the cupboard near the back porch and tied it over her slim figure. She was a tiny thing, not yet developed, no boobs visible. Her front teeth were gapped and her red hair, which probably fell to the middle of her back, was done up in pig tails. She seemed awkward and gawky, but there was something about her, a keen, suspicious intelligence, that bothered Reva. She was always prying, asking questions with just a hint of sarcasm, as if she honestly thought she was somehow smarter than the older girls. Yeah, Reva hated the little twerp.

The two girls began scraping trays, food scraps being pushed into one plastic bin, trash into a lined can positioned near the sinks, silverware dropped into a tub of hot, soapy water waiting in the sink. The kitchen with its low, sloped ceiling was painted white and was nearly spotless. The stove and refrigerators were older, "classic models" resembling something seen in reruns of *The Brady Bunch*. They were gleaming, polished to a bright shine. Miss Naomi, the reverend's wife, insisted on it, spouting the old axiom about cleanliness being next to godliness, but Reva didn't buy it. Fortunately, the cook, a bear of a woman with huge, pillowy breasts resting atop a distended stomach, always complied. "Cookie," as she was called, though her name was Magda Sokolov, wore Coke-bottle glasses, support hose, and a hair net meant to control her steel-gray, always permed hair. The net was an awful spidery-web type all the kitchen helpers were supposed to use if they didn't pull their hair back.

Cookie, who blatantly ignored the ban on smoking, was the sole member of the kitchen staff. The campers and counselors did a lot of the work, either in the meal preparation of chopping and mincing and peeling under Magda's watchful eye, or cleaning the kitchen and cafeteria to Miss Naomi's impossible standards.

Reverend's wife or not, Naomi Dalton was one stuck-up bitch, at least in Reva's opinion.

For now, she left the knife and concentrated on the kitchen cleanup. Pissed that the girls had seen her touching the sharp blade, she wondered if she'd get another chance to pocket it. Maybe after Kinley and Bonnie left for sing-along and prayer a bit later, Reva could "borrow" it. If she could just avoid Cookie's watchful eyes. Kinley cast another look in her direction, but Reva pretended interest in swiping a rag dipped in bleach over the counter. That smarmy little Kinley didn't miss a trick, but hopefully, she'd let the whole knife thing go and find something else to snoop into.

Oh, yeah, because life is so exciting here at Camp Horseshoe, where you get to listen to sermons every *day, do mind-numbing crafts, and work your butt off doing chores.* Even to ride a horse, a camper had to comb it, feed it, make certain it had water and its hooves were in good shape before checking on the condition of the saddle and bridle. And then there was cleaning up after it. Not to mention all the silly songs they had to learn and the flag ceremony and Bible study.

Kinley was giving her the eye. Ostensibly scraping trays, the girl was watching Reva's every move as she loaded the dishwasher and wiped down the surfaces and scrubbed the stove. It was as if the girl had a sixth sense about anything out of the ordinary. What a pain.

Finally, the girls were finished. They stripped off their aprons, then tossed them into an overflowing laundry basket that another set of campers would tend to in the morning. Bonnie, a whining slouch, was in a hurry to leave the kitchen.

Good.

But Cookie had finished her cigarette an was toddling into the kitchen again. "You about done?" she asked, her Russian accent still apparent. She picked up the container of left-over sauce and swept her gaze over the stove.

"About."

"Humph." She carried the container to the refrigerator on the back porch, returned, and eyed the counter where she spied the scraped, but still-dirty trays.

"Why are these not in the dishwasher?"

"I'm getting to them."

"First you wash everything, all the plates and silverware and trays, *then* you wipe down the counters. Otherwise, what is the point?"

Crabby old hag.

"Miss Naomi. She is particular. She likes it"— she struggled for the right phrase and came up with—"spotless, so close to God." With a snort, she went to the long stainless-steel counter where the trays were stacked, and turned on the water. The pipes creaked and water, hot enough to steam, flooded from the spigot. Then she began rinsing each tray. "Kids, what do they know?" she muttered. While her back was turned, Reva snagged the knife. She slipped the long blade into the deep pocket of her apron and prayed the older woman wouldn't catch on as Reva pre-tended to work at removing nonexistent grease on the stove.

But Cookie was busy with her task and mumbling in Russian, probably cussing out the little twerps who hadn't finished their job. Good. A real knife would be a great prop for the little prank they were planning. Reva warmed just thinking about it.

"You!" Cookie suddenly shouted over her shoulder. "Reva! You sweep now. Then mop."

"Sure," she agreed, tossing her cleaning rag into the bin with the other soiled linens. Nervous, she was beginning to sweat as she passed Magda on her way to the screened-in back porch, where in the dirt below the steps were a dozen butts of recently smoked cigarettes. A crow, looking for crumbs in the dirt, squawked and flapped his big wings, flying into the low branches of a pine tree to glare at her. Reva hardly noticed.

The broom and mop were hanging on large nails near the back door, the mop positioned over a bucket, cleaning supplies tucked into a nearby cupboard. Reva stepped farther onto the porch, retrieved the knife, and quickly swiped the handle, in case her fingerprints were on it. Then she ditched the knife in the small space between a refrigerator and chest-type freezer that were used to store extra food. In the dim light of a single lightbulb, screwed into a keyless socket, no one would ever see the knife wedged between the two oversized appliances.

Good.

Grabbing the broom from its hook and snagging the dustpan that was propped near the door, she went inside again. "What took you so long?" Cookie asked, but didn't so much as glance over her shoulder as she started the dishwasher.

"Just getting some air."

"Humph." Shaking her head, she eyed Reva, then wiped her hands on a kitchen towel. "At your age, you need 'air'? More likely you were talking to a boy. That Dustin. I've seen you."

Geez, I was only outside two minutes. What could a person do in two minutes?

"No boy," she said, and was irritated that Cookie, who without her thick glasses was blind as a bat, had noticed a spark between her and the boy who handled the horses.

"Believe or not, I was young once." She tossed her towel into the bin with the other dirty laundry. "You clean up this floor good tonight," she said. "I don't want to hear Miss Naomi say that there was crumbs or dirt on the floor in the morning."

Fighting a sharp retort, Reva started sweeping with gusto and was grateful when the cook peeled off her apron and, tossing it into the laundry bin, headed back outside for yet another smoke before she drove away for the night.

Magda Sokolov was one of the few people at Camp Horseshoe who stayed off campus in the evenings.

As she swept, Reva heard the sound of Magda's old Oldsmobile sparking to life and rumbling away, then, from just outside the front of the cafeteria, the sound of young voices, rising in song. The campers, boys and girls, were gathering for a final prayer after the meal, then they would be allowed to go to their cabins for an hour before they would return to the rec center for games and private discussions and a sermon. Finally, they would be led two by two to the flagpole to sing some more songs, lower the flag, listen to Reverend Dalton give a short sermon, and watch the sun lowering into the ocean. The sun didn't actually set until nine-thirty or ten this time of year, so the campers didn't see it actually sink below the horizon, but they could see the blaze of colors in the sky, magenta, gold, and orange reflecting on the water and any clouds hovering above. "God's easel," the reverend reminded them every night.

So she was alone. Left with a broom and a mop. *And a butcher knife.*

She worked hard and fast, first sweeping up dust and debris, then filling the bucket with hot water and swabbing the floor. She worked from the entrance to the cafeteria and backward through the kitchen, around the butcher block and counters to the back door, where she dumped the water away from the back door and into the side parking area before hauling the bucket and mop back to the porch. She'd just closed the back door when she heard a footstep on gravel.

Whipping around, she spied Dusty standing in the shadows beneath the pine tree where the crow, an hour earlier, had flown.

"Thought I might catch you here," he drawled, stepping out of the shadow of the tree to mount the steps and reach for her.

She batted his hands away and glanced quickly around. "Not here. Not now. Cookie's already suspicious."

"She's always suspicious, and she's gone for tonight." He placed his hands on her waist and this time she didn't push him away, felt the heat of his fingertips through her T-shirt.

"Yeah, well, she mentioned your name to me. She *knows*."

"Big deal."

"We don't want to be caught. You'll be fired and I'll be sent packing." She gave a little shiver at the thought of returning to her family. She was the oldest of eight kids and though she loved her brothers and sisters with all her heart, she didn't relish going back home to become a second mother to them. Here she did chores, but she had some freedom, and she loved her evenings smoking weed and making out with

150

Dusty. She loved the ocean, the adventure, the primitive feel of the place. Well, she liked everything *but* the campers and the rules.

"We won't get caught," he said, and one side of his mouth lifted into that crooked, irreverent grin that she found irresistible.

"I don't know."

He kissed her neck and she felt that little thrill that ran straight down her nerves to the very core of her, a tremor that caused something deep inside to pulse with want. Maybe because it was forbidden, maybe because this was just a summer romance, maybe because she liked being a little naughty. Whatever the reason, Dustin Peters pushed all the right buttons. She didn't love him, she knew that, but so what? For now, he was a damned good time.

"Later," she said hastily, looking around to make sure they weren't seen.

"Ah, babe," he complained.

She peeled his hands away. "I'm serious. I'll meet you later. But I have something I want you to do for me right now."

"What?"

Quickly, she ducked deeper into the shadowy porch and, using the corner of her apron, picked up the knife. She hauled it back and handed it to him.

"What's this?" He rolled the knife over in his fingers.

"What does it look like? Just hold it for me, okay. Take it now and . . . and I'll get it tonight."

"For what?" He was suspicious.

"A prank. To help Jo-Beth. Just do it and don't argue. Now go," she said, sweating suddenly, half expecting that little creep Kinley Marsh or Bonnie to pop up from behind the dumpster, or even that weird Annette Alsace to be looking around the corner, spying on them.

"Okay, okay." He was already stepping off the porch.

"But you'll meet me later, right?" he said, and held out the knife, pointing the blade at her so that anyone nearby could see him. Sometimes Dusty was such a stupid ass.

"Yes!" she promised, and slipped back into the kitchen, where she stood near the door. She couldn't walk across the wet floor yet, but she wanted Dusty to understand that she was serious and just leave.

She thought about the night ahead and the prank Jo-Beth had devised, one to teach that skank Monica O'Neal a lesson. God, the girl was such a pain. Reva would like nothing more than for that sleazy bitch to piss her pants and, she thought with a smile, it was finally going to happen.

All Reva had to deal with was stealing the knife.

Mission accomplished.

Chapter 11

Portland, Oregon
Now
Jo-Beth

"What a fuckin' nightmare!" Jo-Beth said under her breath as she threw things into her suitcase. "Son of a—" She caught sight of herself in the full-length mirror of her bedroom wall and froze. She looked like a madwoman, her short hair uncombed, her makeup fading, her clothes unpressed. Straightening, she told herself to calm down. She had to be in control and look the part.

"Take it down a notch," she told the tall woman in the reflection. "Or maybe like ten notches."

She walked to the windowed wall of her penthouse, placed both hands on the glass, and stared out at her view of the Hawthorne Bridge, one of seven or eight, she couldn't remember, that crossed the Willamette River. Traffic was slow, a trail of brake lights visible on the span. Always, she thought, as Portland traffic had become a perpetual snarl. "Stumptown" had become "Bike Town" and was now cool, somewhere hip people migrated to, and the city was being revitalized. In the process, traffic was now a bitch.

Slowly letting out her breath, willing her frustration to evaporate, she peered over the rooftops of the shorter buildings in her view and swung her gaze to the far side of the river, to the panorama of the city stretching eastward to the Cascades. The mountains weren't visible today, no breathtaking vista of Mount Hood, a peak she'd climbed three times in the past ten years. It calmed her to see the rocky, snow-covered slopes rising above the timberline, but today, with the thick cloud cover, not a single ridge could be discerned.

Decidedly calmer, she pushed off the windows and, walking to the master bath, stripped out of her workout clothes, tossing them into the hamper before turning on the taps of the massive shower. When the spray from the three separate shower heads was the perfect temperature, she stepped inside and lathered up. She hadn't begun to sag anywhere, thank God. Her breasts were still as firm as ever, her abdomen tight, and her ass remarkable, as she'd heard whispered behind her back when she strode into the boardroom of the law firm just last week. She kept her hair short, so that she could run or exercise anytime—at a moment's notice—then shower and pull herself together in less than half an hour. She'd tattooed eyeliner on her lids and used a product that grew her lashes, then touched up those pesky lines on her face with Botox. In the past five years she'd finished six triathlons and two half marathons . . . that was enough. Marathon runners were too weird for her taste, like, *absorbed* with running, and she needed to be a bit more balanced. Her life was much too complicated and interesting to be overrun with one obsession.

Especially when she had dozens of obsessions and compulsions in her wheelhouse.

For a second she thought of Tyler Quade, the boy she'd given her heart to in her youth. Her pang of nostalgia was underscored by a simmering rage, one she'd hidden away in a locked corner of her mind, but that emotion was just behind that latched door, always pressing to get out. How could Tyler have cheated on her? And with that waste of space Monica O'Neal. She shuddered now, under the hot water, just at the thought of it. She was just so . . . well, so trashy and low-class, so plebian. There was no other way to consider it, or to remember her. For the love of God, what had he seen in that bitch? For a second, she remembered Monica as she had been at nineteen, with curling black hair that fell around her face in a way that looked, well, slutty. Her lips had been full and twisted in a come-hither smile, her eyes a cool blue that always had stared a little too hard. So, okay, she did have one of those voluptuous figures. Big boobs, small waist, and a tight ass, but hell, it was nowhere near "remarkable," not like hers.

And still the bastard had strayed, fucking Monica, and impregnating the bitch.

Her fingernails dug into her scalp as she washed her hair and rinsed away the anger. Letting the lather run over her body, she refused to dwell on Tyler's infidelity and couldn't help but wonder what had happened to him. She'd been so incensed at the time that, when she'd heard about the pregnancy, she'd never spoken to him again, despite the fact that they had their own, very private little secret.

You should have married him when you had the chance. He'd asked, hadn't he? And wouldn't he have been better than the loser you ended up with, Eric, the latent hippy? At least Tyler had the same sense of daring, of mischief, as you, would go as far as necessary to get what he wanted.

"We were too damned young," she said aloud, jumping at the sound of her voice over the hiss of the spray. And Tyler hadn't moved in the right circles, couldn't give her what she, even then, realized she needed in life. But he was the one who had been able to make her juices run hot. Not just sexually, but mentally as well, how he liked to experiment, to push the envelope, to prick at another's psyche just to see how much they could take.

Even now, after all these years, she felt a little thrill at what they'd done together, and there was more than a hint of regret that she hadn't explored all that was to discover with him.

Forget it. It's O-V-E-R. Just deal with the issues at hand and those girls, now women. You have to control them. You can afford no loose cannons. No loose lips.

She groaned aloud. God, did she really have to deal with them again? Talk about stress! As if she didn't have enough!

Jo-Beth believed in moving forward with life and didn't like dealing with the hangnails or warts of her past.

Not at all.

"Well, get ready. You're in for it now," she muttered through clenched teeth. She turned the water on a smidge warmer, adjusted the spray, and stood under the piercing needles, letting the hot water beat against her muscles. *You can do this,* she thought silently, going to her daily mantra. In a law firm dominated by men . . . no, make that *old* men, she'd learned to fight and claw her way to junior partner by believing in herself and taking charge. Now, with her sights set on a full partner-ship in the firm of Keating, Black, Tobias, and Aaronsen, she couldn't let anything get in her way, especially not something as insignificant and trivial as a damned church camp and a couple of missing counselors. Jesus, those girls were basket cases anyway. Who knew what had happened to them? As for that horse wrangler, or whatever he was—Dusty? Dustin? He'd probably just walked off the job. Working for that nutcase of a preacher couldn't have been a bed of roses. Who would blame him for grabbing his paycheck and riding into the goddamned sunset?

Jo-Beth had had to take things into her own hands when she'd learned of the discovered body parts. Reva and Sosi were on board, though Sosi had turned *ultra*religious and Reva had her own issues. She'd talked to nerdy Annette, too, who had promised to get in touch with her sister. Jayla, of course, was a problem. She wasn't answering her cell phone or responding to texts, and the last e-mail Jo-Beth had for her had bounced back. She planned to check Facebook or Tumblr or Twitter or whatever social media platform Jayla used. She couldn't be too hard to find. Hell, the private eye who worked for the law firm could find deadbeat dads and spouses who were ducking their alimony payments, and runaway teens, as well as sniff out arsonists and the losers involved in insurance fraud without much trouble, and he was no genius.

Jo-Beth would find her.

And she would convince Jayla to join the rest of them in Averille, Oregon, even if it was the center of no-fucking-where. Together, their story tight as ever, they'd meet with the damned sheriff and whoever else and put this case to bed. For-damned-ever!

She sighed, annoyed. It would have to be a short trip. She couldn't afford to take too much time away from the office. And then there was Eric, who was still her legal husband even if he hadn't lived here in nearly two months.

Why the hell had he decided to have his mid-life crisis now, when her own life was teetering precariously? Between lobbying for a partner-ship in the firm and this mess down at the coast, the last thing she needed, the very last, was a husband who had decided to quit his lucrative job as an investment banker and try to find himself. Why Eric had decided to buy an ancient Volkswagen bus, outfitted as a camper, and go cruising off the grid, she didn't know, but his sudden affinity for weed and an interest in Burning Man, that weirdo festival in the Nevada desert, didn't bode well for their marriage.

She ground her teeth at the thought. Well, if he thought he was going to divorce her and get some kind of alimony just because she was about to get a huge pay increase with the partnership, he could think again.

"Prick," she muttered. Where was the buttoned-up Wall Street type she'd thought she'd married? The man who had worked hard for years to go to graduate school, the man who used to adore her and give her diamonds worth a small fortune, the same glittering gems he now eschewed. Rocks! That's what he'd called her three-carat engagement ring and the earrings he'd given her on their first anniversary.

What the fuck had happened?

So he'd turned forty-five, so what?

Jesus, could nothing go right?

Turning off the spray, she again took a long look in the half-steamy mirror in the tiled bath, liked what she saw, and took the time to locate her phone and take a sexy selfie, full-length, her body still slick from the water, her hair, after she gave it a ruffle with her fingers, looking wet and tousled, her look a naughty come-on. Dear Lord, she should have been a damned model. Could have with those long legs. But she'd known that was a short, hard career, and she'd decided instead to capitalize on her brains rather than her beauty. Much more staying power. Much less competition. Pretty girls were a dime a dozen, or maybe less, but a striking woman with a terrific memory and an acute ability to analyze and solve a problem—the sky was the limit. "Legendary," she said to herself as she always did. This was her daily, if not hourly, affirmation: "That's what you are. Unique and legendary." And, of course, she'd used that beauty to advance herself as well. Whatever it took.

As the fan cleared the moisture that had collected on the mirrors, she applied her makeup in the buff, found a fresh pair of black leggings and a long, cowl-necked shirt that just covered her buttocks, then finished with heeled boots that gave her another three inches.

Then she packed. Neatly. Carefully. Planning the coming days as she folded her clothes and toiletries into her bag. She just had to make certain that everyone, every last one who had been a counselor at Camp Horseshoe, was on the same page to the last paragraph.

"You can do it," she said aloud as she double-checked her suitcase.

Satisfied that she'd left no necessity behind, she zipped up the case, pulled on a sleek, belted jacket, and headed out of the penthouse to drive to bumblefuck Oregon, for damage control.

She took the express elevator to the parking garage, unlocked her sporty white Mercedes wirelessly, and noticed her vanity plate: LGLGDSS, which not too many people could figure out, but that was okay. Smiling, she slid into the cool interior. Who needed the common man to figure out she was a legal goddess?

As long as she knew it, and the senior partners at Keating, Black, Tobias, and Aaronsen knew it as well, then nothing else mattered.

Nothing at all.

She pulled out of the parking garage, easing through the ever-increasing traffic, flipped on the wipers due to the rain, then set her jaw as she merged onto Highway 26. Through the Vista Ridge tunnel that cut beneath the West Hills of

Portland she headed west. Above the tunnel, the forested slopes hid elegant homes of some of Portland's wealthiest residents, mansions tucked between the firs, maples, and spruce trees. Mullioned windows peeked through evergreen branches to peer over the heart of downtown and across the Willamette River to the city spreading eastward toward the rugged Cascade Mountains. The homes on the hillside ranged from contem-porary, to mid-century modern, to classic Portland. All were expensive and grand, but didn't afford the luxury of being right downtown, where one could feel the pulse of the city, the kind of amenity Jo-Beth craved.

From the tunnel, the road ran deep through the forested canyon, then widened. She punched the gas and skirted a huge semi pulling double trailers. Her thoughts turned to Averille and Camp Horseshoe and dealing with the police in that part of the state. Despite the advances in technology over the past two decades, she doubted law enforcement in rural Oregon would be on the cutting edge of a homicide investigation. "Homicide," she repeated aloud. No one had mentioned the word yet, so it was best to avoid it. The road curved upward and she was just cresting Sylvan Hill when her cell phone jangled, bursting into her thoughts.

Answering automatically, she hit the button on her steering wheel to talk through her Wi-Fi.

"This is Jo-Beth," she clipped out as she passed a slow-moving Ford something-or-other, her Mercedes purring and responding like the excellent driving machine it was.

"Hey," a man said as if he'd known her all his life. "I heard you were looking for me."

Her heart nearly stopped, then restarted with a jolt. She recognized the tenor of that voice, despite all the years that had passed, all the time that had slipped away.

"It's Tyler."

Oh. My. God.

When she didn't say anything, he clarified, "Tyler Quade."

"I know," she said in a strangled voice that she didn't recognize as her own. Then she got a grip on herself, took a deep breath, and as she zoomed into the passing lane, barely missing the front bumper of an accelerating BMW, she ignored the angry horn blast from the other driver and said, "And where the hell have you been all these years?"

Chapter 12

Camp Horseshoe
Then
Lucas

It was his fault, Lucas knew as he slammed the door of his battered Jeep Cherokee and pocketed his keys. His fault that Elle had disappeared. If his head hadn't been turned, if he'd been honest with her from the get-go, if he'd been man enough to love her, maybe then she wouldn't have vanished into thin air.

Or run away.

Or been killed.

Oh, Jesus.

He'd tried to let her down easy, but it hadn't worked.

His boots crunched as he walked atop the sparse gravel and a pesky yellow jacket buzzed nearby. With a sense of dread he made his way to the camp's office to talk to the deputy. What would he say?

The truth. You have to come clean . . . about everything. Every last detail. Don't even think of swerving from what you know to be true.

"Hell," he swore under his breath. This was going to be bad. Very bad. Swatting at the damned

164

wasp, he thought about the night the shit had hit the fan and Elle had finally realized it was over between them.

The yellow jacket landed on his wrist and before he could slap it away, the wasp stung him. "Son of a—" He bit back the swear word just in time. No doubt his father was waiting for him with the cop, and he needed to hold on to his temper, despite the small red welt rising near the back of his hand. He rubbed the spot, but his mind was on Elle.

She was missing.

Why hadn't he seen it coming?

But you did, didn't you? You knew she was unstable, that something was wrong, and it didn't stop you.

In a wash of memory, he recalled it all.

It had started when he'd confronted her, a few weeks after Fourth of July, nearly August, when he'd decided he couldn't live a lie, not any longer.

He'd worked up his nerve to end it. Or at least start the process. He and Elle had been a couple for nearly a year, so the breakup wouldn't be easy, even though, he'd suspected, her feelings for him, too, had changed.

At midnight, he'd sneaked over to her cabin and as he had a dozen times before, rapped softly beneath her window. Three short knocks, then two. Then he'd waited. When she hadn't immediately appeared, he'd repeated the signal, then soon heard a rustling on the other side of the thin wooden walls, three rapid-fire taps. Sharp. Distinct. Indicating she'd heard, was awake, and would meet him.

He'd swallowed hard and wished there were some way to get out of this, to avoid the heart-ache of breaking up with her. Would she cry? Hit him? Scream that he was the dickwad he felt like?

Bracing himself, he'd slipped into the shadows, away from the glow of the banked campfire at the center of the ring of cabins, and hustled along the path running behind the cluster of buildings. Jaw set, determined to tell her that it was over, he'd followed the trail, veering at a fork, to hurry through the forest. By the time he'd reached the beach, far below the cliffs upon which the camp had been established, the ocean had been shrouded in fog, the sound of waves tumbling against the shore a rush in his ears, the smell of sea air in his nostrils. He hadn't been able to see the Pacific—nor much of anything else—through the thick mist, but the feel of the sea had been all around him.

As had been their custom, they'd agreed to meet at the point where the bay fed into the far end of the beach, the southern edge of the camp's property. It was nearly a mile from the cabin, and Elle had hated to be that far from her campers, but she would always tell Jayla that she was leaving and instruct the other counselors to watch her girls. Jayla had always kept on eye on Elle's cabin and the campers within, and Elle had returned the favor often enough. The truth was all of the counselors at Camp Horseshoe made a practice of leaving their cabins at night. There was alcohol to consume, weed to smoke, and the opposite sex to flirt and play with.

Yeah, it was dangerous.

Yeah, his father would skin him alive if he ever found out.

But Lucas didn't give a rat's ass what his old man threatened or what he did. These days and nights he was always thinking about sex. *Always.* And Elle, she was beautiful and giving, her pale hair and thin frame almost angelic. He'd known her since middle school, and she'd actually dated one of his stepbrothers before breaking up with Ryan to start dating Lucas. That hadn't gone over so well, and the two boys had come to words and blows, the worst fight resulting in Ryan being rushed to the hospital in the middle of the night because Lucas's fist had busted his nose. While Lucas had gotten by with a couple of bruised ribs and a cut on his chin, Ryan had sported a couple of black eyes for nearly two weeks, but more than his face, his pride had suffered a severe beating.

After the final fight, the reverend had lectured the boys, handed out additional chores, and grounded them each for weeks. Still seething,

Ryan had backed off, though Lucas had caught Naomi's oldest glowering at him when Ryan thought no one would notice. There was sure to be payback, Lucas could feel it, and their younger sister had confided that Ryan had vowed to "get" Lucas. She'd slid through the open doorway to his bedroom, the attic on the third floor that had been converted into a sleeping area, complete with a small window and sloped ceilings that made it impossible to stand unless you were in the very middle of the room.

"That's what he said. I heard him tell David," Leah, all wide eyes, straight blond hair, and upturned nose, had warned as she'd plopped down beside the bed where he'd been staring up at the ceiling and plotting his escape from his father's tyranny.

"Spare the rod, spoil the child." One of his father's favorite adages, and it was bullshit.

He'd slid a glance at his sister. She didn't know it, but he adored her, despite her obvious flaws. And there were many. At eleven Leah was intrigued with everything her older half brothers did and was a bit of a mixer herself, always stirring up trouble. "He was gonna 'get you back' and 'make you pay' and that you 'would regret ever having started the fight.' "

"I didn't start it," Lucas had argued.

Leah had been nodding solemnly as if she understood all the nuances of her siblings' complicated relationships. Of course she didn't. Nor did he. Around her braces, she said, "Ryan said he would 'finish it.' "

Well, so be it. Lucas had welcomed the challenge. Let him try. Lucas had never much liked either of his stepbrothers, and he wasn't afraid of Ryan, who was tough, all right, just not quite tough enough. And neither of Naomi's sons had been blessed with Lucas's wingspan, which really helped in a fist fight. Nor were they as light on their feet. They were both downright naive when it came to street smarts.

So, yeah, Ryan, bring it on, he'd thought.

No doubt he would. Ryan's temper was and had been legendary, and it had flared white hot when his upstart of an older stepbrother had stolen Elle from him. It hadn't mattered that his own relationship with Elle had run its course. Oh, no. In Ryan's mind, Lucas had taken something from him and Lucas had understood even then that he would never be forgiven, that Ryan would always want retribution.

Lucas hadn't cared about his stepbrother's simmering anger. He'd ignored the younger boy, his focus on his new relationship as it had heated and grown in the six months prior to her graduating from high school. Everything had been fine, then she'd hired on at the camp as a counselor and things had changed. Lucas had imagined they would continue to see each other, but Elle, in the weeks before actually moving to the camp, had become moody and grown distant, even snappish.

It was in that period when he couldn't reach Elle, couldn't find out what was troubling her, was the butt of her anger more often than not, that his own feelings had subtly shifted, and he'd begun to question his relationship with her.

And then he'd met Bernadette.

From that first moment of spying her on the other side of the reception desk, he'd been hooked. He'd tried not to notice the length of her neck, her incredibly long legs, and the way her eyes crinkled at the corners when she smiled. However, he hadn't been able to ignore the innocent allure of her, the way her green eyes sparkled or the sharpness of her tongue or how her dark hair turned a deep, fiery copper color when caught in sunlight. She'd been smart, sassy, and opinionated, and though he'd thought she'd given him the once-over, she'd been nonchalant when he'd waited for the two girls to say good-bye to their mother on that first day.

Once Mrs. Alsace's older Volvo had started rattling down the lane that curved away from the center of the camp, Lucas had shown the sisters to their cabins.

They'd walked with him along the wide path leading from the office and rec center, through the thickets of evergreen trees and clumps of salal. He'd noticed then, with sunlight dappling the ground through the branches, the way her T-shirt stretched over her breasts and the movement of her butt when she walked. It was crazy what an effect she had on him. He'd told himself to look away from her, to remember Elle, but he just couldn't. The trail ended at the small clearing with a fire pit directly in its center, benches surrounding the pit. A few yards away, the cabins, like circling wagons, rimmed the perimeter of the open space.

"Here ya go," he'd said, indicating the rustic cabin assigned to Bernadette. He'd waited as she'd stepped inside. This unit, like the others, was basically two rooms, well, actually one large, long room separated by a wall with an open doorway for the counselor, in the smaller "room," to keep track of her charges. Her bed bumped up against the half wall, above which, again, she was able to view the girls under her supervision through the open interior window. On the wall opposite the cot a few shelves and a cupboard had been built next to the exterior doorway.

Bernadette had walked the length of her small space and through the open doorway to the larger area, which would be assigned to the campers. As it had been then, the cots lining the wall were empty, the pegs and hooks from which girls could hang their backpacks were visible beneath two rows of shelves that Lucas, with the aid of Ryan and David, had installed over the winter.

"Six campers to a counselor," she'd said as Lucas had dropped her bag by her cot.

"That's right. Except in the case when there are co-counselors, then it's eight campers to the two counselors. Like in Annette's case."

Her gaze scoured the interior. "No bathroom."

"A shower house is just down the path. Hot and cold running water, showers, toilets, sinks, and fresh towels daily."

"Just like the Ritz," she'd said with more than a trace of sarcasm, but her green eyes had glinted in amusement.

"Exactly like it. The way I hear it, the Ritz copied us."

Her smile had widened, showing off a single dimple. God, she was beautiful.

"So much luxury," she'd commented, surveying the open rafters, windows with wood shutters, and worn floorboard.

"Well, it *is* a camp, you know."

"Hmm. Straight out of the nineteen twenties or thirties." Arching a dubious eyebrow, she'd continued to survey the tight, austere rooms. "Home sweet home for the next three months."

Lucas had nodded. "You got it."

"And the campers?" she'd asked, motioning to the empty beds. "They're not here yet, right? When do we meet them?"

"They're scheduled to show up in about a

week. In the meantime you'll go through orientation and be given a tour and shown around every inch of the campgrounds. The reverend will make certain you know the rules, safety measures, and your duties inside out."

"Oh, joy." She'd dimpled. "Can't wait."

Annette had been standing on the top step and had craned her neck to peer inside. Lucas had nearly forgotten she'd been tagging along.

"Come on in." Bernadette had waved to her younger sister.

Shaking her head, the single braid swiping her shoulders, Annette hung back in the doorway. She'd been taking in the conversation and Lucas had experienced the sensation that she didn't miss much, that she was the quiet type who stood on the periphery of a crowd and made meticulous mental notes. What she'd finally said was, "Where's my cabin? And why am I 'co-counseling'?"

"Right next door." Lucas, irritated that he'd had to deal with her, led the way with Annette following. She was as awkward as her sister was confident.

"Is this cabin smaller?" she'd asked as he'd placed her bag on her cot.

"They're all about the same size—give or take. Yours is actually slightly larger to accommodate the extra campers and counselor. You have bunk beds. You and Nell, I think her name is Nell

Pachis. She's a junior counselor, only fifteen, so basically, you'll be in charge."

Annette was almost eighteen, just as Bernadette had recently turned nineteen.

Annette observed, "It seems darker."

"It's nearly identical to your sister's," he'd assured her, pointing to the counselors' area, where there was an additional slim cupboard and a top bunk mounted over the lower cot.

Annette eyed the open rafters suspiciously. "What about spiders?"

"We've got 'em."

"And rats?"

"Not too many. The snakes take care of them."

As her eyes rounded, her face turning a chalky color, Bernadette had said, "He's kidding, Annette." Then she'd glanced at him and smothered a smile. "Well, at least there aren't any rattlers, probably. But, of course there are garter snakes and others, I guess, nonvenomous."

"Still . . ." Giving a little shiver, Annette had warily eyed the corners of the cabin. She'd swallowed visibly and had appeared as if she were already regretting signing on to the roster of counselors at Camp Horseshoe.

Bernadette had said finally, "You'll be fine. We were just kidding."

Annette had shot Lucas a look that could've sliced through granite. "You shouldn't say those things. Some of the counselors might believe you, you being the son of a preacher and the director of the camp and all."

"Just trying to break the ice."

"Consider it broken." Annette had sniffed and twirled on her heel and, in a huff, half ran outside.

"You're bad, you know that, don't you?" Bernadette's eyes had narrowed and she'd tilted her head to one side as if sizing him up.

"Yeah," he'd admitted, and felt a slow grin pulling at the sides of his mouth. "I sure do. And if I forget? There's always someone ready to remind me." He'd been talking about his old man, but she'd thought he was talking about her. Which had been just fine. He'd let her believe whatever she'd wanted.

"Maybe you should work on how you welcome people when they show up here."

He'd considered it for a second, then shaken his head. "Nah."

She'd laughed.

"Come on. I'll show you around."

"Uh, maybe later. We want to settle in." With a quick glance to the doorway, she'd added, "Both of us."

"You're sure?"

"Yeah, pretty sure."

"You could be missing out."

"Right. And so could you."

Oh, I know it, he'd thought at the time, and from that moment on, his interest in Elle had taken a nosedive. He couldn't help himself. As pretty and intellectual as Elle was, there had been a melancholy about her that he couldn't name, a sadness she'd never explained. He'd asked her several times what was wrong, but more often than not, she'd reply, "Nothing," and manage to scare up a ghost of a smile, or at times ignore his question. As if she hadn't heard it, or just hadn't cared.

Nothing had brought that observation more to the fore than dealing with Bernadette, who was sassy and smart and spontaneous. She gave as well as she got, and he'd found himself arguing with her and laughing with her and finding her so intriguing that he thought about her all the time.

It had caused him immense guilt where Elle was concerned, but he hadn't been able to stop himself from being attracted to the confident, older Alsace sister. All the while Elle grew quieter, more solemn, and began to shrink back into whatever darkness lurked within her mind. Sometimes, when Lucas was with her, Elle didn't seem to be present at all. She was off in her own mind to the point that it seemed she didn't hear him when he spoke to her. He'd wondered if she'd become bored with him, though upon posing the thought, she'd snapped a quick reply.

"No, of course not," she'd told him in irritation as she sat in the passenger seat of his battered

Cherokee. Rain had been pouring from a leaden sky, fat drips drizzling down the windshield. He'd parked in front of her house after what had been a miserable, and mostly silent, dinner. At dinner Elle had been as far away from him as she'd ever been, even though she was seated across from him in a faux-leather booth, paying no attention to her two slices of pizza.

In the Cherokee, she'd asked him querulously, "Why would you think I'm bored with you? I love you, Lucas."

He hadn't returned the vow, too immersed in conflicting emotions, and the atmosphere inside the Jeep grew tense. In fact, he'd never told her he loved her. He just couldn't find the words, which was probably why he'd felt more than a little whisper of guilt whenever he thought of breaking up with her.

That instance had been weeks before he'd met Bernadette, and once he started seeing her, he'd known he'd have to admit to Elle that it was over. For good.

That was the hard part. They'd had sex. At first, all the time. She'd been nearly as horny as he was in the beginning, eager, almost insatiable, but then, a few weeks earlier, something had changed. She'd lost interest and kind of retreated into herself. More than once he'd caught her walking on the beach alone, staring out at the ocean, watching the swells and waves, or the seagulls crying and wheeling overhead, sometimes talking to herself, other times crying, but never once smiling. Gone was the gaiety he'd witnessed in high school, the lighthearted but smart girl with a bashful streak who had caught his eye. It was almost as if the moment she'd set foot on the sandy grounds of Camp Horseshoe, she'd lost her happiness.

No, that wasn't quite right. It had been building in the weeks before the camp had officially opened for the summer.

He'd concluded that things weren't right for her at home and, deep down, he suspected that her change in mood had intensified due to the fact that she'd been working closely with Ryan, her ex-boyfriend, again. Or maybe the responsibility of being a counselor had become too weighty for her.

Whatever the reason, she damned well should lighten up. He'd tried to talk to her and met with a brick wall.

"I'm okay," she'd told him over and over. Then, that night on the foggy beach, she'd said it again and started to walk away. He'd caught her wrist and said, "Elle, what's wrong?"

"Nothing! Nothing's wrong," she'd insisted, exploding, her fury palpable. "How many times do I have to say it?"

He released her wrist then. "Until I believe it."

"Why do you keep hounding me?"

"Because you seem sad."

"I'm not 'sad,' " she'd insisted with a flare of temper. "I've . . . I've just got a lot on my mind, okay?"

"Maybe I could help."

The look she'd sent him then was a mixture of disbelief, disgust, and a bit of despair. "You wouldn't understand."

"Try me."

She'd hesitated and for a second he'd thought he'd broken through whatever wall it was that she'd been building, brick by brick, to make herself inaccessible to him or maybe to the world. "No," she'd finally said, a little more quietly. "I-I'll figure it out. It's my problem, and so I'll come up with a solution." She'd attempted a smile, but it had wobbled and her eyes had started to fill with tears. "Don't worry about me."

"But I do."

"Do you?" she'd asked as the first tear ran down her cheek, one she'd hastily brushed away.

"Of course."

"But you don't love me," she'd accused, the wind blowing off the sea, fog in tendrils, snaking up the shore. "You've never said so."

"It's just not my style."

"Oh, I see, you love me, but you're too 'cool' to admit it." Her words were bitter as she tossed her hair over her shoulder, the strands fluttering in a pale wave. When he didn't respond, she'd said, "Or, maybe there's no love at all. I guess I should've known. Good-bye, Lucas." Her blue eyes were ice. "I'm going to miss you and believe it or not, you're going to miss me, too." And she'd turned away then, headed down the beach, her arms wrapped around her middle.

He'd taken two steps after her, then held up and watched her disappear into the thickening fog. What more was there to say? He did care about Elle, but whatever spark had ignited between them had died weeks before Bernadette had shown up at the camp. That was the real truth.

Still, he felt like an ass letting her walk away into the darkness. Alone. He should go after her, he told himself. Say what she wanted to hear. But it would be a lie, because he was already thinking of Bernadette. Fun-loving, quick-witted, and ready for a dare, Bernadette with her full breasts and long legs and flashing eyes. Her sense of humor was wicked, her skin soft and . . .

He glanced to the beach again, but Elle was gone, swallowed by the night. Squinting into the darkness, he saw no sign of her, so he stuffed his hands deep into the pockets of his jeans, turned inland, and told himself to forget her. It was over.

She'd find someone else.

Someone better.

He made his way to the path that switchbacked up the hillside and as he did, his blood ran hotter.

He would meet Bernadette soon and, with guilt right on his heels, he could already imagine what they'd do when they met.

He couldn't wait.

At least that's how he'd felt two days earlier . . . before Elle had vanished for good the following night.

Now, as he walked up the two steps to the office of the camp, he looked through the windows near the door and spied his stepmother beyond the glass. As if she'd sensed him on the long porch, she glanced up and held his gaze for a heartbeat too long.

The back of his throat went dry.

Quickly, she turned her attention to the mail she'd been sorting. By the time he opened the door, she was retreating, her red-blond hair catching in the light streaming through the windows of the hallway, her heels clicking down the worn plank floor. Without so much as a glance over her shoulder, she started up the stairs leading upward to the second floor, where his father, Leah, and she lived during the summer months when the camp was open.

Lucas's chest tightened a bit. *Not now,* his more prescient mind whispered. *Maybe not ever again.*

"Lucas!" Jeremiah Dalton's voice boomed from the far side of the office, and Lucas whirled to face him. Under the archway between the desk area and a small sitting room stood his father. Tall and ramrod straight, his angular face a mask of severity, his eyes burning like the very coals of hell, he hitched his chin at the shorter, rounder, less intimidating man at his side. "This is Deputy Hallgarth from the sheriff's department."

Hallgarth was blond and ruddy complected, and a tic near his right eye gave him the appearance of winking at you. Which he wasn't. Grim-faced, he nodded stiffly.

Before he could state his business, Jeremiah said, "He's here to ask us all some questions about Eleanor Brady. You're up."

"That's right," Hallgarth said, shooting Lucas's father a look to remind the older man that he was in charge. "Just step into this room over here." He pointed to the sitting area. "I'd like to get a statement from you. As I understand it, you are her friend and more specifically her boyfriend."

"I was," Lucas said as he followed the older man into the anteroom. "We'd broken up."

From the corner of his eye, Lucas noticed his old man tense his fists for a nanosecond.

"I'd like to hear about that," Hallgarth said, and pointed to a stiff-backed chair positioned near a window overlooking the parking area. "Go ahead, son, have a seat. And tell me everything you know about Eleanor." He hitched up the pants of his uniform and took a spot on a sofa situated across a coffee table from Lucas. "Let's start with the last time you saw her."

Chapter 13

Interstate 5, Oregon
Now
Reva

Flipping on the wipers, Reva Mercado tromped on the accelerator of her Toyota Camry. She was driving north on the freeway, twenty miles south of Portland, she guessed, and she pushed the speed limit while passing cars, vans, SUVs, and semis, their trailers laden with everything from gas, to milk, to dog food.

She was anxious and had to keep moving.

Glancing down at her speedometer, she saw that the needle was climbing, hovering near eighty, and she eased up a bit.

Don't get pulled over. Don't get a ticket. You do NOT want to talk to the police! Remember the last time? You don't want that all brought up again. Not now. Not ever.

That part was difficult—the avoiding the cops —because even if she evaded the state police patrol, cops hiding in their cars, radar guns at the ready, she couldn't stay away from some persnickety driver who could phone in that she was speeding or driving recklessly or whatever. So she tried to keep her speed under control instead of hurtling down the interstate at Mach 1.

It really didn't matter if she was the first to land in bumblefuck Averille, Oregon, or the last; she just wanted to make certain everyone's story concurred with hers. She couldn't afford another run-in with the cops. Not after what she'd been through.

The traffic that had been racing along was slowing as she neared Portland, more and more vehicles clogging the lanes, her speed, by necessity, cut by half. Good. She needed to calm down. Think things through. Jo-Beth wanted to meet her first, privately, to get their solidarity strong, their stories rock solid. All good. Reva was in. She couldn't take a chance that any of this would bring back the other nightmare of her life.

"Don't even go there. Do not." She glanced in the rearview, noticed that her brown eyes were worried, rather than feisty. Wasn't that what Theo had always said about her? Now, she looked scared and for good reason.

Theo.

"Love of my life," she murmured, and let out her breath slowly.

Out of habit, she lifted her right hand from the steering while and sketched a quick sign of the cross over her heart, a practice she hadn't given up though her days of catechism and mass were long over and had been since the time of the accident. How could she ever go to a priest and confess her sins when they were so dark? No, better to give up on the trappings of her religion, if not her faith itself.

She saw the exit for 217, cut across two lanes, then slowed as traffic became sluggish at the interchange. The creeping, mind-numbing pace didn't improve much for the few miles it ran between the interstate and Beaverton. Jockeying around other vehicles, she thought ahead to the nightmare that was about to unfold. Jo-Beth had mentioned a reporter, Kinley Marsh—supposedly a camper at the time, but Reva barely remembered her—that she was an investigative reporter or something and that Lucas Dalton, the reverend's sexy son, was now a cop. But what was worse was that he had a partner, according to Jo-Beth, a woman by the name of Margaret Dobbs. The name caused a chill to skitter down Reva's spine. Was it possible? Could she be the same damned detective who'd been a part of the team investigating the accident that had taken Theo's life? Oh, sweet Jesus. That would be a disaster. A total disaster, not to mention what had happened at the camp.

She'd hoped that her church camp experience of twenty years ago had died a quick and certain death. And it seemed it had for twenty years, but now, damn it, it was as if the whole nightmare had been resurrected.

A body had been recovered. It didn't mean that the body was of one of the people who'd gone missing way back in that horrible time warp, right? But if not, why had she and the rest of the damned counselors who had known the missing teens been called to give a statement?

It was hard to breathe, even more difficult to stay calm. She felt as if there were steel bands constricting her chest and as she sat in traffic—the slow inching northward had slipped into a full-blown stop—her fingers tapped nervously on the Camry's steering wheel. She fiddled with the radio dial, started listening to Adele crooning away about love gone sour. She switched the music off and craned her neck to try to see a spot where, within the three clogged lanes, there was any movement.

No such luck. "Great," she said as she stared through the glass to the gray October sky, dark clouds threatening. The rain started slowly, first one heavy drop, then another as her lane began to slowly plod forward; the shower began in earnest, more and more drops pouring from the sky.

"Come on, come on," she said, frustrated. She needed to talk to the damned police and get this over with. She chewed on a fingernail, caught herself, and stopped. She cast a glance in her rearview mirror. Dark eyes glared back at her and she noticed the corners of her mouth were tight. Yeah, she was worried. Who wouldn't be?

If the police pulled up her record and did a little investigating. Holy crap.

She hit the horn just because she could and was rewarded with a rude hand gesture as the traffic began to move again, crawling past Washington Square, then slowing again at Canyon Road.

Reva thought she'd go out of her mind.

Only when she was turning south onto Highway 26 was she able to really start moving again, and she hit the gas, cutting in and out of traffic, trying to eat up the miles. She hoped she could get to Jo-Beth before anyone else arrived. She needed that private conversation to refresh her memory and make certain their story was the same.

Her nerves were killing her. Reva Mercado, the feisty Hispanic woman with her own blog and Saturday night radio show, and soon a segment on a streaming television show about all things Latina, had turned into a wobbling mess.

She couldn't blow it.

Couldn't have the past rise up and bite her in the ass.

Her cell phone jangled just before she angled toward the mountains. Traffic had gratefully thinned, and the rain was now just a shrouding mist that the interval wipers were handling.

She checked the caller ID.

Sosi!

She didn't have Bluetooth, couldn't risk getting pulled over, so she hit the button to put the phone on speakerphone and balanced her cell on her lap. She'd just have to yell until she could pull over. "Hey," she called out, so that Sosi could hear her over the road noise.

"Reva? What's with all the noise? Are you driving? Wait. Oh. Wait. Are you already on your way to the camp?"

"Uh-huh. You're coming, right?"

"I don't know . . . I mean, I'm not sure. I don't know what I'd say to Joshua, and then there's . . ." Her voice faded and Reva couldn't hear her.

"Sosi?"

Nothing. But she saw the phone was still connected. *Crap!* She saw the sign for the next exit. "Hey, look, just hold on. There's a spot where I can pull over." Cutting a pickup off, she veered into the slower lane and while the idiot behind the Chevy truck's wheel laid on the horn, she gunned it onto the exit ramp, sliding under an amber light turning red and cranking the steering wheel when she spied a McDonald's restaurant. "Okay," she said, pulling into an empty parking space near the line for drive-in customers. After killing the engine, she slid the phone to her ear again. "What were you saying? Some kind of lame excuse for not coming?"

"It's not lame. It's that I can't leave my family."

"Why not?"

"Because Joshua wants me at home and I do have Grace to consider."

"Grace?"

"My sixteen-month-old," Sosi said a little tartly.

"Oh, right."

"Besides, I'm pregnant."

Reva rolled her eyes and, with her free hand, scrabbled inside her open handbag to find her pack of Virginia Slims.

"It's another girl," she said proudly. "I just found out."

Bully for you.

"I'm just over twenty weeks."

"Great," Reva said, and tried to work up some enthusiasm.

"Joshua wanted another boy, of course. I think he'd love it if we had a football team, but I love the idea of having another daughter."

"A football team?" Reva repeated, horrified. "Isn't that, like, eight or nine players?" She found her cigarettes and shook one out.

"Eleven," Sosi said with the attitude of a genuine sports nut. Wasn't that the thing now? Sports and God all rolled into one package and complemented with a bucket of popcorn and a supersize Dr. Pepper? "But don't worry," Sosi went on as if Reva cared. "We only want four. Well, maybe five. We've got three—Isaac, Faith, and Grace—and now, the new baby. We should name her Hope."

As if Reva cared. "Haven't you heard about

the world and overpopulation? What are you, a baby-making factory, for crying out loud?"

Sosi gasped and Reva did think maybe she'd gone a little far—her quick tongue and self-protection system kicking in. "Sorry," she said, but Sosi was already defending herself.

"We can afford it and I'll homeschool and—"

"Okay, okay, I said I was sorry, didn't I? Now listen. Sosi, you have to come to Camp Horseshoe. I don't care how many kids you want to have to add to the world's problems, right now, we have our own little situation, and we have to deal with it."

"But—"

Reva cut in. "You've got a family and what would Jacob think if he found out that—"

"Joshua. His name is Joshua! You know, in the Old Testament in the Bible? The leader of the Israelites and—"

"Fine. Fine. Joshua," Reva snapped, not needing or wanting a lecture on the Bible. Not now. Well, not ever. She'd had enough catechism and all the rest of it while growing up in her own family. "What would *Joshua* think if he knew what happened at Camp Horseshoe? As I remember, there was an incident with you and one of the campers and—"

"Oh, dear! No . . . he can't find out." Panic made her voice tremor. "I-I've prayed and prayed about it, done penance. It's . . . It's behind me," she said in a whisper.

"The camper might not think so. Might not have gotten the word from God."

"Reva! You're . . . You're abhorrent!"

"Am I?" Reva said behind a smile, and she could tell by Sosi's little gasp that she got the message.

"We were just kids. Experimenting."

"While two girls went missing."

"I had nothing to do with that."

"I just think it would behoove you to come. We need to be focused and clear and solid. Then we can put any indiscretions behind us." When Sosi didn't immediately respond, Reva pushed a bit. "I thought Jo-Beth explained everything to you. How important it is if you want to keep your secrets and—"

"I know! She did. But I've made my amends through God and—"

"For the love of—! Look, we're not talking about God right now, okay? We're talking about the cops. And I don't think they'll give a rat's ass what your 'penance' or 'amends' or prayers have to do with anything. It's about missing people and the fact that you, Sosi, were there, doing some things we aren't exactly proud of. You and everyone else."

There was silence on the other end and Reva took the opportunity to shake out a cigarette, turn on the ignition, then crack the window before lighting up. As she drew the smoke into her lungs, she watched a minivan pull up to the drive-up and while kids yelled from the back seats, the thirtyish woman placed her order. The nicotine started to take immediate effect and Reva felt instantly calmer, didn't focus on the kids too much, especially the one in the baby seat, turned backward. She slid her eyes toward the building, noticed the paint peeling, and would not look at that infant again. Nor would she think of Sosi—the baby-making machine, the child even now growing in her oh-so-fertile womb.

"I don't know how I'll get away." Sosi sounded worried. But not as holier-than-thou as she had been.

Good.

"I don't either. That's your problem," Reva said, taking another drag. The minivan was replaced by a dirty white sedan with a couple of teenagers in the front seat. *Wash Me* had been scrawled in the dirt on the trunk.

"You know, Sosi, if one of us goes down, all of us will. We weren't exactly forthright about everything that happened that summer."

Another silence.

"Think about it. I'll be there in a few hours. You've got my number, right? It came up on your screen?"

"Y-Yes."

"Good. Find a way to make it work. Make a reservation at the Hotel Averille in the town of the same name. We'll all be there. We're meeting Jo-Beth at five. Be there."

"I-I'll try," she said tentatively, then more firmly, "and I'll pray. For all of us. And the people missing, of course."

"You do that," Reva said, and didn't bother saying good-bye, just clicked off. Then, cigarette clamped between her lips, she thought about going through the drive-up line. She could use a triple espresso. Shit, did McDonald's even make espresso, or just that weak-ass coffee? She didn't really have time, anyway, she thought, and pulled out of the lot, to spy, across the highway, a coffee kiosk.

Good Brews.

And there wasn't a line of cars, none except for a battered green SUV of some kind that was just pulling out. Good. After a quick perusal of traffic in both directions, she hit the gas and shot across the road to the parking lot on the far side. Pulling up to the window, she waited impatiently, made her order to a girl who moved as slowly as a banana slug, and felt her nerves tightening. She finished her cigarette and hoisted the butt out the window as she was finally served. She really didn't have time to stop for anything, even gas, the pressure to get to Camp Horseshoe was that intense, but she needed something to rev her up, make her focus, and figure out a way that she could get herself out of the trap that was the past. The other girls—well, they could fend for themselves. The guys as well. But she had to take care of number one.

"Here ya go," the girl inside the little hut said, handing Reva a hot paper cup that nearly slipped out of her hands in the rain. A chocolate-covered coffee bean was balanced over the plastic lid, and Reva snatched it up with a quick "Thank you" as she handed the girl a bill and added, "Keep the change," which was all of forty cents. After a quick sip of the hot liquid, she set the cup in one of the holders in the console and took off again, finding her way back to the main highway and trying to come up with a plan of action that would save her skin.

Chapter 14

Camp Horseshoe
Then
Sosi

Tears streamed down Sosi's cheeks. She tried to fight them, to brush them aside, but they just kept coming, rolling from her eyes. Tears of embarrassment, tears of shame, and yes, tears of fear. "It's not . . . It's not what you think," she said, swallowing hard as Reva, flashlight in hand, stood over her and the girl she was with, a junior counselor of fifteen.

Nell's dark eyes rounded and she pushed herself away from Sosi, scooting across the carpet of pine needles where they'd fallen, unable to stop themselves from kissing and touching and needing, ending up here under a copse of pines.

They'd been too loud, too aching, too burning with desire to realize that they were close enough to the path running behind the cabins that someone would surely hear them. And someone had.

Reva.

Sosi bit her lip, fought to keep from crying, while Nell, straightening her clothes and climbing to her feet, cast one last glance at Sosi. Gone was the hunger, the raw desire in her wide brown eyes. Now in the moonlight those gorgeous orbs only registered fear and maybe a little shame. Without a sound, Nell hurried away through the night-darkened forest back to the cabin where she co-counseled with Annette Alsace.

"What I think," Reva said, beyond the glow of the flashlight, "is that you'd better get your butt down to the cavern. Pronto." There was an edge to her words, and through her tears Sosi was able to see the flash of her teeth, white in the near-darkness.

"But, I . . . I mean, this never happened before."

"She's fifteen," Reva hissed. "Jailbait." She paused and, when Sosi could do nothing more than sniffle and wipe her nose, she elaborated. "You do know what that means, don't you? Underage."

"Yes."

"Never mind that she's a *girl* and your whole damned family—no, make that the whole damned church you belong to—would at the very least frown on what was happening here, or maybe shun you or turn you in to the police."

"It . . . It was just a kiss." But she fingered the tiny cross swinging from a petite chain at her neck, the cross that was so recently between Nell's teeth.

Oh, dear Lord. What have I done?

"Was it?" Reva demanded, and Sosi crumpled in on herself. "Just a kiss? Innocent? An experiment? Is that what you're saying?"

"Yes." She tried to say the word with some authority and swiped at the last of her stupid tears. She didn't think she was . . . well, attracted to girls, but this one, Nell Pachis, was different. Kind of an intellectual, Nell with her wild dark hair and gorgeous brown eyes loved books, animals, music, and . . . and she was beautiful, in body and spirit—a Greek goddess who was lithe and happy and sexy. Like no one Sosi had ever met. The best part of it was, Nell had also found

Sosi attractive and had come on to her, not the other way around.

But you didn't stop her, did you? Nuh-uh, you wanted to kiss her, to touch her, to see if . . .

"She was touching you," Reva charged. "Her hands were all over you!"

In the darkness, Sosi felt herself blush. Well, there was *that*. The kissing had led to some petting and she'd let Nell touch first her breasts and then . . . oh, dear, lower, into her shorts. Sosi knew that Nell could feel that Sosi was turning on, getting moist. The kissing, oh my, the kissing had deepened and . . .

"Maybe a little."

"Maybe a lot," Reva said, "and you were touching her—No! Don't even try to deny it. I *saw*—okay? Jesus, Sosi, if you didn't want anyone to see you, you could have found someplace a little more private, don't you think?"

Glumly, Sosi nodded. How could she explain when there was no explanation? She'd felt a spark, a sizzling attraction, a raw attraction here in this darned camp. After living under her father's very strict thumb, she'd finally felt that she could breathe a little, step a bit into forbidden territory, learn something other than what her family, homeschool, and church could provide.

"And, by the way, you both stink of weed. Come *on!* Anyone can smell it." Reva let out a long breath. "You'd better warn Nell. Look, just so you know, I don't give a flying fuck who you screw. Really. Boy? Girl? Whatever, but for the love of God, Sosi, use your damned head. Other people do care." Under her breath, she said, "Fucking idiots." Then, more loudly, "Come on, let's go. You're just lucky it was me who heard you and smelled the smoke, not Mother Naomi, that bitch."

"Oh, you shouldn't . . ."

"What? Call it as I see it? Or, more precisely, call her as I see her? Is that what you were going to say? Well, tough. The reverend's wife is a stone-cold bitch, and she'd skin you and Nell both alive if she caught you. She'd bring it up at the next all-camp meeting after discussing punishment and recriminations with her husband, as if he's the damned paragon of virtue. If you ask me, he's one serious pervert. But, it doesn't matter. You two, you and Nell, could be in serious trouble and thrown into religious counseling about the sins of your act. The police might even be called in because Nell's underage."

Sosi gasped.

"Well, maybe not, but your parents for sure and Nell's as well. Not a pretty thought, is it?" Before Sosi could say another word, Reva added, "Move it. We're already late. And Nell has to stay back at the cabins. To be with the campers."

"She doesn't even know we're meeting."

"Good. Let's keep it that way."

Sosi had no arguments. She hadn't done anything wrong, at least she didn't think so, but Reva was making her feel as if she'd committed some mortal sin and God would strike her down at any second. She wasn't sure about that, but she did know her father would kill her. He was a youth pastor in their church and he wouldn't like to know that she was making out with anyone—boy or girl. The girl-on-girl thing, though, that would surely make it worse.

Climbing to her feet, she straightened her clothes, brushed the needles and dust off her. For the first time, now that her eyes had adjusted to the luminescence of the flashlight, she saw that Reva was holding a knife, and not a small pocketknife, but a large butcher knife with a blade that glinted in the cast of the flashlight.

"What . . . What's that?"

Reva cast her a don't-be-dumb look and said, "For something later."

"What?" she asked.

"It doesn't concern you. Come on." Reva was already heading along the path in the direction of the ocean.

Sosi followed, her eyes on Reva's straight back and the glow of the flashlight illuminating the forest. The beam swept across the trail and wind-gnarled branches that curved upward. The smell of the earth from last night's rain was intense, the path below her feet uneven because of rocks and roots just below the surface. "Where did you get it?" she whispered, loudly enough to be heard above the rustle of the leaves overhead as the breeze off the ocean intensified. "The knife? Did you bring it to the camp, or is it one of Cookie's?"

"Let's just say I borrowed it and leave it at that. And by the way, you *never* saw it, or me with it. Got it? *Never*." Reva sounded irritated as she walked quickly along the path, her flashlight in one hand, the hilt of the long-bladed weapon that Sosi was supposed to disavow clenched firmly in the other.

Why the lie?

What was the knife for? To scare someone? Or worse? Maybe she didn't want to know.

Sosi had to half jog to keep up with the taller, more athletic girl. "Where are the others?"

"Duh, Sosi. Already at the cavern, probably," Reva said over her shoulder. "Enough with the questions. We're late already. Hurry up." She increased her pace, kind of race-walking.

"Are any of the guys coming?"

"So now you're interested in boys?" She snorted. "No, this is all girls. Which should be right up your alley."

"Yeah, right," Sosi said, but she felt a cold little shiver run down her spine. Something was wrong here; Sosi sensed it. And it was a lot more serious than her little makeout and petting session. Hurrying, running along the twisting trail, feeling the breath of wind, and spying the veil of clouds slipping over the nearly full moon, she caught up with Reva. "Where's Jo-Beth?"

"She went ahead, told me to get you. She's probably waiting, so come on, move it."

That sounded plausible. Jo-Beth was the ringleader who had planned this meeting, a get-together of all the female counselors to talk about what happened to Elle and make sure that everyone said the same thing, so that no one got caught doing the things they shouldn't.

Like smoking pot and getting sexually involved with another counselor. And not just any counselor, but an underage girl. Oh, Sosi, you idiot! But was it any more of a sin than being with a boy? Most of the girl counselors were hooking up with their male counterparts, and as for the indulgence in weed, they all did it. Okay, a few preferred alcohol or regular cigarettes, but they all did it. And so what if she liked girls? Big deal.

But it was taboo. And illegal, because of Nell's age.

Darn it all, anyway.

Reva had reached the crest of the ridge where the trees gave way and the path angled down the cliff face, switching back and forth to the beach far below. In the darkness it was difficult to see the curving stretch of sand leading to the cape, but Sosi heard the crash of the waves breaking against the rocky point of the cape, where it jutted into the ocean. The air here was damper and smelled of salt.

Coming to a dead stop, Reva halted and positioned her flashlight so that its beam splayed upon the downward grade of the trail. "Go on ahead."

"No, you go. I'll follow."

"I said, 'Go on ahead.' I'm not coming with you. Not right now."

"No," Sosi argued, shaking her head. She wasn't going down there alone, without a flashlight. What if no one else was in the cave. What then?

"I've got something to do. I'll be there soon."

"Uh-uh. No."

"Go!" Reva gave her a little push and Sosi stumbled, her heart clutching in fear. "I'll catch up with you later."

"We're supposed to be all in this together! That's what Jo-Beth said."

"And *I* said, I'll catch up with you later, like in a few minutes. Go on," Reva insisted. Then said, "You're not scared, are you?"

"No." Still Sosi didn't move. She flicked a gaze at the knife again and Reva's fingers gripping the handle tightly. Her skin crawled as she considered the implications, none of them good. What in the world was Reva up to?

"Don't tell me," Reva said, a sneer in her voice. "You need your little girlfriend to come, too."

"Oh, shut up." Sosi had heard enough and she was tired of Reva's innuendos and high-and-mighty attitude. As if she were the boss.

The boss with a very big knife.

Rather than argue further, Sosi turned and started down the trail snaking along the sheer rocks of the cliff face. Her heart was pounding as the climb down was dangerous, but she'd done it ever since she'd shown up at Camp Horseshoe, and the path was wide enough—usually—though tonight with only a bit of moonlight and winking starlight to guide her, she hugged the rock wall and wished like crazy she'd thought to bring her own small, pocket-sized flashlight, but she hadn't, because she'd thought she'd return to her cabin before setting out for the cavern.

She hadn't expected her meeting with Nell to turn into a hot makeout session or that Reva would find them. She shuddered as she made her way in the dark, keeping close to the hillside, angling downward. She told herself it wasn't really that dark and that she wasn't really alone. Soon she'd be with the rest of the female counselors, and later back with the campers and Nell. At that thought her heart did a funny little skip. Should she stand next to her, or act as if they weren't involved?

Whoa! Involved? You're not involved with her. With anyone. Not romantically. Not sexually. Remember that! Avoid Nell when you're in public and in private. . . . The back of her throat went dry and she was so caught up in her thoughts that she hadn't realized she'd reached the foot of the trail, that she'd made it to the beach.

As she stepped onto the sand, she squinted to the far end of the beach, the cape where the cliffs jutted into the sea and a grotto had been carved by the tidewater. Was there some light coming from within? Were the other girls waiting?

As she took a step forward, she sensed a movement and heard, over the thunder of the waves, a sharp, scraping noise, then felt a shower of pebbles raining on her from the cliff high overhead.

Ducking and covering her head with her hand to protect herself, she half ran away from the shadow of the steep hill, where something or someone had kicked the small stones, whether on purpose or by accident.

Reva?

Jo-Beth?

Or someone else?

She looked skyward while trying to convince herself either a stiff gale or some animal had dislodged the bits of dirt or tiny stones that had fallen from the cliff.

No one and nothing was visible. No person. No animal. She squinted, thinking she saw a shadow move at the outermost point of the ridge high overhead, but nothing appeared. "It's nothing," she said, her voice caught by the wind rolling off of the sea, her hair blowing around her face. Still, she was edgy, her skin pimpling as she imagined unseen eyes staring down at her from the deep umbra.

She was just nervous, that was it. She'd been caught with Nell by Reva, who was carrying a big butcher knife and then had left her out here alone.

But there it was again.

A shifting of darkness and light. Movement.

Her heart *ka-thumped.*

Something was up there. Staring down at her.

Heart thudding, she backed up a step, and again the image was gone.

You're a moron, she told herself, but couldn't shake the feeling that she was being observed. She rubbed her arms, trying to convince herself that she was only imagining a dark shape shifting on the ridge, that what she was seeing was a tricky play of muted light, the result of clouds moving slowly across the moon. She started to turn toward the far end of the beach when she caught a glimpse of white. She looked upward again.

There, on the outermost point, was a woman, dressed in sheer white, the moonlight catching in her blond hair, her face as pale as death.

Elle!

Sosi's heart nearly stopped. Her eyes rounded and terror slid through her veins as the waifish figure stared down at her and then, in a blink, disappeared.

Chapter 15

Averille, Oregon
Now
Lucas

"Hey, stop here!" Maggie said suddenly from the passenger seat of Lucas's Jeep. She'd been reading the computer mounted on the dash, but must've seen that they were passing her favorite drive-through coffee kiosk located in the Safeway parking lot, just three blocks from the station.

He wheeled into the lane and saw that the car ahead of him was a grimy Toyota Camry, the back window obscured by helium balloons that shifted with the breeze allowed in through the driver's open window.

"Thank you, thank you. I need a jolt this afternoon," Maggie said as Lucas queued up behind the Camry whose driver got his coffee and drove away. Lucas slid down his window and the barista smiled at him as, along with a stiff breeze, the strains of some jazz tune filtered into his SUV. "Hey, Sheryl," Lucas greeted her. "I'll have a tall coffee. Black. And her—the usual." He hitched his chin toward Maggie, who was still studying the computer screen.

She lifted her head long enough to look past

him and through the window. "Make it a triple shot today, okay?" she said.

"Got it!" Sheryl, a tall, much-tattooed blonde, grinned from within the tiny space of the Coffee Shack. "That's a tall, *triple*-shot mocha with light whipped cream?"

"Right," Maggie said, nodding. "Perfect. Thanks."

Lucas rarely frequented the coffee kiosk on his own, but when he and Maggie were out of the office, driving through the town, she insisted they stop so that she could indulge herself and opt for a "fancy caffeine kick" rather than wait until they got back to the office and the dark brew warming on a hot plate in the lunch room. So here they were.

Lucas handed Sheryl some cash. "Keep the change."

"Thanks!" she said, smiling brightly, the blue butterfly inked onto her neck more visible as she turned her head. "Just a sec."

While the sound of the espresso machine screaming and sputtering filled the air, Maggie asked, "What do you think happened at the camp twenty years ago?"

Lucas glanced at his partner and tried to keep the irritation from his voice. "How many times do I have to tell you? It's all in the statement I made at the time."

"Yeah, but now you've got insight, and it's all

being brought up again and the press, not just Kinley . . . whatever—"

"Marsh."

"Right. Marsh was just first. Others are starting to call. It won't take long for the reporters to connect the dots, that you were there, and when the case is 'officially' reopened, you, my friend, might be in the crosshairs of some of the media."

"I know."

"It makes you look guilty."

He glared at her. "You think I had something to do with that body we found, of it getting there?"

"No, I think you might be . . . not fully transparent."

He felt his jaw tighten. He didn't expect this from Mags.

"Your girlfriend went missing, and Dusty Peters was never heard from again. All on your family's property. That's all I'm saying."

"You think I'd cover up for my old man?" he said, biting out the words.

"No, but you're not giving me anything, so I don't know what to think."

"It's *all* in my statement," he said.

"Okay, fine. I'm just asking you about your take on things now, as an adult, as a cop, that's all. You're not as close to the crime now."

"If there was a crime."

"We've got a body."

"An unidentified body."

"Don't be obtuse, Luke. It's not working with me, okay?" Her back was up and he really didn't blame her as he stared through the windshield. The first few drops of rain began to drizzle down the glass.

"You were Eleanor Brady's boyfriend, and you broke up with her just before she disappeared."

He didn't respond.

"And then you and Bernadette Alsace became a couple and she's also part of the group that seem to have created this air-tight, but unbelievable alibi that they were all together when both women went missing. Not in their bunks, not tending to the campers who were assigned to them, but out partying together, even though they didn't like each other."

"Here ya go!" Sheryl handed the steaming paper cups through the window. "These are recyclable, y'know," she said as she did each time they stopped by. "Same with the lids. Lots of people don't know that and just throw 'em away." She flashed a smile. "Gotta do what we can to save the planet, y'know."

"Thanks." Lucas handed Maggie the frothy drink, held his in one hand, rolled up the window, and pulled away from the kiosk as the rain started to pelt from the sky. "Okay," he said, turning on the wipers and heading back to the station, through the town and past a gas station where a flatbed under the wide awning was gassing up. "You're right. I've held back. Only because I want to do some investigating on my own. It was a long time ago, but yeah, sometimes it feels like yesterday and a lot of crap went on, not that I was in on all of it.

"But you're right. Elle was my girlfriend and I broke it off because I got involved with Bernadette. Once I make sure everyone who knows anything about what went down twenty years ago is either going to show up or talk to us on the phone, then I'll reread my statement, and each of theirs, and you can grill me from here to kingdom come."

"Grill?"

"Whatever. I've got nothing to hide," he said, though he knew he was lying and the truth would come out with or without his help. He just needed a little more time to find out for himself what really happened on those dark days. He wanted to read over the others' statements, including Bernadette's. She was married now, so he assumed any passion they'd shared was long over, any pain of their breakup was water under the bridge. Besides, married or not, they were both adults, for the most part, over twice the age they'd been as counselors at the camp.

Hopefully he would be able to go over the statements, then talk to each of the counselors involved, with Maggie, of course, for impartiality purposes. Like it or not, it was time for the truth to be uncovered. All of it.

"Okay. Let's move on to Waldo Grimes then. He's a loose piece and I'm wondering how he fits in to all of this."

"Yeah, the escaped prisoner." He shook his head. "Convenient, wasn't it? Another one who just disappeared into thin air. At the time the police thought he had an accomplice who helped plan the accident of the transport carrying Grimes and a couple of other prisoners. The other two were caught, almost immediately, but not Grimes. It literally became a real-life *Where's Waldo?* search and he was never found."

Maggie picked up the narrative. "He was from around the area, a hunter, knew all the back roads and creeks. The best that anyone could come up with was that he met someone with a car who drove him to Astoria, and he got on a fishing boat or pleasure craft, either as a stowaway or through someone he knew, and he floated out to sea. Never heard from again."

"At the same time that Monica and Elle disappeared, so there was a lot of talk that he could have kidnapped them or worse. No one ever knew, or if they do, they've never said."

"Weird," she said.

He nodded. "A lot of weird stuff going on back then."

She took another swallow of her coffee, thinking hard. "Not just then. I know this is kind of out there, but you know that people have said they've seen Eleanor Brady over the years . . . or her ghost."

"Oh, sure. If you believe in all of that."

"She—or someone else—has been spotted on the beach, or on the point at the south end of the park, and on Cape Horseshoe itself."

"By a couple of teenagers who shouldn't have been up there in the first place. By the way, they admitted to being stoned."

"Oh, I know. It's just that it keeps happening."

"Averille's rendition of the old ghost story where every year on the anniversary of a deadly car crash at Dead Man's Curve, the ghost of the girl who was killed there appears." He glanced at her. "Oldest one in the book."

"Where there's smoke, there's usually . . . well, at least an ember."

"Don't tell me you've been watching the horror channel on cable."

"I don't think there is even such a thing and no, but I keep my ear to the ground and I'm just sayin' that there's talk."

"What we need are facts."

"Exactly," she said as her cell phone chirped. "That's what I was hoping you could help give me."

"And I keep telling you everything's in the case file."

"And I keep telling *you* that I want your take on it all now, as a cop." The phone rang again and Maggie finally answered as Lucas wheeled into the station parking lot. She listened for a few beats and then said, "Okay, well, let me know." She clicked off and said, "They're still searching dental records on the skull. At this point, we can't assume any of the bones we found on the beach belong to the skull, not until DNA. We know it's a female, and that's where it stands."

Luke nodded, his chest tight.

"Anything else you want to tell me?" Maggie asked, eyeing him.

"When I know something, you'll know something."

She nodded, but didn't take her eyes off him.

Chapter 16

Averille, Oregon
Now
Sosi

The Hotel Averille was the most historic building in town and certainly one of the tallest. Three stories high, the hotel towered over buildings that housed the post office, two taverns, a secondhand store, and a gun shop. On the other side of the main street was an "antique mall," which had once been, as Sosi remembered, a bowling alley. Surrounding the mall were a couple of cafés, a dress shop, and a bakery. This, where the inn was located, was the heart of the town that had, over the last two decades, spread toward Highway 101 in one direction and the ocean in the other. From Averille there was no direct access to the Pacific, but the town was home to a couple of lumber mills, a construction company, and several office buildings that housed insurance companies, architects, an engineering firm, and, a few streets over, two cafés and a gas station, its overhang illuminated by bright lights.

Sosi pulled into the rain-washed parking lot to the rear of the hotel and parked her Ford Escape, its engine smelling hot, the temperature needle having slipped over to the red zone on the gauge the last few miles of her drive north from Roseburg.

So here she was.

Pregnant, two hours early, her room not yet available, the parking lot empty except for a minivan and a Dodge Charger.

Biting her lip, she stared at the clapboard hotel, painted a creamy yellow with white trim around watery windows that were a hundred years old. A broad porch flanked the entire first floor, and an American flag was flying from a mast mounted on a corner post, visible from the main street running through town as well as the side street leading to this parking lot. Raindrops drizzled down the windshield, and she wished she were back home with Joshua and the children, her precious babies.

She'd had to lie, of course, to come here. Joshua didn't know about what had happened at the camp that summer and he never could. She had to make certain of that, so she'd lied that her cousin needed her, was having an existential/ faith crisis and thinking of leaving the church. She'd insisted that she'd be home soon, and thankfully Joshua's mother had taken over the household duties, and her cousin—bless her heart—had covered for her. What a nightmare!

She'd always been religious but had really found Jesus a little earlier. When she had been at her lowest point, finding out that she was pregnant and she was ready to face God and Judgment Day, Jesus had intervened. On that cold February morning, with rain sheeting down from the heavens—God's tears, she'd thought— she'd sat behind the wheel of her mother's classic Mercedes in the single-car garage of her mother's townhouse, the engine running. With the windows down, the carbon monoxide making her woozy, her eyelids heavy, she'd thought she'd heard something, a voice, and had opened a bleary eye to spy the statue of Jesus her mom had hung from the Mercedes's rearview mirror. The little idol had been swinging to and fro, even spinning, and she heard his voice, clear as a darned bell, telling her it wasn't her time, that she had work to do.

His work. She had a baby to birth—a boy—and she could not snuff out that tiny, fragile life, no more than she could take her own. All of her multitude of sins would be forgiven, the voice had said, comforting her. She just couldn't give up. So she'd managed to hit the garage door opener before passing out.

And when she'd come to, she'd seen that the little statue was no longer spinning and rocking, but was quiet again, and a man was opening the door to her mother's car, a repairman who had come to fix the leaking roof: Joshua Gaffney, her personal savior.

She'd practically fallen into his arms as he'd opened the car door and had begun praying over her.

"Dear Father, please have mercy on this beautiful soul."

And in those first few moments, hearing his words of faith and feeling his strong arms surround her, she'd fallen in love.

She hadn't been quite twenty years old, the whole incident at Camp Horseshoe having occurred over two years earlier. And he? He'd been twenty-seven, having served with the army, including two tours in Afghanistan.

As it turned out, Joshua was a traditional man whose father owned his own tire franchise where Joshua worked full time. An industrious soul, Joshua also had a side business and on Saturdays and evenings, he was a handyman, the man her mother had hired.

Had their meeting been divine intervention?

Sosi believed fervently that it had.

Theirs had been a whirlwind romance; their first date his friend's wedding the very next weekend. Though he'd been surprised when she'd admitted that she was pregnant, he'd told her it didn't matter. He'd known she was the one for him the second he'd found her collapsed in the car. When he'd asked her to marry him less than three weeks after that first meeting, she hadn't thought twice about it. He'd claimed her child, born only seven months into their marriage, was his, and no one ever questioned it, at least to her face.

Joshua put his faith in God, loved his country and his family, and expected Sosi to do the same. And she did, though she was a bit more liberal than he and sometimes, deep down, resented the fact that Joshua thought she should take care of the kids, keep the house, work part-time as a waitress, and never want a full-fledged career. That, she thought, was a little backward thinking and it bothered her.

Sometimes she had to remind herself how much she loved him, how he'd literally saved her and her son, if not from death that day in the garage, then from her being a struggling single mother. Because of Joshua she'd never had to scrabble paycheck to paycheck. She did resent the fact that he could spend his free time working out or watching football, or go meet his buddies at the rifle range for target practice, whereas he didn't like it when she met some of her friends for a glass of wine or even coffee, unless they, too, were young mothers within the church.

But Joshua was loving and a good father to Isaac, as well as the two girls they'd had together. Sosi had lied about Isaac's biological father, saying that he was a boyfriend she'd met while working in Portland and who had dumped her upon learning she was pregnant. In fact, Isaac was conceived on New Year's Eve at a party where she hooked up with a good-looking guy and ended up spending the night in his hotel room.

He'd taken off for Chicago the next morning and never called.

Nor had she ever phoned or texted the number he'd left on the bedside table. He didn't know he was a father and he never would. But it was as if God had heard her prayers when Joshua Gaffney walked into her life and took her for his bride.

Joshua loved her with his whole heart, not only accepting Isaac as his own, but fathering their two daughters, Faith and Grace. He'd said he would like another child, a boy, his own biological son even though he treated Isaac so well. Would that change if he actually fathered a son? she wondered. But Joshua was so, so good, she reminded herself. However, if he ever got wind of the truth—all of the truth about Isaac's father, Sosi's partying, and especially her involve-ment with an underage girl and the scandal at Camp Horseshoe—he would never forgive her and, she was certain, he would take her children from her, including the one who was yet to be born.

All because of the sins of her youth. Memories washed over her, memories of first love, sexual titillation, and the resulting shame, whether deserved or not. She knew what her church said about a woman loving a woman, but deep in her heart, in the most private recesses of her soul, she disagreed and wondered about Nell. What had happened to her? Jo-Beth hadn't mentioned her, but was there a chance that Nell, as one of the counselors, might show up?

"Don't go there," she warned herself, and felt her stomach turn over. What was she thinking?

Closing her eyes, she whispered a quick prayer, talked to God, and found her center, then breathed out on a heartfelt "Amen" and restarted her car. With a glance at the dash, she saw that the engine appeared to have cooled a bit, so she backed up and drove out of the parking lot.

The town was small enough that she saw a church spire rising over the tops of trees that were beginning to shed their leaves. Her heart clutched and she fought tears, passing by taverns on opposing sides of the main street as she drove past a wooden sign that listed the population of Averille as under a thousand.

She hit the gas at the outskirts and her Ford leaped forward, sailing along the road as it wound through the foothills of the Coast Range and toward the Pacific Coast Highway. Californians, like Joshua, referred to it as the PCH, while Oregonians called it 101. Either way, it snaked near the coast line offering peekaboo views of the ocean in this part of the Northwest. Traffic on the two-lane road was sparse, but she waited for a motorhome to pass before she pulled onto the highway and headed south. From the juncture, she spied Cape Horseshoe jutting into the ocean.

Three miles later, she pulled into the park on the northern side of the cape, and, after locking the car, zipped up her parka and walked across the parking lot to the series of trails leading through the forest and upward to the ridge, the backbone of this narrow strip of land that fell to the curving stretch of beach abutting the property once owned by the Dalton family. Nell, who had lived most of her life in Averille, had mentioned that the property had originally been part of a homestead and that Naomi Dalton's father had owned it but donated it to the church somewhere along the line.

Sosi didn't know the true story and doubted it

mattered as she hiked up the steep grade. She felt the salt-laden wind pressing against her, rolling inland from the sea, and she knotted her hood under her chin as she reached the summit, where the trees gave way to a headland. She was aware that far beneath her was the cavern where the girls had gathered that night, all waiting, all clutching flashlights, all having abandoned their charges to collect and create a lie with enough elements of the truth in it to be plausible.

How stupid they'd all been.

As she stepped closer to the southern edge, she stared down upon the rocky shelf known as Suicide Ridge, where everyone assumed that Elle had dived or jumped into the ocean and died, her body being pulled by the tide out to sea.

Sosi squinted into the horizon. The ocean rolled and bucked, huge gunmetal swells breaking into whitecaps before thundering inland and breaking noisily against the cliff face. What really had happened that night? And what had she seen?

Elle? Alive and well?

Her ghost? Haunting the camp and all of those who had mistreated her?

Or someone else?

So much had been in play that night . . .

And then there was the knife.

What had become of the butcher knife Reva had "borrowed"?

She leaned over, saw tracks on the beach. The

police? Curiosity seekers? Lookie-loos who wanted to catch a glimpse of a long-ago tragedy? Or someone more sinister, someone intimately involved?

As she gazed across the expanse of beach to the south and the stretch of land that was the old camp, she focused on the spot where so long ago she'd seen the figure in white, a ghost, she'd thought, Elle's spirit awakened from the dead.

But you don't even know that Elle's dead.

Her body had never been discovered, as far as Sosi knew, and now there were bones discovered, a skeleton. Elle's? Monica's? Or someone else's?

She felt a chill and rubbed her arms as the tide rolled in, crawling across the sand in a frothy wave, intent, it seemed, on erasing the prints, of hiding the past, of keeping the truth hidden.

Which, for Sosi, was best.

Chapter 17

The Washington–Oregon Border, Highway 101
Now
Bernadette

"I'm not going to let Jo-Beth bully me," Annette said from the passenger seat of Bernadette's Honda as they drove through Astoria and headed south. She'd gotten more and more quiet as they'd traveled from Seattle, down I-5, then headed west to the coast highway. The moment they'd merged onto the four-mile span of the Astoria-Megler Bridge, Annette had fallen into silence, pretending interest in the steel-gray waters of the Columbia River, watching seagulls wheeling and crying through the rain-spattered windshield.

"No one's asking you to."

"You know how she is."

"Maybe she's changed," Bernadette said, remembering the bossy counselor who had, without invitation, stepped into the role of leader at Camp Horseshoe, as if it were her God-given right.

"Yeah, right." She cast Bernadette a don't-try-to-peddle-me-any-crap glance and searched in her oversize bag to withdraw a pack of gum. "You didn't talk to her. I did."

That much was true. Bernadette had never bothered phoning Jo-Beth; she'd gotten the message and she didn't want to start a long phone call or endless texting thread. Annette had handled the communication between them, but she was right. No more allowing Jo-Beth to manipulate them. Bernadette wondered what the hell that was all about. At the time she was only concerned about saving her own skin. Now, though, that it was all brought up again, she thought it might have more to do with Jo-Beth's self-preservation mode. The deceptions had always bothered her, but since learning about the body being found, all her own doubts and suspicions had come to the fore. Yeah, it was time to take the bossy woman on. No matter what the consequences.

"She's a lawyer now, you know," Annette said.

"So I've heard." That wasn't a surprise.

"And she didn't end up with Tyler," Annette added, "after all of that. Gum?" She was holding out the pack, but Bernadette shook her head and, with a shrug, Annette dropped the rest of the half-empty pack into her open purse. "Suit yourself. It helps. Calms my nerves. Y'know, since I gave up smoking."

Annette was chewing furiously and lapsed into silence as they passed through the town that spread down the river's banks below the bridge, where businesses sprawled along the shore, docks jutting into the steely waters. Bernadette turned south on the highway that cut between the riverfront and the rolling hills, where grand, 200-year-old houses, the original homes of settlers and seagoing captains, stood next to newer, smaller buildings, most with sweeping views of the river as it rolled into the Pacific.

The sky was gray and overcast, and enough of a mist collected on the windshield to cause Bernadette to use the wipers. Annette's somber, reflective mood was infectious; Bernadette felt it as well. Oregon held no appeal for her, no sense of wonder. The beauty of the area was lost in the grayness of it all and the knowledge that the past was about to come to the fore.

She thought about Lucas and her heart quickened a bit despite her dread. She'd had such an intense crush on him that summer. She'd known he was supposedly going with Elle but had accepted the fact that he'd broken it off with her. And she really hadn't cared, she now admitted, her need for him superseding her sense of propriety or decency or whatever you wanted to label it. All she'd known then was that she'd wanted him, had fancied herself in love with him, and when everything had blown up and Elle had gone missing, she'd finally taken a hard look at what she was doing and felt ashamed. By then, of course, it had been too late; the damage had been done.

Even now, though . . . even after another couple of relationships, culminating in a failed marriage, she felt her cheeks heat at the thought of those moments between her and Lucas, what they'd done together, sometimes in broad daylight in the woods or on the beach. Sex with Lucas had been an intense and driving need, despite the fact that she'd heard he was practically engaged to Elle. He had a reputation, rumors had swirled about him, but the whole bad-boy rep had appealed to her, and she hadn't been deterred when she'd overheard Jo-Beth confiding to Reva that Lucas

225

had even been involved with his own step-mother, that they'd had a very taboo and intimate relationship.

"I don't believe it," Reva had said, but there was a breathless quality to her voice. She'd *wanted* the rumor to be the truth. "With his own stepmother? Seriously? *Sick.*"

"Twisted, but true," Jo-Beth had insisted. They had been standing behind the Dumpster just off the kitchen, smoking cigarettes after dinner when they were supposed to be cleaning the kitchen. "I heard it from David."

"He said that about his own mother?" Reva's voice inched up an octave and Bernadette, who had been walking to the dining hall to return a napkin she'd inadvertently stuffed into a back pocket, stopped cold. "He had to be lying," Reva pronounced.

"Why?"

"Shock value."

Bernadette flattened herself on the other side of the Dumpster, the one facing the parking lot and the kitchen, where anyone, especially Cookie if she came onto the back porch, could see her.

"You think?" Jo-Beth asked.

Bernadette's heart had cracked. Could it be possible? His own stepmother? True, they weren't related and Naomi wasn't all that old, but . . . oh, God, she couldn't believe it . . . wouldn't believe it.

"But he saw them," Jo-Beth insisted.

"What?"

"Up over the office. Not in the living quarters, but there's some attic space up there at the end of a hall, like an unused room you can almost stand in. It's got extra stuff for the camp, towels and shit and an old bed. David heard them and peeked through a window on the roof and they were going at it like crazy, his mother holding on to the bars of an old brass bed and Lucas on top of her, sweating and humping, and to quote David, 'Fucking the living hell right out of her. Riding her like a stallion.' His words, not mine."

Bernadette's stomach had turned over, acid crawling up her throat. In her mind's eye she saw them, Naomi, the sexy stepmother, her makeup and hair never out of place, married to the reverend, lying on her back, her mouth parted, her pupils widening as he thrust into her. And wild, untamed Lucas, with his rippling back muscles, sinuous arms, strong thighs, atop her, hands on her breasts, caressing her, twisting her nipples, biting at her neck.

She'd gasped just as she heard a crunch of gravel.

"What was that?" Reva had hissed sharply. On alert.

Bernadette had stopped still, froze.

"What?" Jo-Beth.

Reva whispered, "I heard something."

227

"Fuck. What?"

"I don't know!" A pause.

Bernadette had mentally willed her wildly racing pulse to slow.

"Let's get outta here," Jo-Beth muttered. "Give me a friggin' Altoid and let's go."

Hearing footsteps crunch on the gravel, knowing Jo-Beth and Reva would be able to spot her, Bernadette slipped around the side of the Dumpster away from the kitchen. They were walking away, farther from the building, but it did keep them out of Cookie's view a few minutes longer. Besides, they could claim they were on their way back from the stable. Bernadette had seized her chance to ease her way back around the face of the Dumpster, holding her breath and moving silently and slowly over the tiny rocks. She'd turned a corner and nearly stepped on the camp cat sunning himself near the recycle bin.

With a loud shriek and a hiss, the cat arched its back, then streaked away, a gray blur diving into the brambles surrounding the back parking lot.

"What the hell was that?" Reva's voice reached Bernadette's ears. Heart drumming crazily, adrenaline pumping through her veins, she hadn't dared move a muscle. She'd bitten down hard on her lip to keep from making a sound.

Jo-Beth said, "The damned cat."

"But what scared him?"

"Who knows? Haven't you ever heard the phrase 'scaredy-cat'? Don't worry about it."

"But, I think I heard—"

"So there you are!" Another voice suddenly rang out, cutting off Reva's speculation. Heart in her throat, Bernadette spied Cookie stepping out of the kitchen and onto the porch. She'd been squinting, making a shelf of her hand and holding it to her forehead to shade her eyes.

Bernadette's heart sank and she'd silently prayed that Cookie's attention was focused on the other girls.

"You have work to do!" Cookie had yelled, as Bernadette eased her way along the far length of the Dumpster, still quietly, to stop in the shade near the still-burning cigarette butts, lipstick visible on the remains of their filters. "Hurry! Chop! Chop!"

Closing her eyes, she waited, counting her heartbeats, and finally heard some grumbling under Jo-Beth's breath, then footsteps crunching on the gravel as the two friends headed inside. Floor-boards creaked as they climbed the two steps to the porch; then Bernadette heard the bang of the screen door.

Letting out her breath, she slid down the side of the Dumpster, then angrily kicked gravel and sand over the smoldering remains of the cigarettes and dropped her head in her hands. *How could he? How?* Tears welled in her eyes when she thought of Lucas and his stepmother. Holy crap. What kind of a pervert was he? Was she?

His damned stepmother? Sick! Reva is right. Sick, sick, sick!

She didn't want to believe it, but hadn't she seen them together? Riding horses, on the second or third day of the camp, when she and Annette and Jayla and Sosi had toured the stables? Dusty, the resident camp cowboy, had pointed out the areas where the feed, tack, and equipment had been kept in the cedar plank building with its rough walls. The heat had been sweltering that afternoon, inordinately hot for a June day on the Oregon coast.

Bernadette could recall a creepiness to the old building where sunlight pierced through the gaps and knot holes in the siding to play into the interior that smelled of horses and leather and oil. The four of them had had to walk single file down a long, cement-floored aisle set between two rows of stalls.

Then they'd headed outside to the heat of the day, the sun intense enough that she was sweating and bored with Dusty's speech. Bernadette had glanced overhead to notice a wasp busily constructing a tiny nest under the stable's eave as Dusty droned on in some kind of drawl— Texas, she guessed, as her eyes had moved past him to the closest paddock where three horses stood, tails flicking at flies, ears moving, heads lowered to pick at the barest pieces of grass near the fence.

Dusty had pointed to the horses in the paddock as he'd walked the fence line, the geldings, disinterested, still swooshing their tails as Dusty went on about their schedules. Bernadette had only been half listening, lagging back, caught in her own daydream about Lucas, of course, when she'd caught sight of two riders appearing over a rise in a far pasture. She'd squinted, shading her eyes, and recognized Naomi Dalton, in shorts and a T-shirt, her red hair clipped back, astride a thick-chested palomino. Loping alongside the pale horse was a rangy bay, and atop that horse was Lucas. Bare-chested, wearing faded jeans, his hair mussed, he'd leaned over and said something to Naomi before quickly moving his arms and leaning over his mount's neck. The bay had taken off like a shot and Naomi had responded, giving the palomino free rein and streaking off after the other horse and rider.

Bernadette had felt a bit of exhilaration as she'd watched Lucas move with the galloping horse as they raced across the top of the hillside to disappear below the crest of the hill again. The palomino with Naomi astride was only a few feet behind.

Where are they going?

"Weird. I know," a voice had said from behind her, and Bernadette had physically started. From the corner of her eye she saw Leah, Lucas's little sister, sitting on the top rail of the fence, close to the edge of the stable, half-hidden by a scraggly pine. Bernadette hadn't noticed the girl, or the cat that had been lying in the mashed, dry grass that had grown around the post. "I'm Leah, by the way," the girl had added.

"Bernadette."

"I know. Lucas said."

She'd felt a surprising warmth run through her veins. *He'd mentioned her?*

All of eleven, wearing cowboy boots, cutoff jeans, and a faded pink T-shirt, her teeth seeming too big for her pixie-like face, Leah had followed Bernadette's gaze as she'd stared back at the now-empty field. "Mom and Lucas do that all the time, y'know? Ride together." Her face had pulled into a thoughtful pucker. "It's like they're bonding or something. They didn't like each other much, I guess, when Dad married Mom." She wrinkled her nose. "I wasn't here then, but I was on the way, I guess. Anyway, Mom and Luke fought a lot. That's what David says and he remembers. David's my brother. Technically my half brother, but then they all are. Ryan and David and Luke—er, Lucas."

Bernadette had nodded and Leah had seemed to take that as an invitation to go on. "Lucas's mom, his real mom? She's dead. Been dead a long time, and David and Ryan's dad is a real loser. Doesn't go to church or nuthin'. A real deadbeat, that's what Mom says." Leah had shot another look to the now-empty pasture, where the green grass was already starting to bleach a bit. "Some-times Mom and Lucas take me with them," she'd added wistfully. "Sometimes they don't."

"Hey! We're talkin' over here!" Dusty had yelled, looking over Jayla's shoulder, his gaze settling on Bernadette. "Could be important, y'know? Horse and riding safety? For your campers?"

Bernadette had blushed at the reprimand.

Leah had then hopped off the fence and started toward the stable, tossing a sour look at Dusty before she whispered to Bernadette, "I *hate* that guy."

"Dusty?"

"He's a douche. And a liar. Don't trust him." With that she'd ducked into the open door of the stables and from around the corner the gray cat, tail aloft, had trotted after her.

Bernadette hadn't thought much of it at the time, but after overhearing Reva and Jo-Beth, she'd started to wonder if maybe there was something between Lucas and his stepmother.

But then she'd gotten involved with Lucas herself, had spent most of the summer either being with him or wishing she were. Even when she was with the campers, helping with crafts, or discussing Bible stories, or riding horses or kayaking, even during prayer service, her thoughts had zeroed in on Lucas.

She'd thought he'd felt the same.

And the uncomfortable feeling that had disturbed her, that sensation that something was not quite right that had slithered through her soul whenever she'd seen Lucas and Naomi together, she'd ignored. Bernadette had told herself not to trust the sensation that something was happening between Lucas and his stepmother or the idle musings of a preteen. After all, Leah hadn't said anything sexual was going on; she'd just intimated that Lucas and Naomi spent time alone horseback riding.

But the seed had been planted, lying fallow despite the looks she'd caught between them, or the trill of Naomi's laughter whenever she would see him, or the way her fingers surrounded his biceps when she gave him an affectionate, motherly squeeze.

It wasn't until the day she'd overheard Jo-Beth confiding in Reva about the supposed affair, though, that the seed had germinated. After they left, she'd sat on the gravel lot trying to sort out what she was going to do, a montage of images of Lucas and Naomi together—in the office, on horseback, seated next to each other in the dining hall, Lucas fixing a loose pipe as Naomi stood over him, the little touches and smiles, all growing fast and ferociously, like the magical beans in the cartoon version of *Jack and the Beanstalk*—filling her head. That afternoon, as Reva and Jo-Beth were hustled back into the kitchen by Cookie, Bernadette had kicked at their smoldering cigarette butts and decided then to break it off with Lucas. She'd been aware of the irony of it. Elle was missing, ostensibly because Lucas had broken up with her because of Bernadette, and now, if the rumor she'd just heard was true, Bernadette was going to dump him. She just had to figure out how much, if any, of Jo-Beth's gossip was true.

Her heart had ached at the thought, a physical pain, but she had to do what was right. She'd climbed to her feet, dusted off the seat of her pants, and spied the cat, who had scrambled up a fence post in the shade of a pine tree to stare at her with wide, knowing eyes. As if he knew the truth.

Now, as she drove, Bernadette remembered that day vividly. She recalled her emotions, the soaring highs and crashing lows of thinking she was in love. She'd thought breaking up with Lucas would be easy. But, truth to tell, back then? All his wild, raw, primal energy, his natural sexuality, had only heightened her curiosity, her interest. The fact that he'd slept with his stepmother wasn't a true crime, except in Reverend Dalton's eyes, and the fact that he'd gotten away with it had only added to his bad-boy allure.

There had been a dark side to Lucas Dalton, one she'd only seen in the barest of glimpses, secrets he kept under wraps. She'd found him dangerous and absolutely fascinating.

Well, at the time.

"God, you were a fool," she said under her breath.

"What?" Annette, who had been caught in her own private thoughts, turned to stare at her.

"Nothing." Bernadette hadn't realized she'd spoken aloud. "Sorry."

"It's all right." Annette stifled a yawn and stretched her arms out in front of her, then rotated her neck and tilted her head, her chin-length hair falling to one side. She'd grown prettier over the years, the coltiness that was still with her in her teens replaced by a gentle, adult grace with her long, supple limbs, her hair no longer wild but trimmed, her features even. She'd never married. Come close a couple of times, engaged once but broke it off explaining only with, "I just couldn't see myself waking up next to Connor every morning for the rest of my life." And so she'd remained single. So far. Which was probably better than getting married and a few years later divorced.

So much for their mother's "Nothing ventured, nothing gained" motto.

"So, what do you think really happened that night?" Annette asked thoughtfully.

"That night?"

"You know, the one we never talk about, the one that we're all going to make certain we remember 'correctly'?" She sighed. "It's all a bunch of bull, y'know. Because I remember vividly. I know who was at that 'meeting,' " she said, making air quotes with her fingers, "the one at the cavern and who wasn't. Jo-Beth, she wasn't there. Reva had to take over. Remember? And Monica, she didn't make it either. And that's not all," she said, her face crumpling as she struggled against sudden tears, an inner emotional war waging. "And I know . . ." She glanced out the window, her jaw jutting forward as she thought for a long minute.

"What?" Bernadette prodded.

"I know that . . . that I saw a ghost, Bernadette. I never said anything because you all thought I was just some stupid kid who spied on everyone and took notes and was a total useless geek. But I saw her. It. Elle's ghost. That night after the damned meeting." She turned to stare directly at Bernadette. "And she's haunted me ever since."

Chapter 18

Bend, Oregon
Now
Nell

"Look, it's not that big a deal, okay?" Nell was pulling off her Under Armour fleece, then peeling out of the tank top that had wicked the sweat from her body from her run, 8.75 miles, nearly 20,000 steps according to her Fitbit, and it wasn't noon yet. Good. "I'll just be gone a couple of days," she yelled from the bedroom, toward the hallway leading to the living room of the condo she shared with her partner, Tasha, who was now pouting, ostensibly upset with Nell's leaving.

So what else was new?

Picking up her clothes, she carried them into the bathroom and dropped them into the hamper. More loudly, she added, "You can get Elise to take over my classes or do it yourself."

"Very funny," came the response, and Nell grinned. So Tasha *was* listening. Not quite as miffed as she'd pretended when Nell had announced she was taking a trip to the coast for a couple of days and she needed to do it alone.

Stepping naked onto the scales, she eyed the digital readout and frowned. 118.7. Up two tenths of a pound. She'd have to take care of that. She caught a glimpse of her lithe figure in the mirror, was satisfied that not an ounce of fat showed and that her tan, compliments of the state-of-the-art tanning bed at the gym she owned with Tasha, was perfect. Not a blemish.

Reaching into the shower, she turned on the tap; then she waited. As the water reached a warm temperature, she managed to knock off ten slow squats and just as many lunges. Steam rolled upward from behind the glass.

Into the hot shower she popped, quickly scrubbing the sweat from her body, skimming her legs with her fingers as the water rolled over her body. No stubble yet. Good. A quick shampoo and she was out, toweling off, drying her hair quickly, applying zero makeup, and turning on the fan. She double-checked her weight, just in case she'd misread the scales, scowled at the results— the same—then, mentally telling herself not to obsess, pulled on leggings and a tunic, wrapping a long belt twice around her waist. A little gel in her hair, to make it stand up a bit and look a little wild and sexy, and she was out.

Her bag was packed and she snapped it shut, then rolled it into the living room, where a fire was burning in the fireplace that ran up an interior wall to a soaring ceiling some twenty feet above. In front of the fire, Tasha was lying on their sleek couch, a glass of wine on the long ottoman that doubled as a coffee table. Next to the half-empty glass was a plate with two chocolate-chip cookies, crumbs visible; Tasha was munching on a third.

"What're you doing?" Nell asked, trying to keep the irritation from her voice. They owned a gym for crying out loud; they couldn't afford to not be fit and trim. Cookies—chocolate chip or otherwise—were not on the diet and exercise regime they'd both agreed to.

"I'm coping." She took a bite from the cookie and with a rebellious glare silently dared Nell to argue. Long and lean, well, so far, Tasha was six feet tall, Nordic-looking with a broad, beautiful face, flawless skin, piercing blue eyes, and blond hair so thick she had trouble taming it. Yet she did. Rather than cut it, she grew it so that even in a thick braid running down her back, the tip nearly reached her waist. Right now, her locks were spread around her in a pale golden cloud as she sprawled on the couch, a sloppy stack of those idiot women's magazines on the floor near her, her iPad balanced on her flat abdomen. She was dressed in her favorite old, much-too-large sweats, faded navy blue. As if she didn't give a shit. Which she very much did.

"Doesn't look like you're coping all that well. Aren't you supposed to be at the gym?" *Calm down. She's upset. Don't say anything. Don't be baited. You can deal with this little break in routine.* Trying to cool her jets, Nell glanced out

240

the window and through a copse of lodgepole pines to the golf course, the tenth fairway, where the clipped grass spread like a green carpet.

"Go to work and not stick around to say 'good-bye'?" Tasha cocked an eyebrow at Nell, then glanced at the screen of her mobile device, where she was absently scrolling through some social media site.

"It's not like I'm going on a world cruise. I'll be back the day after tomorrow, or the next day at the very latest. I'll text you when I know for sure."

"Ummm." She took another bite of the cookie. A bit of chocolate hung on her upper lip.

Nell, standing near the front door, prodded, "The gym? You're going in today?"

"Elise and Guy are handling it." Tasha licked off the chocolate, her icy blue eyes fixed on Nell, the tip of her tongue flicking and disappearing. A come-on? Maybe. It had been several days since they'd had the time to really get into it.

"It's our business, Tash. One of us should be there."

"But not you. Right? So I put up all the money to buy the place and you just come and go as you please, leaving me to run it."

There it was again: the money. Her inheritance was used to purchase a failing, out-of-date gym and retrofit it, adding new carpeting, new machines, new desks, and make it shiny, bright, and hip. Never mind all of Nell's sweat equity.

Who'd painted and laid the tile in the bathrooms, cleaned and polished the pool and showers? Who had trimmed and replanted the landscaping, adding a fountain near the front door? Who had come up with the idea for a climbing wall?

Tasha shoved the iPad off of her body and stood up, her hair falling around her. Her beautiful face was set, her chin hard, every muscle in her body flexed beneath the dull clothing, and Nell was reminded that when she'd met her, Tasha had been a bodybuilder—all glistening overbuilt muscles stuffed into the scrap of a tiny hot-pink bikini.

They had both been in Las Vegas, at a convention for all things geared to women's sport. Spying Tasha on the stage, Nell had been awestruck. Watching her go through her routine, flexing and stretching, Nell had felt as if her heart were pounding so hard it might jump out of her chest.

For her, it had been love, or at the very least lust, at first sight. They'd hooked up after the competition, consuming more than a couple of mai tais, though neither of them were big drinkers. Tasha had been bold enough to whisper in Nell's ear, "Damn you're sexy," before sliding her tongue around the shell.

The rest had been history—their history. They'd been together ever since that one fateful night and here they were four years later, owning a small, successful gym in Bend, Oregon, and engaged to be married.

Everything had been perfect. Not a single bump in their blissful road, or at least nothing more serious than a tiny pothole, which was always about the money—Tash's damned money. But even that wasn't a serious problem. Her relationship with Tasha was rock solid. She'd felt that way until two days ago, when she'd heard about the bones being found at Camp Horseshoe.

A flood of memories as intense as the tides near that cavern had washed over her, and Nell had done some quick investigating online through social media. She'd found Sosi Gavin Gaffney living in southern Oregon. Married, it seemed, with three kids, a boy and two girls. Still petite and freckled, her reddish hair longer now, in some kind of a mom bob cut, chin-length and feathery. Still pretty. Stupidly, Nell's pulse rate had escalated while she scanned the photos.

From what she had gleaned, Sosi was really into her kids and her church. The husband, Joshua Gaffney, didn't have a page, but there were a few pictures of him scattered within the photos of children on Sosi's page, either with the kids or toting a rifle. One shot particularly stood out in Nell's mind, the husband, Joshua, dressed head to toe in camouflage, his rifle slung over his shoulder, bending down on one knee next to a dead deer—his kill—and holding the animal's head up as the picture was taken.

Nell had studied the man. He was handsome in that neo-Aryan sort of way, blond, clean shaven, etched jaw, intense gaze, and she guessed, just a gut feeling, that she wouldn't like him.

She thought about the nights she and Sosi had been together—learning, experimenting, not understanding where their relationship might lead . . . so long ago, so romantic.

Until you got to the missing girls.

And the scream.

And what she'd seen that night when she'd followed that awful Reva with Sosi in tow. Nell had been worried because Reva, who had seemed mental at the time, her temper legendary, had snarled at them, gripping a huge knife in one hand so intensely that her knuckles had shown white in the darkness. Nell had initially panicked and run away, rolled off Sosi and headed back to the cabins, expecting Sosi to follow.

Nell's steps had slowed when she'd realized Sosi wasn't coming. Something was going on, and Nell had decided to find out exactly what it was. She didn't like Reva or anyone else sneaking up on them, and the whole attitude that because they were not only smoking a little weed, but also girls doing their girl thing, making out with girls was somehow worse than what the rest of them were into.

That had burned Nell then and it sure as hell burned her now.

She'd gotten some of her nerve back about half-way to the cabins, so she'd turned and followed Reva and Sosi and had seen Sosi almost pushed down the trail to the beach.

But Sosi hadn't been harmed.

At least not at that point.

Whatever Reva had intended to do with the knife, it hadn't been to butcher Sosi, and Nell had taken heart in that knowledge, backtracking once again toward the cabins and the campers they'd left unattended.

Until the scream.

Sosi's bloodcurdling shriek had reverberated over the rush of the ocean.

At that moment, Nell had done a one-eighty and barreled along the path and, without a second's thought, taken the switchbacks to the beach below to find it empty. Desolate. The wind rushing in, clouds covering the moon. She'd felt she was all alone, her heart trip-hammering with fear until she'd spied the footprints, several trails of them, sometimes next to each other, other times crossing, almost braiding along the pristine beach.

Something was going on, something that made her blood run cold, but she'd followed that trail, feeling the push of the wind, adding her own footprints to those of the others. She tried to sort out exactly how many sets, but it was impossible in the darkness and didn't matter anyway as she saw they all continued across the stretch of sand to the north end of the beach where Cape Horseshoe curved out to the sea, whereupon its narrow headland, at a rocky shelf called Suicide Ledge, rumor had it that Elle Brady had leapt to her death.

Swallowing back her fear, Nell had trudged ever onward, reaching the narrow opening leading to the cavern and seeing a slit of weak, watery light that seemed to beckon her forward.

She'd had to force herself to move forward. For Sosi, and for herself.

She'd never never wanted to ever think about that horrid camp again. Yet . . . here she was. The truth was, she needed to go to back to Camp Horseshoe now and that bumblefuck little town of Averille to make sure that the truth came out and that it had nothing to do with Sosi or herself. She was starting a new business here, in Bend, which was not the most liberal spot on the planet, so she didn't want the least whiff of a scandal touching her. So far her clientele didn't care that she was gay, but in this part of Oregon, unlike the metro area surrounding Portland, the attitude was definitely more redneck and conservative—and proud of it. So, she and Tasha didn't throw their sexuality into others' faces.

"I'll be back soon," she said, and lifted up on her tiptoes to deposit a kiss on her fiancée's cheek, but Tasha pulled away and Nell felt a little jab of disappointment in Tasha's pissy attitude. "I promise."

"I won't hold my breath."

Fine. Be that way, Nell thought as she picked up her bag and walked out the door to the bright sunshine and blue sky that was typically central Oregon. *Drown your bad mood in red wine and store-bought cookies. See if I care.*

But she did. Care.

She slipped on a pair of sunglasses and climbed into her older Subaru, parked outside, of course, as Tasha's BMW was in the garage. She knew she loved Tasha. Probably too much. Despite her bitchy mood. But these little things really got under her skin.

Switching on the ignition, then backing up while strapping on her seat belt, Nell cast a quick glance in the side-view mirror to the two-story cedar condo that Tasha had bought and she felt a little pang. Maybe she shouldn't be driving to the coast, maybe Tasha was sensing that things would go wrong—she did have a little weird ESP thing going on—maybe she should play it safe, or at least safer, and stay here, where she belonged, with Tash.

Then again, she thought, ramming her little Forester into drive, when the hell had she ever played it safe?

And besides, truth to tell, she wanted to see Sosi again.

Chapter 19

Camp Horseshoe
Then
Lucas

Something was up. And it wasn't good.

Lucas could feel the electricity, the sizzle of a disturbance in the night air.

Lying on his messy bed in the bunkhouse, he was alone, the windows open, the sounds of the night creeping through. Crickets chirping, frogs croaking, and a mosquito buzzing around his head and something else, something he couldn't hear, couldn't see, but sensed. Heat from the warm day seeped through his window, and he thought about the difference in the summer weather, about how the night before a storm had passed through, the wind howling, the rain lashing.

The night Elle had disappeared.

Guilt tore a hole in his gut as he stared through the window over his bed and heard, far off, over the distant rush of the sea, the sound of a semi, engine rumbling, brakes growling and echoing off the hillside as the trucker slowed and descended from the high point on the ridge near the cape, driving closer.

As was the case these nights, he thought of Bernadette and he felt his cock twitch, start to harden. He was always horny this summer, always, sex forever heating his blood. Just the sight of one of the counselor's butts in their tight shorts, or a glimpse of a breast held in place by the flimsy straps of a swimsuit caused his blood to heat and drove him to distraction.

He fought his urges and tried to avoid temptation by working doubly hard around the camp, cleaning the stalls, fixing the fences, chopping and hauling firewood, repairing the roof or porch or stacking hay, grooming the horses, swinging a hammer, anything physical to keep his mind off sex. He swam, rowed, ran for miles, pushed himself to the brink of exhaustion, and was in the best physical shape of his life.

Throwing off the top part of his sleeping bag, he rolled out of bed and stretched his muscles, thought about Bernadette less than a quarter of a mile away. He was focused on her now, wondering if this is what love felt like, then reined in his thoughts, wouldn't let them wander too far down that dangerous path.

But he'd love to go to her cabin, tap on her door, and pull her out into the night. They could come back here and explore each other's bodies —make love—all night long. He was getting hard again just thinking of the possibilities. Her lips, her mouth, her wet, warm tongue, and her breasts, and the curve of her rump, the hollow of her back, the way her hair curled and fell around her face . . .

And . . . yep, he was rock hard, his boner stiff to the point of almost being painful.

Just like that.

He should go for a run, swim in the lake, jump into the ocean, or take a damned cold shower—*any*thing! His mind was whirling, but the need for sex, for release, was still there, front and center, a damned ache teasing him, reminding him that Bernadette with her perfect, warm, willing body was just five minutes away. . . .

Angry, still feeling that something wasn't right tonight, he pulled on his jeans, dealt with his cock, stuffing the damned thing under his fly, then reached for the T-shirt he'd flung on the floor. When he caught a whiff of rank BO on the grubby cotton, he tossed it into a corner and grabbed a cleaner shirt from a shelf mounted on the bare cedar walls.

Telling himself he wasn't going to see Bernadette, that he was just going to walk off the heat in his blood and the guilt in his heart, he slipped on tennis shoes and headed out. With a look over his shoulder, he glanced toward the stable and the patch of light glowing from a high window—Dusty's room. So the ranch hand wasn't sleeping either.

He took a path that skirted the cluster of

buildings near the parking area, which was lit by a few security lights, their bluish illumination casting the structures and the surrounding trees in an unearthly light.

He swung his gaze toward the rec center and office. The second story was dark, his father's little family tucked in for the night, except that Naomi wasn't sleeping with her husband. Not tonight. Temporarily at least, she was bunking in the cabin that had been assigned to Elle, to try to comfort the worried campers who had been assigned to the missing counselor and assure the girls that they were safe, that "Sister Elle" had just taken sick for a few days. Elle's charges, and the rest of campers, weren't buying the story. It was just a stopgap measure at best, but, for now, Naomi was bunking down with the girls.

Not that he cared where his stepmother claimed a bed.

Not anymore.

As for Elle? God, please, that she'll show up. And soon. That she was safe.

She was, and always had been, a little weird. Beautiful, but off-beat, a devout girl, Elle was a member of his father's congregation, and Jeremiah had wholeheartedly approved of his son's involvement with the girl.

"She's a good one," Jeremiah had told him on more than one occasion. "I couldn't have picked a better woman for you."

251

The last time had been here, at the camp, when his father had come into the stable where Lucas had been brushing Blondie, the palomino mare that both Leah and Naomi favored.

Jeremiah had leaned over the rail of the stall, watching his son with a practiced eye.

"I take it you're not talking about the horse," Lucas had said, guessing where the conversation was going.

Jeremiah chuckled, but it had sounded phoney, false to Lucas's ears. "No, son, I was remarking about your interest in Eleanor. She's the good one I was talking about."

Lucas hadn't responded.

"You know," his father had said, his voice lowered for reasons Lucas couldn't fathom. "Her father is a deacon in the church, her mother teaches Sunday school and Bible study. I really couldn't have picked a better woman for you if I'd tried."

"We're just dating," Lucas had pointed out.

"So far, son, but y'know, when it comes to picking out a wife and a life partner—"

Lucas whipped around, startling the horse that had shied and backed farther into the small stall. "I don't think you're the best one to suggest who I should pick. First of all, I'm not lookin' for a wife, not yet, and secondly, you don't exactly have a great track record in that department."

His father's congenial expression had changed,

his lips tightening, his eyes narrowing, his face reddening. "You're an insolent pup."

"Probably."

"You need to learn to respect your elders."

"Then maybe my 'elders' should handle themselves in a manner where they earn my respect."

"You little . . ."

Lucas's eyebrows raised as he'd silently encouraged his father. "What?"

"God will be your judgment."

"As He will be yours."

Lucas had braced himself, ready to vault the gate to the box and tear into the old man, but nothing had happened and he'd relaxed a bit, turning back to the mare. "It's all right, girl," he said, taking up the currycomb again and sliding it gently along the palomino's back. As he listened he heard his old man take his leave.

He liked Elle. A lot. But the fact that his old man approved of the relationship, had almost insinuated that he'd handpicked "Eleanor" for his wayward son, had made Lucas second-guess his choice. And no way was he thinking of marriage. Funny how his father had talked about Elle being a good choice for a wife about the same time Elle had started pressuring him to commit, had told him she wanted to get engaged or get married. She'd even suggested eloping a couple of weeks before he'd met Bernadette. What the hell had that been about? Neither one of them was old enough or mature enough to think of marriage.

Now, as he made his way along the path, Lucas hoped to hell she would show up soon. With each passing hour that Elle wasn't found, he grew more anxious, more worried, more guilt-riddled.

What had happened to her?

Had he been the last one to see her?

He thought about the rumor of a prisoner at large, a murderer no less, news he barely believed. Really? A killer just happened to escape a transport a few days ago and ended up here at Camp Horseshoe to what? Kidnap Elle? Or . . . worse? It seemed unlikely. Really unlikely.

And yet he couldn't discount it. Not completely.

He broke into a jog once he was past the kitchen and on the familiar path that eventually led to the girls' cabins. The light was dimmer here, no glow from the lights at the hub of the camp, and he squinted to make out the twists and turns in the trail.

The howl of a coyote rent the night air and he felt his muscles bunch. A primal reaction. That was all. He was on still on edge and . . .

A twig snapped.

Nearby.

He stopped. Listened. Ears straining.

Nothing out of the ordinary, just the hiss of the wind sighing through the fir-needled boughs.

Just his nerves.

And the feeling that the universe was a little off-kilter tonight.

One more step and he heard a rush of air. *Whoosh!* And frantic footsteps above a primal growl.

What the hell?

BAM!

He was knocked off his feet. An assailant, all muscle, sinew, and anger, knocked him onto a carpet of needles and pinecones.

"You cocksucker!" his attacker hissed. David. His stepbrother. Furious. Out of control. "You fuckin' cocksucker!"

Bam! A fist landed against his jaw.

Crack! Pain exploded through Lucas's face.

In a blinding instant his own fingers clenched into fists. Pummeling upward, he tried to land his own series of blows to the angry swinging blur that was now attached to him. Striking him. So incensed that there was murder in David's eyes.

"You stay away from her!" David snarled, managing to straddle Lucas and pin his arms to his side, making further attempts to hit the bastard futile.

Lucas squirmed and rocked, trying to dislodge him. Though David's strong legs were holding him down, Lucas still was able to move and kept kicking, trying to pull his arms free, to no avail. David was tough, worked out, rode horses, had thighs of steel, and they were banded around Lucas's chest.

"You hear me? She's fuckin' off-limits!" Incensed, David hauled back and swung again, but Lucas shifted and the blow slid down his face.

David drew back to hit him again and in the shadowy moonlight Lucas caught a glimpse of the hatred, pure and bitter, seething in his step-brother's eyes.

With a ferocious growl, David threw the punch just as Lucas flexed every muscle in his body, arching his back like a bucking bronco. Too late! David smashed his fist into Lucas's face. The blow glanced off his nose. Something popped beneath his skin and a sickening warmth gushed out his nostrils.

But the force of the blow coupled with Lucas's gyration caused David to lose his balance. His legs slackened their grip a bit as he tried to right himself.

Again Lucas arched, his back muscles screaming in pain as he flipped over and David toppled. In one quick motion, Lucas rolled to his feet and swung around, ready to tear his stepbrother limb from limb. He leapt as David was staggering to his feet and they went down again, this time rolling and landing blows, Lucas giving far better than he got.

He felt his chin split with one of David's jabs, but he cocked his fist and swung back and struck hard, pain bursting in his hand as his knuckles smashed into his stepbrother's cheek with a sickening, splitting crack.

David howled and tried to scoot away. Hand to his face, blood streaming from his chin, he yelled, "You just stay away from her, you hear. Leave my mother alone!"

Naomi?

This is about Naomi?

They hadn't been together in a long while. Lucas had stopped seeing her when he and Elle . . .

"I saw you humping her. Fucking her! You stay the hell away from her!" He was on his feet now, walking quickly backward. "Or next time . . . next time I'll . . . I'll fuckin' kill you!" He backed up, pointing an arm and accusing finger at Lucas. "You hear me, Dalton, you try it again and you're a fuckin' dead man!" Turning, he took off running and was swallowed into the dark forests while Lucas caught his breath and wiped his nose, deciding whether or not to give chase.

To what end?

To teach the little prick a lesson?

Yeah! He deserved it, Lucas thought, spitting, the coppery smell of blood in his nostrils. His brief but hot affair with his stepmother was months over, but apparently not in David's small mind.

Jaw set, Lucas broke into a run, but after less than ten strides he slowed to a stop. What would he do if he caught up with David? Really wail on him? Maybe involve Ryan as well? His jaw worked and his fists curled, a fight still burning in his gut. He'd love to punch both their smug lights out.

But you did screw with their mother.

"Shit." He kicked at a clod of dirt. It didn't matter to them that Naomi had been the seductress and really, did he blame them? If one of them had hooked up with his mother, how would he have felt? Would his reaction be any less volatile? He closed his eyes as he thought about Isabelle. She was gone. Dead. His stepbrothers would never . . . "Oh, fuck!" he growled under his breath, and pressed the heels of his hands to his forehead at the thought. "Fuck, fuck, fuck!"

Though his blood was still boiling, and if he were honest he would have loved to beat David to a pulp, he restrained himself, tried to cool his blood. He ran both hands through his hair and stared up at the moon. What the hell was wrong with him? Why couldn't he leave women alone? Especially those he knew to be trouble, those with red flags plastered all over their tempting bodies. He glanced down at his once-white T-shirt and even in the dim starlight noticed the blood and dirt smeared all over it.

As the shirt was ruined, he tore off a strip

around the hem and used it as a bandage, holding it under his dripping nose as he took a deep breath and decided to call it a night, even though he was still on edge, still randy, still itching for a fight. If anything, David's attack had only heightened his restlessness, his need to do something.

And the night still seemed uneasy, a raw, malevolent energy in the air.

It's just because your blood is up. Because of the fight.

But, no, he'd sensed it before and knew the girls had been planning something.

Should he try to find Bernadette? Rubbing the back of his neck, the urge to see her strong, he glanced down the fork in the trail, now dark, but one branch leading to the girls' campgrounds. Maybe . . .

He heard a footfall.

Shit! David is back.

Good!

Involuntarily, he flexed, turned on his heel, cracked his neck. Bloody fists curling so hard they hurt, his teeth clenched, he was ready. *Bring it on, you dumb fuck. Bring it on!*

Another footstep.

But not from the path where David had disappeared, from the other direction, where the trail split and angled into the web of pathways leading to the cliffs above the sea.

So the dickwad had doubled back. Good. Lucas

259

spun, ready to leap, every nerve ending humming.

A dark figure appeared, the shape of a man emerging from the shadows. Moving oddly, nearly staggering, it stumbled forward.

What the hell?

"Lucas . . ." The voice was raspy, almost guttural. "Lucas . . . help . . . God, help me."

Tyler? This is Tyler? Not David, returning to the fight?

What the fuck?

Groaning, shuddering, falling to his knees, Tyler Quade looked up at Lucas, his face pale and bloodless, his mouth gaping. "I-I'm fucked," he spat out, blood on his lips as he fell forward, dropping facedown into the dirt, the hilt of a knife visible in his back, the blade buried deep.

Chapter 20

Portland, Oregon
Now
Jayla

"Excuse me, who are you again?" Jayla asked the small woman standing on her front porch. The wind was picking up, pushing the wet leaves around the yard, and she noticed a small black car—maybe a Chevy—parked in her drive. "Kylie who?"

"Kinley. Kinley Marsh," she replied. "I was a

camper when you were a counselor at Camp Horseshoe."

A camper? Oh. Lord. Jayla's heart skipped a beat and her throat was suddenly dry. She hadn't thought about that damned camp for years. And with good reason. Well, until a female detective named Dobbs had called just yesterday, asking questions, snooping around, suggesting Jayla return to Averille to make a statement. After twenty damned years. Now this. An ex-camper on her doorstep, asking Jayla if she remembered her. "I guess."

"I was kind of a pain in the butt back then," Kinley said with a grin. "Now, I'm with *NewzZone*, out of Astoria?"

"Okay." Where was this going?

"I guess you haven't heard of it." A gust of wind swept over the yard, making the leaves dance and playing with the hem of Kinley's long coat. "*NewzZone* is a small, independent, online newspaper."

"In Astoria you said?"

"Yes, but we have an online audience that's worldwide."

Jayla doubted it. She waited, wondering what this reporter wanted. She did remember Kinley now. The red hair was the giveaway. No longer in long pigtails, but highlighted and cut to her shoulders, her freckles diminished with age and makeup, her teeth now straight, Kinley was

261

dressed in designer jeans, boots, and a sweater and the overcoat. She'd sophisticated herself up, but, Jayla suspected, she was probably the same nosy person she had been all those years ago.

A reporter.

Wouldn't you know? But not exactly the big time.

"I don't know if you've heard, but there have been some bones found near the camp, a skull."

Jayla felt her heart clutch, her palms turning suddenly sweaty.

"It's been ID'ed, but the sheriff's department hasn't released the identity pending notification of next of kin. However, the conjecture is that it will be Eleanor Brady or Monica O'Neal—I do know that it's a female. That's been confirmed."

Oh, sweet Jesus.

Jayla tried to keep her expression blank. She didn't need this.

"I'm doing a story about the camp and since you were there when those two women went missing, I'd like to ask you a few questions."

"Me?"

"Everyone who was there, of course," she said. "But I was in Portland, had your address, so I thought I'd look you up, see what you remember."

A car drove by the front of the house, spraying water from a puddle on the street that ran between Jayla's house and the park.

"I really don't remember much."

"It won't take long," Kinley cut in. "And I assure you it's in your best interests."

"How's that?"

"It's always best to have the press on your side."

"My side of what?" This was starting to sound like a snow job, and it was feeling awkward with her standing on the porch so long.

"The story. The truth. Justice."

"Should I start waving my American flag?" Jayla said. The reporter or whatever the hell she called herself was beginning to seriously bug her. "Look, I gotta pick up my sons from school and basketball practice, so I don't have much time."

"It won't take long, promise."

Jayla didn't like it, but she wanted to get rid of the woman quick-like. She recognized the glint of determination in Kinley's eyes and didn't want her husband to come home to some kind of twenty-year-old freak show. "Fine. But I've only got ten minutes."

"Great!" Kinley's smile widened. Jayla had barely gotten out of the way and didn't have a minute to second-guess herself before the woman slipped into the house, boot heels clicking across the marble of the foyer and past a center table, where a huge bowl of potpourri gave off the scent of magnolias. Past the foot of the stairs she walked unerringly into the living room. "Nice view," she said, glancing out the bay window to the park beyond.

"We like it."

"Anyone would." Kinley eyed the columns separating the living room from the foyer and staircase, then surveyed the coved ceilings, bay windows, and an antique fireplace located on the far wall. Flanked by bookcases with beveled glass doors and crowned by a thick mantel supported by ornate corbels, the fireplace was the focal point of the large room. "And this house—spectacular."

Jayla knew that, had known it from the moment she and DeMarcus had bought the place from his parents. Three stories of an old Portland Victorian overlooking Laurelhurst Park. The place was old and creaky sometimes, and Jayla was half-certain there were ghosts haunting the attic, but she'd kept that mostly to herself. Her belief in the spirits trapped here on earth was a major bone of contention between her and her husband, a man of science.

Jayla asked, "So what is it you want to know?"

Without being invited, Kinley dropped onto a corner of the sofa that faced the fireplace. "I'm doing a series about what happened at the camp that year, the last year it was in operation. If it turns out the body, or partial body, that's been discovered is one of the women who went missing that night, it'll be a much larger story than I originally imagined. I'm talking to everyone who was there." She reached into the pocket of her jacket and pulled out a small recorder, then her phone. "So, if you don't mind, I'm going to record this interview."

Jayla didn't like the sound of that. "I thought you were just going to ask a couple of questions."

"I am. Really. But I want to be as thorough as possible." She placed the phone and recorder on the glass-topped table in front of the couch, pushing aside a vase of pale roses. "Please, come in. Sit down." She actually waved Jayla toward the nearby sofa. "You can sit there, the recorder will pick up your voice."

"I really don't have much to say. I told the police everything I knew."

"Twenty years ago. Okay." She fiddled with the phone and recorder, pressing buttons so that the red light on the recording device was burning bright. "Interview with Jayla Williams Robinson at her home in Portland." She rattled off the address and date before smiling at Jayla.

"You said you were at a meeting that night, the night after Eleanor Brady disappeared."

Slowly, Jayla dropped into a side chair. How much could she divulge?

"At the cavern below Cape Horseshoe?" Kinley prodded, and Jayla felt her insides turn to jelly. They'd had a pact. Was it still in force? Now that someone might really be dead?

"I was there."

"So you left your campers alone, unattended,

and met with a group of other counselors?"

"Naomi, er, Mrs. Dalton was still there. She had taken over Elle's cabin and we all figured since she was the reverend's wife and all, y'know a real adult, the girls would be fine. And Nell was supposed to be there. She was the . . . the junior counselor, in the same cabin as Annette Allen . . . er, Annette Alsace."

Kinley just stared at her for a second and Jayla felt like a fraud. Kinley had been one of the campers they'd left unattended, abandoning their responsibilities just as they had every night. As teenagers it hadn't seemed such a big deal, but now, as a mother of two boys about the same age as the campers had been, Jayla felt major pangs of guilt. How had she been so selfish? So reckless? So damned irresponsible? And the rest of them as well.

"So you went to the cavern. Alone?"

"Yes." She was nodding, remembering being pissed that she'd been dragged away from what she wanted to be doing by that Jo-Beth's whims.

"And when you got there? Who was there?"

"Uh . . . not everyone, but . . . me and Sosi and the Alsace sisters, Bernadette and Annette for sure, and Nell showed up, later, though, when she wasn't supposed to be there." She frowned at how everything had turned upside down that night.

"Bernadette is Bernadette Alsace Warden, and her sister is Annette."

"Yes."

"No one else?"

"I don't think so . . . No, no, wait. Reva was there. She came in and explained that Jo-Beth wasn't going to make it, that she had cramps or something, and really, the whole meeting was Jo-Beth's idea."

Kinley nodded, her face impassive. "What about Monica O'Neal?"

"She never made it."

"Anyone say why?"

Jayla shook her head.

"You'll have to speak. The recorder can't see you," Kinley reminded.

"No . . . Uh-uh."

"Did anyone ask?"

"Yeah, I think so. I think Bernadette . . . asked. Look, it was a long time ago and—"

"Did anyone answer?"

"No . . . I mean, I don't think so. We met, Jo-Beth didn't arrive. We all agreed to say we'd been together the night before, that no one had seen what happened to Elle."

"So you lied?"

Oh. Dear. Jayla was starting to panic. "Yes and no."

"You can't have it both ways. Either you did or you didn't."

"The truth is, we were together, but not all of us all the time." Oh, this was going badly. She'd ignored the calls from Jo-Beth, didn't want to go back to dealing with the past, and yet here she was with a reporter, a damned camper who had been at Camp Horseshoe and was now in her home. She should've called Jo-Beth back, agreed to meet at the camp.

"So where, exactly, were you? Where was everyone else?"

"I went directly to the cavern. Alone. And then I went back to my cabin."

Lie, lie, lie! Oh, Jayla, God is gonna punish you. And if DeMarcus ever finds out—

"Directly back?" Kinley seemed skeptical.

"Of course." Jayla's phone rang at that second, and she scooped it up, pressed it to her ear, and answered. "Excuse me," she said quickly to Kinley, "my son." She walked into the foyer while Kinley snapped off the recorder and phone. "Hey, honey," she said into the phone as the recorded telemarketer told her about some fabulous cruise to the Bahamas that she'd just won. "Yeah. What?" She made a big show of looking at her watch. "But I thought you said practice lasted another half hour. Say what, Taye?"

The telemarketer was babbling on.

"Slow down, honey. What about your brother? Is Malik with you?" She paused. Then said, "What? Oh, for the love of God, Taye. No, don't . . . You stay there. Got it?" A beat. "Do *not* leave! I'm on my way . . . Okay, okay! I said, I'll be right there." She hung up and, sweating bullets, grabbed her coat from a front closet. As she stuffed her arms into the sleeves, she said to Kinley, "I've got to go."

"But I just have a few more questions." The reporter made no move to pick up her devices.

"Sorry." Jayla buttoned up, found the scarf in a pocket, and wound it around her neck. "You have to leave."

"I can wait. You pick up your kids and I'll go grab a cup of coffee or hang out here and—"

"No!" Jayla cut her off. "This interview is over." She was firm as she walked to the living room.

"Then tomorrow—"

"Sorry. I'll be out of town." She arched her eyebrows and waited, standing over the coffee table as, reluctantly, Kinley finally grabbed her things, tossing both her phone and recorder into her bag.

"You really want to talk to me," Kinley warned. "The police will be calling and they can rail-road you. I can tell this story from your point of view."

"My point of view? Why?" Jayla was really nervous now, but she held it together.

"Well, there's talk that the head of the victim was severed from the body. No one's saying that—"

"What?" Jayla interjected in horror. "No body?"

"Just a skull, other scattered bones, not yet identified as belonging to the skull."

Jayla thought she might be sick.

"As I was beginning to say, no one's saying yet that the head was cut off the body, but—"

"Oh, my God. Are you really in my house telling me this? Discussing some kind of dismemberment?" All of Jayla's fears congealed while standing in the middle of her living room on her thick Turkish carpet. "I . . . I have to go."

"There was talk that you had a bit of a problem back then."

Jayla's heart nearly stopped and she realized in that split second how fragile her hold on her life—her marriage, her children, this huge historic house—was, that it could all be snatched from her with one whisper about the past. "I don't know what you mean."

"Some things went missing at camp."

"You mean campers lost things."

"I mean *some*one took them, and then there's the missing knife."

"What?" Jayla whispered.

"A butcher knife. Big one. Stolen from the kitchen according to the cook at the time. You remember her? Big Russian woman, Magda Sokolov? Went by Cookie?"

"Of course I remember her!"

"She reported a knife missing."

"So?"

"Back to your problem."

"You're saying that . . . that I'm a thief? Is that what you're accusing me of?"

"No accusations. I just know that you were accused of taking things, that you might have been dealing with kleptomania or something."

"I have to go," Jayla said again.

Kleptomania?

Or something.

"Now. My son Taye is waiting." Jayla stood by the door and reluctantly, it seemed, Kinley strolled through the foyer, past the bowl of potpourri. Jayla opened the door for her and wanted to damn near push her through it.

The second Kinley was over the threshold, she shut the door firmly and locked the deadbolt with a loud click.

Then she made her way to the kitchen and out the back door, across the porch and breezeway to the detached garage. Once inside, she let out her breath, and though she wasn't due to pick up either of her children for over an hour, she hit the button on the garage door and backed out. She wouldn't put it past Kinley to follow her; there was just something sneaky about the woman that bothered Jayla.

She melded onto Cesar Chavez, drove twice around the traffic circle, then angled off and took back streets, heading west, keeping an eye out for Kinley's little black car as she took the Burnside Bridge across the Willamette River, then turned onto a side street, where she parked and walked the two blocks to Voodoo Doughnut. Inside the funky brick building trimmed in a variety of colors, she waited in the inevitable line before ordering half a dozen odd-shaped and decorated doughnuts. All the while, as she stood beneath the chandeliers, she surveyed the crowd and the traffic through the window, her heart nearly seizing when she spied a black Chevy, only to realize the driver was an Asian girl who didn't look old enough to be at the wheel.

"Calm down," she told herself, then waited another ten minutes just to make certain she hadn't been followed. Finally she headed back to her car, where she devoured two of the doughnuts without really tasting them. *Get a grip. So a nerdy ex-camper reporter tracked you down and started poking around, asking about that summer. So what? Remember: You've got nothing to hide. Well, nothing anyone knows about. It's over. Done. Ancient history. Even if that body turns out to be Monica or Elle, none of this is about you.*

For a second she thought about the ghost she'd heard walking in her attic, the floorboards creaking, the old boxes and memorabilia and Christmas decorations moved from one area to the next. Could those ghosts be Elle? Or Monica?

No—she didn't even know that they were dead, and ghosts didn't travel like that, right? Didn't they haunt the area where they'd died? Wasn't that how it was supposed to be? But with ghosts, who knew?

She felt her skin crawl at the thought and picked up her cell phone. She didn't know how she'd get away from her job at the hospital, where she was a nurse, but surely someone could cover her shifts. She worked twelve hours straight and had today and tomorrow off. She hadn't wanted to go down to Averille, but now it felt imperative. However, if she was gone longer than two days she'd need someone to cover for her. DeMarcus and his sister would have to see to the boys.

Dear Lord, she didn't need this now.

Nor ever, she supposed as she searched for Jo-Beth's number, then texted: I'll be there tonight.

What about the police? No doubt you'll have to talk to them. Her head swam. Kinley Marsh, Jo-Beth Chancellor, or whatever her name was now, and the damned police?

Her blood chilled at the thought of talking to the cops.

But she would have to.

To end this thing.

She started her car and eased into the flow of traffic, making her way back to the Burnside Bridge and heading east where the cloud cover obscured the view of Mount Hood, some sixty miles or so distant.

Not that she could appreciate the sight even if the sky was clear. Not today. Not with her entire future at stake.

Chapter 21

Averille, Oregon
Now
Lucas

Caleb Carter was pissed as hell. At himself. What the hell had he been thinking? Bringing the police into the cove. Now the place was crawling with cops, and it would probably only get worse.

Mentally cursing himself, he drove to the south end of the old camp, to an old access road that was supposedly locked from the public. Years ago, he'd fixed that with a bolt cutter and new lock. He'd hidden the key under a rock near the gate post and came and went as he pleased, entering the private property at will.

Now, he drove onto the overgrown lane, parked at the gate, found the key where he'd left it, and, after wiping the little scrap of metal on his pants, slid it into the lock where, with a *click,* it released the chain, which slithered to the ground like a dead snake.

Then he drove through without bothering to lock up behind him. This trip wouldn't take long.

He'd left some crab pots off an old bridge and wanted to retrieve them in case the police fanned out and increased their search for more body parts. He shivered involuntarily at the thought that more dead people or *parts* of dead people could be lying around, shallowly buried in this solitary stretch of land. He thought of the oysters and clams he'd dug in the soft sand near the ocean and how easily he could have found other body parts.

"Shhheeit." He'd drag his pots from the spot they were hidden near the bridge and haul ass outta here, take whatever was trapped inside. Caleb wasn't all that picky about the size or sex of the crabs he hauled in, despite regulations. He figured if he caught 'em, the little buggers were his.

Once inside the gate, he drove along the twin ruts that wound through thickets of pine and fir on a path toward the sea. Beach grass and weeds scraped the undercarriage of his vehicle and the gloomy sky seemed more leaden than usual.

Probably just his imagination.

He'd been more than a little spooked since finding the jawbone, and today the normal coastal weather seemed more oppressive, a bit of fog creeping between the trees, moisture collecting on his windshield. He needed to get in and get out. He didn't consider himself a wuss by any means. Hell, he could beat anyone at arm wrestling down at Spike's Bar and had taken a guy twice his size. And he never backed down from a fight, but he still didn't like disturbing the dead.

Telling himself he was a fuckin' fraidy pants, he parked in a clearing near the inlet, where a good-sized creek dumped into a small bay that opened to the ocean. He cut the engine and reached under the seat, pulled out a half-drunk pint of Jim Beam that he kept hidden in the frame beneath the cushion, uncapped the bottle, and took a quick, long slug. Then, his courage up a bit, he left the bottle on the passenger seat, grabbed his cooler from the back of the truck, then hurried through the dense, dripping foliage to the broken-down bridge that someone a generation ago had built across the stream, where it flowed into a narrow neck of the bay. He didn't know how much time he had, but probably not much. Already there were reporters nosing around in town, too. Already some woman reporter from Astoria had left him a couple of messages that he'd ignored. Goddamned circus, that's what it was. Pretty soon the whole camp would be crawling with cops.

Shit, he'd done it to himself by reporting the jawbone.

Better hoist up the pots and haul them back to the truck, then lay low for a while, wait for all the interest to die down, let life as he knew it here in the outskirts of Averille return to normal.

All in all, it was a big pain in the ass.

The trees opened up to the creek—almost a river, he thought—and the beach grass lined the shore. He headed to the trail, scared a couple of rabbits, and wished he'd brought his shotgun as one hopped into the brambles, its tail disappearing into a hole, the whole nest of salal and berry vines disappearing into the fog rolling in.

Caleb made it to the bridge and started hauling up his pots. As the first emerged from the clear water he counted five—no, six—of the little buggers trapped within. A great haul, and some of them were good sized.

His spirits rose as he lifted the cage, water cascading back into the stream, the surprised crabs clinging to the netted sides, when he felt a change in the temperature. And not just from the spray of water that had splashed over him, but something else, like the breath of an unseen predator whispering up the back of his neck. He glanced up quickly, his eyes searching the surrounding woods.

Did he hear a soft moan, a quiet sob, something out of the ordinary over the dull roar of the ocean just over the rise?

He swallowed hard.

Saw nothing.

No one visible.

And yet . . .

Barely audible, he heard it again, a low groan, like an animal in pain, the sound murmured on the stiff ocean breeze blowing inland.

Where the hell was it coming from?

Had someone come up behind him?

He froze, looked over his shoulder, half expecting to see a game warden standing on the bank, his pistol drawn.

But again, nothing. No officer of the law drawing a bead on him.

Despite the cool temperature, he began to sweat.

"Jesus," he whispered, surprised the single word sounded like a prayer. It was time to get the hell out of here.

"Ooowwwwwaaaahhhh . . ."

The sound was louder now, a definite moan. He turned quickly to stare at the spit of land that jutted between the inlet and the ocean, where the beach grass danced against a backdrop of sodden gray.

His heart clutched as he spied her.

A wisp of a thing, in a long white dress, her pale hair playing wildly around her face, obscuring her features.

But he knew.

Goddamn, he knew.

"Elle," he whispered, his eyes rounding, his basket of crabs dropping back into the creek, icy water splashing. He backpedaled, gaze fixed on the apparition, the heel of his boot catching on the lip of the bridge. He fell backward, landing on the soft, wet ground when in a blink, as the fog settled in closer, she vanished. Evaporated.

"Holy *Christ*." He scrambled frantically away, climbing to his feet and running as if Lucifer himself were on his tail. What the hell was that? Her *ghost?* Frantically he got into his truck, turned on the ignition, and started backing up, the pickup's tires spinning in the sandy soil before finding purchase. He gunned the engine, then half turned in the seat, his hands clammy on the steering wheel as he steered backward.

At the gatepost, he twisted on the steering wheel, backing so quickly that his back bumper hit an exposed boulder. He didn't care. Not even if he'd bent his towing hitch. Too damned bad. He slammed his gear shift lever into drive, and with his tires kicking up mud, tromped on the accelerator.

Glancing into the rearview mirror, he saw the image again—the ghostly, waifish figure. "Shit!" he cried, and nearly rammed into an RV lumbering down the county road. The driver of the coach, a guy who had to be eighty, maybe ninety, scowled at him and shook his finger at him.

Caleb didn't care. He just hit the gas again and, while driving one-handed, snagged the bottle of Jim Beam from the passenger seat. He flicked off the cap and took a long belt, drinking several throat-searing gulps, draining what was left of the bottle.

Only then did he check his mirror again.

This time, he saw only the ribbon of asphalt and the huge RV disappearing into the fog.

No woman's figure.

No ghost.

No nothing.

Yet his damned heart kept drumming as if the very maw of hell were about to swallow him whole. He glanced at the empty bottle he'd tossed into the well in front of the passenger seat. Not a swig left.

But he needed another drink.

He drove into Averille and pulled into a free parking spot in front of Spike's Bar and Grill. He'd go inside, have a couple of whiskey neats, then, once his nerves weren't so jangled and he'd calmed himself, he'd drive back to the access road and little bridge, grab his crab pots and what was left of his catch, drive out again, and lock the gate behind him.

Or, maybe not.

No big hurry, he decided, race-walking past a couple of guys in jean jackets and baseball hats smoking near the doorway.

Inside he was met with a wall of heat, and a cacophony of sounds—rumbling conversation, clicking billiard balls, hissing soda guns, and bursts of laughter. Flat-screens flickering with some ball game were mounted between neon beer signs and racks from long-dead deer and elk. The bartender, Monty, was on duty and swabbing down the polished length of century-old oak that was the bar. Bald as one of the cue balls, a full black beard making up for the lack of hair on his head, he glanced up and grinned. "The usual? PBR?"

"Nah." A little calmer, Caleb slid onto one of the bar stools. He needed more than a beer, even a Pabst. "Whiskey. Jack Daniel's. Rocks."

"Black label?"

"Whatever."

Within seconds the glass was in front of him, amber liquor over ice cubes. He took a calming sip, then let out his breath.

"So I heard you were the one who found the body," Monty said, and the muscles in the back of Carter's neck tightened.

"Just a jawbone."

"And later a skull?" Monty let out a long whistle. "Man, oh, man, that would have scared the spit out of me."

Caleb took another drink, nearly emptying the glass.

"You know, there's been some people in here asking for you."

The hairs on the back of his neck lifted. "That right?"

"Yeah, a reporter of some kind. Works for

an online newspaper. Kelsey something or other."

"Kinley," Caleb corrected. He knew. She'd left messages on his phone.

"Yep, that would be the one."

"She came in here?" He finished the drink and crunched one of the ice cubes.

"Yeah, said she heard you were a regular. Asked a few questions, you know, about the body being discovered, but I didn't know much. Then she told me if I saw you that she'd like to talk to you."

Shoving his glass toward Monty, Caleb tried to ignore the feeling that somehow he'd stepped across an invisible barrier separating this world from the next, that in digging up the jawbone, he'd crossed a forbidden line and now he was cursed. He let out his breath slowly and wondered what to do. Then it hit him and he said, "I'll have another."

For now, he'd just get wasted.

It had been a long night that had spilled into the morning. Inside his cabin with its peekaboo view of the ocean, Lucas had spent hours at his desk or on the couch with his laptop, a fire blazing in the hearth. He'd called the state crime lab, gone over the old files, surfed the web, and come up with more information on the witnesses and suspects who'd been at Camp Horseshoe.

Lucas had double-checked on Waldo Grimes,

making certain that the prisoner was still indeed missing, and he'd coordinated everything he'd done with Maggie, so that they covered every detail, but didn't waste too much time going over the same information.

Now, it was past noon and after only a few hours' sleep between one a.m. and five, he was propped on his old couch. Roscoe, his rescued shepherd, was lying near the fire, the remnants of take-out food spread on the coffee table in front of him, not exactly out of the danger zone of Roscoe's quick attacks. For now the dog was keeping an eye on the white sack, where only a few leftover French fries were congealing in spilled catsup.

Lucas clicked on the television and checked the local news. As expected, the discovery of a partial skeleton was the headlining story, with an anchor in the newsroom in Portland questioning a reporter who was standing in front of the Neahkahnie Sheriff's Department.

He'd seen the reporter before, an African-American woman with short hair, dimples, and intelligent gold eyes, and now focused on her words: ". . . still not identified, though the skull is definitely female and the sheriff's department is focusing on what was once Camp Horseshoe, a Christian overnight camp located just south of Averille, Oregon. The camp, whose minister, Dr. Jeremiah Dalton, was also its owner, has been closed since three people associated with the camp went missing twenty years ago." At that point, the screen split, the reporter on one side, and on the other, an older picture of Lucas's father standing in front of the rec center, Naomi at his side. Lucas felt a surge of conflicting emotions as he stared at the faded image of Jeremiah and his wife. God, how young they both appeared. Jeremiah had been in his early forties, not that much older than Lucas was now, and Naomi had been in her thirties. His gut twisted as the reporter continued, and the picture of his father and stepmother was replaced with single head shots of Monica O'Neal, Eleanor Brady, and Dustin Peters, the victims who had vanished.

He listened to the report, then using the remote, clicked off the television and walked to the French doors that led to a small deck, beyond which was his view of the bay and ocean beyond. Today, the panorama was distorted, fog rolling in, the whitecaps, waves, and horizon invisible.

Roscoe gave up his vigil at the table and followed Lucas outside. He held his nose to the salty breeze, his tail wagging gently. Lucas had adopted the dog six years ago, or, more correctly, the shaggy black and tan stray had adopted him, showing up at the old house when he'd been renovating the floors, refusing to leave and just hanging out. Lucas had tried to find the dog's owner, had gone to the local vet and newspaper, had checked with the dog shelters, and then had finally accepted the fact that, like it or not, Roscoe was his.

Best decision of the dog's life, he figured.

Maybe the best of his own as well.

They were pretty much inseparable, except when Lucas was on the job.

After a few moments, he turned to the dog and said, "Come on, time for a break."

He went inside, grabbed a jacket, made sure there were a couple of tennis balls in the pockets, then tied on running shoes and, with the dog at his heels, took off through the French doors and down the steep steps to the yard. Together they ran the back roads to the bay, around the edge of the water to the jetty, and out onto the beach. Once there, winded, Lucas threw the tennis ball and Roscoe, who never seemed to tire of the game, took off after it, scaring up a flock of birds who'd been wading along the shore, to retrieve the ball and return to drop it in the wet sand at Lucas's feet, only to take off running again, so Lucas hurled it after him.

Today, as he gave chase, the shepherd disappeared into the fog and Lucas was reminded of the night Elle disappeared. His jaw clenched and he wondered if the skull that had been discovered would prove to be hers and, if so, what had happened to the rest of her body?

Severed intentionally? Or had it naturally, over the years of deterioration, become detached?

Or was it someone else's entirely? Monica's? Dustin's? Or some other unlucky person whose body had ended up in this part of the Pacific?

The breeze off the sea slapped at his face, chilled his hands, and kicked up whitecaps, making the pewter-colored ocean appear restless, striations of darker gray reminding him how deep and deadly were the waters.

Had Elle ended up in the Pacific that night? A wave pulling her out to sea? He hated to think so and had found some kind of ludicrous solace that her body had never been found, which left a glimmer of hope she was alive and well some-where.

"Yeah, right," he muttered sarcastically. From his years on the force he knew better.

Even with all the time that had passed, he still thought about her, wondered about her, and despite the fact that he'd told himself over and over again that what had happened to her wasn't his fault, he'd never quite bought it.

Now, it was all dredged up again.

And yes, he'd found any information he could on Bernadette Alsace Warden, who, court records claimed, was divorced. Not that it mattered, he reminded himself, as he watched Roscoe loping back with the now wet and sandy tennis ball.

Scooping up the ball, he flung it in one swift motion. "Last time," he told the dog, who took off, sand and foam flicking up from his paws as he raced along the edge of the tide. Lucas heard the familiar *whump-whump* of a helicopter's rotors and spied a Coast Guard chopper flying low, skimming along the coast line.

"Roscoe, come!" he yelled over the crash of the waves as the helicopter passed, but the dog wasn't listening, was still chasing the ball, which he caught up to, grabbed in his mouth, and spun around, returning. Lucas, his head clear, started jogging across the beach to the dunes and the bay, heading inland. He glanced over his shoulder. Roscoe was following, gaining on him, and would probably beat him to the stairs.

Lucas would shower, take a final look over his notes, then give Maggie Dobbs a call and let her ask any and all of her damned questions.

It was time to revise his statement of twenty years earlier.

No more secrets.

Chapter 22

Seaside, Oregon
Reva
Now

Reva could've picked Jo-Beth out of a throng of a thousand strangers. She was still tall, slim, and, from the tilt of her head, just as much of a snob. Her hair was shorter and there were the barest traces of lines near her eyes, probably spots that Botox couldn't fix, but she was chic, almost elegant as she sat in a booth in the back. If she'd wanted to blend in with this crowd of loggers, fishermen, and regular barflies, she needed to take it down a notch. The designer outfit, perfect makeup, and chic hairstyle were at odds with the common man's or woman's jeans, T-shirts, hoodies, and battered work boots or tennis shoes.

The crowd in Barnacle Bob's was thin—it was still early. The seven flat-screens bolted to the rough cedar walls were each flickering with different ball games and, if the sign outside was to be believed, broadcast via satellite dish, which was somehow sign worthy.

She wended her way through a few scattered tables, then slid into the booth opposite Jo-Beth, who had stood, as if she'd expected a damned hug or something. Reva was too keyed up for niceties and really, did she want to hug Jo-Beth? No. Besides the whole point of this meeting was to blend in, not be noticed.

"I need a drink," Reva announced, and searched for a waitress or barkeep or anyone who would bring her some damned alcohol.

Country music was playing through speakers mounted on the walls while the various games continued and a waitress, a pencil-thin woman with white-blond hair streaked with green, strolled over. She wore jeans and a black T-shirt with BARNACLE BOB'S embroidered over an appliqué of a winking shellfish, presumably a barnacle.

"What can I get you?" she asked, not bothering with a pad or pencil.

"A mojito," Reva said, noting that Jo-Beth was sticking with some kind of white wine. Well, fine and dandy, but she needed something stronger. "Make it a double."

"Well, alllll right! Ready to get the party started?" She grinned, her eyes brightening. "Anything to eat?"

"Maybe some pretzels or popcorn or whatever it is those men are having," she said, looking pointedly at a couple of guys at one of the tables positioned in front of the largest flat-screen. They were guzzling beer, a half-drunk pitcher sitting between their near-empty mugs, a glass wine carafe being emptied of some kind of party mix.

"You got it." The waitress actually twirled and headed to the L-shaped bar situated near two unoccupied pool tables.

"A double?" Jo-Beth said.

"Uh-huh, and it might not be my last. What the hell is going on?" She was anxious and didn't understand why the other woman could be so calm. Or was it just an act? "I mean, they find freaking Monica now?"

"Part of her. I heard it was just a skull. Or maybe just a portion of the skull. There was something about a jawbone being disconnected or missing, or found and then lost or something."

Reva shivered. "After all this time? And she really is dead. Jesus H. Christ, I can't believe it."

Jo-Beth took a sip of her wine. "So we have a problem."

"You think we have 'a' problem. I can think of a few more than that." She lowered her voice as the waitress returned and placed Reva's drink in front of her. "What about you?" the blonde asked Jo-Beth. "Ready for another?"

"I'm fine, thanks." Jo-Beth's glacial smile was enough to get the waitress to leave. When she was out of earshot, Jo-Beth said, "So we're on the same page here, right? What happened that night is that I had cramps, you went to the meeting, everyone agreed to say they were together on the night Elle disappeared, and that's all we know of it."

"But—"

"We just have to keep it simple. Don't veer from the story. Not an inch. That's where we'll get into trouble."

"What about Tyler?" Reva took a long swallow from her drink, felt the cool rum slide down her throat, the flavors of mint and lime erupting in her mouth. It tasted like heaven.

"What about him?" Jo-Beth's voice was sharp.

"What's he going to say?"

"That he didn't see me. I was in the latrine, with the damned cramps. Remember?"

"I get that, yeah, but what's he going to say that *he* was doing?"

"That he went to meet Monica, to break it off with her, at that old chapel, and she never showed up." Something ugly flashed in Jo-Beth's eyes, a hint of the same emotion she'd displayed twenty years earlier. "I talked to him. He's in Coos Bay now, still on the coast, just farther south. Owns a sawmill down there."

"I thought he came from money."

"He did. His father owned a string of mills, but they were mortgaged and he lost them during the recession. Now there's only one, and Tyler owns it."

"He married?"

"Was. No kids."

"And he's going to back us up? Our story?"

"I said it's the truth, so remember that," Jo-Beth stated coldly.

Reva took a sip of her drink. If she was to guess, she'd say that Jo-Beth had never gotten over Tyler Quade. "So, what did you talk about?" she asked casually.

"Nothing much. Just the fact that he was coming up here and confirming the truth."

Reva didn't believe it, but decided not to press her luck as Jo-Beth was starting to become more and more irritated. She twirled the ice in her glass, watching pieces of lime and mint swirl, but couldn't just let the subject die, so she ventured, "I thought you and he, y'know, might end up together."

She snorted. "No."

"You were crazy about him."

"He cheated," she stated flatly, trying, it seemed, to keep her expression calm and neutral, but the tiny tic at the corner of her eye, barely discernable in the dim light of the bar, gave her away.

Reva pushed. "You would have done anything to be with him."

She took a swallow from her glass. "I was young and dumb. We all were."

"But you knew each other in high school."

"Exactly. High school romance." She lifted a shoulder. Sipped again. "Not real life. I figured it out."

"When he nearly died?"

Jo-Beth's cool snapped. "When he got another girl pregnant. Now, drop it. All of that's ancient history."

"Which we get to relive."

"Right."

"So you're sure Tyler will stick with that—the story—that he never saw Monica that night?"

"It's what happened," Jo-Beth said tautly, as if the obvious lie were a no-brainer.

"What about the knife?"

"What knife?"

"The knife from the kitchen that I stole and gave to you and—"

"Oh. Tyler's handling that. As far as you and I know, there was no knife." Jo-Beth's voice was cold as ice, her gaze hard, her lips flat, the tic going a mile a minute.

"But if the police have it?"

"If they have it, they've had it for years, right? And there hasn't been a problem, has there? No fingerprints?"

"But now there's DNA."

"So what? As I said, Tyler's handling the knife. I talked with him." Jo-Beth's face softened just a fraction. "Seriously, don't worry about it. If the police ask about it, then you say that you knew nothing about it. Got it? *Nothing.*"

Reva was going to let that sleeping dog lie. For now. As some tinny country song played through speakers mounted in the ceiling, a football game being broadcast on one television, a baseball game on another, the video poker machines glowing in a row on a far wall, she drained her drink and lifted the empty glass, catching the waitress's attention as she passed.

"Double?" The server held up two fingers and raised her eyebrows.

Reva nodded back.

"Since Tyler's story is solid, then we're good," Jo-Beth said, frowning a little at the exchange.

"Almost."

Across the booth, Jo-Beth's eyes narrowed. She'd picked up her wineglass, but before it reached her lips, she stopped, held her drink midair. "What do you mean, 'almost'?"

"I know Lucas Dalton is on the case—he's a detective."

"My guess is they'll throw him off. Conflict of interest."

"Great." She let out a long breath. "Just effin' great."

"You want him on the case?"

"Hell, yeah." She gathered her courage, wondered where the hell that second drink was. "He's got as much to lose as the rest of us, and that other detective, Margaret Dobbs, she and I have a history."

"And I take it that it's not great." Jo-Beth's voice was clipped, her lips tight, but she stopped speaking as the waitress returned with Reva's second drink, which would be, if you were counting, and Reva really wasn't, four shots.

"Nope."

The waitress removed the old glass, glanced at Jo-Beth, whose countenance was stony, then said, quickly, "Two guys over there, at the pool table, they'd like to buy you two a drink."

Jo-Beth shot the two men an appraising look. Sipping from frosted mugs, holding pool cues in their free hands, the men, in their fifties in grungy jeans, beards, and T-shirts, were watching the conversation. "Tell them, 'No, thanks,' " she said tightly. "We're busy here and definitely not interested." She gave a little shudder and muttered under her breath, "In their wet dreams. Looks like they're only missing Tom."

"What?"

"Don't you recognize Dick and Hairy?" When Reva didn't respond, Jo-Beth looked irked and said, "It's a joke," then swept on. "Never mind. I guess it was a piss-poor attempt at humor. It doesn't matter anyway. What happened between you and Dobbs?"

Reva took another long drink, felt the alcohol warming her blood. "There was a car accident, and she must've been working in the valley at the time. It happened in Clackamas County, one of the back roads between Oregon City and Canby, and she was the investigating officer."

"You were involved, I take it?"

"I was in the accident—two cars—as was Theo, who was my husband. We'd been married just a short while. He, um, didn't make it, nor did the driver of the other vehicle. But her kid, five-year-old girl in a car seat, she survived with minor injuries and so did I."

Jo-Beth glanced at the fresh mojito that Reva was sipping. "Who was driving?"

"Theo!" she shot back. Then more softly, "It was his fault. Swerved over the center line on a curve, both . . . both cars went spinning," she added, remembering. "It was determined both cars were traveling over the speed limit and each ended up on the opposite side of the road, in brush. It . . . It was awful." She recalled the crash, the twisting groan of metal, glass shattering and spraying, the world, in those few seconds, spinning wildly. She'd screamed as the SUV rolled down an embankment. Neither she nor Theo had been wearing seat belts . . . and Theo, dear, sweet Theo . . .

"You said Dobbs was the investigating officer?" Jo-Beth prompted.

"Yes."

"And?"

"We'd been drinking. Theo . . . was over the limit." Reva's skin felt hot. She still tried to forget it, but in that last second before the crash, she had seen the child in the minivan, her little face full of fear and confusion at the sight of Theo's careening SUV.

"Then I don't understand," Jo-Beth said. "So what?"

Reva took another belt as she contemplated just how much of the story she could reveal to Jo-Beth. "Dobbs was really pushing it with me. She, uh, she seemed to think there was something fishy about the accident."

"Fishy?"

"She kept asking me where we had the drinks, how many each of us had, why did I let Theo get behind the wheel. You know. Cop stuff."

"That's what happens and you'd better be ready for it now," Jo-Beth said. "Just keep to the story. It's what happened."

"Dobbs isn't easily fooled."

Jo-Beth pushed her wineglass aside and leaned over the table. "Is that what you did, Reva? What you're still doing? Trying to fool a police officer?"

"No, no, but—"

"Then you don't have to worry. You didn't lie then and you're not lying now." She checked her watch. "Look. It's time to go. Stay strong. On point." She motioned to the waitress. "Check please. We're done here." Standing, she added, "You might want to leave the drink, Reva. We still have a few miles to go and it probably wouldn't be smart to get involved in another accident." The waitress walked up and slipped a bill onto the table. Jo-Beth gave it a cursory glance and rather than use a credit card, peeled a couple of bills from her wallet. "Keep the change," she said. Then to Reva, "Let's go."

The men at the nearby table gave them each a long look and seemed about to say something, but the hard glare Reva sent their way stopped them cold, and a few seconds later she and Jo-Beth were making their way to their cars.

She climbed into her Toyota, tossed back a handful of the Tic-Tac mints she kept in her console, just in case she got pulled over, and wheeled out of the lot behind Jo-Beth's Mercedes.

She tried to concentrate on driving, on keeping up with Jo-Beth, but maintaining a safe distance behind. She snorted at the thought. Wasn't that how she'd always played it? One step behind the ringleader, always in the army, but never leading the charge?

And how has that worked out for you? Huh?

Glancing in the rearview, she caught her own gaze, saw the hard lines of her visage. She'd have to be careful or all of the pain and anger of her life would start showing up in the set of her jaw, the wrinkles around her mouth, the fearful, almost feral, glimmer in her eyes.

She thought of returning to Averille, and not only facing Lucas Dalton as a detective, but also that freaking Maggie Dobbs. Why the hell did it have to be Dobbs?

Because, Reva, your past always catches up to you.

Isn't that what her grandmother, her *abuela* Maria, had told her? "You remember that God sees everything," the old woman had reminded her when she'd caught Reva attempting to ditch catechism once. "Trust me. The past always catches up with you. Now go on. Back into the church. To confession." And with steely, wrinkled fingers digging into Reva's shoulders, she'd marched her up the steps of the church and said, "Talk to Father Matthew and do whatever penance he sees fit." With that, she'd opened one of the heavy wooden doors with one hand and pushed her granddaughter into the darkened apse, where, swallowing hard, Reva had passed the table filled with flickering votives and made her way to the confessional.

If Abuela Maria could only see her now. Taking her right hand from the steering wheel for just a second, she sketched the sign of the cross over her chest and wished to high heaven she could avoid the woman detective.

Dobbs would remember Reva Mercado Vicari.

And all of Jo-Beth's assurances that she wouldn't be lying would be out the window. Biting her lip, she followed Jo-Beth's sleek car past the city limits, heading steadily south, past an RV park, and a fruit stand, beyond the on-ramp to Highway 26, and steadily south along the jagged coast. But she was driving by rote, remembering another time when she'd been at the wheel, Theo in the passenger seat. She'd been buzzed, not really drunk, but feeling good after an afternoon of wine tasting. Theo, as usual, had been too drunk to drive, as he'd topped off the wine with two martinis. "You handle it, babe," he'd said, and had climbed into the passenger side of their older Ford Explorer. She had tried to be careful, had only sipped at her wine, she thought, cognizant of the fact that she was pregnant. She'd known she shouldn't drink anything, but she'd been trying to work up the courage to tell Theo about the baby. She was barely pregnant, after all, and booze was probably the reason she'd gotten herself into this mess in the first place.

It had happened in the week that she and Theo had broken up and she'd gone out on the town, hooked up with an old boyfriend, and . . . wouldn't ya know? Then, Theo had come back to her and since she was married to him and the boyfriend was a bad-boy loser, she'd slipped on her wedding ring never to take it off again.

So she'd driven that day and the skies had opened, rain pouring from the heavens, water shimmering on the road, the wipers unable to keep up with the torrent. She probably should have pulled over, waited out the storm, but in Oregon that could be hours, so she'd kept driving in the darkness of late afternoon in winter, twilight really. She'd thought she'd spied a deer at the side of the road, ready to leap onto the shiny asphalt in front of her. She'd swerved slightly as she'd rounded the corner, hitting her brakes just as the oncoming headlights flashed in her eyes. A woman driver. Kid in the back, in a car seat placed in the middle of the vehicle.

The minivan had been close.

Too close.

"Move over!" Reva had yelled, and saw terror in the little kid's eyes.

"Huh?" Theo, slumped against the passenger door, had opened a bleary eye.

"Not you! That idiot!" she'd screamed, even though it had registered that her vehicle had careened over the center line at the corner, placing her SUV in the path of the oncoming minivan. She'd stood on the brakes, tires screaming, the SUV sliding wildly, her gaze locking with that of the child at the moment of impact!

BAM!

With a sickening crunch of metal, the vehicles had collided. Glass shattered. Steel had twisted and groaned. Tires had exploded. The SUV had reeled wildly, Reva seeing for a nanosecond the look of sheer terror in the girl's eyes. As the Explorer shuddered and spun, crunching metal, someone's screams filling the air, she'd been flung through the windshield, pain screaming through her body.

She'd come to, seconds later, dazed, bloody, but with the horrendous knowledge that the accident was her fault. Theo, too, had been flung from the Explorer, his body crumpled against a tree. She crawled to him to find no pulse, no signs of life in his broken form.

Touching his neck, feeling the blood warm against her fingers, she'd been sobbing hysterically when, clear as a bell, she'd heard his voice, as if he were still with her, still alive.

"Babe, you have to save yourself and the baby. You can't go to jail for this. Tell them I was behind the wheel. For me, it doesn't matter. Do it. Now. Why punish yourself? Why punish the baby? Love you . . ."

With his words as her impetus, she'd used all of her strength and with supreme effort, had gone back to the SUV and forced the driver's seat back, as if someone with longer legs than hers had been driving. With the dirty napkin from Starbucks she'd found wedged in the seat as rain had pelted her from the leaden clouds overhead, she'd wiped down the steering wheel.

Only then had she turned her attention to the other vehicle, on the far side of the road. The driver had been slumped over the steering wheel, the air bag deployed around her. Staggering and limping, Reva, still dazed, had started across the road. Vaguely, her head still echoing from the impact, her limbs seeming detached, she'd stepped onto the wet pavement and thought she'd heard something over the hiss of the rain and the splattering of raindrops peppering the asphalt.

An engine? Is that the rumble of a big engine?

She'd stopped, turned slowly, and seen, coming around the curve, the headlights of a vehicle, beams cutting through the curtain of rain. Squinting, holding her arm up against the bright lights, she'd teetered, then seen the old pickup slide, brakes shrieking as the driver had narrowly missed her and slid to a stop barely ten feet away.

He'd been out of his truck in an instant, a farmer in bib overalls, his pallor white beneath a day's growth of beard, rain beating down on his baseball cap.

"Holy Mother of God!" he'd cried. "What the hell happened here?" Quickly sizing up the situation, he'd seen that Reva, feeling a warmth ooze down her legs, had been about ready to collapse. "Oh, geez, honey," he'd said, and had caught her just before she fell and passed out. The next thing she knew she awoke in the hospital to the news that Theo and the driver of the other vehicle had died at the scene. The little girl had survived, thankfully, as had she, though she'd lost the baby. Maybe that had been for the best.

Now, as she drove by rote, following the glowing taillights of Jo-Beth's Mercedes, she remembered the next few months, recovering, dealing with the grief of losing Theo and the accusatory looks she'd received from his sister. And the baby . . . even now, her heart split at the memory of losing it.

She swallowed hard and tried to pay attention to keeping her Camry on the road. She didn't look forward to dealing with Dobbs again. There was little doubt in her mind that the officer who had left a message for her on her voice mail, "Detective Margaret Dobbs" from the Neahkahnie County Sheriff's Department, was one and the same as Deputy Margaret Dobbs of the Clackamas County Sheriff's Department a few years back. She had been a snippy little investigator who had looked at her intently with disbelieving eyes, who had seen beyond the new widow and woman who had miscarried her first child. After listening to the voice mail, Reva had Googled the detective. Sure enough, one and the same.

Reva hadn't returned the detective's call.

Didn't want to talk to her.

Now, of course, it seemed inevitable.

She would see the woman face-to-face.

Steeling herself, she saw the familiar peekaboo view of the ocean through the trees as she approached the outskirts of Averille. Oh. God. Somehow, she had to get herself together and make sure that all of her ducks were in a row, even if they were really just decoys.

Chapter 23

Camp Horseshoe
Then
Annette

With Bernadette only a few steps behind, Annette reached the cavern. Hearing voices echoing from within, she slipped through the cave-like entrance. Inside, tiny flashlights gave the wet interior walls a bluish glow, and a group of girls were huddled near the small tide pool beneath the high, rocky ceiling. A stream, merely a rivulet now, wandered in from a crack in the sea wall, allowing water to filter into the grotto and pool near the center of the cavern.

Annette had thought they were late, that the "meeting" Jo-Beth had called would be in full swing. However, that wasn't the case. The group was small; not only were Jo-Beth and Reva missing, Monica hadn't yet joined them and, of course, they were missing Elle, her disappearance the very reason they'd gathered.

"Where is everyone?" Bernadette asked over the roar of the surf. Though the tide was out, the pounding of the ocean on the shore echoed through the cavern.

"Good question!" Sosi, in a gray University of Oregon hoodie, was shaking her head. "You'd think Jo-Beth would have been the first one here. I mean, this was all her idea, right, and it's nuts. I don't even know why I decided to come here. We *all* shouldn't be away from the girls."

"We *all* aren't," Jayla said. "Mother Naomi is in Elle's cabin and then there's Nell. Jo-Beth intentionally left her out as she didn't know Nell all that well and there needed to be at least one counselor at the camp."

Sosi hesitated, as if she were going to say something, then held her tongue and walked to the cavern to peer outside. "Where are they? You don't think this was all part of some big prank, do you? Jo-Beth's big on pranks."

"I don't think so," Annette said, but understood. Jo-Beth was a vicious, angry girl. She'd heard somewhere that Monica was seeing Tyler and had wanted one of them, most likely Sosi, who was small and petite like Elle, to dress up as the missing girl and act like her ghost, carry a bloody knife or something, and come after Monica. But Sosi had put the kibosh on the prank, and the rest of them had agreed not to go along with it. Jo-Beth had calmed down a bit, and had instead come up with this alternative plan to meet down here, in the middle of the night, when they could all get together without the eyes and ears of the campers upon them.

Jo-Beth had insisted they had to meet and get their story straight about the night before and stupidly, Annette now thought, they'd all capitulated. The only stipulation had been that one of the counselors stay back at camp for the girls. Nell, being the youngest and out of the loop, had been elected, even if she didn't know it.

Sosi had agreed to bring Nell up to speed tomorrow.

Jayla rubbed her arms, glanced nervously overhead, where, because of the watery beams of the flashlights, the reflection of the tide pool shimmered eerily on the rocky ceiling. "Let's . . . Let's go back. I don't like it here. This is nuts. And . . . Jo-Beth and Reva? Maybe they're not coming."

"No one's going anywhere!" Reva said breathlessly, slipping suddenly into the cave. "Not until we sort this all out."

"About time," Jayla remarked, still edgy.

"Sort what out?" Bernadette stared pointedly at Reva. "What's to 'sort out'?"

"We just need to be on the same page." Reva motioned to all of the girls.

Sosi asked, "Where's Jo-Beth?"

Reva waved off the question. "She's . . . She's got cramps."

"She's not coming?" Annette demanded as the surf pounded ever louder. "This was all her idea!"

"That's it. I'm outta here." Jayla's eyes were wide. "This place gives me a serious case of the C-R-E-E-P-S!"

Sosi agreed, "Let's just leave."

"No, no! Wait!" Reva practically shouted, and Annette had the feeling she was stalling. But that was crazy—well, everything about tonight, and last night, was off, creepy, even. She felt her skin crawl. "We need to figure out what we're going to say to the police," Reva insisted.

"The truth!" Annette threw up her hands, her shadow dancing eerily on the rocky walls behind her. "I don't care what we've all done. We have to do what's right. If we lie, we'll all get in worse trouble."

They started arguing, Annette getting hot and adamant that they tell the truth, and Bernadette trying to calm everyone down. "Let's not argue," she said. "Come on . . . think this through. What are the guys going to say? Are they all going to be a part of this lie, too?" Obviously Bernadette, always the peacemaker, felt at a loss. She was finding no one here, including Annette, who wanted to calm down. Everyone was edgy, everyone was worried about what had happened to Elle and getting antsy about leaving the campers alone so long.

"We can't stay here all night!" Jayla said, her eyes darting around in her head. "And what about that murderer on the loose, huh? Do you all think he had something to do with Elle? Oh, sweet Jesus, I can't think about that."

To Annette's surprise, Reva nodded. "Me

neither," she said, and made a deft sign of the cross over her breasts.

"Lying's not going to help." Annette was firm. "We have to help the police find her."

"Let's figure this out quickly," Bernadette said. "The campers are bound to wake up. Therese will have to go to the bathroom soon again, I just know it. And Arielle, she's always having nightmares about monsters."

"Amen, Sister," Jayla said, holding up a hand. "I hear you on that one."

Bernadette said, "Any one of the other kids could wake up from a really bad dream and come screaming in search of a counselor. And not find one. How would that look? And then Mrs. Dalton will wake up and go through the roof."

"We'll all be screwed," Annette agreed, noticing that the rivulet was growing steadily, the trickle of water quickly becoming a larger stream as the tide had apparently turned, the waves moving closer to the shore. "I think we should leave."

"Not yet!" At that moment, Jo-Beth hurried into the cave. "Sorry. I was . . . sick."

"I told them about your cramps," Reva cut in quickly.

"Right. Miserable."

But she didn't look sick. If anything, she seemed out of breath and jazzed, nervous. Maybe from running to get here? Annette wasn't sure, but she'd decided to mention it in her journal when she got back to the cabin. One thing was certain, Jo-Beth, as always, was determined and ready to be in charge, which she obviously thought was her rightful place, here and probably anywhere else she set foot. "So now," she said, looking at each of the other counselors in turn. "We have to come up with our story and we have to stick to it."

"I'm not going to lie," Sosi stated firmly, short reddish hair poking from beneath the hood of her sweatshirt. Her little chin was angled up determinedly and though nearly half a foot shorter than Jo-Beth, Sosi seemed ready to take on the taller girl. No surprise there. Annette remembered Sosi had four older brothers whom she claimed tried to bully her from the time she'd been able to walk, and she tried to resist taking guff from anyone, including know-it-all Jo-Beth Chancellor.

"Of course you are." Jo-Beth advanced on the shorter girl. "We all are. For the greater good. And we're going to say that we were all together to . . . to commune with nature and to feel closer to God and to, you know, bond with our 'sisters.' "

"While we just left the girls? Nuh-uh." Jayla was shaking her head.

Jo-Beth reminded, "For a few minutes."

"Everyone but Elle," Jayla pointed out. "No one's going to buy that."

"Sure they will. The Reverend Dalton will want to believe we were trying to connect with God. With Jesus. What better place than here, in God's backyard, isn't that what Reverend Dalton calls this place?"

Sosi glowered up at Jo-Beth, her voice barely audible over the rush of the ocean. "I don't think we should use Jesus as an excuse. It's just not right."

"Amen," Jayla agreed, springy dark curls bouncing around her face. "We don't use Jesus."

"It's not Jesus per se," Jo-Beth argued. "We'll just say we all wanted to experience a connection with God, through nature. Reverend Dalton's faith has inspired us. All of us."

Jayla arched a disbelieving brow. "At midnight?"

"Yes, we couldn't sleep." As if anticipating the next obvious question, she added, "Okay, so maybe a couple of us couldn't sleep and woke the others." Nodding to herself, she added, "Yeah, that makes it more plausible."

Sosi frowned. "So the story is that two of us— let's say Bernadette and Annette, since they're sisters—they had a lot on their minds and couldn't sleep."

Bernadette cut in, "Just because we're sisters doesn't mean—"

"Let her finish!" Jo-Beth snapped. "We don't have a lot of time." That was the first honest thing she'd said, as it was obvious from the ever-growing stream of water they needed to leave and soon or be trapped. "We can work on the details later." Then, seeing Bernadette was about to argue, said, "Fine, we'll say Monica couldn't sleep. She's not here to say differently."

"And that's weird, don't you think?" Annette said. "Where is she?"

"Oh, for the love of—Who knows? We all know how she is." Jo-Beth let out a huff of disgust. "She's probably just late."

"Maybe she didn't wake up. Shouldn't someone go back and get her?" Annette suggested nervously. "Since we're all in this together. And you're going to say that she's the one who woke everyone up?"

Jo-Beth waved away Annette's argument as if it were as insignificant as a fly. "Forget it! We don't have the time to go find her and get back here just to start the discussion all over again."

"You got that right." Jayla was nervously eyeing the rising stream.

"So then," Jo Beth said, "fine. Use me. I'm the one who couldn't sleep."

"So you woke the rest of us and we all decided to find Elle and not worry anyone," Jayla said.

"You mean, we'd just leave our girls—" Sosi started to put in.

"Yes! Yes! Of course!"

"And we were doing it to find God." In the

weird glow of the flashlights, Jayla rolled her big eyes. "Oh, sure, that's believable."

"It is!" Jo-Beth looked at each girl in turn. "We didn't go far, just . . . say to that clearing near the flagpole, okay? So . . . So we could hear any of the girls if they called or needed us. And we . . . we weren't just communing with God—no, you're right—but we were worried about Elle, okay?" Jo-Beth was finding her footing now, the tale—the lie—unfolding in this cavern far below the cliffs. "She'd said some things to us that concerned us, so we got together to discuss what to do about it, how . . . how to help her." Jo-Beth snapped her fingers as if the idea had just struck. "That's it. We didn't know she was missing."

"We didn't," Bernadette said.

"What did she say to us?" Jayla asked, not convinced, one eye on the rising water.

"Boyfriend problems," Jo-Beth said. "Lucas. She was worried about Lucas. I mean really upset. Everyone knew she was involved with him."

Annette saw Bernadette pale as if her heart had stilled. For her, Annette suspected, this was too close to the truth. "I don't think we should lie about that."

"It's not a lie," Reva said. "She admitted it to me that Lucas had broken up with her and she was 'devastated,' that's the word she used, 'devastated.' She was really upset. I was afraid she would do something."

313

"Like what?" Annette prodded.

"Like, I don't know . . ." Reva said. "Like maybe kill herself or kill Lucas. Maybe kill him, then herself."

Bernadette blurted, "That's crazy. And besides, Reverend Dalton will wonder why we didn't alert him or his wife."

"Because we were scared. Didn't want to get her into trouble." Jo-Beth was really going now. "Like we thought we could help her, just the way he's always preaching about. We were . . . you know, taking control of the situation."

"Instead of covering our asses," Annette said dryly.

"We all know Elle's a little crazy," Reva put in to silence any opposition. "That's the point."

"When?" Bernadette demanded. "When did she say that they—she and Lucas—had broken up?"

Reva lifted a dismissive shoulder. "I don't know. A couple of days ago. Like on the day she disappeared."

"Yesterday then?" Bernadette said, her voice a little higher than usual.

Annette had to wonder, was it possible? Had Elle gone missing because of her sister? Is that why she'd just taken off? Or had she really killed herself? Oh. Dear. God. Her gaze met Bernadette's and she knew her thoughts were mirroring her sister's.

Reva nodded, catching Jo-Beth's eye. "We were coming out of the cafeteria and she saw Lucas. He was helping fix the stairs on the front porch of the rec center."

Annette witnessed Bernadette swallowing hard. She knew why. She, too, remembered spying Lucas hammering the new step into place, and Reva had been talking to Elle after lunch.

Oh, God, was it true?

Bernadette looked stricken.

Sosi, though, wasn't convinced. "This is a dumb idea," she said, and Annette nodded her agreement as a particularly loud wave crashed against the rocks and the little stream widened. "Jayla's right. Nobody's going to buy it."

"I don't see you coming up with a better idea," Jo-Beth said crossly. She glared at Sosi. "You want to tell the truth, about what you were really doing?"

Sosi opened her mouth, then shut it. "I'm telling you," Jo-Beth insisted, "we need to stick together on this."

"Why? What did you do that makes you so sure we should lie?" Jayla asked.

"Like everyone here, I wasn't where I was supposed to be last night, and I don't want to admit it and mess up my future." For the first time Jo-Beth seemed sincere. "That's what this is really about. What happened to Elle? We don't know, right? But we'll all look compromised, guilty, if we start blabbing about what we've really been doing."

Annette didn't like it. None of it.

Nor did Bernadette. "I think we should just tell the truth," she said. "I mean, what are we going to say if they break us up and interview us one by one? Won't they ask each of us what the other was saying?"

Nobody answered Bernadette, so Jo-Beth went on. "Just stick to the story. We were all worried about Elle. And you all can say that I mentioned she'd been desperate, even suicidal, and that I was worried. I'll say she confided in me. So if you get asked anything, dump it on me. I can handle it. Both of my parents are lawyers; I know how the system works."

"This is never going to work," Annette said.

"Not if we don't all stick together. Look, this is the best plan I've got. Do you have something better?"

"We could tell the truth," Sosi said.

"Hey, you all. The water?" Jayla said. The stream was rushing more wildly now, the tidal pool taking up more and more space in the cavern. Jayla edged closer to the entrance to the cavern, but no one, aside from Annette, was paying any attention.

"Okay. Fine. Let's explore 'the truth,' " Jo-Beth suggested, using finger quotes for emphasis. "If we're going to go with 'the truth,' then it's going to be all of it. Think about it. What it means if everything we've ever done here comes out. *Everything.*" Her eyes narrowed a bit as the surf echoed through the chamber. "How do you think your parents would like to know that you've been smoking weed?" she asked Sosi. "Isn't your dad like a mucky-muck in that church you belong to?"

"An elder," Sosi admitted, head bowed.

"Right. So what would he say if he knew the truth? And what about your girlfriend? Don't deny it. We all know. Everyone in the camp knows it except for Reverend and Mrs. Dalton. Can you imagine what he'd say? What he'd do? What would happen to you? To *Nell?*"

"Dear God," Sosi whispered.

"And what about making the gymnastic team at Oregon? That would be over. Right?"

Sosi's eyes rounded. She tried to argue but couldn't.

"And you." Jo-Beth turned to Jayla. "Don't act so innocent. I've seen you pick up stuff that doesn't belong to you."

"What?" Jayla looked stricken.

"Wasn't one of your campers missing a necklace? Something her grandmother gave her before the old lady died?"

"Yeah, but I didn't—"

"And another one couldn't find some of her money, right?"

"I didn't take anything!"

"Save it, Jayla. We all know you have a problem."

"I don't!" Jayla insisted, hoisting her chin up a notch, but she quit arguing when she noticed that none of the girls standing in the ring came to her defense. Not one. Because they all knew. And there was more, Annette thought to herself. She'd seen Jayla with Dusty on more than one occasion, sharing cigarettes and kisses behind |the stables. Annette had been on horse duty one day and had come across Dusty and Jayla on the side of the stables near a watering trough. At the sight of her they'd broken off their embrace.

It was true, Annette thought. Every one of them had something to hide, something that could change the course of their lives. It had all started out so innocently, nine girls thrust together in this small camp on the Oregon Coast, all being dropped off by their parents and entrusted with the lives of younger girls. Annette remembered Bernadette stepping out of the front passenger seat of her mother's battered old Volvo while Annette bounced out of the back seat.

And then she'd observed Bernadette catch her first glimpse of Lucas in the office. He'd just walked in the back door and, after a hesitant introduction, had offered to carry the Alsace sisters' bags to their assigned cabin. In faded jeans and an equally scruffy black T-shirt, he'd lifted the two duffels as if they weighed nothing, tossed each onto a shoulder, and walked away. Bernadette hadn't been able to drag her gaze from his retreating form, his wide shoulders, straight back, and slim buttocks moving easily beneath the pale jeans hanging oh-so-low on his narrow hips.

Witnessing her sister's transformation, Annette had realized that Bernadette had felt a thrill then, a little tingle of awareness that surprised her and caught her off guard, the same awareness Annette, too, had felt. She'd been so entranced herself that she hadn't realized her mother was introducing her to Reverend Dalton and his wife, Naomi. So much so that she'd barely noticed Leah, Naomi's eleven-year-old daughter, who was holding a gray cat desperate to scramble out of her arms.

Now, Annette blushed. Of course Lucas had never even noticed her. She pushed all those memories aside for the moment and decided to divulge one of her own secrets. Since the group seemed deadlocked, it was time to admit the truth no matter what the consequences. "What about if we've seen Elle?" she asked, and felt the weight of everyone's gaze land on her.

Jo-Beth demanded, "What do you mean? Like, since she disappeared?"

"Yeah." Annette was nodding, hating to have to tell them all.

"But we haven't. No one has." Jo-Beth paused. "Wait a sec. *You? You* think you saw her?"

Now that everyone was staring at her, Annette wished she'd never told them. "Look, I mean I saw something or someone. Last night."

For a second no one said a word. Stunned, they just looked at her as the tide pool, like a living thing, grew larger, then shrank with the incoming and retreating ocean.

Much as she wanted to, Annette couldn't backtrack now. "It was dark of course and raining, and so . . . so I'm not sure."

Jo-Beth pointed at her. "You just said—"

"I know, I know!" Annette regretted mentioning it. "I think . . . I mean, it could have been Elle or someone who looked like her or . . ."

"Or what?" Reva demanded, dark eyes flashing.

Annette screwed up her courage. "Or . . . or her ghost."

"Oh, for the love of God!" Jo-Beth groaned. "We don't need this kind of drama or crazy talk, okay?" She shook her head. "I mean, I expected something like this from Jayla, but not you. So, don't even go there."

Sosi looked concerned. "Let her speak. What do you mean? What did you see?"

Annette set her jaw. "It was just after lights out and I had to pee. I didn't want to, because it was raining like crazy, but I . . . I left my cabin and headed toward the bathhouse when I thought I heard something."

"In the bathhouse?"

Annette shook her head. "It was before I got to the turnoff for the latrines. I'd just reached the fork in the trail. And there, up ahead, on the main path was a girl, I think, in white, like a long dress, running. Away from me."

"Say whaaat?" Jayla said, her eyes as big as saucers.

Reva shook her head. "Around eleven?"

Annette nodded. "She was far enough away that through the rain and the dark and the trees, I couldn't be certain, but I followed for a few steps and then she was gone."

"Gone?" Sosi repeated. "Did she see you?"

"Don't know."

Jayla asked, "Like she disappeared? Vanished? Poof?" She snapped her fingers. "Into thin air?"

"Yeah," Annette admitted. "Like I said, a ghost."

"Jesus. You're serious, aren't you? A damned ghost. Holy shit." Jo-Beth actually laughed, a deep cackle that seemed to echo through the cavern.

Annette took a step toward Jo-Beth. "I saw her!"

"And you know it was Elle?" Jo-Beth didn't bother to hide her disbelief. "Even from a distance?"

"I said I think it was her."

"Or a ghost through the rain and the trees on a dark night," Jo-Beth mocked.

Sosi said, "You have to tell them. The police."

Jo-Beth rounded on her. "Why?"

"So they can find her!" Sosi declared.

"You think this could help? Look, Annette isn't even sure that what she saw was a girl, let alone Elle! What do you think the cops would say if she started talking about ghosts?"

"I just don't know!" Annette said, her voice rising an octave, and she noticed Bernadette visibly cringed. She was used to Annette's hysteria, her need for attention, her lies, Annette knew, but tonight she was only saying the truth. "Okay! Forget I said anything!"

"We will," Jo-Beth agreed sternly, and looked from one worried face to another. "We," she said, "all got together last night and we didn't see any girl, or ghosts or anything. We met by the flagpole and we all said we were worried. We tell the truth about yesterday, okay? Keep it simple. Tell the cops when the last time you saw Elle was, but then we all went to bed, made sure the kids were asleep, and met to try to figure out what had happened to her. That's it." She eyed everyone. "We were back in our bunks by eleven."

"Why even say we met?" Sosi asked. "Why not say we all just went to bed?"

Jo-Beth's mouth tightened. "Because someone might have seen something, okay? One of the guys, or Mrs. Dalton, or a camper might have woken up and seen that her counselor wasn't in bed. Who knows? This way we cover our asses."

"Jo's right," Reva inserted. "If we admit we were out, it'll seem like we're coming clean, that we're not perfect and not pretending to be."

"Right." Jo-Beth was insistent. "So let's do it."

Bernadette asked, "What about Monica? Where is she?"

"Don't worry about her," Jo-Beth said. "She'll go along."

"How can you be sure?" Bernadette wasn't convinced.

Jo-Beth smiled, her teeth visible in the bluish light. "She has more to lose than anyone. So come on. Now, let's go. Before anyone figures out we're missing. Besides, if you haven't noticed, the water's rising. We'd better get out of here before we all drown."

Jo-Beth didn't wait for a consensus, just figured everyone would follow her from the cavern and they did, keeping close, shutting off their flashlights, heading back to the campground with their weak-as-crap story. No, make that weak-as-crap lies.

And that was the story they'd kept to all these years.

Chapter 24

Averille, Oregon
Now
Lucas

Desolate.

That was the word to describe the camp-grounds, Lucas thought, walking around the rec hall, now boarded and locked, but once filled with campers, counselors, and workers, voices and laughter rising to the ceiling. He remembered the smells coming from the kitchen where that old grouch of a woman made the most amazing dishes, everything from piroshky—fried buns with meat fillings—and cabbage rolls when she was feeling a longing for the mother country, to baked salmon and fresh crab, or spaghetti and pizza. The cuisine had been eclectic and not exactly kid-friendly, but there had been enough work and exercise at the camp and no snacks that even the pickiest eaters had dived in at mealtime, complaining mightily but filling their bellies.

Music had been a staple at the camp, with Naomi playing traditional hymns on the piano in the rec center, and a ragtag group of campers and counselors playing guitars and harmonicas, the braver or more gifted ones singing hymns or, on occasion, pop songs approved by the reverend. Back then, Jeremiah was in control of every second of every hour of every day.

It wasn't a surprise that the counselors—teenagers who loved to rebel against any kind of authority—ignored the camp rules when they could, especially after "Lights Out," when night stole across the land.

He walked past the kitchens and along a path to the stable, now empty, once home to a small herd of horses and donkeys, animals the campers could ride but had to care for. He felt a bit of nostalgia that he immediately tamped down. Things weren't always bad here, he knew. Hadn't he met Bernadette on this very scrap of land, and hadn't he fancied himself falling in love with her that summer?

And Elle had disappeared, probably died. Possibly because of you. And you were involved with your stepmother, remember that? Around the time you were supposed to be with Elle and before you and Bernadette got together. Nonetheless you and Naomi had a brief and very hot affair.

He rubbed his jaw, felt a day's worth of whiskers, and told himself not to think about Naomi. That she'd seduced him didn't matter. He'd been all too eager to tumble into bed with his father's second wife. He wondered what some shrink would say about that? Was it retribution for Naomi turning Jeremiah's head while he was still married to Isabelle? A divorced parishioner, Naomi had sought solace, comfort, and advice from her minister and Jeremiah had willingly complied. No matter that Isabelle was still his wife and that in comforting the young divorcée, he'd crossed a moral line—well, make that several moral lines.

So Lucas's parents had split and his mother had died a few years later, after hiking along the Pacific Crest Trail, trying, she'd told him on her deathbed, to find herself, to reinvent herself after being married to a pastor for nearly ten years. She'd broken her leg and several ribs in a fall and had been life-flighted to a hospital. As it turned out, she'd developed an infection that had raged and eventually, after nearly a week of antibiotics and hospital care, her heart had stopped and she was dead before she turned forty.

Jeremiah, in all of his hypocrisy, had visited her three times and invoked prayers over her.

Now, thinking about that bleak period in his life, Lucas fought the anger that always fired whenever he thought of his mother's last days. Would he have wanted his mother to stay with Jeremiah? No. But it pissed him off to no end thinking that Isabelle probably died unhappy and lost.

His jaw slid to the side as he looked toward the cluster of buildings that had been the heart of the campus, not only the rec center and kitchen, but the office and suite above, where his father, wife, and their daughter had lived. He and his stepbrothers had been relegated to the bunkhouse when the campers weren't on-site, and to individual cabins if there was a need for extra counselors. That summer, twenty years ago, when he'd met Bernadette, he'd been living in the bunkhouse, alone, David and Ryan having been assigned to cabins, and Dusty, the hired hand, was living in an attic space above the stable. He glanced upward now, squinting at the bit of sun filtering through the clouds. A window was cut into the weathered siding, the only window to the room that had been carved into the hay mow.

He wondered what had happened to Dustin Peters, who had left with his last paycheck, cashed in a bank in Roseburg, to the south on the I-5 corridor, and was never heard from again. The department had searched for him twenty years ago and hadn't found hide nor hair of him. There had even been a question as to whether he'd ever really cashed that last check, as the handwriting on the back, the endorsing signature, seemed different. The presumptive theory, at the time, was that the check, along with Dusty's ID, had been stolen from him.

Who knew?

The trail was not only cold, it had turned to ice, cracked, and disappeared.

Now, he saw headlights cutting through the trees and made his way back to the central parking area, where along with his Jeep, a van from the crime scene unit was parked between two cruisers and an SUV owned by the department.

Driving a county cruiser, Maggie Dobbs parked next to his Renegade and, spying Lucas, cut the engine and threw open the door. Holding up one finger in his direction, she stepped outside, cell phone to her ear. An autumn breeze tossed her hair in front of her eyes as she kicked the door shut, listened to a one-sided conversation, and approached him.

". . . yeah, we got it . . . um-hmm . . . with him now." She glanced up at Lucas and mouthed, "Locklear." ". . . Don't know for sure," she said into the phone, eyeing the western sky, the horizon blocked by the buildings and ring of old growth surrounding this part of the camp, clouds moving to shroud the pale sun. "Yeah, we're at the camp now. Okay. Got it." She hung up and slipped her phone into a pocket of her jacket. "The boss."

"I heard."

"Why are we out here?"

Lucas had called her and asked to meet. "Because you think I've been ducking your questions."

"You have."

He inclined his head in acceptance. "I wanted to go over the files, reread the statements, see for myself where everyone who was involved ended up."

"And did you?"

"Enough." In truth he'd spent hours sitting at his kitchen table, the files spread before him, his laptop nearby and a cold beer close at hand. Maggie had done a great job at locating most of the people who had been here, had come up with their current names, addresses, phone numbers, employment as well as marital status, family members, and whether they'd ever had an arrest. He'd seen pictures on driver's licenses and tried to match them to the campers and counselors, workers and visitors—to the people they once were, many of them kids. Including himself.

"Okay, back to my question. Why here? Couldn't we discuss this at the office?"

"Sure. But I wanted to remember a little more clearly. Let's go inside."

"You've got keys?"

"Saved 'em."

"And the locks haven't been changed?"

"Not all of them, but I suppose if the place gets sold, as Jeremiah wants, the new owners will rekey the place." He glanced around the older buildings. "Or, more likely, bulldoze it. Some investors are talking resort, golf course, the whole nine yards. Come on." He led her around the office area and sitting room, where Deputy Hallgarth had interviewed him all those years ago, to the back porch that connected the rear sides of the kitchen, dining hall, office, and eventually rec center. The church and stable and barn were separate buildings, but these were connected.

Slipping a worn key from his ring, he unlocked one of the French doors to the rec center and stepped inside, where the air was dead, spiders had spun webs, and a layer of dust had settled over tables, benches, and chairs. He flipped on a switch and a few overhead lights gave off some watery illumination.

"You really want to talk here?" she said.

"Yeah." He nodded, his gaze sweeping the grimy windowsills and the conversation pit where his father had held court, Naomi at his side. If he tried, Lucas could envision them standing at a dais, the counselors and their charges sitting on the built-in benches. Lucas walked to the pit and dropped onto one of the top benches.

"So," he said, "my statement."

"Do I need to record this?" Dobbs was already removing her small recorder from her pocket and set it on the bench between them.

"If you want. It doesn't divert much from my original one." She doubled up with her cell phone. That was Maggie—belt and suspenders all the way. She identified herself, the date and time, and space, then spoke his name and said, "Okay. Let's go. Start with Eleanor Brady."

"We had been dating, a couple, for not quite a year. I'd known her from high school," he said. "But I broke up with her that week, the day before she disappeared."

"And why was that?"

"I fell in love with someone else, a new girl, one of the counselors, Bernadette Alsace."

Maggie didn't appear to be surprised. She had read through the case file, all of the witness statements, the reports by the officers, the newspaper clippings at the time.

Lucas went on. "That night, when everything happened, the night after Elle disappeared, I was in my bunk, for once. I was upset. Elle was missing and it wasn't like her to just leave without telling anyone, at least not for good. She was"—He thought hard. Conjured up her image. Pretty, blond, model-thin, on the shy side. And a little off-beat—"unique, to say the least. Very serious. Though, yes, she would sneak out of her cabin like the rest of us. We were all so . . . irresponsible and self-centered. Young. Didn't think anything bad could possibly happen." He hesitated, glanced out the filmy panes to the empty yard outside. "We were wrong. Elle had always been moody, and our relationship had really changed. She wanted me to commit, to think marriage, and I . . . shit, I was what? Not quite twenty? I had a whole lot of living to do before I was ready to settle down. So we fought. A lot. And . . . and then I met Bernadette."

"Bernadette Alsace," Maggie clarified, as she swept the bench with her hand. "One of the counselors."

"Right."

"Her name is Warden now."

"Yeah, married I guess."

"Divorced," she supplied, and his head snapped up.

"I know." His pulse quickened at the thought that she was single and he mentally kicked himself.

"Go ahead."

He drew a breath and then launched in, telling her everything he could remember. About feeling restless and leaving his cabin, about noticing the light burning in Dustin Peters's room, about the fight with his stepbrother, David, and then about stumbling on Tyler Quade, bleeding, losing consciousness, falling facedown in front of him on the path, a knife protruding from his back.

"I sounded the alarm," he admitted. "Ran here, woke up my dad, who called nine-one-one. It seemed like it took forever for the EMTs to arrive, when I think it was less than ten minutes. Tyler was in bad shape, barely alive. The whole camp was woken, and it was discovered some of the counselors weren't in their bunks. I went with

Dad and Naomi to the hospital. While we were waiting there and Tyler's parents were called, I talked to a deputy. Her name was Althea Jones."

Maggie was nodding. "I read her report on the accident."

"I had to talk to another deputy, Hallgarth, again, along with all of the other kids and counselors who were staying at the camp. It was easier than hauling everyone down to the station, I guess."

"I read over his notes as well as Jones's," Maggie said.

Lucas nodded.

"And no one, not a soul, saw Monica O'Neal that night, the night after Eleanor Brady's disappearance. O'Neal was around the day after Eleanor vanished. Everyone agrees that she was at the camp, with her campers, that she attended every meal, did her chores, prayer service, lowering of the flag, and was seen going into her cabin after lights out, or whatever you want to call it. Then, there was a group of female counselors who admit to being out of their cabins, that they met down at the cove, where Caleb Carter found the skull, but they all claim O'Neal wasn't with them, that they waited for her, but she never showed up."

"That's the story they all stuck to."

Maggie tilted her head to one side and surveyed him. "Did you believe it?"

"No one told me any differently. It was a mess then. Everyone gave their statements, the police were all over the place, investigating, and Jeremiah closed the camp."

"For good?"

"Yes." Lucas stared down at the bottom of the conversation pit, remembered his father saying a final prayer for Monica and Eleanor, asking God to keep them safe and lead them back to the camp. Candles had been lit, all the campers holding hands, the girls who had been in Elle's and Monica's cabins integrated into a larger circle overseen by Naomi.

"We all said good-bye here. Final prayer and all, the campers already packed, a few of them already gone as their parents had arrived to pick them up. It was all kind of surreal at the time." He scratched the back of his neck. "I tried to say good-bye to Bernadette, y'know, because we had a thing, but she would have none of it. She blamed me for Elle's disappearance. At the time, some of the girls thought Elle had committed suicide. Some of the campers swore they saw her, or her ghost, that week. It was in the statements."

"Yeah, I read that." Her face was noncommittal. "What about you?"

"Did I see her? Her ghost?" He snorted. "Come on." The whole idea was bizarre and the subsequent "sightings" of her ghost over the years? Never had they proved to be founded, which didn't surprise him. All of it was just local lore or legend.

"And the last time you saw Elle?"

"Was when we broke up. On the beach. It's in my statement. Hasn't changed. She just walked away from me, taking off into the fog."

He remembered the night all too vividly.

"Good-bye, Lucas." He could still hear her voice—breathy and sad—foretelling the future in a way he'd never thought possible. *"I'm going to miss you and believe it or not, you're going to miss me, too."*

"Disappearing into the mist?"

"I know it sounds weird, or overly dramatic. Whatever. That's what happened."

"And no one ever saw her again, except for all the ghost business, which, near as I can tell, happened right after she disappeared, the rest of that summer, and then not again for years, over a decade."

"I can't explain the sightings."

"It's just kind of strange," Dobbs said.

"What isn't?"

"About this case?" With a half smile, she said, "Nothing." She asked a few more questions and he answered them, but, of course, there wasn't much new to add.

"So, I just want to get this straight. Your story, like your statement, is that you couldn't sleep, knew something was up or had a feeling. Is that right?"

"That's about it," he agreed. "I'd heard some whispers that the girls were meeting that night."

"And you ran into your brother, had a fight, but didn't see anyone else until Tyler showed up with a knife in his back?"

"Yes, he was rushed to the hospital, like I said."

"What about his attacker? Did he say who that was?"

"No, it was dark. You read his statement, right?" Lucas had gone over it, as well as everyone else's.

"He was waiting in the chapel, not the main one, but the older, smaller one that wasn't supposed to be used. He had a rendezvous, he claimed, with Monica O'Neal, but he was attacked before she got there and woke up dazed. Pulled himself together and showed up on the path, where he met you." Maggie regarded him silently a moment, then said, "So, his attacker could have been a man or a woman."

"I guess."

"But probably not a ghost."

"Probably not," Lucas said evenly.

She grimaced. "It just doesn't add up, not really. Almost all of the female counselors were out meeting at the cavern. Your brothers were obviously not in their bunks either, nor was Tyler Quade, and you said Dustin Peters's light was on, but we don't know if he was in his room or not. And then Tyler is almost killed. Would have been, had the knife blade hit a vital organ. Lucky for him."

"Yeah."

"The crime scene? In the old chapel? They found Tyler's blood there and what appeared to be a woman's footprint running out of the chapel, blood on the bottom of a Nike running shoe. The tread pattern is consistent with the sole of one of Monica O'Neal's. Meredith O'Neal, her mother, confirmed that, but since no shoes were found with Monica's belongings when her cabin was searched, it is assumed she was wearing them and was in the chapel with Tyler before she disappeared."

Lucas nodded again.

"But there were no other shoe prints, or finger-prints. No DNA, cigarette butts, or hairs, nothing. No sign of a struggle. Tyler apparently was jumped from behind and didn't see his attacker. He said he fell, bumped his head, and blacked out. Later, when he came to, he stumbled out of the church and ran into you."

"He was headed back to the main part of the camp to get help." It had been a frantic night, he thought now, as he stared at the empty room with its dirty window, scarred tables pushed into the corners, spider webs, and dust motes.

Maggie also looked around the once-vibrant, now-empty, nearly forgotten building. "What do you think happened?"

"I don't know."

"Take a stab at it."

"The police concluded—"

"I know what the prevailing theory was, that somehow Waldo Grimes showed up here, but that seems just too convenient to me, where there's no evidence to support it. He what . . . ? Attacked Tyler Quade and left him for dead, a knife in his back? Why not take the weapon? And then, what? As Grimes was finishing up with Tyler, he's interrupted by Monica O'Neal and takes off after her, which could explain why Tyler wasn't killed; Grimes didn't have time to finish the job. And what about Dustin Peters? He disappeared the same night, having been paid earlier in the day. Maybe he took off . . . maybe he was done. You saw his light on, but no one saw him again. We know he was alive because he cashed his check, unless, of course, someone had his ID."

She was regarding him expectantly. Lucas said, "I think there's more to it than that. Four people disappeared off the face of the earth within a couple of days—Grimes, Monica, Elle, and Dusty. . . . I've always felt there're big pieces missing."

"I agree. It all starts with Eleanor Brady, Elle," she said. "We've been assuming she was heartbroken that you broke up with her, that her disappearance was linked to the fact you called it off."

"Nothing else had changed."

"That you know of. You were barely more than a kid yourself. Wrapped up in your own teenage angst. Maybe it just seemed like you caused Elle to vanish. The girls at the camp said you thought she was despondent because she knew you were seeing Bernadette Alsace even before you broke up with her."

Lucas's jaw was tight, but he gave a curt nod. There was a thumping across the roof, a squirrel or rat or maybe even a bird scurrying overhead.

"What if she disappeared for another reason?" Maggie asked, her eyes narrowing. "Her family is still around, right?"

"Yes." He'd checked. "Just her mother. Her father died a few years ago. Heart attack, I think." Lucas remembered the man. Tall, stern, protective of his daughter, Darryl Brady had been an elder in the church. The mother, Jeannette, was tiny, like Elle, and had worked in a fabric store in Averille, but the shop had closed years earlier. He'd heard she now worked part-time at the preschool and volunteered at the local library. "They gave statements and were questioned over and over again."

"And they blamed you."

"Yep." He hadn't had to read their statements to know that much. Elle's father had been very clear as to why he thought his daughter had "taken off," as he called it, never wanting to believe she might have died.

"Your stepbrother dated her first."

"Yeah, Ryan."

"How'd he take to you moving in on his girl?"

"Maggie, what is this? We were kids. We'd both known Elle forever. She was always hanging out at the house. Ryan and I fought about it, yeah, and he was pissed as hell. We came to blows, but he backed off."

"Quit seeing her?"

"Yes," he said with more conviction than he felt. He'd known that Ryan had harbored a grudge, but believed his stepbrother had gotten over it.

"You're sure?"

He gazed at her hard. "Why? Do you know something?"

"I read his statement, too." In the report Ryan had admitted to fighting with Lucas. "And I talked to him. He admitted that he saw Elle that night, earlier, before you caught up with her on the beach."

"That wasn't in his original statement," Lucas said.

"It came later. He said he was just a scared kid who was trying to stay out of trouble at the time."

"We all were, but we didn't lie."

"No, Lucas. You didn't lie. I'm not so sure about the others."

He had a bad feeling about this. Who had lied? And why? Could Monica and Elle still be alive? And what about Dustin Peters? "Come on," he said, standing. "I'll show you around the place. Give you the personalized tour. Let's start here, the heart of the camp," he said, and walked her through the connecting hallways from the rec center, past the bathrooms, and into the reception desk and office area with its door to the back of the building. "Over here," he said, leading her into the small anteroom, now devoid of furniture. "This is where we were all interviewed by Deputy Hallgarth, who served as the detective at the time." From the office, he showed her upstairs to the suite of rooms that had housed his father's family. The floors of the rooms creaked, hardwood that hadn't seen a mop or duster in years. A chair sat near one of the windows, and a table had been left in the small dining area, but the rest of the space, two bedrooms with separate bathrooms, was empty. Windows opened to the front of the building to overlook the parking lot, and to the back gave a view of the trails that skirted the buildings.

"What's in here?" Maggie asked as they left the apartment and stood in the short hallway at the top of the stairs. She was pointing at a closed door that led to the attic space, and in his mind's eye he saw himself on a brass bed with a bare mattress behind that door, the space hot and close, a yellow jacket buzzing angrily as it flung itself over and over against the dusty windowpane. Naomi naked and breathing hard, her body slick with sweat, lay beneath him, her arms wrapped around his neck, her legs tight around his torso. Even now, so many years later, he felt a heated blush steal up the back of his neck as he remembered his own feeling of sick ecstasy, a kind of sizzling rapture heightened by the knowledge that their lovemaking was taboo.

"Storage closet," he said, and swung open the door. The space was empty and dirty, smelling dry, the air stale, the bed long gone. "Come on." Down the stairs they went and he showed her the dining room and kitchen, then outside to the grounds, the stable, and Dusty's living quarters, a small room tucked under the eaves of the barn, accessed by the ladder to the empty hay mow, a cavernous space with a small, open window located at the highest point of the ceiling. It was located over the rafters, where evidence of a barn owl—feathers, droppings, and pellets—was visible.

"This camp hasn't been occupied since that summer?" Maggie asked as she switched on her flashlight.

"Not that I know of."

"Why?"

"At first, no one was interested in the property," he explained as he opened the door to the room

Dustin Peters had occupied when he'd worked at the camp. Maggie swung the beam of her light over the rough walls and single grimy window. Pegs lined the walls; no closet had been built into the small, confined space. "Lots of people were interested, the police, the television stations, news reporters, and then every kind of conspiracy nut on the coast. It didn't help that Grimes was on the loose, but no one wanted to rent the place for any kind of camp or retreat."

"Camp Horseshoe was owned by the church."

"That's right. And my father basically was the church."

"But your stepmother's family owned it all originally. Her great, great great whatever grandfather homesteaded it?" Maggie asked in the tight place where Dustin Peters had once resided. Little more than a closet with a few nails driven into rough plank walls, the space was dry and airless and empty, no evidence of the cot or tiny desk that had once been inside.

"Uh-huh." He eyed the small window where he'd seen a patch of light on the night he'd run into David, the same night Monica O'Neal, and apparently Dusty, had disappeared, not unlike Elle the night before.

"Naomi's father inherited this piece, the rest of the section was divided between his brothers. He was ill when Naomi married my father, but he signed over the deed to the church, as part of a wedding gift, I guess. She'd been married before. Her first husband was a low-life who left her and the kids, and Naomi's father looked upon Jeremiah as some kind of savior for his only child."

"Kind of an antiquated way of thinking," she observed.

"Naomi thought so, but her father was insistent. She'd already been through one divorce and her father hadn't liked that. No matter that husband number one was a low-life. So Jeremiah comes along, and Naomi's father's prayers have been answered. His little girl will be married and not only that"—Lucas held up a finger— "she was marrying a man of God, a man with his own Christian church. He wanted the church to have the property."

"You remember this?" she asked skeptically.

"I heard," he said, "from her. And the plan backfired. When Naomi and Jeremiah divorced, he essentially owned the camp, as he was the church."

"How'd that go over?"

"How do you think? Like the proverbial lead balloon. Naomi fought him in court and lost. But they battled it out for years. Now, I guess, he's given up on whatever plans he had for the place and is trying to sell it."

"After all this time?"

"As I said, it was stained with the scandal, and

that went on for years. The parents of the missing girls? The O'Neals and Bradys? They sued the church and my father and my stepmother for everything from negligence to mismanagement of funds, anything they could try. They kept at it for years, but since there were no bodies, there was no real crime. Sure, there wasn't a lot of supervision and all of us were totally irresponsible teenagers, but each parent and counselor had signed iron-clad agreements when they signed on, and those agreements basically absolved the camp, church, and Mr. and Mrs. Jeremiah Dalton of any responsibility. The court battles continued for years and, since you've gone through all the files, you know Monica O'Neal's mother, Meredith, has been a thorn in the side of the sheriff's department for years, demanding answers every three or four months or so."

Maggie nodded. "But without a body . . ."

"Right. Kind of a 'no harm, no foul' situation."

"But now that we have a body, or at least a partial one . . ."

"She'll be all over it, and I don't blame her." He was frowning, rubbing the back of his neck. "She's been missing her daughter longer than she had her. Not knowing what happened to her. The same with Jeannette Brady." He felt the same familiar hollowness, the guilt that had been his companion for two decades. Now, at least, if nothing else, there would be some answers.

345

And probably a lot more questions.

"Were you close to Dustin Peters?" she asked.

"Nah, we just worked together. I didn't meet him 'til Dad hired him. He was from central or eastern Oregon, I think, maybe around Pendleton, and was looking for a job, at least for the summer. Dusty was good with horses, a hard worker who had spent time around ranches, so Jeremiah hired him just before the campers arrived."

"What about his personal life? How'd he get on with everyone?"

"Okay. He was a little on the macho side," Lucas remembered. "Had a swagger about him and rode a horse like a Hollywood stuntman, always working without his shirt."

"He have a girlfriend?"

"Hard to say. I saw him with Reva Mercado a lot." He frowned at the thought, remembering Reva sneaking up the hayloft ladder to this very room.

"You didn't approve?"

"Reva was a schemer. And had a hot temper. She and Jo-Beth Chancellor were like this." He crossed his fingers. "Tight. Always up to something. Throw Dusty into the mix and I don't know. Dusty played the field, and it might have rubbed some people the wrong way. I saw him with Jayla, too. And I think he made a run at Elle."

Maggie's head snapped up. "Were they involved?"

"No, but she told me about it. Dusty seemed to think any girl over sixteen was fair game. He liked the chase, the 'hunt,' he called it."

She made a face. "So the girls here were prey."

"I don't know if I'd go that far, but . . ."

"What?"

"He was flirting with Naomi, my stepmother, but Leah was there and she was only about eleven, and I didn't like the way he kept glancing over at her. I almost called him out, but he saw me and stopped. I don't know."

"You think he was coming on to your sister?"

Lucas shook his head. "It was probably nothing. We done here?"

She gave the space one last cursory glance. "Yeah."

They made their way out of the tiny closet of a room and climbed down the ladder. He showed her the trails leading to the flagpole and the cabins on either side, one grouping for the women and girls, the other, on the opposite side, for the males.

"Why were there more girls at the camp than boys?"

"Just how it broke up that year," he said as he walked between the cabins, now falling down, roofs collapsing, siding rotting, interiors exposed. He thought of how many times he'd hurried down the path at night, making his way to the doorway of Bernadette's cabin, his heart racing, his blood up, anticipation of the night ahead in his brain. "That's why there were fewer male counselors than female. They put more boys into each cabin and my stepbrothers, Ryan and David Tremaine, they each had a cabin, as did Tyler Quade, Demarco Lewis, James Becker, and Rob Engles. Dustin and I filled in as counselors if they needed extras."

"I've talked to them all," she said. "Except Quade. I left a message, but he hasn't responded. Becker is in the navy, stationed in Hawaii, giving a statement to the local authorities there. Engles is in Wisconsin, and his statement will come via the Milwaukee PD. Lewis said he'd show up here. Like the girls. That's the odd thing," she said, thinking aloud as they walked toward the parking lot. "All the women have agreed to come into the station and talk, but the men? Not so much."

He started to voice his opinion, but she held up a finger. "Don't give me any crap about the women staying home, able to get away, because most of them have jobs and families just like the men, but somehow they seem more . . . compelled to come and talk about it." And then, as if she guessed where his mind was heading, added, "It is *not* because women talk more than men. No . . . there's something else going on, I think. They didn't immediately respond, but when they did, they agreed. Almost as if they'd decided among themselves to arrive down here en masse. Got any idea why that would be?"

"No."

"You don't think it might be because Kinley Marsh is on the story? That she might be pressuring them for interviews?"

Lucas shrugged. They reached their vehicles. Maggie glanced at the overcast skies and said, "Well, something's up. It feels like they're circling the wagons."

"After twenty years."

"Their statements were all so much the same that I wondered if they'd come up with one story between them and just stuck to it."

"Wouldn't one of them have broken?"

"Maybe they were threatened or had something to lose."

"All of them?" he said, thinking of the girls, now women, that he'd known. Some of them had pretty strong personalities. "Seems unlikely."

"Teenagers run in herds and have an us-against-them mentality. I'm gonna bet there was a ringleader." She glanced up at him. "Any guesses?"

He thought. Saw where she was going. "Maybe Reva Mercado."

"I've dealt with Ms. Vicari née Mercado before."

"Yeah?"

"Umm-hmm. Accident in Clackamas County, a few years ago. Her husband and another woman died and there was always something fishy about it; something that didn't feel right."

"How so?"

"She claims her husband was driving and the evidence seemed to point that way, but the kid in the other vehicle, the five-year-old who lost her mother in the crash? She swears the driver was a woman. No one really believed the kid because of her age and the trauma of the accident, how everything's out of kilter when you're going through it." Maggie's face set. "It never felt right to me, but then I was transferred and my replacement bought Reva Vicari's story. So, I believe she's conniving, yeah, and a liar, able to cover her own ass and break all the rules, but she never struck me as the type who could influence people."

"She influenced your replacement on the job."

"But he's a wuss. And let's just say an 'uninspired' investigator." She unlocked the door of her car. "You got any other ideas? What about Bernadette Warden? You knew her."

"Yeah, but . . . she's not that . . ."

"Devious? Ambitious?"

He shook his head and took one last glance at the aging buildings, with their mossy roofs, boarded windows, and rusted, needle-clogged downspouts.

"Would she go along with someone else? Maybe her sister?"

"If you're looking for a ringleader," he said, coming to the same conclusion he had when he'd gone over the files, "I'd look at Jo-Beth Chancellor Leroy. My money's on her."

"I'm way ahead of you," Dobbs admitted as she opened the car door and slipped inside. "I just wanted your take on things. Next up, I'm going to talk to your family, or ex-family. The good preacher, his ex-wife, and all the kids. Unless you want to tag along, be there for the interviews."

He didn't have to think twice. He was heading to his Jeep when his cell phone buzzed and he answered, expecting to hear something from the lab, or an update on the case. Instead a familiar voice said, "Hey, Lucas, sorry to bother you. This is Monty, down at Spike's. Got a bit of a situation here. It's Caleb."

"Yeah?"

"He's, um, had a few and he's started going all buggy on me, y'know?" There was a bit of worry to Monty's tone. "Claims he's seen a ghost. That he was out crabbing and ran into the damned spirit of Eleanor Brady. I don't want to get him into trouble. Hell, I usually just take his keys from him and serve him coffee until I know he's sober enough to drive. But, with all that's been going on, I thought you'd want to know."

"I'm on my way."

"Oh, and there's one more thing."

"Yeah?" Lucas was already sliding behind the wheel of his Renegade. "What's that?"

"There's a woman down here, hanging out, trying to talk to everyone, and she's zeroed in on Caleb. Name of Kinley Marsh; I checked her ID. Claims she's a reporter for one of those online newspapers, this one out of Astoria, and she's real interested in what Caleb's sayin'. Real interested."

"Got it," Lucas said, jabbing his keys into the ignition and backing up. Nosy Kinley Marsh. Drunk Caleb Carter. The makings of a lethal combination. "I'll be there in ten, maybe less." Then he hung up, rammed the Jeep into drive, and hit the gas.

Chapter 25

Camp Horseshoe
Annette
Then

This was crazy, Annette thought as she snuck into her cabin. She hadn't seen a ghost. Had not viewed any kind of apparition. Nor had she caught a glimpse of Elle in the flesh. Her mind was just playing tricks on her, that had to be it.

But no matter how she tried to convince herself

that she'd dreamed up the image of Elle on the cliff, she knew in her heart she'd seen something . . . something that she shouldn't have.

Trying to calm herself, she slid into her bunk and noticed that Nell appeared to be sleeping, one pajama-clad arm hanging down from the top bunk. Nell, the junior counselor, hadn't been invited to the meeting tonight, as if she were insignificant.

"Why not make her come?" Annette had asked earlier in the day when she'd caught up with Jo-Beth hurrying out of the rec center.

"Someone's got to stay for the girls, and besides, she's not trustworthy," Jo-Beth had snapped. Annette hadn't argued. Jo-Beth had obviously been on edge, spoiling for a fight, and Annette knew Jo-Beth thought she was just Bernadette's nerdy little sister, someone to be tolerated, but never accepted. Someone so immature that she had to be saddled with a secondary counselor.

Well, they'd find out differently, because she knew all their secrets, had worked to find out exactly what made each of them tick—their strengths, their weaknesses, and most especially their lies.

After freaking out about seeing what she'd thought was a ghost, Annette had ditched the others and headed back to camp. She'd slunk quietly into Monica's cabin to find that Monica wasn't in her bunk, her girls left unattended.

Where was she?

More jittery than ever, Annette had returned to her own cabin and had tried to calm herself, telling herself that everything was going to be all right. She was letting her imagination get the better of her, but the night had seemed to close in on her, and the dying embers of the campfire, a few sparse glowing coals, had pulsed like red, ghoulish eyes.

Stop it! For God's sake, pull yourself together!

Letting her breath out slowly, she did a quick bed check to see that all of her charges, those quirky, well, let's be honest, nerdy, little eleven-year-olds were still sleeping in their bunks. Once satisfied that all were safe, she kicked off her boots and slid into her open sleeping bag, where she listened to the sounds of the summer night and wondered about the events of the last couple of days. First Elle going missing and now Monica . . . not in her bed? Was she with Tyler? Someone else? Or had something happened to her?

Don't go there. She's fine. Just because Elle is missing . . . She swallowed hard. There had been talk of a murderer on the loose, an escaped prisoner. Could he have sneaked into the camp and kidnapped the girls? Could he even now be waiting outside one of the unlocked cabins, waiting to pounce again?

Her heart drummed wildly and she thought of

all the murder mysteries she devoured, the cable TV channels devoted to true crimes that she watched. Her imagination ran wild and she wondered if, even now, Waldo Grimes was lurking near the doorway to this very cabin.

She clutched the edge of the sleeping bag with sweaty fingers.

Ears straining, she listened for any sound that was out of the ordinary. Above the rush of the wind and the ever-present roar of the ocean, crickets chirped, frogs croaked, and far in the distance a coyote gave off a plaintive howl.

Her mind was whirling and she knew that sleep would be elusive, if not impossible. A counselor had gone missing and might be dead, for God's sake. Geez, what were the others thinking with their stupid deception? And why were Jo-Beth and Reva, who came late to their own meeting, so adamant about it? What did they have to hide, and what did it have to do with Elle? With Monica? Could they have done something to the missing girls?

Monica's not *missing! You know how everyone leaves their bunks at night. Don't jump to conclusions!*

She forced herself to calm down by reminding herself how stupid the other girls were. Things would work out. They always did. No matter what bossy Jo-Beth ordered, they couldn't very well just lie to the police about a girl gone missing and everything would be fine. No freaking way. They should all tell the truth, no matter how hard it was or what the consequences were.

Of course, things could get pretty damned dicey for some of the girls, but that was just too bad. As Mom always said: "You make your bed, you lie in it." And there was the sorry fact that Annette herself had done more than her share of things she wasn't proud of. She'd been snooping and spying on her older sister and the other girls. If she hadn't heard confessions or seen nefarious deeds, she could hazard a pretty damned good guess as to who was doing what to whom. And she'd kept a little diary of all of it. Why? She didn't really know, but she considered the information she'd gathered important, even valuable. Who knew when she might need a little help from one of the others?

You would resort to extortion?

"Maybe," she murmured under her breath.

What about bribery?

"Definitely." Then she zipped her lips. No telling what Nell might overhear, or one of the campers; she wouldn't put it past the little whiners to be feigning sleep.

Wouldn't you be? If you were on the other side of this half wall? Come on, Annette, you know yourself too well. You'd be the first in line to stay awake and keep an eye on what's going on in the dark of night—just like you are now.

She knew she was an outcast, one of the youngest counselors aside from Nell, only tolerated because she was Bernadette's little sister, which only served to make Annette feel like a damned albatross around her older sister's neck.

But then, Bernadette wasn't exactly playing by the rules. Annette knew because she'd followed her, seen her meet with Lucas Dalton, watched them doing the nasty even though everyone knew Lucas was Elle's boyfriend, at least according to Elle. And it broke Annette's heart to think that Lucas, if he were going to cheat on Elle, would do it with Bernadette, not her.

She yanked the covers over her head and tried not to think about Lucas. It was stupid, really, the way she felt about him, but she felt it was more than a simple schoolgirl crush. From the second she'd seen him in the office, when she and Bernadette had been dropped off by their mother, Annette had noticed him. How he carried himself, the way his jeans hung low on his hips, and his butt, yes, for the first time ever, she'd observed the fluidity of his movement in those nearly worn-out Levi's. She'd looked quickly away, hadn't wanted him to notice how she was staring at him, but in a blink, she had a fantasy, of him on top of her, him pushing into her, her grabbing his butt and—oh, God, now in the dark, alone, she was blushing. Never had she had such a raw and sexual fantasy. She'd kissed a couple of boys in school, even let Anthony Sinclaire touch her breasts, but she'd pushed him and his greedy hands away when he'd gone for the waistband of her skirt. She hadn't been that into him anyway, and he'd been a fumbler and a groper, so she'd never seen him again, shunned him in school.

Lucas was a cut above any of the boys she'd dated, more like a man.

Still, he was out of her league.

And apparently fit right into Bernadette's.

She knew. She'd seen them. Followed them just this past Sunday, in the afternoon, after church services when the campers were busy with projects and the counselors had been given a few hours to themselves, ostensibly for rest and reflection, to get in touch with God or something.

Lucas and Bernadette had met at an abandoned cabin, one close to the ocean, and their makeout sessions had steadily progressed.

After following her sister through that part of the forest, Annette had waited until Bernadette had slipped inside, then discovered an open window near the staircase and had climbed up stealthily, then slid across the loft floor to watch the display on the floor below. They'd started out talking and touching, then Lucas had kissed her and when Bernadette hadn't stopped him, he'd kissed her harder and pushed her onto her back. His hands had slid under her sweatshirt and Bernadette had moaned as he'd kissed her.

Annette had felt her own pulse quicken and her blood heat watching them. She'd wondered what it would feel like to have a man kiss her so passionately, to press his knee between hers, to fondle her breasts. She'd swallowed hard at the thought, felt a little ache deep within and told herself to quit watching, but she was transfixed at the sight of lovemaking.

Bernadette's hair had been pulled back and banded at the back of her neck, but now was escaping, framing her head. Her eyes had been closed and she'd moaned as he'd kissed her neck, then moved lower, unzipping the sweatshirt and pushing up Bernadette's pink T-shirt.

His hands had found her bra and he'd skimmed the lacy edges with his lips before somehow unclasping it, allowing Bernadette's breasts to spill free. They were white beneath her tan line and the nipples dark buttons that Lucas had found fascinating enough to kiss and nip at.

Annette had bit down on her own lip not to cry out as she watched her sister let this boy she barely knew remove her bra and toss it aside. *As if he'd done it a hundred times before!*

But what about Bernadette? Was this new to her, or had she done this before with Joel, her boyfriend back in Seattle? Weren't they practically engaged, and here she was kissing and touching and moaning with this Lucas Dalton?

As she'd watched, Annette had seen Lucas's hand move lower, his fingers discovering the button of her jeans. Deftly, he'd slipped the button through its hole, then a second later Annette had heard the soft hiss of a zipper being lowered.

Bernadette had grabbed his wrist. Stopped him.

Good. About time!

"No," she'd whispered. "I don't think . . ." she'd said, and as he'd lifted his head and had started to pull back his hand, Bernadette had opened her eyes and looked into his. As if she'd read some unspoken vow in his gaze, she'd wrapped her fingers around his wrist once more, but this time she'd guided him back to her, parting her legs so that he could slip his fingers into the opening of her jeans.

"You're sure?" His voice was a whisper.

She'd nodded and urged softly, breathlessly, "Please."

He'd complied, slipping those long, strong fingers into the opening. She gave a soft little cry as he began to touch her. He shifted, moving over her, so that he was half lying atop her while ministering to her with his fingers.

Annette, her own heart tearing a bit, had

360

watched in fascination as his hips had started to move to the rhythm of his fingers. She'd witnessed the cords in his neck stand out and his jean-clad buttocks flex as if he were straining against the fly of his own jeans.

Oh. My.

Her gaze had drifted to his shoulder, where the top half of Bernadette's face had been visible. Her sister had looked up, her eyes rounding, her breath coming in quick, short pants, her gaze as it had focused, landing in the darkened loft, zeroing in on her sister's face.

Shit!

Annette had frozen. Had Bernadette seen her? Would Bernadette keep letting Lucas touch her so intimately knowing her baby sister was watching?

Praying her sister hadn't caught her being a voyeur, Annette had quickly closed her own eyes, hoping to shutter any reflection in them. She'd eased backward very slowly, not making a sound. Holding her breath, she'd pulled away until the toe of her tennis shoe discovered the edge of the staircase; then she'd noiselessly crept down the dusty steps to the open window where she'd slipped through, and silently dropped to the soft earth outside the cabin.

She'd felt a little dirty watching them groping and breathing hard, and told herself she wouldn't follow Bernadette again. But as she made her way back to the heart of the camp, she felt a new, unfamiliar ache deep inside of her. She'd slipped into her own bunk and, using her flashlight, a pen, and her small notebook, written down what she'd seen. As she'd finished she'd wondered when, if ever, she would meet a man who would touch her as Lucas had Bernadette.

The thought had been as titillating as it had been worrisome.

Maybe she'd never meet the right boy. Maybe she'd never lose herself in the throes of passion.

Then again . . . she'd begun plotting just how to make that happen and had even started spinning a story about her imaginary lover, all of which she'd written in the diary that she kept in a secret little cubby in the wall on the far side of the bed. The niche was hidden by the mattress and springs, and just wide enough for the diary to slip inside.

Now, as she lay in her bed she closed her mind to the memory of Bernadette and Lucas, wondered what it would have felt like if he'd touched *her* so intimately. She would be so much better for him than her sister. And why not her? If Elle were gone and her sister as fickle as ever, why not true-blue Annette, the girl who believed in fairy tales and happily-ever-afters? She would do right by Lucas, she would! If given half a chance. But the fates were always against her, it seemed.

And as much as she would like to fantasize and fall asleep to dream about the feel of Lucas's work-roughened hands on her body, she had more important things to think about, like what had happened to Elle, what she would tell the police, and how in the world she would live a lie, if that's what the others wanted.

Oh, for the love of God, get over yourself, that nasty little voice in her head warned. *You know as well as anyone that you've been living a lie most of your life. In fact, "Annette," you thrive on it. You loved spying on the others, seeing their secrets play out, writing them down. It makes you feel better about yourself, right? Makes you feel superior? When all your life you've felt like a faint shadow in your sister's wake?*

She knew that much about herself and decided, since she was keyed up after the meeting in the cavern, and the campers as well as Nell were asleep, that it was time to write in her diary again, make note of what had been said in the cave and the fact that Monica wasn't in her bed. It seemed her fears about the escaped prisoner were unfounded, at least for the night.

Good.

But where was Monica? Why hadn't she shown up at the cave? Why had Jo-Beth been late? Annette didn't believe for a second that it was because of monthly cramps. No, Jo-Beth was too tough. So where had she been? And why had

Reva arrived a few minutes late and breathless, too? It didn't make sense. Annette intended to write down every little thing that had happened, along with her suspicions about what was going on beneath the surface. She knew that Monica had been seeing Tyler and had heard bits and snatches of a late-night campfire conversation between Monica and Bernadette. They had kept their voices low and between the rumble of the surf, crackle of the fire, and someone snoring in Jayla's cabin, Annette, lurking behind the rough bole of a giant fir tree, had only heard partial sentences.

"I'm . . . about six weeks . . . more like eight. I'm not sure. . . ."

". . . false alarm . . . late."

". . . cycle . . . on the dot . . . infirmary . . . can I?"

From what she could gather, Monica was pregnant, and the father? No doubt Tyler Quade, Jo-Beth's boyfriend. So it was odd and very, very interesting that Monica was knocked up.

And now she didn't show up to the meeting?

Was it related?

She'd have to find out.

Annette fished in her hiding spot for her diary, feeling around the small niche, and came up empty.

What?

Quickly, she ran her fingers over the space again. Nothing!

Panic started to swell in her chest. Her most private thoughts were on those pages and all the secrets . . . ? No, no, no. The diary had to be here! She'd just misplaced it. Holding her breath, her heart beating faster than a hummingbird's wings, she found her flashlight, clicked it on, then waited. Nell didn't move. The kids in the other room didn't so much as stir. Good. Frantic, trying to keep herself calm, she shined the tiny flashlight's beam into the crevice and found it empty. Her pen wasn't even in there. Telling herself to stay calm, she stealthily shined the yellowish beam around her bed, flipping back the sleeping bag. Nothing. Under the cot, no sign of the diary, just dirt, sand, fir needles on the solid, old floorboards, no holes where the diary could slip through to the ground.

Oh, no!

It couldn't be gone.

Could *not* be!

She had to have misplaced it. That had to be it! However, as she quietly searched through her jacket pockets and backpack and bag, she found nothing, and the dawning realization that the diary was really and truly missing made her realize she hadn't lost the damned thing. Someone had taken it.

Oh, God.

It wasn't fair!

She was in love with her sister's boyfriend.

She'd seen what probably was a ghost.

A girl had gone missing, maybe a second one.

A maniac killer was on the loose.

And now, the one thing she held dear, her private thoughts all locked away in a diary, had been stolen.

Annette wanted to scream with fear and fury, but she stayed still and lay awake in the dark.

Chapter 26

Averille, Oregon
Now
Lucas

"I'm tellin' ya, man, I saw her. Elle. Big as fuckin' life," Caleb insisted from the passenger seat of Lucas's Jeep.

Lucas didn't believe him. The man was three or maybe four sheets to the wind. "And you're sure it was Elle?" he asked as they made their way through the back roads to Caleb's house.

"Aren't you listenin'?" Caleb smelled like a brewery and looked as if he could use a shower, fresh set of clothes, haircut, and . . . well, the list went on and on.

"At the spit by Crown Creek?"

"Yes! I told ya. Where the damned creek dumps into the ocean."

"Let's go see."

"No way, man!" Caleb's little piggy eyes rounded in his flushed face and he shook his head violently. "I want nothin' to do with that! Take me back to my fuckin' truck."

"You walk back and get it. When you sober up."

"No way. You can't do this."

"You're lucky Monty called me and not one of the more by-the-book officers who would have loved to run you in for being 'drunk and disorderly' or some other charge. There were quite a few violations."

"Didn't do nothin' wrong! I just saw a fuckin' ghost and had a drink or two."

"Or seven or eight," Lucas said as one tire hit a pothole and the Jeep bounced. Caleb hit his head where he'd already cracked it getting into the Renegade.

"Ow! Sheeeit. Damn it, Dalton, be careful!" Jaw set, red cap square on his head, he rubbed his forehead and stared out the windshield, where the rain was coming down in sheets.

"And you should be careful talking to reporters."

"Wha—?" Caleb said. "What reporter?"

"The woman you were talking to."

"That li'l thing? A reporter?" He let out a disgusted breath. "Nah."

"You think she was talking to you because she was interested in you?" Lucas asked with a skeptical lift of one eyebrow.

"Maybe."

"When pigs *and* cows fly."

Lucas found the lane cutting into the acres that Caleb had inherited. The sparse gravel drive wound through fields spotted with weeds and Scotch broom, and separated from the drive with a wire fence stretched between steel fence posts decorated with old hubcaps showing varying degrees of rust. Lucas said, "She was playing you, trying to get information."

"You don't know nothin'."

"I know that Kinley Marsh is always working an angle." He'd felt lucky in the fact that he'd avoided talking to her by hauling Caleb out the back of Spike's before the reporter could ask any questions. She'd been at the bar, talking to Caleb, leaning into the older man as if she were interested in him. It was no wonder that Caleb, at his level of drunkenness and with his inflated ego, had thought she was flirting with him. When Lucas strode into Spike's and taken stock of the situation, Kinley's focus had shifted. She'd obviously recognized him, zeroed in on him, and tried to ambush him by introducing herself.

"Detective Dalton!" she'd said, pasting on a winning smile. "I'd like to talk to you." She'd stuck out a small hand. "Kinley Marsh with the *NewzZone*, out of Astoria. You've probably heard of it."

"No," he answered, giving her hand a quick shake, then hustling Carter off his bar stool.

"I'd just like to talk to you about the bones that were found on the beach. The skull."

"No comment." He said to Carter, "Come on, Caleb. You've been cut off."

Carter glowered at the barkeep, who had been filling a short glass with soda from his bar gun. "For Christ's sake, Monty. What the hell's going on? You called the cops on me?"

Monty shrugged. "It's for your own good."

"How's that?" Caleb had eyed Lucas hard and realized he had no choice in the matter. "Oh, man," he'd whined as he nearly fell while Lucas kept urging him toward the back door.

"I've left you messages," Kinley had called out, trailing after Lucas and Caleb as they passed four video poker machines, screens glowing bright. Caleb had nearly knocked a woman's drink from an unoccupied stool.

"Hey!" the blonde had shouted, her overly made-up face a mask of fury. "Oh, for the love of—! Look what you did! And I was on a winning streak."

"Sorry," Lucas had said automatically.

"Well, watch where you're going!"

"Not goin' anywhere," Caleb had protested, but Lucas had hold of him by the collar and forced him out the back door to the gray afternoon, where rain had started to pepper the pockmarked parking lot.

"Excuse me, Detective!" Kinley wasn't one to

give up. She'd followed them outside, a short thing in jeans and an oversized jacket, staring up at him belligerently, her chin jutting forward. "I'd like a word or two with you. Not only are you investigating the skeleton that washed up on the beach, but your father owns Camp Horseshoe, where it was found."

"It was in the cave," Caleb had said petulantly. "Didn't I tell ya? And not a skeleton, just a fuc—effin' jawbone!"

"But a skull was discovered later." To Lucas, she'd asked, "Have you been able to ID it yet?"

"No comment." Not wanting to get into it with her, Lucas had opened the passenger door of his Jeep and forced Caleb inside. The bigger man bumped his head getting in and it hadn't improved his already bad mood. "Hey! What the fuck?"

"You'll live," Lucas had assured him and, leaving Kinley standing in the rain, had climbed into his Jeep. Through the open window, he'd added, "Call the station. Talk to the Public Information Officer."

"I tried that!" she'd yelled after him, only to reach in her pocket for her cell phone.

Lucas hadn't waited to see if she would follow him and luckily she hadn't. He'd spent most of the night before nursing either black coffee or a beer while reading over all of the statements and reports in the missing persons' cases of Monica

O'Neal and Eleanor Brady, going over every detail that was online, which wasn't complete, while waiting for the actual paper records and evidence to be hauled out of the basement, where the archived cold case information was kept. There had been no file on Dustin Peters, the drifter, as no one had bothered to file a report, at least not in Neahkahnie County or the State of Oregon, and the records for Waldo Grimes were all pertaining to his prior arrests.

Still, Lucas had scoured all the law enforcement databases, as well as the Internet in general, for information on all four of the people who seemed to have vaporized into the air that summer.

He hadn't learned much more than he'd already known, but he'd barely slept since first hearing about the jawbone that Caleb Carter had discovered. He felt the ache in his bones from lack of sleep, sensed a headache coming on, and as he glanced at his reflection in the rearview mirror he noticed that the crow's feet at the corner of his eyes were more pronounced, the one day's worth of beard stubble working its way to two.

And he was irritated and grouchy, didn't want to deal with Kinley Marsh or anyone else from the press. Not now. Not until the media could be of some help solving the case. Of course he knew he'd have to deal with Kinley and other reporters at some time in the future, but it wasn't going to be today.

Over a slight rise and Caleb's home came into view. The single-storied house squatted in the middle of the clearing, its sagging roof covered in moss, the siding made of graying wood that had never seen a paintbrush, the porch covered in leaves and old furniture, including a washer and dryer circa 1965 or so. An open garage had been built at a ninety-degree angle from the house, and trucks in various states of dismemberment— hoods up, tires missing, dents visible—stood in attendance. Past the house, near a dip in the land where a huge puddle had collected, a lonely windmill missing several blades turned unevenly in the wind.

"Here ya go," Lucas said, and with a grunt, Caleb opened the passenger door and rolled out, his boots landing with a squish in the soggy grass. "Sleep it off."

"Fuck you, Dalton."

"I could still arrest you."

"Shit." Caleb turned too quickly, nearly fell, then righted himself and headed a little unsteadily for the house.

"You're welcome," Lucas yelled, and thought he heard another "fuck you," before he reached across the passenger seat to pull the door closed.

He hit the gas, leaving Caleb to his own devices as he backed onto the highway, then headed to the old access at the south end of Camp Horseshoe that led to Crown Creek and the spot where Caleb swore he'd seen Elle. The usually locked gate was wide open. Lucas drove through and parked his Jeep at a wide spot on the overgrown road, then squared a hat on his head and made his way to the old bridge and the spit. The wind was up and brisk, heavy with the scent of salt, the rain pouring from dark clouds as they scudded inland.

He thought of what he hadn't told Maggie earlier in the day, the information he'd kept to himself for twenty years, information about a man who'd gone missing. Not that it was relevant, or at least he'd told himself that over and over again, but he should have given Maggie the full account anyway, rather than just starting the story, leaving his own part of it out. Hell, he was a police officer now, a damned detective, and the information still didn't seem to have any bearing on Dustin Peters's disappearance.

That day he'd come upon Peters grooming the palomino mare outside near the stable, the horse tethered to the fence where Naomi and Leah had been perched on the top rail . . . there was more to it. Naomi and Leah were talking to Dustin, watching him work, Leah's ever-present cat slinking along the fence line in search of a mouse hiding in the clumps of dry grass that grew near the posts.

Lucas remembered the day. Vividly. It was the afternoon before Elle had disappeared, a hot, muggy day, the air laden with the promise of a storm that had been forecasted.

Horseflies had buzzed around the mare. The horse was edgy as if she, too, sensed the coming storm. Her ears had been pinned back, her wheat-colored tail flicking. Heat had shimmered over the surrounding hills, the summer sun beating down, and Dusty, naked from the waist up, his jeans riding low on his hips, had been sweating, his hair at his nape wet and curling. His smile had been almost predatory as he combed the horse's coat, his own muscles gleaming.

At the time Lucas had experienced a cold feeling in the pit of his stomach.

And it hadn't abated over the years.

Dustin had been talking to Naomi, ostensibly about a trail ride scheduled for later in the week, but his gaze kept landing on Leah in her cutoff shorts, cowboy boots, and thick ponytail. She'd been awkward and coltish, long legs and skinny arms, but there was just the hint of a woman beneath her freckles and innocence.

Lucas had never noticed her blossoming womanhood until that second, when he, understanding male sexual needs all too well, had observed Dustin eyeing his sister.

Spying Lucas walking toward them, Naomi had scowled slightly, the corners of her mouth pinching. "What's up?" She'd been dressed in tight jeans and a sleeveless pink T-shirt, huge sunglasses hiding her eyes.

"Nothin'. Just letting Dusty know we need help with the truck. It's misfiring."

Naomi's eyebrows had drawn even closer together. "You need him *now?*" she'd asked, obviously seeing through his lie.

"Dad wants to run into town," Lucas had lied. It had been so easy to bend the truth back then. "Magda needs some supplies."

"We get deliveries." Naomi's lips had twitched in exasperation, and she seemed to glare down at him imperiously from behind her retro Jackie O sunglasses.

Lucas had held up both hands in surrender. "I'm just the messenger."

"I'm done here anyway," Dusty had said, his eyes narrowing on Lucas as he'd snatched his shirt from the ground, then untied the horse and had begun leading her through a gate opening to the corral at the back of the stable.

Naomi had clearly been irritated, but she and Leah had hopped to the ground. Naomi had shot him a dark look from behind her shades as she'd dusted off her rear, then, with Leah in tow, had started heading toward the office and rec center.

Lucas had followed Dustin around the corner of the stable to find the cowboy allowing the mare to drink from a water trough while he'd begun pulling his T-shirt over his head.

Without another thought Lucas had jumped him, pushing the muscular man hard against the stable wall.

Bam! The back of Dusty's head cracked against the graying boards.

"What the fuck, man!" Dusty had cried, the top of his head poking through the neck of his shirt, his arms still midway through the short sleeves. "Back off!"

Lucas had shoved the cowboy harder, pinning him against the rough, weathered boards, his forearm jammed firmly over the smaller man's throat.

He'd felt Dusty's Adam's apple bob, seen him sweat.

Shoving his face to within an inch of the cowboy's nose, Lucas had hissed, "Off-limits." So furious he'd been spitting, he'd repeated, "Got that, Peters? Leah is *off-limits!*"

"Whoa, man—" Dusty had fought furiously to free his arms, but with his body pressed against the side of the wall he could only struggle and squirm futilely. "I didn't—"

"Shut up," Lucas had ordered, throwing all of his weight onto his forearm, his body shoved firmly against Dusty to keep him from breaking free. "She's just a kid. Not even a damned teen-ager yet. So you just stay the fuck away from her."

"You got it all wrong!" Dusty had choked out,

his face red, his eyes bulging, his head finally emerging from the neck hole of his shirt. "I don't give a shit about her. It's your stepmother. Naomi. *She's* the one. C'mon, man, you know how hot she is . . . sitting up there on the fence, watching me from behind those dark glasses. She wants it. I can tell."

"Shut up."

"I bet she's got one wet, sweet pussy, doesn't she?" His thick eyebrows had arched suggestively. "You know, right? She's a real she-cat in bed."

Lucas's free hand curled into a fist and he struck swiftly, landing a hard punch in Dusty's gut.

Smack!

"Ooooph! Oh . . . gawd . . . Jesus, Dalton!" He'd gone limp.

Lucas had wanted to beat the living shit out of the guy, to pummel Dustin with his fists until he was spent, because he knew, he damned well *knew* the cowboy had been ogling his kid sister. "Perverted son of a bitch," he'd ground out just as he heard approaching footsteps. He'd glanced over his shoulder to spy Naomi rounding the corner of the stable, heading straight at them.

And then he'd heard a sniggering laugh. Not from Naomi, from above. Squinting, he'd glanced skyward and caught sight of Ryan with his head out of the tiny window of the hayloft looking down at the scene unfolding below him.

Damn, damn, damn!

"What's going on here?" Naomi had demanded, her lips glistening and pursed tight. Her lips were a thin line as she said with barely suppressed anger, "The truck is fine. I just spoke with your father. No one needs it to go into town."

Caught in the lie, he hadn't responded.

She'd looked at Dusty. "For heaven's sake, are you two fighting? Really? Well, stop it. For the love of . . . just stop it."

Still hot under the collar, feeling the need for a fight boiling through his blood, Lucas had reluctantly lowered his arm and taken a step back.

"That's better. But you lied, Lucas," she'd charged. "And it's not the first time. You know, the Bible says, *'The wages of sin is death.'* Romans 6:23. God is watching. He sees all, and you'll pay, Lucas, for your sins."

"What about yours?" he'd asked, and her lips had flattened.

"That's enough." She'd let out an angry breath and glared at him from behind her glasses. Then, deciding not to push it, Naomi had turned and stormed off, leaving them as quickly as she'd come.

Coughing, sagged against the wall, Dusty had finally pushed his arms through his sleeves. "You're a fuckin' idiot," he'd choked out.

Lucas, muscles still tense, had warned, "Stay away from Leah."

Dusty had shaken his head and doubled over, hands on his knees, propping himself up.

Backing up before he tore Dustin to pieces, Lucas had pointed an accusing finger at the ranch hand. "You hear me? Just stay the hell away. From both of them."

"Or what?" Dusty had croaked, straightening and trying to regain some of his disappearing dignity. "Didn't you hear her about all that Bible stuff? About sins? That you're gonna pay? She's right, you know. You will." He'd straightened a bit then, challenge in his eyes. "So what was it you were gonna do?"

"You keep away from my sister, or I'll kill ya," Lucas had threatened. "I'll rip your fuckin' head off." And then, before he got himself into any deeper trouble, he'd left Dusty coughing and leaning against the wall of the stable.

Lucas had taken off at a jog, rounding the corner of the stable, keeping to a well-worn path and passing his stepmother, who was still striding back to the heart of the camp. He'd caught sight of his own reflection in her sunglasses.

"Lucas!" she'd called after him, but he'd ignored her. He was going to catch hell from his old man for his actions later, so what did it matter. "Lucas!" she'd screeched more loudly, but he'd just kept running and had tried not to notice the familiar scent of her perfume wafting in the hot summer air.

Now, two decades later, he wondered about Dustin Peters and what had happened to him, just as he wondered about the women who had vanished. In less than a week, all three who had been part of the camp were gone. There had been a media circus over their disappearances, but it had faded with the passage of time; until now, the only person still actively demanding answers was Meredith O'Neal, Monica's mother. Meredith had even moved to Averille years before to be "close to the investigation" and keep the story of her daughter's disappearance in the news. Over the years, of course, interest had waned as the case had gone cold. Ice-cold. That had all changed, of course, with the discovery of the skull.

He eyed his surroundings, where, on this lonely spit, Caleb Carter had been certain he'd seen Elle. Lucas spied no one, of course, and certainly not Elle. What the hell was the deal with that, her ghost supposedly appearing? Why the sightings over the years? The incidents had been spotty and he'd dismissed them, chalked up the supposed appearances of her ghost as either misconceptions, hopeful sightings, or out-and-out lies. Some had claimed to have seen her walking along the edge of the sea, near the camp. There had been differing reports over the years. One from a group of teenagers having a bonfire on the beach three years after her disappearance.

Two girls had sworn they'd seen a weird figure dressed in white running through the dunes as they walked from their car and along a path to the beach. Another time a fisherman, hauling his gear back to his car, had caught sight of "something eerie, a woman in white," on the strand where Lucas had watched her disappear into the fog years before. Another report had come from a twenty-eight-year-old kite surfer who had been riding the waves and had sworn he'd seen a lonely woman in white standing on the edge of Cape Horseshoe, on Suicide Ledge, the very spot where, people had speculated over the years, Elle had leaped to her death into the ocean.

Had she taken her own life?

Had someone murdered her?

Were her bones being examined in the lab even now?

Jamming his fists into the pockets of his jacket, Lucas walked through the shivering grass to the headland and eyed the ocean, ever moving, swells and whitecaps visible.

Was Maggie right? Was Elle at the center of it all, her disappearance the crux of all the disappearances? Had her vanishing been caused by more than his rejection of her? Was it even possible that she had not vanished, but had somehow been a part of whatever the hell happened the following night?

He didn't know, but as he watched a storm

roll in from the west, he decided he was damned well going to find out.

With one last glance at the steely waters, he turned and started for the path leading to his Jeep. He walked across the sandy dune to the edge of the tree line, where in the shadowy gloom he noticed a scrap of white caught on a berry vine. Thinking it was a bit of paper, litter that had been carelessly dropped, he stopped to take a closer look. Not paper, he realized as he approached, but some kind of filmy cloth.

As he bent down, he saw that there was lace attached to the thin cotton and the edges were ripped as if the fabric had been caught on the thorn . . . the hem of a long dress left because whoever was wearing it was fleeing?

Goose bumps crawled up the back of his neck.

In his mind's eye he pictured Elle as Caleb had described her, wind in her hair, standing alone on the dune. But why? And how?

He shook his head. Just because he found a scrap of white material on the ground didn't mean it was torn from Elle's dress, that she'd been here. Caleb *may* have seen someone, and even that someone *may* have caught her hem on the thorn, but the idea that this bit of cotton belonged to Elle Brady, that she'd been out here, was a big damned leap.

Telling himself he was an idiot, that he was letting a drunk's hallucinations influence his own judgment, Lucas took a picture of the bit of cloth with his cell phone, then picked up the scrap by one corner. His jaw tightened when he saw the stain on the ripped edge. Red. *Blood?* Or was he again jumping to conclusions, ideas implanted by a drunk? He held the torn piece to his nose and sniffed, a faint coppery smell evident in the sea air.

What the hell was this all about?

He couldn't believe it had anything to do with Elle Brady. Still, he carried the bit of cloth to his Jeep, where he kept a box of plastic bags, and sealed the scrap in one of the small sacks, then slid behind the wheel and fired the engine. As he drove toward town he knew one thing: If the ripped piece of fabric had been worn by some woman who Caleb thought was Elle, then whoever she was, she certainly was *not* a ghost.

Chapter 27

Averille, Oregon
Now
Kinley

"Damn it!" Kinley was pissed as she made her way back to the hotel. Make that beyond pissed. Just when she was about to get a little insight into this piss-ant town, learn what the locals knew from Caleb Carter, Lucas Damned Dalton had swooped in, hauled Caleb out—literally by the scruff of his neck—and pulled that "no comment" bullshit she was sick of. Obviously everyone had something to hide including Detective Dalton and they were stonewalling her.

But it wouldn't last long. She wouldn't let it. She was going to ferret out the truth, write the story of her lifetime, and have it streaming on the Internet so fast that the Portland TV stations who were on their way here would be playing second fiddle, if that. The glory and fame for breaking the biggest story to hit this part of Oregon in years would be hers.

And those big leaguers in Portland could just suck it!

Little did anyone know that Kinley Marsh had more than an ace up her sleeve. In fact, she had the whole effin' deck! Smiling to herself, knowing this little misstep with Dalton would soon be straightened out, she hurried across a street, jaywalking as there was like zero traffic in this tiny town.

Her advantage in solving the case was compliments of Annette Alsace, though poor little Annette didn't know it: *her diary!* Yes, Kinley had taken it all those years ago and had held on to it, sure that someday it would be worth something to somebody. And that day had come. That day was here. It was going to make Kinley famous. She'd always known it was important, more than just the faded diary of a lovesick little twerp of a counselor. Those pages with their loopy script held secrets about what had gone on at Camp Horseshoe twenty years before and might just hold the key to the current investigation. Yes, the diary was important, but just one part of what she considered her upper hand. The other cards in that fabulous deck, the ticket to her leaping to the big time? Her own skills, her ability to read people, to get what she wanted, and of course, if she had to, to bend the law a bit. Not that she would ever admit to as much, and she never had to. What with her sticking to "not revealing her sources" and her editor's disinterest in "how" a story was discovered, she was able to work the system—just enough.

And then, the best part, Kinley was not only going to interview all of the family members of the victims, but she intended to spy on the other women here, at the hotel, those very women who had been the irresponsible counselors in the middle of the night doing what Annette had thankfully described in minute detail. She'd been a snoop and the secrets in the pages would be more than helpful in painting a picture of the debauchery, carelessness, and intrigue that had been Camp Horseshoe twenty years before. However, Kinley had been forced to steal the diary on the night that Monica O'Neal had vanished, so there was no entry about the secret meeting in the cave down by the beach.

Too bad.

That would have been the coup de grâce.

So now, she would have to count on her interview skills, her investigative ability, and . . . yes, the spy equipment she'd planted earlier.

Kinley had managed to swipe a house key to the hotel rooms from a careless housekeeper, who, as it turned out, was afraid to lose her job and had lied about how she'd "misplaced" the card at home.

Which had been perfect, Kinley thought now as she crossed to the side of the hotel away from the street, her boots sliding a bit on the wet grass.

She'd had other help as well, a stroke of luck! Kinley had recognized Jacqui, one of the desk clerks at the hotel. They'd met briefly in college before Jacqui had dropped out, so she'd made a big point of being thrilled to reconnect, insisting on having drinks and "catching up." As things turned out, Jacqui had just broken up with her decade-long boyfriend, was heartbroken, and needed a single friend to whom she could pour out her heart and hatred of Brad, while scoping out new candidates for "Mr. Right." Jacqui was pathetic and bored Kinley to no end. Come on, did the woman have no backbone? Wonderful Brad didn't have a job, owed her money, and had ended up leaving her for someone with a brighter future. Kinley thought "good riddance to bad news," but Jacqui didn't quite see it that way . . . yet. She was still hung up on the loser, a man-boy in whom she'd "invested years of my life," as well as, probably, what could have been a nice little nest egg.

Kinley hated her evenings with miserable Jacqui, who had lost ten pounds and had begun wearing decidedly more makeup, along with low-cut tops and a push-up bra. For a more dramatic effect, Jacqui had also dyed her naturally black hair a weird shade of straw blond, just to "show him." Like Brad gave a rat's ass that his once-plain-Jane of a girlfriend was now sporting a way more slutty demeanor in her attempts to look sexy and younger.

Jacqui had started opening up over a few drinks, admitted that the hotel was booked for the next couple of days, lots of out-of-towners showing up for some kind of a reunion, which wasn't usual for this time of year. At least not midweek.

Kinley had put two and two together and come up with seven, as in seven female counselors from Camp Horseshoe from twenty years ago: Bernadette and Annette, Jo-Beth Chancellor, Reva Mercado, Jayla Williams, Sosi Gaffney, and Nell. The only two missing would, of course, be Elle Brady and Monica O'Neal.

Still, it was good to confirm what she'd suspected, that the lot of those pathetic "counselors" would be within these hundred-year-old walls, and it helped to know exactly which rooms to bug.

Jacqui's brokenhearted, desperate emotional state had been a big help to Kinley with the layout of the hotel, how the security worked. With the passkey she'd lifted and Jacqui's loose tongue after a few drinks, Kinley had not only gleaned that the female counselors from Camp Horseshoe were all staying at the Hotel Averille—well, duh, it was the only game in town, the nearest Motel 6 being thirty-five miles north—she'd also learned that Jo-Beth Chancellor had wanted a suite where she could have a "meeting" with some "old friends." Bingo. Luckily, the suite next door, identical aside from being a reverse layout, had been available and Kinley had booked it, getting a BFF discount from Jacqui in the process. Because she felt that this story had the potential to launch her career far beyond what *NewzZone* could supply, she'd rented a room on the third floor even though she lived only about fifty miles north in Astoria.

The room was an extra place to keep her things, collect her thoughts, write her notes, and most importantly, observe those who came and went through a discreet wireless connection to minuscule hidden cameras and microphones. She'd bought her equipment in Portland and returned to the hotel, where she'd been camped out, ever since hearing about the partial body being discovered on the beach.

Now she entered the hotel through a side door and slipped into the staircase used mainly by the staff. She hurried up the stairs, her wet boots making entirely too much noise, though she came across no one. On the third floor, Kinley slipped into her room, locked the door behind her, and checked the hotel safe, where she'd put her notes and the small diary. Half-filled with Annette's scrawl and dozens upon dozens of decades-old secrets, along with the sick musings of a girl in love with her sister's boyfriend— that lousy cop Dalton.

Flopping onto the bed, propping herself with pillows, she turned on the television, a poor excuse of a flat-screen perched atop an ancient dresser that was supposed to be antique, but just looked cheap.

For what had to be the hundredth time, she started rereading the diary. She'd taken pictures of every page and kept them on her computer, as well as on a backup drive. Just in case. But holding the actual little book with its filled pages of teenage longing and worries and observations could only help in Kinley's mission, which was to solve the mystery of the disappearances at the camp and divulge all of the dirty little secrets that had played a part in two girls and one ranch hand seemingly falling off the face of the earth.

She picked up her cell phone, saw no messages, and fumed a bit. Why hadn't there been an ID on the body? In this day and age it wouldn't take too long, despite the whole holdup with DNA. They had the skull, right? So wouldn't the old-fashioned dental records come through? Or some hair samples, if there were any? She shuddered inwardly at the thought of the decomposition of the skull, then went back to what she sarcastically referred to as "light" reading: Annette Alsace's diary.

From Annette's perspective, no one had much liked Monica O'Neal, and Annette had over-heard Monica reveal to Bernadette that she was pregnant, with Tyler Quade's baby. All very interesting since Tyler had been practically engaged to Jo-Beth at the time. So how did that play out? Did Jo-Beth know? The Tyler/Jo-Beth/Monica love triangle was just one, what about the other? Elle/Lucas/Bernadette? And then there were rumors about Naomi, Lucas's step-mother, that she'd had a fling with her stepson.

The juicy details, well, those that Annette had surmised, were captured in her little once-pink book. Studying words she had practically memorized, Kinsey flipped through the pages and thought about her next move. She'd considered, in doing her piece for *NewzZone*, or maybe some other bidder, using some of Annette's quotes, spinning the story so that it would show from a teenage girl's eyes and pretend that those eyes were hers. She had, after all, been at the camp during the time in question.

"So many options," she said, and wished she had a glass of wine. The Hotel Averille was short on amenities, however, and room service was one of them. Even the Wi-Fi, though offered, was untrustworthy, the connection poor at best, and probably not all that secure. Not that it mattered to her. Kinley had brought her own portable connection. Completely private. Which was essential.

The familiar words in the diary couldn't keep her attention this afternoon. She was restless, wanted action, was a little edgy as she waited. She should have had a glass of wine at the bar when she'd been trying to pry information from Caleb. Tossing the diary aside, she slipped off the bed and walked to the French doors that led to a long deck shared by all the residents of the third floor. A staircase was positioned at one end, grounded near the parking lot, to be used as an emergency escape if this tinderbox of an ancient building ever caught fire. The doors opened to a beautiful view of the rapidly going to seed parking lot.

She'd already observed Sosi Gavin, now Gaffney, in her Ford SUV, an Escape, which was parked in the lot. A sleek Mercedes was in a spot near an older Toyota of some kind and as she watched, she spied an older, smaller SUV, a

Subaru, wheel into the lot, splashing up water from the various puddles. Behind the wheel? Kinley narrowed her eyes and focused as the woman parked and climbed out, then reached into the back seat to pull out a bag before swinging toward the front of the hotel.

Nell Pachis.

Interesting.

But she spied no vehicle she could ascribe to either of the Alsace sisters. She was certain they were on their way, but so far she couldn't see any evidence that they'd arrived. That knowledge bothered her. She was itching to get started, to write this story, to break the case wide open, but she needed all of the players. Time was fleeting and even now some of those greedy, corporate-ladder-climbing, step-on-anyone's-back-who-got-in-the-way reporters were no doubt on their way. She clamped her jaw at the thought. No way were they going to horn in on her exclusive. No way were they going to get the jump on Kinley.

A smile played at the corners of her lips and she picked up the diary again, flipped through the faded pages, and found a familiar section where Annette had speculated about Nell and Sosi after catching them swimming topless in the pond when they'd thought they were alone.

Nell was here, and Sosi . . . most of the others.

They would collect in the room next door, the room that shared the deck with this one, the suite rented oh-so-conveniently to Jo-Beth Chancellor Leroy. Kinley reminded herself to be careful. She didn't want to blow her cover. She needed to hide in the shadows until she collected all the information she could for her exclusive—at least she thought it would be an exclusive due to her intimate knowledge of the witnesses, who were probably considered by the sheriff's department as suspects.

She noticed another car sliding by on the street, a dark sedan that she couldn't quite make out, but the driver slowed and eyed the parking lot, surveying it just as Kinley had a few minutes earlier. For a second, Kinley thought the car would pull in and either one of the women she'd known way back when or another hotel guest would arrive. But no, the dark vehicle rolled on.

No big deal, she told herself but couldn't help having an uneasy feeling about it, and that sensation only increased when she spied the car easing past again, going in the opposite direction. A cop maybe? Another reporter? Or just someone out for a lazy drive? She saw her camera with its powerful lens on the bureau and she reached for it, intending to take a picture of the car and driver when they drove past again, but though she waited a full ten minutes, staring outside into the rain and descending night, the dark sedan didn't reappear.

"It was nothing," she said aloud, her breath

fogging on the panes of the French door. She put the camera away. For now. She'd use it later.

Soon, the damned Alsace sisters would arrive and then it would be "game on." She could hear, through the thin walls, that the women were gathering. Perfect.

One way or another the truth about the dead woman found on the beach was going to come out, and she would have an exclusive because she was there and, of course, she had the diary to back her up. "Showtime," she told herself, and double-checked her connections, her laptop, iPhone, and the external Wi-Fi and hard drive, making sure, again, that everything was working, and gaining audio from the hidden microphones and from the minuscule camera, a wide-angle view of the room next door.

She spied Jo-Beth in leggings and a tunic walking from one end of the room to the other, heard her curse under her breath when her computer case slid off the ottoman near a side chair. "Shit!" she said in a whisper that the tiny microphone picked up clearly.

Kinley's equipment was working perfectly.

Trying to tamp down her own excitement, reminding herself that she didn't have anything earth-shattering, or case-cracking, or even newsworthy *yet,* she took in a deep breath and hit the record button on her phone.

Things were about to get interesting.

Chapter 28

"Register us both," Bernadette said as she slid her Honda into a long parking space in front of the hotel. She jammed the gearshift into park, but didn't shut off the car, just let it continue to idle as rain drops slid down the windshield.

"What?" her sister asked from the passenger seat.

"Use your credit card for now, and I'll come back and put mine down."

"Wait . . . what're you doing? Where are you going? Oh, God . . ." Annette rolled her eyes. "This is about Lucas, isn't it?"

"I just need to straighten some things out."

"Seriously? After twenty years? Don't you remember what he did?"

Bernadette shot her sister a glare meant to melt ice. "Of course I do, but this is something I need to do."

"He's a cop."

"All the more reason. You were the one who wanted to talk to the police, remember?"

"I know. I know," she muttered, "but maybe we should hear what Jo-Beth has to say."

"And let her bully us? Like she used to? Nuh-uh. I've been thinking about it, all the way down from Seattle. Well, for the past couple of decades, you know, how she bullied us into doing what she wanted, but no more."

"If you say so." Annette looked uncertain.

"I do."

They stared at each other a moment, Annette not making a move to get out of the car, Bernadette waiting, hands white-knuckled around the steering wheel.

"Jo-Beth's gonna be pissed."

"Let her be. And anyway who cares? We're not scared little girls any longer."

"Aren't we?" Annette said, holding her gaze. Then, "Oh, screw it. Do what you want."

"I will."

"I know." Annette was already yanking on the door handle and stepping onto the curb and sidewalk that ran in front of the tiny picket fence, short lawn, and wide front porch of the Hotel Averille. "But you can check in yourself." She opened the back door and grabbed her bag, leaving Bernadette's on the seat. "I'm not your damned slave."

"But you are Jo-Beth's."

Annette sucked in a breath, offended. "That wasn't fair."

"This time we're telling the truth. All of it."

"But you're coming to the meeting with Jo-Beth?"

"Oh, yeah. Wouldn't miss it for the world," Bernadette said, feeling a sense of anticipation. It was time someone knocked Jo-Beth down a peg or two, and if it had to be her, fine. All the better. She, for one, wasn't going to be running scared. No longer.

"What if you're late?"

"It's been twenty years. Jo-Beth will wait."

"How're you gonna find him?" Annette asked, hesitating, standing in the rain, her head still poked into the interior.

"I've got his number. He called. Remember?"

"But you never talked to him."

"I'm planning on changing that."

"It's your funeral."

"*Namaste.*"

"Oh, for God's sake, Bernadette." Annette slammed the door shut, then pulled her roller bag up the brick walk. Bernadette watched her sister, head ducked against the rain as she climbed the two front steps and passed through a set of French doors, the entrance to the hotel.

She shouldn't piss off Annette, she supposed. Her sister might be the only friend Bernadette had in Averille. Well, so be it. Pressing her foot firmly on the accelerator, she pulled away from the hotel, leaving Annette and all of her insecurities behind.

There was a lot of strain between them, and some of it stemmed from Annette's jealousy, a piece that had always been there, the friction amplifying as their mother had slipped into dementia, her symptoms worsening to the point that she didn't recognize anyone, couldn't walk, talk, or feed herself. Round-the-clock care wasn't enough as she slowly died by inches. Hospice had come in, morphine prescribed, and as their mother's state had worsened they'd agreed to up the dose, a little more each injection.

When she'd passed, Annette had experienced instant guilt, complete regret, and had blamed everyone for the unfairness of it all, but mostly she'd pointed an accusing finger at Bernadette, claiming that it had been Bernadette's idea. That much had been true, Bernadette had thought often about helping her mother cross over, but she'd never acted upon it. Then came the day their mother was out of her mind, in pain and desperation, moaning and completely out of it. Annette was the one who suggested they up the dosage, "Just to calm Mom down." From there, the pattern had started, and within a month Bess Alsace's agony was completely alleviated. She'd slipped away to join her husband in whatever ever after there was. Bernadette hoped it was heaven. Annette still struggled with the tough decisions they'd made, and Bernadette was first in line to shoulder the blame.

Now, Bernadette sighed. Like Annette, she really couldn't believe she was going to meet

Lucas Dalton. As recently as when she'd left Seattle, she was pretty certain she never wanted to see Lucas Dalton again. However, as she'd driven south, her little car moving steadily closer to Oregon and the summer when she was all tied up emotionally with Lucas, she decided it would be best to talk to him. Face-to-face. Clear the air. Before she dealt with Jo-Beth and whatever agenda she'd concocted.

Bernadette and Lucas had parted without really saying good-bye, a maelstrom of fear, recriminations, emotional upheaval, and the ominous cloud of mystery surrounding the missing girls, making it impossible to talk or see each other. Everyone had been shell-shocked, the police had arrived, the press nosing around, parents worried sick and shuttling their kids—campers and counselors alike—home as quickly as possible. So she'd left and never responded when he'd tried to reach her.

Until now.

She bit her lower lip. Maybe this was a mistake, but she felt she had to talk to him *before* she dealt with the others.

Ignoring the no cell phone rule while driving, she punched out his number, then waited, hearing the phone ring once, then twice, her heart pounding. Would he pick up? Would he agree to meet with her? Annette was right, he was a detective with the sheriff's department and—

A third ring.

"Hello?" His voice was low and deep. And familiar. Stupidly her heart started thudding. Oh. God. "Bernadette?"

"Hi," she replied quickly, clearing her throat. "I'm here, in Averille," she said as she drove by a gas station on the outskirts of the small town. "And . . . look, I know you've called and I've ignored you, but I think, I mean, it would be best . . ." Oh, quit beating around the bush. "I wanted to talk to you. Alone. Not . . . not officially. Not because you're a detective. It's just that . . . we never have spoken and now . . . I just think it would be a good idea. You know, to clear the air and sort some things out . . ." Oh, Lord, why was she rambling on? She gripped the wheel harder with her free hand and stared out the windshield to the old-growth Douglas fir trees guarding the narrow road.

"Okay," he said. "So when?"

"Now? Would that be okay? Can you make it?"

A beat.

In that moment of hesitation she doubted herself, felt her heart nosedive.

"Sure," he said. "You're in town?"

"Just leaving. Turning onto 101." The rain increased, blurring her windshield, and she flipped on her wipers automatically and caught a glimpse of a car following her in her rear-view. "How about we meet at the camp? Camp Horseshoe?"

Another hesitation. Then, "All right. I can be there in about ten minutes."

"Me too. See you then." Then she clicked off and let the phone drop into the cup holder wedged between the two front seats of her Honda. Ridiculously, her heart was still pounding and she was transported to another time and place, when it was summer, the days hot, the sea wild, an energy running through the camp where preteens laughed and talked and ran.

And you fell in love.

"Yeah, a million years ago," she said, glancing at her eyes in the rearview and hoping to quell the voice in her head.

That's what this is all about. Seeing Lucas again. Finding out if that white-hot attraction you felt as a teenager still exists.

"No," she said quickly, but knew there was more than a little truth in the allegation.

She drove without seeing, passing cars heading in the other direction, the beams from their headlights cutting through the late-afternoon gloom, the vehicle behind lagging back but still following. Had it been parked on the street and, when she pulled away from the curb in the front of the hotel, fired up and started tailing her?

Oh, geez, Bernadette, you've watched one too many cop shows. This is the main road along the coast, so quit being so paranoid.

Still . . .

It didn't turn off and now her attention was split between the car behind her and the road ahead, a wet, slick strip of black asphalt winding along the coastline and hugging the forested mountains. She needed to focus as she drove where rocky tree-covered cliffs rose on the east side of the pavement, while to the west there was no shoulder, just a thin guard rail separating the edge of the road and the sheer drop-off. Through the patchy trees she saw the Pacific, a vibrant and vast gunmetal ocean roiling with whitecaps.

She guided the Honda by rote until the highway curved inland a bit. Darkness was threatening and she hadn't been in the area for years, but she caught sight of the turnout, now covered in wet leaves, the fence surrounding the property mossy and sagging in places. Slowing, she cranked the wheel toward the ocean and checked her mirrors. The dark car sailed past and as it did she caught sight of the driver, a woman with white-blond hair.

Her throat went dry as she thought of Elle, with the same light hair.

But she'd only caught a quick glimpse of the woman at the wheel and she knew her mind was playing tricks on her.

"Power of suggestion," she told herself as she continued down what seemed to be a forgotten driveway, little gravel remaining, weeds sprouting, grass growing, potholes threatening the tires. She noticed the sign that had once welcomed people to the camp, now faded, barely legible, and not nearly as bold as the NO TRESPASSING sign.

Pushing all thoughts of Elle Brady aside, she ignored the sign's warning, concentrating instead on keeping her silly heart from racing at the prospect of seeing Lucas again. She knew he wasn't married, well, at least he wasn't the last time she'd Googled him. She'd also learned that he'd stayed in this neck of the woods, worked on various farms and ranches, gone to college at Oregon State University, then began working twelve years ago for the Neahkahnie Sheriff's Department, and now was a detective. She'd kept up with him, at least virtually, even though she'd been married to Jake for five years.

Getting involved with Jake hadn't been a rebound thing. He'd come along much later, after a few other romances had quickly burned out with men she hadn't much thought about in the intervening years. Not like Lucas, who came to mind at the oddest of moments.

No, Jake had been the natural choice, the right man, handsome and affable, and the timing had been right because she'd been of the age to think of marriage and children. Besides, she'd believed she'd never see Lucas again and had tried to think of him only as a teenage fling, the first boy she'd ever loved, but certainly not a life partner. She always told herself that it was best to forget him. It just hadn't happened. She'd met Jake at twenty-seven, nearly ten years from the last time she'd seen Lucas; she'd liked him immediately, fallen in love slowly, gotten married filled with hope and dreams that had all crumbled horridly after the miscarriage. So here she was and, as the nose of her Honda broke through the mossy trees to the clearing of what had been the camp, she reminded herself that Lucas was a different person than the boy she'd left, just as she was a very different woman.

There probably wouldn't even be a spark between them.

But she had to know.

And she had to tell him the truth—all of it. He needed to be informed, not only because he was someone who had been at the camp when the girls had disappeared, but because, more importantly, he was a cop.

It wouldn't be easy.

She caught sight of a Jeep, a much newer model than the one he'd driven years before, parked near the old rec center, in the rutted parking lot where recent tire tracks were visible in the mud.

Lucas stood near a post on the porch, protected by the roof from the rain. He was just as tall as she remembered and just as lean. He'd matured, of course. His hair was now darker and a little wet, but still thick. In jeans, a T-shirt, and jacket, a beard shadow covering his jaw, he looked more cowboy than cop, and though his expression was grim, one side of his mouth lifted as she parked and cut the engine.

Oh, man.

Her damned pulse was racing, her hands damp from being clenched around the steering wheel, all of which was just plain idiotic. Pasting on a smile she didn't feel, she forced herself out of the car. Flipping up the hood of her jacket, she dashed through the puddles.

"Lucas," she said a little breathlessly as she mounted the two steps. When she met his eyes, she saw something flicker in their hazel depths, something recognizable and fiery.

"Hey," he said in return. And then, "Jesus, Bernadette, you look great."

"Thanks." She was nodding, feeling awkward. God, why had she called him? "You too."

He cocked his head, waiting.

Shrugging her shoulders, she said, "You know, I thought this was a good idea, that you and I— we meet and, you know, clear the air, but . . . now . . . I don't know—"

Before she could finish her thought, he said, "I get it. Me too." Then, to her surprise, he wrapped his arms around her, pulled her close, and kissed her. Just like that. She was still trying to catch a breath, still dying a thousand deaths and wishing she hadn't called him, when his lips came crashing down on hers and he kissed her as if he'd been waiting a lifetime.

Warm.

Firm.

Urgent.

The scent of him filled her nostrils, the feeling of his body against hers stripping away the doubts and insecurities of the past twenty years. She closed her eyes for a second, felt the old longing, the ache to be with him, and almost let herself sag against him.

Almost.

For the love of God, Bernadette, what are you thinking?

Stop.

Now.

This is nuts! Alarm bells went off in her head, but she didn't back away. Strong arms held her tight and his warmth invaded her body. She didn't respond, or tried not to, but his lips were strong, pliant, and warm, and her crazy heart was beating a thousand times a minute.

The world shrank away and she was caught in memories of a simpler summer, when all that mattered was Lucas. If she let herself . . . *No, no, no! This is insane!*

As if he'd heard her inner thoughts, he lifted his head.

"No," she whispered shakily.

"No?"

"Yes, no."

He took in a long breath, then released her slowly and took a step back.

"Wow. What the hell was that?" she asked, crashing back to reality as she tried to calm herself. Dear Lord, her heart was thundering in her ears and images of making love to him were still teasing at the edges of her mind. "Are you out of your mind?"

A slow grin grew from one side of his mouth to the other. "Maybe. I've been accused of worse."

"By other women?"

"Mainly my boss. And, oh, my partner, too."

She almost laughed. "Well, they're right." For the love of God, what had he been thinking? What had she?

"I just thought we should get that out of the way."

He was so calm. Irritatingly so. She wished to high heaven that she wasn't breathing so hard that her chest was rising and falling rapidly. "Okay, well . . . don't do that again."

He waited, the only sound being the rain splashing against the roof and gurgling in the overflowing gutters.

"I mean it, Lucas." Did she? Right now she didn't trust herself to know up from sideways.

"All right." He was nodding, his gaze held hers, but there wasn't a bit of regret in his expression. "Won't happen again."

"Good," she declared. Then added lightly a moment later, "Well, not unless I want it to."

He laughed. "Deal." Then he stared hard at her, one of his eyebrows arching.

She knew what he was thinking, read the challenge in his eyes. He'd felt her response, knew that she, too, had been curious.

She let out a breath, then held up one hand in surrender. "Okay, okay . . . let's start over."

He nodded, shoved his hands into the pockets of his jacket, and asked, "So why did you call?"

"I thought we should clear the air. Jo-Beth wants all the ex-counselors, the women, to get together to make certain their story is the same and I don't know . . . it feels wrong somehow. She manipulated all of us back then, and now we're adults living our own lives and . . . living our own lies." She looked around the buildings that surrounded the parking area. Where once there had been children and teenagers laughing and talking, on their way to horseback-ride on the trails, or to swim or kayak in the lake, or assemble for flag service and prayers in the fading daylight, there was only the quiet of the surrounding forest, the low rumble of the Pacific in the distance. The place was gloomy and dark, seeming to have no vibrance, no soul.

"And . . . there is something I wanted you to know," she admitted, and bit her lip.

"As a . . . friend? Or a cop?"

"Both." She walked to one of the few windows that hadn't been boarded to peer into the darkened interior and Lucas followed. She couldn't make out much, not even when she brushed away a layer of grime, but noted a few remaining tables and chairs and the huge rock fireplace that still climbed to the soaring ceiling, its grate cold and empty. "Wow," she said, and in unspoken agreement they walked past the office where she'd first met Lucas. "Lots of memories in here, well, in the entire camp." They paused at the door and through the remaining glass she saw the peninsula of the reception counter. "It's kind of nostalgic, but a little . . . eerie, for lack of a better word." A chill, like a blast of arctic wind, blew through her soul and she shuddered.

"You had something you wanted to tell me," he reminded her.

"Yeah."

"And—I'm just guessing here—you wanted to get it out privately before you make an official statement, right?" The look he sent her was assessing, almost clinical.

She nodded.

"Regardless of what you tell me, you'll still have to talk to someone at the station."

"I know. I texted Detective Dobbs and asked to meet with her tomorrow. I think that will be cleaner than talking to you in an official sense."

"Makes sense," he agreed. "She get back to you?"

"She left some phone messages earlier, before I decided to come here, and I finally responded that I'll be around tomorrow morning. So we're on. At nine. At the sheriff's department."

"Good."

"You'll be there?"

"In some capacity."

She straightened, quit peering into the windows to face him. As she did a gust of wind kicked up, scattering damp leaves. "I heard that they think the skull belongs to a woman."

He nodded, squinting. "It has to do with size of the skull, shape of the orbits, the eye sockets, as well as the temporal lines."

"ID'ed?"

"Not yet, but according to the lab, they're just waiting to hear on the dental records. Probably today, I'd guess. DNA will come later."

Stuffing her hands into her pockets, she got to the reason she'd phoned him, had wanted to meet. "I don't know if you know this or not, or if the sheriff's department wants the information, but about a week before she went missing, Monica told me she was pregnant."

"I didn't know."

"It wasn't common knowledge. I'm surprised she told me, to tell you the truth. But she did say that the baby was Tyler Quade's, and I think she'd told him about it." She searched his face but saw no reaction. "I thought maybe Tyler mentioned it, you know, when he first gave his statement."

"First I've heard of it."

"Don't you think that's odd, that he wouldn't say anything?"

"He was laid up in the hospital, but yeah, you'd think he'd say something."

She went on. "Anyway, so Monica's pregnant and worried, and then Elle went missing, and the next night, when we, the counselors for the girls, were all supposed to meet? Monica didn't show up at the grotto, you know, under Cape Horseshoe."

"Where we found the jawbone."

"I guess," she said. "I don't really know about that. But everyone was supposed to show up to get our story straight. Jo-Beth's idea. She thought, and we all agreed, that we should hide what really went on from our parents and the owners of the camp and even the police." She walked to the edge of the porch and stared toward the ring of trees surrounding the parking lot. "It was a stupid, stupid idea. Not everyone wanted to go along with Jo-Beth's plan, but she convinced us all. Except for Monica."

"Because she never showed up."

She realized he'd no doubt read the reports that the girls had met at the cave on that night. Everyone knew about it.

"So what was really odd about the whole thing," she went on, remembering the girls gathering in the cave with its eerie light and tide pools, "is that the instigators, Reva and Jo-Beth, were both late. Jo-Beth said she was sick with cramps, I think, and Reva backed her up, but . . ." She shrugged, unsure of herself, just as she had been twenty years earlier.

"You don't believe her."

"I think that Jo-Beth, and maybe Reva, too, had their own agendas. What those agendas were, I don't know."

"You think it has something to do with Monica's pregnancy?"

"Maybe. Jo-Beth had found out that Tyler was seeing Monica and she was furious, but I don't know if she knew about the baby. Anyway, I heard her talking to Reva after Elle went missing. The next day they thought they should do something to Monica. Really scare her, ya know? Like have someone dress up as a ghost of Elle or something and then get a big laugh about it. But no one wanted to go along. Elle had just gone missing and it seemed . . . heartless and cruel and just too mean. So, she scrapped it."

"But a couple of girls thought they saw Elle that night, right? Didn't Annette say she saw her?"

"Yeah, and maybe Sosi. And this is weird," she added, hesitant to even bring it up, "but as I was driving here, a car was following me, like a dark blue Ford, I think, I'm not really good with cars, but . . . well, it seemed to be behind me all the way from the hotel and I thought maybe I'd seen it pull out behind me when Annette got out of the car, but I'm not sure about it. Anyway, it blew past me as I turned off and that's when I saw the driver, a woman, I mean a blond woman who reminded me of Elle." She glanced at him and saw the edges of his mouth tighten. "I didn't get a good look at her and I'm not saying she was Elle, for God's sake, but, I have to admit it, she reminded me of Elle." She shivered inside. "Maybe it's just being back here, y'know with all the talk about her and the whole ghost story thing. I . . . I shouldn't have brought it up."

"No, you're not the only one, although," he admitted, "some of the people who thought they saw her aren't the most reliable of witnesses." He seemed worried.

"It's probably nothing."

"But maybe not. I'll look into it." His eyes narrowed as he rubbed the back of his neck in a gesture she remembered from her youth, and she tried not to let her mind wander back to that time when she spent her days getting through her chores and dealing with the campers, trying to be enthusiastic for the girls, when most of the time she was anticipating the nights alone with Lucas. She'd been an idiot then, head over heels in lust or love or probably both, and it surprised her that those raw emotions, the insecurities, the highs, the lows, the tingling sensation whenever he was nearby were not dead, but still simmered just under the surface. She was now an adult, twice the age she'd been when she met him, but still, that same needle-sharp awareness, a sexual energy, still existed.

Which wasn't just odd, it was a pain in the neck. And now she'd almost thought she'd spied the ghost of the girl he'd broken up with twenty years earlier? God, she was losing it. That was insane. Seeing Lucas again was destroying her equilibrium, her rational thought, and being here at the camp where she'd fallen in love with him and all hell had broken out wasn't helping.

She'd come down here to talk to the police, to see him again, to do what she had to do to put her past to rest, and now she feared all she'd done is roiled it up, bringing back the ghosts that were better off buried.

His cell phone chirped and he pulled it from his pocket, read a message, and said, "Duty calls."

"Okay." She had to get going as well.

"You'll come into the station and give an official statement?" he asked as they walked off the porch, shoulders hunched against the rain as they hurried to their cars.

"Yeah, of course." She reached for the door

handle and felt his hand catch in the crook of her elbow. Her reaction was immediate, her pulse quickening.

"Bernadette?"

"Yeah?"

His face was serious, his hazel eyes dark, and she felt the back of her throat go dry. Her heart began to thump again.

Oh. Dear. God.

Without the hint of a smile, he said, "It was good to see you again."

"You . . . You too." She waited, half expecting him to draw her into his arms and kiss her again, but instead he turned on his heel and hurried to his Jeep. As she climbed into her own car and surveyed him through the window, she saw him slide behind the wheel of his rig and press his cell phone to his ear. She drove out of the camp with a feeling of nostalgia for what might have been had tragedy not struck.

Would she and Lucas have continued to see each other? Would her life have been here, in some small coastal town rather than in Seattle? Or would they have broken up anyway?

What did it matter, Bernadette thought, her little car bouncing down the rutted lane. Would-have-beens? Could-have-beens?

All fantasies. Now she had to deal with reality.

And Lucas Dalton was very much a part of it.

Chapter 29

Averille, Oregon
Now
Lucas

The second Lucas stepped into the sheriff's office, Locklear, from behind her desk, ordered, "Into the conference room." Maggie, who had been sitting in one of the visitor's chairs, shot to her feet and threw him a "don't ask" look.

Maggie had called him while he'd met with Bernadette at the old campgrounds. His partner had been curt and told him to hightail it to the department. He'd complied but had spent most of the drive thinking about Bernadette while dealing with all the old emotions that had come to the fore. He'd been a damned fool and had mentally kicked himself over and over again for kissing her so impetuously. That had been a mistake and she'd called him on it, even though she'd responded. He'd felt her warmth and desire, at least for a second, but he'd been out of line. It was almost as if he'd reverted back to his randy teenage self at the sight of her. Then again, she was still gorgeous with those long legs, intelligent eyes, and lips that were quick to turn into a smile. Thankfully, Maggie had phoned and told

416

him to get his butt back to the dep[   ] door
he made a complete fool out of hin[   ] them
Locklear glared at him. Her featu[   ] his j[a
in stone, lips thin, dark eyes with[   ] and s
humor, her bad mood radiating off l[   ] "W
anything you need from your offi[   ] Mag
on the way. The body's been ID[   ] him
Monica O'Neal."   "I

"Jesus," Lucas said, his muscl[   ] leng[t
reflexively, though he'd been half-[   ] floo
news. The lab had concluded the sk[   ] "C
to a female and had been buried f[   ] Th
Lucas had already come to the co[   ] roon
skull found on the beach belonged [   ] "S
Elle. Still, the confirmation, the cer[   ] "ple
blow, and he realized he'd held out [   ] head
that the victim wasn't one of the girls[   ] her.

"Okay." Maggie nodded and hea[   ] com
the door. "Now we have something co[   ] at t
on."   mor

"Right. An identifiable victim." L[   ] the
out of her chair and rounding her des[   ] win
that we know who she is, we're goin[   ] and
the case. Top to bottom. Her mother [   ] A
be informed ASAP, and the press will [   ] app
enough. So let's get going." She beat l[   ] we
door and gestured him through after [   ] O'1
"Everyone's going to bring me up [   ] pic
Including both of you." With that, s[   ] the
into the corridor behind them, pulled [   ] blu

hut, then took the lead, walking ahead of
down the short hallway. Lucas stripped off
ket, dropped it in his office along the way,
abbed up a notebook.

at did I tell you the other day? Warpath,"
ie murmured, hanging back to wait for
the doorway.

ard that." Locklear's voice came down the
of the corridors, echoing off the polished

reful," Lucas warned under his breath.

y caught up to the sheriff in the meeting

," Locklear ordered, then tempered it with,
se," as she dropped into the chair at the
of the broad table, a laptop open in front of
large screen hooked wirelessly to her
uter was on the wall at her back so anyone
table could view what she saw on her
or. Aside from the table and a slim credenza
oom was devoid of furniture, the only
ws cut high overhead next to the ceiling
howing that night was rapidly falling.

Locklear typed into her keypad, images
red for all to see. The first photographs
of Monica O'Neal. Lucas recognized
al's driver's license photo and graduation
e, both shots of a beautiful, vibrant girl on
sp of womanhood. Black curly hair, bright
eyes, and a smile that was almost sexy.

The picture of youth. The next pictures were grim: several photos of a deteriorated skull and jawbone, both of which Lucas had seen in person.

Acid crawled up his throat.

Footsteps sounded in the hallway. A short man with a soul patch, thin sideburns, and rimless glasses stepped into the room—an African-American tech from the crime lab by the name of Winslow Tatum. He was carrying an iPad and slid into one of the unoccupied chairs as other approaching footsteps could be heard.

Ryan Tremaine appeared next and took a seat across from his ex-stepbrother. Their gazes clashed for a second before another set of footsteps, accompanied by a low, rumbling voice, could be heard. Half a second later, Junior Detective Alejandro Garcia strode into the room, a cell phone pressed to his ear. "Call you back later," he said as he dropped into the chair nearest the door. Short and stocky, with buzz-cut black hair and deep-set, dark eyes, Garcia pocketed his phone.

"Okay, let's get to it," Locklear said, touching the screen of her computer. "This is gonna be a long one, so I've asked Dottie to bring us coffee, sodas, whatever. If you want something else, something not on the cart, like iced tea or whatever, let her know." She shot Lucas a hard glare. "And if you were going to suggest something stronger like whiskey or a beer, either because you're serious or even just as a joke to break the ice, forget it. I am *definitely* not in the mood. We all may need a drink later, but for now, we've got work to do. Serious work."

"Excuse me." A tap on the open door indicated Dottie had arrived. She stuck her head into the office.

"Come on in," the sheriff said, waving the receptionist into the conference room.

In heels and a crisp gray suit, a remote phone headset buried in her white curls, Dottie pushed a cart laden with cups, carafes, and bottles of water into the room. Also on the cart's surface were small baskets of tea, a variety of sweetener packets, and a pitcher of cream. "Anything else?" she asked as she parked the rolling cart in a back corner. The aroma of coffee mixed with the faint scent of the receptionist's signature perfume sifted through the air.

"That should do it. Thanks," the sheriff said.

"If you're certain . . ." Pursing her lips, probably trying to find some excuse to stay, Dottie reluctantly made her way back to the switchboard and front desk, her heels clicking down the hallway.

"Okay." Locklear stood, walked to the cart, and grabbed a bottle of water. "Get what you need, and let's go over everything we've got."

Lucas didn't bother, but Maggie poured herself coffee with cream while Winslow snagged a Diet Coke. Tremaine abstained. After picking out a regular Coke, Garcia snapped the tab and returned to his seat.

As Garcia scraped his chair into place, Locklear started in. "I know what we're doing here is a little unusual. But then we've got a unique situation. The reason I've called this meeting and that I'm running it is because this is the biggest case that we've seen and I've briefed myself on it so that I know what's going on. Just for today, so that we're all on the same page. However, the detectives, of course, will be running the show. But first things first." She stared directly at Lucas. "You're officially off the case. Your family is involved and you're involved, so after this meeting where we get the ground rules set, see that the work you've done to date is complete so that Detective Dobbs can take over with Detective Garcia as her partner. This isn't a reflection on your work, Dalton. It's purely to prevent a scandal of someone calling foul because of a perceived conflict of interest."

She turned her head and skewered Ryan with her uncompromising gaze. "Same with you. I've only included you today to get your input, but, like Detective Dalton, Mr. Tremaine, you're officially off the case as well. I've already talked to the DA and the brass. Everyone agrees. Understood?"

Lucas's back muscles tensed and he bit his tongue with an effort. He wanted to argue that he knew better than anyone what had happened at Camp Horseshoe twenty years earlier, but he didn't. He was lucky to be allowed to stay in this meeting as it was. So, as Maggie stirred her coffee, he gave a quick nod. "Got it."

"And you, Counselor?" Locklear again looked hard at Ryan Tremaine. "Have you 'got it,' too?"

His eyes flashed and, beneath his goatee, Ryan's jaw turned to granite. "I'll talk to the DA."

"You do that. Now, let's go over what we've got. As I said, I've allowed you two in here because you might have some information or can give us some insight into what we've got so far, but that's it." Turning her attention to the computer screen, she said, "Okay, now that the preliminaries are over, we'll go over what we've got, what we need, and then, later, you two"—she motioned with an index finger to Lucas and his once-upon-a-time stepbrother—"can leave."

For the next two hours, as the screen showed pictures of the others who'd gone missing, with Maggie refilling her coffee cup, stirring in cream, then chewing on the plastic stir stick, they discussed the case, including the dental records that proved the jawbone belonged to Monica O'Neal and that the rest of the skull was apparently hers.

Winslow, on his second diet soda, explained that some of the other bones located in the sand

422

and driftwood on the beach appeared to be from a female of the approximate same age and size. They could be Monica's, but only through DNA testing would that information be conclusive. There was always the problem of other bones being discovered and Lucas thought of Elle again.

Once Winslow had talked about the examination of the skeleton, the sheriff told them that the Public Information Officer would handle calls to the station from the press. Deputies had already been sent to Meredith O'Neal's home. Jeremiah Dalton, too, had been informed that the entire acreage that had once been Camp Horseshoe, along with the area of the beach, cavern, and state park abutting the beach, would be considered potential crime scenes and searched.

"He's not happy about it," Locklear admitted, speaking about Lucas's father. "He's trying to block our excavating on the beach legally, but it won't happen."

"He doesn't like the negative publicity," Ryan said. "He's got a couple of potential buyers. One out of LA and one out of China, and is afraid of the negative publicity."

Lucas sent the prosecutor a look. It was odd how close he and David had remained to his father, their ex-stepfather, considering the acrimony surrounding Jeremiah's divorce from their mother. Naomi had fought tooth and nail, hiring the best Portland attorney she could find, to reclaim the acreage associated with the campground, a piece of her history, homesteaded by one of her ancestors who had actually come out by wagon via the Oregon Trail. That bit of history and connection to the land hadn't been enough to help her reclaim what she considered rightfully hers. In the end Jeremiah's lawyers had prevailed by showing the court that the property had been deeded to the church by Naomi's father not long after the wedding. Since Jeremiah was essentially the church, the judge had decided, Naomi had no legal rights to the valuable land. Her own father's actions couldn't be reversed.

Naomi had been bitter about the loss, not only of her husband, but her family's home and, she'd claimed, her heritage.

Still, both David and Ryan remained fairly close to the man who their mother was certain had swindled her out of her inheritance, all in the name of God. In this one case, Lucas was inclined to agree with her.

"The records are pretty old, but it seems like the last person to see her alive, who's admitting it, was Naomi Dalton." The sheriff paused to glance at Ryan. "Mrs. Dalton says she saw Monica come out of her cabin, once all the campers were asleep. She was gone for about ten minutes; then Mrs. Dalton said the girl returned and went back inside. Then Mrs. Dalton retired to the cabin that had been assigned to Eleanor Brady. We think Monica waited and then either left her cabin on her own or was forced to, though according to reports there was no sign of any struggle any-where.

"We also know that she was supposed to meet the rest of the female counselors at the cavern at the base of Cape Horseshoe but never showed up. No one saw her again after that."

Lucas said, "There's a new little piece of information that I wasn't aware of. It could be that Monica O'Neal was pregnant. I just spoke to Bernadette Alsace—"

"Warden," Maggie interjected, pushing her empty cup aside.

"Yes, Warden now. She claims that Monica confided in her." He explained about his conversation with Bernadette and saw the sheriff's face cloud over.

"So this pregnancy?" the sheriff said. "If it was real. A possible motive?"

"Maybe."

"Anyone else know about it?" she asked. "Like the father?"

"I don't know for certain, but Bernadette thought so. Monica had said so."

"Something to check out." She glanced at Tatum, who took his cue.

"If there was a fetus, it wasn't discovered with

any of the bones we located." Tatum flipped through several screens on his own laptop and shook his head. "Since we only have a partial skeleton, we can't confirm or deny. If conception occurred close to the time of death, very early in the first trimester, there would be no sign of calcification, no bones, and, of course, the pelvis wouldn't have begun to widen. I assume that this would have been her first pregnancy?"

"If it even existed," the sheriff said. "In all the conversations the department has had with Meredith O'Neal, the victim's mother, there was no mention of a previous pregnancy or birth."

"Do we know what the cause of death was?" Maggie asked, and Winslow shook his head.

"Impossible to determine without more tests as there was a lot of degradation of the bones, but there were some nicks to her left radius and ulna, potentially from a knife. Not conclusive yet."

"Tyler Quade was attacked with a knife," Dobbs reminded everyone.

Winslow said, "We've got that knife in evidence and we're checking to see if it's a match."

Maggie's eyes narrowed. "That knife was purportedly taken from the kitchen, right? A butcher knife that, according to the cook, Magda Sokolov, was used in the dinner prep that night, but when she looked for it the next day, it couldn't be found."

"It ended up in Tyler Quade's back," Lucas said.

Her eyebrows pinched together in thought, Maggie said, "Quade said he was to meet Monica at the old chapel where he was attacked. He claims he didn't see his attacker, that the guy leaped out from behind a pew, stabbed him, and took off, leaving him to bleed out. He passed out for an indeterminate amount of time and woke up in a pool of his own blood before somehow stumbling outside and running into you." She looked at Lucas.

"That's right," he said. "He was a supercilious jerk."

The sheriff, who had been screwing the cap back onto her now-empty bottle of water, asked, "Your opinion, Detective, or general knowledge?"

Lucas glanced at Ryan, who nodded curtly and added, "I wasn't a fan. Quade thought he was God's gift."

"Finally," Locklear said, "something you two finally agree on. Do we know where Quade is now?"

"He lives in Coos Bay," Maggie said. "Single. Well, actually divorced. Went to college, graduated, and ran some of his family's sawmills, most of which were sold in the last recession. When his father died, he inherited the last of the mills." She checked her notes and glanced up. "He's driving up. Scheduled for an interview tomorrow. Along with the women counselors who came up. And Jeannette Brady again, as well as the Dalton family. Those who didn't come here will be interviewed by police in their local jurisdiction and if there's anything interesting or inconsistent with previous statements, we'll interview them again."

"Looks like we're going to be busy." Locklear tossed her empty water bottle into a bin near the table. "Interviewing the Dalton family would include you two." She motioned her hand to include both Lucas and Ryan. "You're both part and parcel to this case. Makes it complicated. As a matter of fact, Counselor," she said to Ryan, "you claimed that you heard Detective Dalton threaten Dustin Peters."

What? Lucas felt the muscles in his neck stiffen.

Ryan stared right at Lucas and said, "I saw Lucas beat Dustin to within an inch of his life and then warn him that if he looked at his sister or my mother again, he would kill him. Something about ripping his head off."

Lucas's jaw clenched.

"Did anyone else hear the threat?" Locklear asked.

"Dustin Peters and possibly my mother, Naomi Dalton."

The sheriff's gaze swung back to Lucas. "Even if I pass this off as a teenager getting into a youthful scuffle, I can't ignore it, Detective."

Maggie, maybe to deflect the attention from Lucas, or maybe because she needed to know, brought up the missing prisoner. "No one's seen Waldo Grimes since he escaped from that transport," she reminded them all. "But his weapon of choice was a knife. He was doing time for the slaying of his ex-girlfriend and her new lover, both with a kitchen knife."

"Those were crimes of passion," the sheriff said slowly.

"But if he were cornered, if Monica had stumbled upon him? He might have reacted the same way," Maggie argued. "In digging through his records, I discovered that he'd put another acquaintance in the hospital, someone he attacked with a machete when he was in high school. The kid survived. Grimes, who was a juvenile at the time, did some time in juvie and so he has a history."

"Except he, too, is missing," Garcia finally said.

"Then maybe we can find him, or Eleanor Brady, or damned Dustin Peters." Maggie was tense.

"Maybe we will," Winslow agreed. "The crew is going to go over the whole stretch of beach, metal detectors, dogs, whatever we've got. Rolling in before dawn tomorrow. Monica O'Neal might not be the only body hidden in the sand."

Sheriff Locklear eyed everyone at the table. "Do we have anything else that is pertinent to the case, or cases, before we wrap this up?"

Lucas thought about the scrap of fabric he'd recovered and Caleb Carter's insistence he'd seen Elle. It was probably nothing, but he decided that the best way to approach this whole case was to bring up all the theories as well as any potential evidence, despite the fact that it might not lead to anything. He reached into his pocket and pulled out the scrap of bloodied fabric in its plastic bag. "I found this down at the spit near Crown Creek, a tip from Caleb Carter, who claimed he'd seen Eleanor Brady down there or her damned ghost."

"Again," the sheriff said.

"He was drunk as hell and I drove him home before taking a look. I found this out there. It could have nothing to do with Elle Brady or this case or anything, but I marked the spot and brought it in." Lucas dropped the bag onto the table. "Just in case."

Ryan snorted. "Jesus, Dalton, you're supposed to be a detective, not some idiot who believes in ghost stories and collects . . . what? Bits of trash on the beach because some drunk hallucinated about seeing a damned ghost." He glared at his ex-stepbrother. "This is a police department not a psychic hotline call center."

"It could be nothing," Lucas agreed, managing

to hold on to his temper, "but others have seen her." He wasn't going to bring Bernadette's name up, not with the sketchy information she'd given him.

"Yeah, yeah, and some people still believe in Santa Claus and the Easter Bunny, Dalton," Ryan said. "This is a police force for crying out loud!"

"I'll check it out," Maggie said, snagging the bag and eyeing the scrap through the clear plastic. "If there's blood on it, we can type it, check it for DNA."

Ryan said, "If it's blood, it's probably from an animal."

Maggie sent him a brittle smile. "Well, we'll find out, then."

"Just what we need. Another Elle Brady sighting," Locklear said with a frown.

"By a known drunk. And you followed up the lead," Ryan said to Lucas, unable to let it go.

Lucas offered the man a lazy smile. "No stone unturned."

"Yeah, right," Tremaine said.

Locklear didn't bother to comment any further, but checked her watch and Lucas noted that it was dark beyond the window. Night had fallen, only a bit of a glow from security lamps appearing in the wide panes.

"Anything else?" Locklear asked.

When no one came up with anything, the sheriff

exhaled and said, "Okay, that's it for now. As Detective Garcia said, the department is going to do some more digging on that stretch of beach between the state park and Camp Horseshoe. For what it's worth, we're putting out metal detectors and cadaver dogs, but those are a long shot. There's new technology available, but any that relies on a change in the foliage of the area won't work well on the beach." She sighed. "Twenty years of tides and winter storms and shifting topography. It's needle in the haystack time. But we'll have excavation equipment ready to go and an army of deputies with shovels."

She leaned back in her chair and backtracked a bit. "The women who were counselors at Camp Horseshoe are now in town. They'll be interviewed by us. As Dobbs said, those who didn't come to Averille will be interviewed by officers from the jurisdictions in which they reside. I want everyone who was questioned back then to have their statements revisited. Also everyone who worked at that camp, or who delivered to the camp, or was related to the victims. Report back to me." With that she stood, silently signifying the meeting was over.

Chapter 30

Averille, Oregon
Now
Jo-Beth

"Where's your sister?" Jo-Beth demanded of Annette Alsace, the mouse. Jo-Beth was antsy, wanting to be through with this ordeal. Truth be told, everything about Averille, Oregon, and the camp located a few miles south gave her a bad case of the creeps. She'd even had the feeling she was being followed earlier today, but that was just her nerves stretched to screaming. She sat in the largest chair in the room, the one positioned near the French doors, where if she wanted to, she could observe the deck, visible through thin sheers that fluttered due to the uneven flow of air from an overused and ancient heater.

God, what she wouldn't do to put all this quickly behind her.

The other ex-counselors were sprinkled throughout the sitting area, crammed together in Jo-Beth's "suite," if that's what you could call the pathetic group of rooms that took up half of the third floor of this for-crap two-bit hotel. Not exactly the Ritz. Then again, what could one expect in a tiny town located so far from the rest of civilization?

"Bernadette's on her way," Annette assured her. "She just texted me five minutes ago."

"Didn't the two of you come down together?" Reva asked. Dear God, was she sidling over to the minibar again?

Annette said, "She had something she needed to take care of."

It didn't take a super sleuth to determine that she was probably hunting down Lucas Dalton, which was just plain wrong. And scary as hell.

Even Reva, already tipsy again, figured it out. One of her dark eyebrows raised, and the smile that curved over her lips was nearly a smirk. That was the problem with her, she was so damned arrogant and transparent about it. Yeah, Reva was willing to do just about anything, and she could lie with the best of them, was an ace of an actress when she wanted to be, but she also loved to play the superiority card, liked to let others know she was on to them with her cat-eating-a-canary smile.

Then there was Reva's worry about Maggie Dobbs, the cop, about her previous accident. Whatever had gone down with the wreck wasn't good. Not at all. Which was a problem. Jo-Beth needed Reva to keep the big lie going, but Reva was unreliable and could become another liability.

Just like Tyler Quade. There was just no telling what he might tell the cops and Jo-Beth needed him, along with the others, to stick with the story.

What the hell was wrong with everyone? Couldn't they just keep their mouths shut, repeat the same story they'd sworn to years before, be cool, and go home? Then, maybe, this nightmare would be behind them for good. As she took stock of the women in the suite, all losers in her opinion, she tried to keep her blood pressure under control. God, she hated working with morons!

Sosi, pious, wearing a gold cross dangling from a chain around her neck and her religion on her sleeve, was seated in a side chair with Annette perched on the ottoman in front of her. Sosi was still pixyish, aside from the bump in her belly—yet another baby on the way. So much for her dreams of being an Olympic gymnast. Now she was just the winner of the overpopulation of the earth award as she tried to avoid Nell's eyes, all the while fingering the little cross.

Of course Reva was already nursing something pathetic from the tiny refrigerator—a wine spritzer—God, did they still bottle those things? Disgusting.

Nell, slim and athletic, prettier than Jo-Beth remembered, was on one end of the rust-colored hide-a-bed, casting furtive glances at Sosi, who was steadfastly ignoring her.

Jayla just looked scared. She had gained about ten pounds since the last time Jo-Beth had seen her and was decked out in an expensive gray pantsuit, orange scarf, and a little too much jewelry. But at least she took care of herself, and her mocha-colored skin had a warm glow to it. Irritating as hell. Wedged into the other end of the sofa/hide-a-bed, Jayla kept looking at the door while folding and refolding her hands. Nervous. Well, she should be. They *all* should be.

Of course Bernadette was MIA and—oh shit, why couldn't they all just do what they were told?

It was up to Jo-Beth to herd them, including the missing Bernadette, in the right direction, but it would take all of her people skills, which weren't all that great to begin with. She would have to be patient despite her anxiety that everything she'd worked so hard for could very well be destroyed. Her marriage was already a shambles, but her career was on track. Or had been. The partners at Keating, Black, Tobias, and Aaronsen wouldn't be thrilled if this scandal broke and her name was plastered all over it.

"Okay," she said, getting everyone in the group's attention just as the heater rumbled on again. God, the room was stuffy. "Let's assume Bernadette will be here soon and get started."

Nell glanced at her fitness tracker/watch strapped to her wrist. "About time."

So she, too, was going to be a pain. Ignoring the comment, Jo-Beth said, "I just thought we should go over the details, you know, refresh our memories."

"You mean lie," Sosi corrected, having more backbone than Jo-Beth had anticipated.

Jo-Beth inwardly sighed but pasted on her sincerest smile. "It's just that I've had a lot of experience with this kind of thing, you know. Being a lawyer. I've taken depositions, and dealt with pre-trial testimony, as well as spent time in courtrooms. I've negotiated with the opposing counsel, talked to witnesses, and been in the judicial process from the first day of selecting a jury until the verdict's read. And further. On appeal. So I know the ropes and, believe me, from my experience, I know it's important that we're all on the same page." She saw the skepticism in Sosi's eyes and knew she'd have to appeal to the woman on a different level. "What we need to do is pare what we say down to the simple truth, which is to tell the police exactly what we know. Not what we think we know, not . . . conjecture or hearsay or supposition or anything like that." She took the time to look at each woman in turn, just as she would a jury when making a critical point during a trial.

"This is serious business now that we know, or suspect, the body discovered on the beach is someone we know, someone who went missing while we were at the camp, so we want to help the police as much as we can, and the easiest way to do that is to be concise and true. We all need to reiterate what happened the night that we all gathered at the cavern."

Clouds were gathering in Sosi's wide eyes and she looked about to argue but stopped when they all heard a sharp rap on the door.

Reva answered the knock and Bernadette Alsace strode into the sitting room. Her eyes were bright, her face flushed, and she brought with her the scent of rain and the sea. Ridiculously, Jo-Beth felt a small sliver of jealousy burrow into her heart.

Bernadette had grown into a striking woman, with a firm chin and high cheekbones. Her hair and rain jacket were spattered, her green eyes bright. Damn the woman, she exuded a healthy exuberance that no amount of abdominal crunches, weight lifting, spa treatments, expensive creams, or hours spent with a personal trainer could replicate, the damned joie de vivre that Jo-Beth, herself, found so elusive. Jo-Beth immediately hated her. Way too confident.

"Sorry I'm late," Bernadette said, breezing in and peeling off the jacket to toss it over the back of the couch.

"Where were you?" Reva had sidled up to the minibar again.

"At Camp Horseshoe. I met with Lucas Dalton."

Jo-Beth suddenly wanted to strangle Bernadette. "For the love of God, why?"

"To set the record straight."

"You made your official statement?" Jo-Beth asked, fighting the urge to scream.

"No."

With all the effort she could muster, Jo-Beth forced her face to remain impassive, just as she did when she was in front of a jury making a case, just as she had when her sorry excuse of a husband had first told her about needing to "find himself" on the open highway in a ludicrous Volkswagen bus/camper/whatever. "So what did you tell him?"

Bernadette said, "I just told him the truth, exactly what I remember, which is basically everything I've said all along."

"Hopefully you didn't embellish it," Jo-Beth said. God, why was it so hot in here?

"I didn't. Nor did I hide anything." Bernadette held Jo-Beth's gaze and didn't seem to be intimidated. "I said everything I should and though it wasn't an official statement—I'm giving mine tomorrow to Detective Dobbs—I just wanted to clear the air between us."

"Dalton's a cop," Jo-Beth reminded.

"I know. I don't see that as a problem."

"Then you're blind. Not only is he a damned detective, but he's got a personal stake in this," she said, wondering how Bernadette, who looked like an intelligent woman, could be so damned dumb. "So . . . from now on the story is this," she said to the group at large. "We all met at the cavern the night Monica went missing because we wanted to discuss what had happened to Elle. We were all worried that because we'd been sneaking around a bit, at night, away from our cabins, that we might be in trouble. But no one saw anything on either night that would help. We didn't see Elle. We didn't see Monica. Simple. End of story. This is what we tell the cops. This is what we tell any reporters. They'll come nosing around, like that Kinley Marsh. She's been calling around."

"She came to my house," Jayla said.

Jo-Beth's heart sank. "And?"

"I told it like it was, just like you said, and then I got a phone call and acted like my son needed a ride immediately so she would leave."

"Good thinking. I don't trust her."

"You don't trust anyone," Bernadette said.

Jo-Beth agreed. "It doesn't hurt to be a little cautious."

"Or suspicious." Bernadette was really pushing things.

"Fine, call it what you want. But trust me, Kinley Marsh is trouble. She'll do anything to get a story. And she's not the only one. I've already had reporters from Portland, Vancouver, and even Seattle calling me." Jo-Beth walked to the thermostat and tried to adjust the heat, pushing various buttons. Nothing happened. The damned heater kept purring, pouring out hot air.

Annette broke in with, "What about if we saw Elle after the night she went missing?"

Jo-Beth turned from the wall with the thermostat to stare at the younger Alsace sister. "Not this ghost thing again."

Annette was nodding.

And then Sosi said softly, "I did, too."

The two exchanged looks and Jo-Beth felt her control over the meeting slipping through her fingers. "You're both kidding. Right?"

"I told you I thought I'd seen her," Annette said. "The night Monica vanished she was on the ridge on the south end of the beach, not the cape, but in the property owned by the camp, and she was dressed all in white and looking out to sea. I thought it might be Elle's ghost."

"Give me a break," Reva muttered, and took another drink from her tiny bottle.

Jo-Beth laughed shortly. "You can't be serious."

"I am."

Jo-Beth shook her head. "We can't complicate our statements with ghosts or spirits or any of that paranormal crap. We have to keep it simple. Keep it to the truth. The facts."

"I said I saw her, too." Sosi was clutching the little cross now. "And you're right," she said, looking at Annette. "She was dressed in a white dress, or maybe a nightgown." She turned on

441

Jo-Beth. "And for the record? It's not paranormal crap, Jo-Beth. If you had any faith at all, you would understand that there are ghosts and angels and spirits walking among us."

"You're saying she's dead, then?" Jo-Beth demanded, taking a step in Sosi's direction. She had to cut this crazy talk off now.

To her surprise, the shorter woman climbed to her feet and inched up her chin. "What I'm saying is that I saw her. Dead or alive, I don't know."

"How do you know it was Elle? How close did you get?" Jo-Beth asked, aware every eye in the room was on her. "As close as I am to the deck?" She motioned to the French doors.

"No, but—"

"Then, what? Ten yards maybe? Twenty?" Jo-Beth asked.

"I don't know, a distance, I guess . . ."

"And you?" she demanded of Annette, swinging her gaze to the younger Alsace sister still seated on the ottoman. "You saw an 'apparition' on the ridge? You were up there?"

"No." Annette was shaking her head, her brown hair brushing the tops of her shoulders. "I was on the trail below."

"So, fifty, maybe sixty yards away from the ghost, right? At night?" She didn't bother hiding her skepticism. Slowly, she moved her gaze from one of the women in the room to the next. "Impossible," she said before swiveling to face

442

Annette again. "You couldn't possibly have seen who was there. It could have been anyone. Don't you think, doesn't it make sense that since it was the night after she'd gone missing and that we were all worried about her that it could have been your own imagination? I mean, we'd even floated the idea around to scare others by dressing up as Elle, remember? Just a dumb, adolescent idea that we scrapped, but it could have been planted in your minds and so—"

"You think we didn't see her?" Sosi demanded, cutting Jo-Beth off.

"I'm saying you don't know what you saw. Sure, you probably caught sight of something or maybe even someone. But when you consider everything logically, don't you think it's possible that your subliminal mind conjured up the idea that whatever you saw—a person, place, or thing—was twisted into the image of a missing girl or a ghost? Like maybe a tree caught swaying in the wind, maybe someone walking . . . became Elle, and over the years you've convinced yourself that you saw her ghost?"

"I know what I saw," Sosi said, but she swallowed hard and Annette was biting her lip nervously. Good. That was better. If only it wasn't so damned hot in here!

"I believe her," Jayla cut in, and Jo-Beth wanted to bean the woman. Why was she chiming in now? "There are ghosts. I've . . . I've heard them.

443

At my house. I never admitted it, but . . . I know there are spirits here on earth. Everywhere."

"But you didn't see Elle that night, did you?" Jo-Beth said, and noticed a hint of indecision in Jayla's dark eyes. Good.

"No," Jayla said carefully. "But I believe—"

"It doesn't matter what you believe," Jo-Beth cut her off. "The important thing to remember is that we're here to: One, tell the truth." She held up her pointer finger. "Two, keep things as simple and straightforward as possible for the police." Another finger shot up. "And three, go back to our own personal lives and lay this all to rest." A third finger joined the others. "Keep those things in mind."

"Some things aren't easily laid to rest," Jayla said. "That's why there are ghosts in the first place."

This wasn't working. There was no arguing against those whose faith, however weird it might be, was strong. Jo-Beth had to take another tack, be more pragmatic. Forget theory. "Well, yes, Jayla, you're right, of course," she said, nodding. "But the trouble is, none of this will help the police find the truth. All the paranormal talk might even be counterproductive in finding out what really happened on those nights." Jo-Beth managed to keep her voice even, though the concerned-for-everyone face she'd forced into place felt like the mask it was.

"I saw her again," Sosi admitted. "Today."

Oh. Jesus.

Jayla gasped, her splayed hand flying to her ample chest.

"Oh, my God," Annette whispered. "Really? *Today?*"

"Now wait," Jo-Beth said. "You didn't." This *couldn't* be happening.

"It was earlier this afternoon, I went to the park and looked across the beach toward the old camp and there was a woman in white on the ridge again, on the path we all used to climb down to the beach."

"An angel," Jayla whispered. "I told you," she said to Jo-Beth. "They're everywhere."

Jo-Beth felt a trickle of sweat run down her neck. "Okay. But—"

"Hey!" Reva cut in loudly. Somehow she'd come up with yet another drink, her fingers wrapped around a tiny bottle of vodka. "K-I-S-S, I say." She poured it into a plastic glass left by the coffeemaker, then added a can of V8 juice from the small refrigerator. "Keep it simple, stupid," she added as she dropped the empty can and bottle into a waste basket, then lifted her concoction to her lips. Jo-Beth shuddered. Reva, despite her efforts, wasn't helping convince the women.

Bernadette, the would-be purveyor of truth, was beginning to appear agitated. She said,

"What if Annette and Sosi saw Elle, not her ghost, but the real woman?"

"Today?" Jo-Beth nearly laughed. "After all this time?"

"Other people have seen her." Sosi was insistent.

"And when we all just happened to be here?" Reva asked, rolling her eyes and taking another swallow.

"That's right." Sosi was getting bristly. "After I got back to the hotel I Googled it—'ghosts' and 'Camp Horseshoe' and 'Eleanor Brady' on my iPad. Annette and I aren't the only ones who've see her. There have been others who have described a ghostly figure in white around the same area and people assume it's Elle's spirit."

"Someone followed me today, in the car while I was driving, and I know it sounds crazy, but the driver looked like Elle," Bernadette said.

"Last I heard, ghosts don't drive," Reva said.

Bernadette shot back, "I'm not saying it was a ghost, I'm just saying what I saw, okay?"

"I believe you," Nell said earnestly, looking from Sosi to Bernadette and back again.

Great. Jo-Beth was out of options and she was so damned hot! She walked to the French doors, unlatched them, and cracked one so that cold air could seep into the room. "Fine," she said. "Tell the police about 'Elle's ghost' "—she actually used finger quotes to make the point that Sosi's story was silly—"if you think it will help." She was done with these idiots. What were they thinking? But she'd seen it over and over again in her lifetime. *No good deed goes unpunished.* "I was just trying to make it easier for all of us, so we could do our civic duty and go home to our families."

"Wait a sec," Bernadette cut in, and Jo-Beth felt the skin on the back of her neck tighten. "I think we should put all our cards on the table."

What was this?

Bernadette looked around the small room. "Some of you may not have known that Monica was pregnant at the time she went missing. She told me about it, a week or so before she went missing."

The other women exchanged glances.

"I didn't mention it to the police at the time because Monica swore me to secrecy, and I really believed that she would show up again. Then we were all hustled out of the camp, Monica was never found, and in the chaos, and because I wanted to push this behind me, I never told the police. I used the excuse to myself that I didn't want to break that confidence and, truthfully, because I was scared, I didn't want to bring up something I couldn't back up." She looked from one woman to the next. "It was a mistake. The police need to know everything from pregnancies to sightings. Let them sort out the fact from fiction, but we have to give them every bit of information we have so they can solve the case."

Bernadette, damn her, had everyone's undivided attention. The room went so silent, you could have heard a pin, or maybe a cotton ball drop.

"At least one woman is dead," she went on. "And we all know that the body that was discovered on the beach could very well be either Monica or Elle." She glanced at Jo-Beth. "You're right. We have to tell the truth. All of it. What we think, what we saw or overheard, it matters."

Sosi said, "Okay. I saw Tyler alone with Monica—not doing anything really, but walking with her, and I didn't think a lot about it at the time, but they were . . . you know, into each other. Like people in love are. They don't notice anyone but the one they love." Her gaze flicked to Nell for just a second, then quickly away.

Jo-Beth's throat constricted.

"I saw Tyler and Monica, too," Jayla said, moving her head in agreement as she remembered. "You know, at the time I thought it was weird. They were really close together, like maybe they'd been hugging or kissing, I wasn't sure."

Jo-Beth wanted the floor to swallow her.

Jayla was gathering steam. "I was just coming out of Columbia Hall, I remember it was a really hot day and I came around the corner to the back of the building and they were together, holding each other. Tyler's shirt was off and Monica had her arms around his neck, but she saw me and pushed him away. Real fast. It was kind of guilty-like, y'know?"

Jo-Beth wanted to deny it, even to this day, because her pride had been so battered at the time. She felt Bernadette's eyes on her—the weight of all of the women's gazes on her. "Did you know she was pregnant?" Bernadette asked. "You were supposedly going with him."

Jo-Beth felt her fingers curl into fists but managed to straighten them. "I don't know it now," she hedged.

"You think I would lie about this?" Bernadette was coldly serious.

"I think *she* would."

"Monica? Why?" Bernadette wasn't letting this go. "*She* seemed convinced. I asked about it and she didn't say she took a test or anything, I mean, there probably weren't any at the camp, but she definitely told me she was pregnant and then before I could talk to her again, she . . . she was gone."

"But you never told this to the police, right?" Jo-Beth said. It would be better to discredit Bernadette now as best she could. "Because you were keeping her secret."

"That's right and it was a mistake. So now it's way past time to come clean with everything," Bernadette said. "And about this meeting that you called, I can't help but wonder why. It's almost like you're afraid that someone will say something wrong, that you're covering your ass. You showed up to the meeting in the cavern late, because you had cramps? And, Reva"—she turned to look at the other girl, who was fishing in the minibar again—"you came in late, too."

Reva let the door to the refrigerator close. "I need a cigarette," she said suddenly. She snagged her purse and phone from the credenza where a tiny flat-screen was mounted and made her way to the balcony. A blast of cold air seeped into the room as the door opened wide for a second.

Jo-Beth watched as she lit up, her image visible through the sheers, the tip of her cigarette a red dot in the night as she huddled under the overhang of the roof. Suddenly Jo-Beth wished she, too, could escape. And God, what she wouldn't do for a deep lungful of smoke, though she'd given up the habit ten years earlier. Her nerves were shot and she could use a strong hit of nicotine. It didn't help that Nell suddenly was on her feet and in Jo-Beth's face. "What the hell is this all about, Jo-Beth? Why did you call us here to make sure we'd tell the police what you wanted?" Nell hadn't been a part of the deception, had supposedly only learned what had happened the day after the meeting at the grotto, but Jo-Beth knew better. She'd overheard a conversation suggesting Nell, too, had abandoned her charges and sneaked to the cavern that night to listen in. That's why she, too, had been invited. And now she was suspicious. "Do you know what happened to Monica O'Neal? To Elle?"

"I wish I did," Jo-Beth said.

"But you were supposedly almost engaged to Tyler." Nell scowled. "You knew each other from high school. If Monica was pregnant with his kid—"

"But I didn't know it. I still don't," Jo-Beth said. "And neither do you. For all any of us knows, Monica could have been lying or mistaken."

"Why?"

"Because . . . I don't know, maybe she wanted Tyler, intended to trap him. She didn't make it a secret that her home life was crap. Drunk of a father, whacked-out mom."

"That's sick." Nell took a step back.

"Much as I hate to say it, because she did disappear, Monica O'Neal wasn't a very nice person. We all know that. No one here really liked her." She swung her gaze around the room, challenging each woman in turn.

Bernadette said, "It doesn't matter who felt what about her. The thing is, she vanished and maybe because of foul play, we don't really know. The police need to know the truth because they need it to find out what really happened."

"Oh, God," Jo-Beth whispered, understanding. "You already told Lucas Dalton about this supposed pregnancy, didn't you?" Jo-Beth had to fight the rage that threatened to consume her.

"That, too, but I'm with Nell. I can't help but wonder why you think you have to tell everyone here what to say. Why is that?"

"I was just trying to make things simple. I thought we could all get this behind us and go home to our normal lives, if we all just kept our statements to the bare bones of the truth," she said. "I was trying to streamline the process, that's all. For everyone."

Bernadette's eyes challenged her, silently accused her of lying.

"But hey," Jo-Beth said, "I guess I made a mistake. Maybe Bernadette's right, we should just all go on our own memories of that night, even though it was twenty years ago, and we can bring up ghosts and possible pregnancies and admit that we were out smoking weed or drinking or having sex while we left the campers to fend for themselves."

"I think we owe it to Elle, to Monica, and to ourselves to tell everything," Bernadette said, picking up her jacket and heading for the door to the hall. "That's what I'm going to do."

Great.

"Then go ahead. Do it. Be some kind of hero," Jo-Beth said, "And don't forget the ghost of Elle Brady motoring around Averille." But Jayla and Sosi were nodding, and Jo Beth knew she'd lost them. Annette was already out the door after her sister, the others following.

Reva returned from the balcony, the scent of cigarette smoke still clinging to her. Surveying the nearly empty suite, she shut the door. "How'd it turn out?"

"A disaster."

"Idiots," Reva said, stuffing her cell phone and pack of cigarettes into a front pocket of her purse. "You did what you could."

"I guess."

"Anything else?"

"No."

Reva made her way to the door. "It is what it is."

"You gonna be okay, with the Dobbs thing?"

"I hope so."

"What happened exactly?"

"I think she thinks I lied about the accident, that maybe Theo wasn't driving, that I was behind the wheel when it happened." She thought for a second, then reached for the handle of the door. "I'll see you in the morning." And then she was gone. Jo-Beth was alone. All of her well-thought plans laid to waste. Well, screw 'em. She'd tried to help.

Kicking off her boots, she flopped onto the king-sized bed and leaned up against the stacked pillows. She'd just pulled out her iPad, fired it up, and was checking her e-mail when her cell phone, tucked into her back pocket, vibrated.

Expecting a message from Reva that she'd lost her key or something, she checked the screen.

The text wasn't from Reva.

Tyler Quade's name came across the screen and she couldn't help the little uptick in her pulse as she read the message.

Made it to bumblefuck. Hate this place.

In room 216.

Drink?

She thought of the disaster of the meeting with the women, and of the catastrophe of her marriage and the debacle that was certainly about to be her career. Nothing was going right for her. Nothing. So why not meet an old friend? Even if, after nearly twenty years, she was still slightly pissed at him. It was just for a drink, right? She'd meet him, have a drink and a laugh, stiff him for the bill, and if he made any moves on her, give him the cold shoulder. Maybe even play with him a bit. Flirt, make him think she was into him, that he had a chance, then dump his ass.

He deserved it.

She didn't have to think twice.

But she couldn't take the chance of being seen with him, she was still married, unfortunately. And she didn't want to complicate things any more than they were already with the sheriff's department or her damned job. She couldn't afford to be involved in any more of a scandal than she already was.

How about my room? 302. Be careful. Bring booze. Take back stairs. Don't let any cameras see you.

Maybe I should wear a disguise.

Oooh. Kinky.

Could be.

She felt a little thrill and then reminded herself that she was still legally married. What a drag. Then again, Eric was off to who-knows-where doing who-knows-what with who-knows-whom. Maybe he was in Big Sur or driving his old bus through Colorado or Utah, off to find the Four Corners and discover the meaning of life or whatever.

What a load of crap.

Eric was in the wind.

Tyler, however, was here in damned Averille, Oregon.

On his way up to her room.

A slow smile curved across her lips and she checked her hair and makeup quickly in the poor excuse of a bathroom—God, the lighting was awful.

Then?

She waited. Nerves strung tight, anticipation causing her heart to race and her palms to sweat, she waited.

Chapter 31

Averille, Oregon
Now
Lucas

Lucas was driving home as the dreary day was quickly turning to night. He replayed the day over and over in his mind, meeting with Bernadette at the camp, then the meeting at the office where he'd been kicked off the case.

After being dismissed by the sheriff, Lucas had had to fight his first instinct, which was to drive to the hotel and find Bernadette and tell her about the body being identified as Monica O'Neal. She'd been honest with him and he wanted to return the favor.

Oh, sure, Dalton. You just want to see her again.

The voice in his head was right, he thought, as he drove on 101, heading for his cabin in the hills. Seeing Bernadette again had kick-started all those heightened emotions of his youth and he didn't want to go there. Couldn't. So he'd headed to his cabin instead.

They'd been kids, high on life, love, and lust.

Now, though, they were adults.

And he was a cop, even if he wasn't working the O'Neal case. At least not officially, but he'd still investigate. Hell, he couldn't just let it go. No way. But no one at the department needed to know that.

He drove by rote to the ten acres he'd owned for the past five years. Located in the hills on the east side of 101, the property offered a peekaboo view of the ocean. After turning off 101, he picked up his phone, found Bernadette's number, and called her.

She answered before the phone rang a second time. "Lucas? Hi." So she either recognized his number or had programmed it into her phone.

"Hey," he said, and decided there was no time for small talk as the afternoon shuttered into evening. "How are you?"

"Fine. Just got out of a meeting with the other women."

"And?"

"And everyone's ready to come into the department tomorrow and tell their stories. Jo-Beth wanted everyone to stick to a script. Which wasn't a lie, of course, but—I don't know. I think she either has something she's hiding or is the ultimate control freak. Maybe both."

"I'd love to interview her," he said, negotiating a sharp corner, the beams of his headlights washing over the rocky wall of the cliffs rising from the sea. "There's something else I wanted you to hear from me," he said as the turnoff to his place came into view.

"What?" Her tone was suddenly wary.

"The skull's been ID'ed. It's Monica O'Neal."

He heard a sharp intake of breath. "No."

"Yeah."

"Oh . . . God . . . I mean, I know it's to be expected, but still . . . Oh, God."

"Look, I probably shouldn't have called you; I jumped the gun a bit, but a couple of deputies are giving Monica's mother the bad news, so the story will break within the hour. I wanted you to know."

"Thanks."

"Well, you did give me some information about Monica and the pregnancy, so it's only fair."

"I guess." He heard a hesitation in her voice.

"Thanks."

"Lucas!" she said quickly, as if she expected him to hang up.

"Yeah?" His fingers tightened over the wheel.

"It was . . . It was good to see you today."

So there it was. He nodded, as if she could see him, and hit the low beam of his headlights as an oncoming car approached. "Maybe when this is all over we could get a drink or a cup of coffee?"

More hesitation, the seconds ticking by.

"Bernadette, you still there?" he asked as he turned off 101 and onto the county road leading to his house.

"Yeah, I'm here. And sure, I think that would be okay, getting together, I mean," she said, which wasn't exactly a ringing endorsement of the idea, but he'd go along with it.

"Good." Negotiating the ess curves in the slick road, he said, "There's something else you should know: I'm officially off the case."

"What? No!"

"The sheriff thinks there's a conflict of interest, so she threw me off, the same for Ryan Tremaine, who's a local assistant DA."

"Can she do that?"

"Legally? For me? Yeah. I don't know about Tremaine, but he's a lawyer, so he'll figure it out."

As he drove over a familiar rise he saw the turnout to his house appearing in the twin beams of his headlights. Easing onto the brakes, he thought about telling her about the scrap of cloth and Caleb Carter thinking he spied Elle, but held his tongue. Until the fabric was analyzed, until it was connected to the case, he wouldn't say a word.

There were just too many damned things he wanted to tell her and most of them he should keep to himself. "Okay, gotta run," he said, and heard her say, "Yeah, me too." Then he clicked off and turned onto the gravel lane.

Lucas thought about the case that was no longer his and the woman who, too, was no longer his, a woman who still, unfortunately, caught his eye, and if one kiss were telling, could still turn him inside out.

"Don't go there," he warned. He couldn't be distracted by Bernadette, or anyone else.

Besides, he had work to do, with or without the sheriff's blessing.

No one in the department knew what had gone down at Camp Horseshoe twenty years ago more intimately than he did. Not even Ryan Tremaine. As far as conflict of interest went? To hell with it. He, as much as anyone, needed to find out what had happened to Elle, Monica, Dustin Peters, and Waldo Grimes.

He pulled into his carport and hopped out to be greeted by his dog. Roscoe had been waiting on the front porch and jumped near the Jeep as Lucas stepped onto the concrete. "Hey, boy, slow down. Yeah, I missed you, too," he said, petting the squirming mass of fur as the dog gave off a couple of excited yips. "I know. I know. Now, come on, we've got work to do." The dog raced ahead and was bouncing as Lucas unlocked the door and dropped his laptop case and wallet on a table near the kitchen, then walked through the house to the back door. Roscoe trotted expectantly to the hooks near the back door in the kitchen where several leashes dangled. "I don't think we need those today." He opened the door and Roscoe took off like a shot, scaring up birds and bounding through the wet grass. As Lucas whistled to the horses, Roscoe returned with that boundless energy and enthusiasm reserved for dogs. Lucas scratched him behind the ears, as the two geldings trotted into the paddock near the barn. "Hungry?" he said to them and the bay tossed his head, jangling his halter and snorting while the older sorrel gave Lucas a stony look that Lucas interpreted as, "What do you think?"

"Well, let's go." Dog in tow, Lucas made his way inside the barn as the horses ambled in through a separate entrance.

He snapped on the lights as the familiar smells of oiled leather, horses, and dry hay reached his nostrils. While Roscoe snooped around the tack area beneath the bridles hung from hooks and saddles mounted over sawhorses, Lucas scooped out measures of oats and spread hay into the mangers.

He'd done the same chores most of his life and still felt a sense of satisfaction, listening to the geldings' teeth grinding, smelling the rain on their coats. Even the odors of wet horse, urine, and dust were familiar and somehow calming. Leaning on his pitchfork, he watched the animals, patted their long noses, and eventually left them to throw a ball for Roscoe for twenty minutes in the darkness.

All the while he thought.

About the case.

About Monica and Elle.

About Dusty, the loner of a hired hand, and

Grimes, the murderer who might have stalked the woods surrounding Camp Horseshoe twenty years ago.

Other than the camp, how were the four of them connected?

And had whoever nearly killed Tyler Quade also murdered Monica and possibly the rest of them? Why those five? Random? Or some deeper connection? Or, possibly, remotely, no connection at all?

Now, finally with the discovery of Monica O'Neal's body, the search for more corpses ongoing, and the investigation ramped up again, maybe there would be answers.

"Come on," he finally said to the dog, "it's your turn." He led Roscoe inside and fed him, his bowls always at the ready in an alcove that had once been a walk-in pantry near the back door, the only closet of any size in this hundred-year-old cabin. The layout was simple, a rustic bathroom, kitchen out of the forties, one bedroom, and over the living area, a small loft he used as an office. A wood stove was the original heat for the place, but he'd added a small furnace after his first bone-chilling winter in the place. Now, he grabbed a beer from the refrigerator and twisted off the cap.

His stomach rumbled and he opened the refrigerator, saw the box with remnants of a pizza he'd picked up two nights before, heated a couple of slices, and carried a plate of pizza and a bottle of beer to the loft. Roscoe, having mown through his cup of dog food, was right on his heels and took up his position near the desk as Lucas fired up his computer. As it clicked on he bit into the pizza and washed the first slice down with a long swallow of the beer.

Then he pulled up the files for the missing persons, reread statements, and went over evidence, all of which he'd pulled together over the years while the cases of the four individuals went colder and colder. He typed in the information he'd gotten today at the meeting and as he finished his beer and the so-so pepperoni pizza, remembered that night. So Monica had been pregnant and was meeting Tyler. On the night after Elle had gone missing, the night that he'd broken up with her, Monica hadn't shown up, had maybe been abducted on the way, or something, and Tyler had ended up with a knife in his back, managing to walk nearly a quarter of a mile, bleeding, the blade lodged between his ribs.

If Waldo Grimes had been around, no one reported seeing him.

Lucas leaned back in his chair, ignoring the screen, thinking back. Roscoe whined and Lucas dropped a hand, letting the dog lick off the remnants of the pizza from his fingers.

All of the girls were each other's alibis. They all were together for most of the night, huddled in the cavern, with the exception of Nell, who they claimed they'd left at the cabins so that one counselor had remained on duty, though that, according to her statement, was a bunch of bull. She, too, had gone down to the cavern, leaving Naomi as the only adult in charge.

At the thought of his ex-stepmother, he paused. She claimed she'd been at the cabins all night long, tending to the children, but she wasn't sharing a bed with her husband and she, too, could have been a part of this . . . but what? He couldn't quite put that together, but it bothered him. Though she'd sworn to be dutifully in the girls' camp, no one could prove it.

Or maybe he was making too much of it because of his own past with her.

Frowning, he thought about the female counselors again. They all agreed that Reva Mercado had come into the grotto later than planned, and Jo-Beth Chancellor had shown up even later. Jo-Beth had explained away her tardiness to the very meeting she'd called because she supposedly had menstrual cramps.

Maybe.

What if she and Reva were involved in something else? What if the damned meeting was to provide an alibi?

But for what?

A murder?

An attack?

A prank gone wrong?

If Jo-Beth had found out that Tyler was screwing around on her, knocking up another woman, would she go as far as to kill Monica and, with Reva's help, dispose of the body? Nowhere in the statements of the counselors was there any evidence of blood on either Reva or Jo-Beth.

No, the person who was covered in blood was the man with the knife in his back. Could he and Monica have fought, struggled, and she plunged the butcher knife into his back in a fit of passion?

Or had someone else been involved? A third, or even maybe a fourth player?

He felt that he was missing something.

Realizing the dog was still licking his fingers, he said, "Enough, okay? I'd like to keep my skin if it's all the same to you." Then he climbed to his feet and took the empty bottle, plate, and fork downstairs, where he dumped them all into the sink. He'd spent too many hours staring at the computer, rereading information he knew by heart. Now they had a body, the corpse of one of the missing four individuals. And most of the people involved were here, in Averille.

He couldn't just sit around, he needed to act.

What was it Maggie had said when she'd interviewed him?

Start with Eleanor Brady.

Why not? Maybe Elle was the logical place to begin, a spot he'd ignored due to his own involvement. Maybe he should check with her mother, Jeannette Brady.

"You're in charge," he said to the shepherd, who followed him to the door. "Not this time, buddy, okay? I'll be back soon." That statement could have been a lie, but he didn't need the dog to pile any guilt his way. He was able to do that well enough by himself.

The night was thick, rain having stopped, but moisture was heavy in the air. He backed out of the carport and with a quick glance in his rearview saw the silhouette of his dog's head in the light of the window. If only people were as loyal as dogs, he thought, then maneuvered through the trees, his headlights illuminating the dual ruts of his lane. Just as he reached the county road, his phone chirped and Leah's name appeared on the screen.

"Hey, shortcakes," he said, calling up a nickname he'd given her in her youth, one he hadn't used in years.

"Brother dear," she responded in kind, then became serious. "Hey, look, I just saw on the news that the body has been ID'ed. So it's really Monica O'Neal?"

"Yes."

"Wow . . ." She cleared her throat. "I mean, I knew she was probably dead, that they all were, or they would have shown up by now, right? But . . . it's still kind of surreal. I guess . . .

I guess I was holding out some kind of hope."

"I know. Kind of a sucker punch."

"Exactly. It makes me feel weird."

He frowned. "Need me to come over?" Ever since her boyfriend, a musician with dreadlocks and several tattoos and the inability to hold a job, had moved out, she'd lived alone in a small apartment in the heart of Averille. Lucas hadn't minded the hair or tattoos, in fact he'd admired the one on Craig's shoulder, but the not working and Craig's disinterest in holding a job longer than it took to start collecting unemployment, over and over again, that really bothered him. Lucas thought Leah could do better. As it turned out, she'd come to the same conclusion all on her own and had sent Craig, his tattoos, guitar, and probably whatever stash of weed he'd had at the time packing.

"Nah, I'm fine," she said, but she definitely didn't sound like it.

"What's up?" He flipped his lights on bright, illuminating more of the road. Though the rain had stopped, the asphalt still shimmered in the glare of the Jeep's headlights.

"I know this is a long shot, but have you seen Mom?"

"Naomi?" he clarified, frowning.

"I only have one," she pointed out.

He eased off the gas as he came to the intersection of the county road with 101, and after a quick "California stop," seeing no one approaching, made the turn. "Give Jeremiah time, he never goes long without a bride."

"Ha, ha. Not funny. Just listen, okay? The deal is, I've been calling her all afternoon and she hasn't answered."

"Well, she . . . wouldn't be with me."

Leah let out an audible breath. "I *know*."

"And she wouldn't tell me what she's doing. Wouldn't give me an update on her plans. Leah, I haven't talked to her in . . . God, maybe years."

"Yeah, yeah, I get it, 'no love lost' and all that, but I've called around. David and Ryan haven't heard from her, and so she's kind of MIA, I guess."

"How long?" he asked as a car came up quick behind him, too quick.

"I talked to her this morning. Around ten. She was going shopping and meeting someone for lunch—she didn't say who—and then she said she'd check in with me later. So far, she hasn't."

He negotiated a turn, clicked his lights to dim as the car, a truck it turned out, sped around him, fishtailing a little as the driver had to pull in front of the Jeep quickly because of an oncoming car coming over a rise.

Lucas hit his brakes, the Jeep sliding just a bit, his heart thudding. "Shit."

"Hey—are you okay?"

"No thanks to the asshole who just passed me

on a hill." He slammed a fist onto his steering wheel. "I should pull him over."

"You should calm down. Road rage isn't good for anyone."

He snorted. "You were saying, what? Naomi's not returning your calls?"

"Yeah."

"It's early." Leah, by nature, was kind of a worrywart.

"After seven. And neither Ryan or David have heard from her."

"I didn't think they got along with her. They seem more interested in Dad."

"She's their mother! Dad's not even related to them."

"Sometimes that doesn't mean much."

"It does to me."

"I know, I know. But your brothers—"

"Are all a bunch of dicks. Including you," she said vehemently, her temper finally showing.

"Can't argue that."

"I hate you," she grumbled, and he laughed, knowing she was kidding.

"Sure you do. Every time you don't get your way."

"I just want to talk to Mom. She's going to be upset when she hears that the body belongs to Monica."

That much was true.

"Well, kiddo, you're barking up the wrong tree.

I have no idea where she is, and I'm pretty sure I'd be the last person she would call."

"But you're a cop."

"Still. She would still call Ryan if she wanted information."

"He's not a cop."

"So what're you asking? You want me to put out a BOLO for her?"

"A what?"

"Be On the Lookout," he explained. "But I think we should wait a bit on that."

"I wasn't talking about something so official, but thought, I don't know, that you could do something!"

"Hang tough. Naomi can take care of herself."

"It's just not like her."

"She'll be fine," he said.

"A lot of help you've been!" She clicked off in disgust just as he found another side road leading into the hills, a narrow lane that he turned onto. Two miles inland, he spied the bashed-in mailbox without a name on it. Just the address, hard to read as the box had been hammered and re-hammered into shape after being the target of rocks or beer bottles over the years. But he knew this was where Elle's mother, Jeanette Brady, now a widow, still lived. She'd spent all of her married life in the little bungalow and, after her husband's passing, hadn't moved. She and Darryl had stayed in the home even after their daughter had gone missing and along with law enforce-ment and the press, the curious hadn't given them a rest.

Steadfastly, the Bradys had remained in their home despite any scandal. Eventually interest in the case and their family had waned, and an insurance policy on Elle had finally been paid, though the stress had taken its toll. Elle's father died a few years back from a heart attack, he believed.

As he turned into the drive and the little, shingled house came into view in the beam of his headlights, he felt an unexplained sense that caused the hairs on the back of his neck to raise. Just like the night when Monica O'Neal had gone missing, he had the feeling that something was off, a sense that something was about to happen.

And it wasn't going to be good.

Chapter 32

Averille, Oregon
Now
Maggie

Maggie Dobbs's dining room was a disaster area. Though she was usually neat, her work at the office kept in even stacks that would make even the most OCD patient appear untidy, when she worked at her condo, things got messy. Real messy. The TV in the attached living area was turned on, volume low, the screen giving off a flickering light. As she worked, she checked the television every so often.

She'd sorted the statements, not alphabetically, but in groups: Counselors. The Brady family. The O'Neal family. Workers other than counselors. The Dalton family. Then she'd figured out where the groups had intersected and how, if at all, they were related.

So far, she thought, seated at the table, the overhead light fixture casting a warm glow over the reports, statements, files, and notes scattered over the faded walnut finish, she hadn't caught a glimmer of anything that would help her. She shoved her computer glasses onto her head and rubbed her eyes. She was getting nowhere fast. Her white cat was lying on the counter separating kitchen and dining room, a spot he loved and was usually taboo. Tonight, Maggie didn't want to fight with him. She muttered a quick, "Get down, Mr. Bones," but he ignored her, staring at her with his gold eyes, his legs tucked under his body, his long tail with its one black spot twitching slightly. "Fine. Suit yourself." Picking up the half-drunk cup of tea from a cleared spot on the table, she took a sip and realized the tea had grown cold. Not that she cared. She was too wrapped up in the case.

Cracking her neck, she considered the victims.

In the case of Monica O'Neal, the only connection to the others was that she'd been a counselor. Monica hadn't been friends with anyone before she showed up at the camp and no one had seemed to like her much. Though her file was large, it was mainly because of the "information" and "tips" her mother, Meredith, had left over the years. She'd had no boyfriend, but she was obviously involved with Tyler Quade as he'd admitted, and she'd come to see him on the night she disappeared, the night he'd nearly been killed by the very knife that had gone missing from the camp's kitchen. So Monica was loosely associated with the other counselors, the girls in her cabin, and some of the workers, as well as more intimately with Tyler Quade.

On the other hand, Eleanor Brady had several connections. Her father had been an elder in the church where her boyfriend Lucas Dalton's father had been the preacher. "Elle," as she was called, had spent a lot of time with the Dalton family, and like her father she was a member of the church. She was a counselor at the camp but knew Lucas and his stepbrothers, Ryan and David, as they all had attended the same schools, though not all at the same time. Elle, having grown up near Averille, had known people in the town, whereas Monica hadn't. And Elle, according to the other counselors, had been liked while Monica hadn't been.

The two missing girls didn't have much in common.

Except Camp Horseshoe.

And their files were very different. Monica's was much thicker, mainly due to Meredith O'Neal's constant phone calls and "tips" that the officers had diligently checked out over the years, though none had panned out.

Elle's family, on the other hand, had been quiet and reclusive. Their daughter's disappearance had affected them profoundly and they'd pulled ranks. Her father, a millwright, had retired early and her mother had been a homemaker. They broke off with the Dalton family, including Jeremiah's church, and belonged to another small sect twenty miles away. Odd how their response was the direct opposite of the O'Neal family's. While the O'Neals were vocal and always calling the department, taking interviews with the press and, while Monica's father was alive, organizing search parties, the Bradys had drawn in on themselves and had been hardly seen. They'd accepted their daughter's unknown fate calling it . . . what? God's will?

Maggie fished out the interview with Darryl Brady and flipped through the pages. There was a tape of the interview as well, but she found the quote, "It's hard for her mother and me, but we believe in God's will that He will care for Eleanor and if He's seen fit to call her home, then so be it."

"Really?" She read the quote aloud and looked at the cat. "That's a little weird, right?" Flipping through a few more of the old pages, she found a similar statement by Eleanor's mother, Jeanette, and read the quote. "Who am I to question the Father?" she'd said when asked about her daughter's disappearance. "I know that He will take care of her and she'll come home to us, or God will protect her." Maggie shook her head. "I don't think so," she said aloud, and knew that if she had a missing daughter, or son for that matter, she would move heaven and earth to find that kid. She wouldn't be counting on God to step in.

Now, of course, Darryl was gone, felled by a heart attack, but his wife had continued to be reclusive.

Maggie tapped her pencil on the table and thought, the wheels turning in her mind. Even though the partial body recently discovered had turned out to belong to Monica O'Neal, she needed to talk to Jeanette Brady again. After all, it was the ghost of Elle that people had reported seeing. Not that of Monica O'Neal. Maggie riffled through the papers, the reports of people who had thought they'd seen Elle. Quite a few in the beginning and then sporadically over the years until now when Caleb Carter was certain he'd seen Elle or her ghost earlier today.

But no one had ever reported seeing a woman who looked like Monica O'Neal.

"What's that all about?" she asked Mr. Bones, and got no reaction.

Not coming up with an answer, she mentally threw Dustin Peters and Waldo Grimes into the mix. Dustin Peters was loosely tied to the camp. Only there for a summer, to work, then disappear. As for Waldo Grimes? Who knew if the convict was even ever close to the area of the camp?

So why would all four of them disappear in the same damned week?

What fate had they all suffered?

It seemed to make sense that they had all been caught in the same mysterious trap, but maybe that theory was wrong. "Damn it all to hell," she muttered, pushing her hair out of her eyes. She wanted to solve this case so badly she could taste it, but wondered if it were possible after all this time. She glanced at the television again and saw that the news was on, so she found the remote under a loose stack of papers and clicked the volume up, then ran the DVR back to the beginning of the segment where anchors were discussing the identification of Monica O'Neal as a victim of the crime.

Pictures of O'Neal were shown; then the television screen split in half. On one side a serious-looking female news anchor sat at a broad desk, a fake scene of Portland at night in the background. On the other half of the screen, a clean-shaven male reporter stood outside, wearing a red jacket with the station's logo emblazoned upon it. Hatless in the wind and rain, he was positioned so that the gates of Camp Horseshoe were in the background.

". . . and this is what remains of a Christian summer camp, Camp Horseshoe, where Monica O'Neal was a counselor and disappeared along with several others in a case that started twenty years ago and has, over the years, gone cold," the reporter was saying. "Today, investigators identified bones found in a cavern below Cape Horseshoe and the beach stretching from the cape to this property as belonging to Monica O'Neal." He gave out basic information about the case, all fed by the Public Information Officer from the department, just as the sheriff had indicated. As he continued his report, pictures of the beach where the bones had been located and the cavern beneath the cape were flashed onto the screen.

There was more speculation by the anchor as the reporter signed off; then the image of the Public Information Officer for Neahkahnie County making a statement on the steps of the sheriff's department filled the screen. Finally, short footage of a thin woman with a reddened face and curly brown hair streaked with silver appeared.

Meredith O'Neal. Monica's mother. Dabbing at her eyes, which were covered with dark glasses, though there wasn't much sunlight, and holding her chin up as she tried not to fall apart, she answered a reporter's questions.

". . . Closure?" she whispered, sniffing loudly. "No, I don't feel any closure. What has just happened is that all hope that my daughter was still alive is gone and . . . and . . . there are still so many questions that need to be answered about what happened to my dear, sweet Monica. . . ." Her voice cracked and she turned into the waiting arms of a barrel-chested man, her live-in boyfriend, Ray Smith. Beefy arms folded around her and through his own photo-gray lenses, Smith said, "We're done here," then rotated Meredith in his arms and led her into a double-wide modular home, his thin gray ponytail visible against the back of his camouflage jacket.

"Damn," Maggie said, feeling for the woman. Somehow she, now that she was the detective in charge, had to solve this crime, whatever it came down to. She thought so hard her head began to pound, so she scooted back her chair, went into the kitchen, and downed a glass of water.

Once seated at the table again, she called the lab. She'd delivered Lucas's scrap of fabric to a tech there less than three hours earlier, but he'd said he'd get right on it. Yet he hadn't called. On the third ring, he answered. "It's Dobbs," she said.

"Oh, I was just about to call you."

"And?"

"First off, let's start with the skeleton."

"The body? Okay. You found something?"

"The nicks on the bones we found, the ones we're still trying to connect with Monica O'Neal? We can say with some certainty that they did *not* come from the knife that was embedded in Tyler Quade, the butcher knife that was missing from the kitchen. That knife was sharp as a fillet knife. The cuts on the bones were made by a different blade, most likely a smaller weapon."

"Hmmm. And that's confirmed as the blood on the butcher knife was only Quade's? Did you check the blood on the knife that was embedded in Quade's back? To see if it matched Monica O'Neal?" A second knife?

"That's the thing. There was a screwup either at the hospital or in transport of the weapon to the lab. There was no blood on it when we got it twenty years ago. Of course that hasn't changed with the passage of time."

"But how could that have happened?"

"Someone wiped it clean. Either a mistake, an accident, or because they wanted to hide something." As they talked Maggie was going through the old notes, flipping through reports, finding the report on the knife and the attack on Tyler Quade, and there it was in black and white—no blood on the knife. She'd never noticed that notation before. It hadn't seemed significant.

Now, it seemed crucial.

Why would the blade be wiped clean? A mistake?

She was more than disappointed. And she was suspicious. Who had wiped the knife clean? Why? She wasn't buying the possibility of it being a mistake. Nope, that just didn't feel right. And yet the weapons were different. Whoever attacked Quade had left the knife in his body and then taken off after Monica O'Neal. Or killed her first, before Quade.

"What about the scrap of fabric that I sent over? The one with the stain?"

"Yeah, it's blood. Verified. I won't have a type until tomorrow."

"Is it human?"

"Don't know. Again, tomorrow. And that's pushing it."

"Okay. Thanks."

She clicked off and tossed the phone onto the table. Something was very wrong here, something deeper than she'd first imagined. The too-clean knife was the clue. But what was it? A cover-up? By whom? She wondered what, if anything, Tyler Quade would say about it. Did he even know? He'd been in the hospital overnight, so the weapon used to attack him would be out of his control. But not so the doctors, or anyone who worked at the hospital . . . or someone in the police department. That last thought stopped her cold. Surely not. But the officer in charge was long gone, and no one currently at the department including the sheriff had been on staff during the time when Monica O'Neal went missing and Tyler Quade was attacked.

The only person now employed by the sheriff's department who had been a part of the investigation was Lucas Dalton, her partner. The last person to see Eleanor Brady alive, a kid who had threatened to kill Dustin Peters.

"Huh." She trusted Lucas, didn't think him capable of anything brushing this kind of violence, but what did she know about him as a younger man? She chewed on the end of her pencil as she thought, but she couldn't come up with any likely conclusions.

Yet.

She was banking on murder rather than an accident, and the knife certainly pointed in that direction. She thought about the other victim that night, the night Monica O'Neal had disappeared. Maggie had talked briefly to Quade on the phone and he'd agreed to an interview, at the department tomorrow, scheduled between some of the other ex-counselors. She would love to hear his version of what had happened from his mouth. She thought there were some inconsistencies in his version of what had gone down, but then she didn't trust any of the statements made by the counselors; there was just something too pat about them. As for Quade, his statement was made after he was conscious at the hospital and he stuck to his story that he was attacked at the chapel. There had been enough of his blood there to confirm the attack, and bloodstains had been found on two cushions from an old couch that had been left in the chapel, in an old cloak room. Not a lot of blood, but enough to take notice. The blood matched Tyler's and he said he'd cut himself shaving earlier in the day and had fallen asleep on the couch waiting for Monica.

Maybe.

But there had been scratches on his face that could have been from a human. She studied the pictures of Quade's injuries and the couch cushions where they'd been found, where the stain was, and it seemed unlikely that his face had been in a position to get both of the upright cushions a little bloody. That couch was long gone unfortunately, only scraps of the fabric in evidence. Too bad. Because she would have liked to have looked at it.

Tyler had been an athlete, strong and muscular. Had played football and wrestled and according to the attending physician in the ER's notes, had a high pain tolerance, hadn't needed any medication despite the fact that he'd had a knife lodged in his back. A butcher knife that hadn't hit a vital organ.

Lucky. So lucky.

For a second, a random, almost impossible thought flitted through her head. Could the wound have been self-inflicted, well, with the aid of an accomplice? Jo-Beth was late to the meeting she'd called. Could she have helped? Actually stabbed him with the precision to not kill him? But no one had reported seeing or finding any blood on her or her clothes. The blood had been mainly contained to the old chapel and then the trail Tyler had left on his mad, stumbling dash to the heart of the campus to get help.

Maybe.

But as far as Maggie could tell, the source of the weapon had to come from someone who had access to the kitchen, not that it was always locked. She studied photographs of Tyler Quade and his wounds, then reread his statement. The weird thing was that there had been no finger-prints at all on the weapon. None even from anyone who worked in the kitchen. So odd. Whoever had plunged the blade into his back had to have been wearing gloves or wiped the hilt clean. Also, he was stripped naked. That had never been explained. Why were his clothes left on one of the pews? When asked about it, he'd claimed that he wanted to surprise Monica, that they were planning to get together and have sex.

Maggie thought the excuse weak at best. Would

he really strip in anticipation of sex? What if someone else came along? Then again, Tyler had been a teenage boy at the time. Who knew what went on in their brains when it came to sex?

She found Tyler Quade's driver's license picture. He was handsome and strong-jawed, and even in the poor-quality DMV photo there was an air about him, an attitude of superiority. He was smart, too, a GPA good enough in high school for the honor roll and decent grades at Colorado State. Why did the description "arrogant prick" come to mind as she stared at his picture? Because he radiated smugness. Any other photo had the same hint of arrogance about it. Like he thought he was smarter than everyone else and could pull a fast one on them. Hadn't Lucas said the same, that he'd never much liked Quade?

And, when it all came down to the case, Tyler Quade had the motive to kill Monica O'Neal. She'd told him she was pregnant. All of his dreams would have been put at risk if he had to support a child.

Would he have really endangered his own life by murdering Monica and his unborn child? Whom could he trust with so big a secret? A friend? Jo-Beth, who was probably pissed as hell about the pregnancy? *Who?* Whoever it was, they'd kept their silence over the years . . . or disappeared themselves. Her mind spun scenarios involving Dustin Peters and even Waldo Grimes.

Whoa. Whoa. Whoa. Slow down. It's not even been proven that Monica was the victim of homicide.

"B-effin'-S," she said aloud. She felt it in her bones that Monica O'Neal had been killed, her body tossed into the ocean.

Maggie tapped her fingers on the desk and stared at the computer screen. A thought came to mind and she pushed it aside as too far-fetched. Too nuts. But this was a boy who "had a high pain threshold," a desperate kid who was a known risk taker. Who did extreme sports. Wasn't afraid of death. Considered himself invincible.

Could he have actually done this by himself? She Googled "self-inflicted knife wounds" and found a YouTube video where a young man actually demonstrated how to plunge a knife in your own back using a very sharp blade, incredible nerve, and the cushions of a couch. The knife had to be placed just so to avoid life-threatening injuries, and it had to be propped up and held fast as the "victim" actually threw his body back against the couch with enough force that the razor-sharp blade sliced through the skin, into the muscle, and wedged against a rib.

"Holy crap," she whispered, watching the video five times, four in slow motion, studying the idiot daredevil showing the Internet how to fake a stabbing. All you needed was a very sharp knife and a whole lot of nerve. She thought about

485

it; didn't like it. The idea seemed so far-fetched.

She found the pictures of the couch that had been in the chapel and eyed the cushions with the weird bloodstains, in perfect position.

Adrenaline rushed through her and she felt that singular anticipation she always experienced when she sensed she was on to something important, when she knew she was about to crack the case. Rubbing her temples, she watched the damned video one more time. "You son of a bitch," she said as if Quade could hear her.

Yeah, she was looking forward to talking to the Adonis who had gotten one girl pregnant while nearly engaged to another.

But Quade was only one of the interviewees. There were others, and they could have been part of the hoax, if there was one. All of those counselors who left their campers, to meet and collude together? Why? Who was hiding what? She thought of them all, reading the statements Detective Hallgarth had taken, deciding Jo-Beth Chancellor Leroy was the ringleader. According to all of the statements, Jo-Beth had taken charge, had called the meeting for them all to get their stories straight. Two of the girls, Sosi Gaffney and Jayla Williams, had said as much when they'd talked to the police. The others had con-firmed. And they'd lied—at least partially. Maggie could smell it. And didn't she already know that one of them, Reva Mercado, was untrustworthy? There had been that car accident that Reva blamed on her husband, claiming he was at the wheel when the kid who lost her mother swore over and over that she'd seen the driver—a woman—just before the crash. There just hadn't been enough evidence to nail Reva as she'd sworn up and down the husband had been driving.

And now this homicide. Okay, *potential* twenty-year-old homicide. Though the ME hadn't come out and said it, Maggie felt it in her gut that Monica O'Neal had been murdered. She just had to figure out who'd done it. If the killer was Tyler—and she was definitely warming to that theory—she had to prove how reckless, unstable, manipulative, and calculating he was. Otherwise, it was all just conjecture. And if he didn't spill his guts, then someone else who had known what he was up to might be able to confirm a theory that Sheriff Locklear would think was ridiculous.

And how in the world was the *potential* homicide tied to the other people who had gone missing?

Maggie needed evidence. Was it possible one or more of the counselors knew the truth and had kept it hidden all these years? But who?

"Eenie, meenie, miney, mo," she said, flipping through the dusty pages. She could only hope that someone knew something they hadn't admitted as scared teenagers; maybe Monica O'Neal's confirmed death would loosen a tongue or two.

The news on the television moved to the local weather, more rain predicted, temperatures falling, and she punched the mute button.

She was determined to solve the case.

So what if others had tried and had failed?

She knew she had a reputation in the department of going with her gut, that sometimes things just didn't seem right to her. This was one of those times.

Thankfully her headache was receding and she stretched in her chair and noticed the cat wasn't looking at her any longer, but staring past her to the sliding door that led to her patio. He was still, his tail no longer flicking. She turned, followed his gaze to the darkness outside the panes.

And saw nothing but the reflection of the dining room and her own pale visage.

Still, she reached for her service weapon, which was in her purse lying open in the chair next to hers. Slowly, holding the pistol against her side, she walked to the door. With a flip of a switch the deck and small yard of her condominium were illuminated. She saw no one lurking in the shadows.

"Liar," she said to the cat, but felt that little frisson of fear skitter down her spine, as if there were unseen eyes lurking just beyond the pale light cast by the porch lamp. Searching, she still saw nothing, not even the movement of shadow. She checked the door, found it locked, told herself that there was no one out there, no one staring in at her.

The case was getting to her, that was it. Now she was jumping at shadows. Nonetheless, she snapped the blinds shut.

Chapter 33

Averille, Oregon
Now
Lucas

"Lucas Dalton?" Jeanette Brady whispered, the screen door to her house a thin barrier between them. "What're you doing here?" A dog stood at her side, a black and white border collie, his gaze fixed on the intruder standing on the porch. He growled low in his throat and Jeanette snapped, "No! You, Oreo, you go to your bed!" The dog gave one final look at Lucas through the screen, then, tail tucked, padded to a dog bed positioned near the fireplace.

Lucas said, "I need to talk to you."

"Now?" she asked. "I was about ready to settle in to watch TV."

"It'll only take a minute."

Her eyes narrowed. "Well, all right. But make it quick." And she didn't move. She'd aged over the years, her once-blond hair now graying and lank, her skin more sallow, twenty pounds or so added to her figure.

"Can I come in?"

"Well . . . I suppose." She was flustered, her fingers fumbling as she undid the simple lock on the screen. "I assume this has something to do with Monica O'Neal. I just saw on the news that it's her body that was found."

Standing like a soldier, she held the door open for him. He stepped inside and was transported to a time two decades earlier. The furniture hadn't changed, just become more dingy and scarred, an Early American motif with maple tables and chairs in earth tones and floral prints, antique vases with fake roses and daisies, splashes of white in a dingy room of earth tones of rust and avocado green and gold. Darryl's picture graced the mantel of a used brick fireplace and a family portrait, of the young family taken when Elle was around seven, was still hanging on the opposing wall, near the staircase.

He remembered coming here, waiting for Elle in this room, eating dinner at the dining room table that still stood on the far end of the living area, just steps off the kitchen. How many times had he sat at that table, next to Elle, feeling her bare toes rubbing his calf as Darryl gave the blessing and all Lucas could think about was scarfing down the meal and getting with Elle alone to have sex?

The thought was disturbing.

"Have a seat," Jeanette offered without much enthusiasm.

Lucas shook his head. "No, thanks. This won't take long. I just wanted to tell you that yes, the body that was found is Monica O'Neal. Also, Caleb Carter swears he saw Elle earlier today."

She looked up sharply, her lips pinching. "Today?" She took in a long breath, glanced at her husband's picture.

"That's right. Carter swears he saw her at the spot where Crown Creek flows into the ocean."

"Why on earth would she be there?" she asked, almost angrily. "And who can trust that man? He's a drunk."

"I know."

"No one should ever believe him. Caleb Carter? Of course." She let out a long, world-weary sigh. "Elle is gone. And that's all there is to say about it. What happened, it's a shame, but there it is. You know Darryl blamed you?"

"I figured."

"Well, he wasn't alone, Lucas," Jeanette was saying. "I did, too. If you would have done right by her, married her, then . . ." She waved a hand toward the family portrait on the wall, the three of them: stern, long-faced Darryl; pretty, petite

Jeanette; and Elle, with her white-blond hair in a ponytail, her teeth too big for her small face.

"If it's any consolation," Lucas said, "I'm sorry."

"I just bet you are." Her eyes flared behind her glasses. "You're the cause of it all. It started with you. All of Elle's troubles. Her leaving. And Darryl. He never was the same after all of the trouble. It killed him, y'know. I lay the blame at your feet, Lucas Dalton, and I pray every night that when Judgment Day comes, God reminds you just what you did to my family, that you'll pay for your sins." Her face was turning red with her words and she, nearly shaking, reached for a pack of Salem cigarettes on the coffee table.

In the years he'd known her, Jeanette hadn't smoked or drank, or even worn the slightest bit of makeup. Now lip gloss was visible on her lips and through the open pocket door to the kitchen, he spied a bottle of wine on the counter, a half-full glass, and a corkscrew next to the bottle of red. Things had changed in the Brady house. Where once there had been faith and happiness, there was now only sadness and anger. Somehow despair and grief had morphed into a seething fury that the mere sight of him seemed to have ignited.

"Now," she said, shaking a cigarette from her pack with trembling fingers. "Was there anything else?"

"Nothing concrete." He wasn't going to mention the bit of stained fabric, as it wasn't, as yet, connected to anything.

"What's that supposed to mean?" she asked, sticking the filter tip between her lips. Her hands were still quivering as she reached for her lighter, flicked it, and when the flame appeared, drew hard on the cigarette.

"That we have nothing more to report. We don't even know the cause of death or anything, but I wanted to let you know this is probably going to roil things up again. Elle's name and her disappearance will probably come up. You said you saw the press conference on TV?"

"So?" Smoke drifted from her nose and mouth.

"News people are going to be interested in everything associated with the camp, including Elle."

"Tell me something I don't know," she spat. "I've already had several calls from some woman from Astoria. A reporter. Kinley something or other. She wants to talk to me and I said, 'Nuh-uh. No way. You just leave me out of it,' but she didn't seem the kind to let it drop, y'know?" She was calmer now, either from the nicotine racing through her bloodstream or because she'd had her say, been able to blame him for her family's woes.

Lucas was nodding and, as he did, he thought he heard something, a footstep on the stairs? He glanced to the darkened staircase but saw no one, heard no more footfalls. "Is someone else here?" he asked.

"No," she said quickly. "Not that it's any of your darned business. I could be having a party and it wouldn't be any concern of yours."

But she was lying, taking another puff as if her life depended upon it. The dog had lifted his head and was looking toward the bottom steps that protruded into the hallway.

"It's just that I thought I heard something." He started for the steps. "If you think you're alone—"

"Hold on right there!" she said, and was on her feet in a shot, almost blocking the path upstairs. As if she were hiding something.

And then he got it. The lipstick, the wine-glasses, her furtiveness and anxiety. Jeanette had a lover. Well, hot damn. Lucas was never one to judge anyone for a relationship; in fact, he thought it was a good thing, especially in Jeanette's case, after losing her only daughter and then her husband. But she was a woman of faith, and he didn't doubt that people of the church she attended out of town might not approve of her new love interest.

"If there's nothing else, Lucas, I think you should leave. You're not welcome here, you know that, so maybe next time, if anyone from the department wants to talk to me, they can phone or send someone else."

Message received. "Okay." He hadn't come in an official capacity, but she didn't need to know that. "Then I'll be on my way."

He almost expected to hear "Good riddance" as he left, but she had the grace not to say the words even though they were evident in the set of her jaw. Instead, she stubbed out her cigarette angrily in a clean glass ashtray and then, as he let him-self through the door and screen, she locked each behind him. He heard the dead bolt click loudly as he made his way down off the porch and got into his Jeep.

She'd been anxious to get rid of him, worried that he might figure out she was entertaining.

As he backed up in the small parking area, he noted no car parked in the lane, no sign of a visitor. The garage was a single and Jeanette's Buick wasn't visible, so he assumed it was parked behind the closed garage door. There were no other outbuildings large enough to hold a car, so he decided she must've picked up the boy-friend . . . or he was living in? But there had been no signs of a man in the living room. No slippers, no newspaper opened to the sports page, the television a small, bubble-faced, portable model most men wouldn't adjust to, no male jacket on the hall tree, or baseball caps or anything that suggested Jeanette wasn't living by herself.

As he slid the gearshift into drive, he took a final look at the house. Though the two dormers poking out of the sloped roof were darkened, a bit of light filtered into the one on the right, as if a door had been left ajar and slight illumination from the hallway was seeping into the space. Elle's room, he remembered.

Then there was movement. Shadow on shadow. Narrowing his gaze, he thought he could make out a person standing in the window, backlit just slightly.

The lover? No. Wait. Not a man, he thought, more likely by the size and shape, a woman. A slim, petite woman . . . In that split second his heart froze. *Elle?* Holy crap! Was the woman in the window Elle? Hadn't he seen a hint of white-blond hair? What the devil?

And then she was gone.

As quickly as she'd appeared.

His heart was hammering as he turned his attention to the lower floor and living room, where the television flickered and lights glowed. Behind the pulled curtains, a shadow drifted, the figure of a larger woman. Jeanette.

But upstairs? He swung his gaze upward again, his eyes narrowing, trying to pierce the darkness. The silhouette had shrunk away, whatever light that had backlit her no longer existing. Either a door had been closed or the light snapped off. If the woman was standing behind the glass and staring down at him, he couldn't see her.

He threw the Jeep into park and cut the engine,

intending to barrel up to the front door and demand answers. But he held back. He couldn't go bursting into Jeanette's home. She'd throw him out, the dog would raise a ruckus, and if the woman who was hiding upstairs intended to remain hidden, she damned well would. No way could he force his way up the stairs and confront whoever had been watching him.

No. He had to tread carefully. He'd thought Jeanette's reaction to him had been all wrong. She'd been angry and almost panicked at first. Now, he was certain the anger and blame were all masks to hide her anxiety. Something was definitely going on.

Rather than arouse suspicion, he started his Jeep again and headed away from the house. In the rearview he caught Jeanette opening the curtains just a bit to ensure he was really leaving. Fine. He'd be back. On the sly by setting up his own private stakeout.

In her hotel room Sosi asked God for strength. She needed His guidance now more than ever. After the meeting with the other counselors, she had walked two blocks to a deli she'd spied earlier in the day, ordered a Sprite and a sandwich made with fresh chicken, then returned to her room. She had called Joshua and talked to each of the kids, grounding herself again as they had happily babbled about their day and fought for the chance to talk to her. Joshua had been forced to remind each of them about taking turns.

Sosi had started to tear up at the sound of their little voices and had blamed her emotional state on the stress she was under and her raging pregnancy hormones. She had tried to convince herself that she wasn't emotional because she'd seen Nell today. No way.

"So they're doing okay without me?" she'd asked her husband after little Grace had finally surrendered the phone back to him.

"They miss you. Bad. Like me. But they're tough," he'd said, and she'd heard the pride in his voice. She'd dashed her tears away with her free hand and admitted where she was and why.

"You're at the camp?" he'd said. "Why didn't you say so?"

"I was afraid you'd be mad."

"No." He'd paused and she'd waited breathlessly. "You have to do what you have to do. Just know that we're waiting for you."

In that moment she'd remembered why she'd fallen in love with him.

"I'll be back tomorrow, just as soon as I get through the interview with the police."

"I've been following the story," he'd admitted. "And I heard they found out who the body belonged to. I heard it on the news."

"What?" she'd said, glancing to the windows. "I . . . I haven't had the TV on or seen a recent paper."

"I just saw it a few minutes ago. The skull and some of the bones belong to that Monica girl. Monica O'Brien."

"O'Neal," she'd whispered, and dropped to the bed.

"Man, that's rough." He hadn't sounded all that concerned, but then, he'd never met Monica, hadn't been around the camp. "You okay?"

"Yeah, sure." Sosi had tried to pull herself together.

"I hope this doesn't make the interviews take longer."

"Me neither."

"Miss you, babe."

"Me too," she'd said distractedly as she'd reached for the television remote and heard, through the phone, one of her children crying in the background.

"Oops. Better go, before World War Three breaks out," he'd said, then had added a quick "Love you" and had cut her off before she could tell him she loved him as well.

Sosi had turned the channel to the local news, found a station that was reporting about the case, and watched in stunned horror as someone from the Neahkahnie Sheriff's Department had explained about the identification. There hadn't been any more information than what Joshua had told her.

It was enough to kill her appetite.

And so she'd dropped to her knees and braced her elbows on the blue-patterned quilt that covered her bed. She'd prayed for Monica's soul and family and for herself and her kids, all the while wondering what in the world had she been caught up in?

No sooner did she climb to her feet than her cell phone started to go crazy, the phone chirping crazily as text after text came in. All of them about Monica O'Neal.

OMG—just heard that body on beach ID'ed: Monica O'Neal. Awful! from Annette.

Prayers for her, for everyone was Jayla's response, and she included an emoticon of praying hands.

Bernadette wrote: Can't believe it. So sad.

Vigil? Jayla asked.

Reva: Any family?

Bernadette: Mother?

Jayla: Only Mom I think. No siblings. Dad passed. She added three cross emoticons and five prayerful hands. Prayer vigil! More emoticons, this time kitten angels, complete with wings, halos, and heart eyes.

Rap. Rap. Rap!

Sosi glanced up from her phone and headed for the door. Standing on her tiptoes she peered through the fish-eye hole; she expected to find Jayla, candles in hand, ready to start a vigil.

Instead she saw Nell in the hallway.

No. Her heart leapt to her throat. No. No.

She tried to get a grip on herself, one hand poised over the lever to open the door. Maybe she should just ignore the knocking and if Nell asked about it later, she could explain that she was sleeping and wearing ear plugs and—

Rap! Rap! Rap!

Nell wasn't giving up.

Great. The last thing Sosi wanted was anyone else from the old camp to see Nell hanging around in the hallway by her hotel room. Before the pounding started again, she threw the bolt and swung the door open to find Nell looking absolutely miserable. Her eyes shone with unshed tears and her face was red. "Did you hear?" she asked.

Sosi nodded. "Yeah. Joshua called, told me, and I was just watching the news."

Without another word Nell stepped over the threshold and threw her arms around Sosi's waist. "It's so terrible," she whispered, her breath hot against Sosi's neck. "So, so terrible. I can't help but wonder what happened to her. Who killed her."

"But we don't know that she was murdered." Sosi's pulse went into overdrive.

"What then, an accident?" Nell was still holding

her, but lifted her head and stared straight into Sosi's eyes. "What the hell happened?"

"I don't know . . . I think the police will sort it out."

"After all this time?" Her breath, smelling slightly of some kind of alcohol, was warm against Sosi's face.

"They have to. We'll help," she said, and tried to extract herself from Nell's embrace, but the other woman held on tightly and damn it, Sosi's heart was knocking wildly, the smell and feel of this girl she'd loved in her youth surrounding her.

"God, Sosi, I've missed you," Nell admitted, before taking a step back and visibly pulling herself together. "You know, I think about you often and now . . . this brought it all up again."

"What?"

"Us for one thing," Nell admitted, walking into the room and taking a seat on the foot of the bed where Sosi had so recently lain. Nell had grown to be beautiful, naturally so, her features even, her dark curls still a little wild, her eyes large and intelligent, her body trim and fit. She looked as if she ran marathons in her sleep while Sosi, pregnant with her fourth child, felt dumpy in comparison. "And the fact that you all lied to me. Even you." She held her gaze and Sosi drifted onto the single chair by the window. "You all met at the cavern and came up with this bullshit story about being together so that you

wouldn't get caught out. I know. I followed you."
She glanced away. "So I lied, too. I didn't let
anyone know I was there; didn't call you all out.
I should have, but . . ." She clasped her hands
over her knees. "I didn't want to get you into
trouble."

"You never told anyone."

"Of course I did, but not the police."

"You lied for me?" Sosi said.

"Essentially, yeah. I know, dumb, huh?" She
cleared her throat. "I just hope that it wasn't
because of what we did, or didn't do, that Monica
ended up dead."

"Oh! No, that can't be." Sosi was shaking her
head, but she, herself, had wondered the same
thing. Had they inadvertently caused Monica's
death? No . . . that didn't make sense.

"Think about it," Nell said soberly. She'd
always been smart.

"I . . . I don't want to."

"We have to make it right."

"What do you mean?"

"I'm telling everything I know tomorrow. I'm
not sticking to Jo-Beth's bullshit story, not for a
second. If you ask me, she might have had
something to do with it. I mean, don't you
think? Why's she so frantic to stay in control and
make everyone say some kind of rehearsed
piece like we're all robots who can't think for
ourselves?" She was shaking her head.

"I just hope we find out what happened. And to Elle."

"Yeah."

Nell was staring at her and the silence between them stretched. Sosi felt the atmosphere in the room shift a little, and she was all too aware of Nell and how touching her could make her feel. Her throat thickened and images of the past invaded her mind—Nell's laugh, her lithe body, the water sliding over their skin as they swam naked in the pond.

Their gazes held and Nell slowly got up from the bed and walked to the chair, where she knelt down and pressed her head into the crook of Sosi's neck. Her tongue slid over Sosi's bare skin and Sosi had to fight to keep from moaning. Images continued to flash through her mind and she was tempted to let go. Oh, so tempted. Nell's lips were so warm and pliant, her breath a whisper.

"I . . . I don't think . . ." she whispered.

"Don't." Nell's face moved closer, her mouth brushing over Sosi's.

Oh, dear Lord, why was she thrumming inside? Throbbing? Her blood running hot. "I . . . I just can't." She saw a sadness in Nell's eyes. Sosi grabbed Nell's hand and placed it over the bump of her abdomen where her sweater stretched tight. "I'm having another baby," she said, her throat clogged, "and I have three other little ones at home. With a husband who loves me. I can't . . . I won't cheat on him." At that moment the baby kicked. Twice.

"Oh. Wow." Nell didn't move for a second, her fingers splayed over Sosi's baby bump. A smile teased the corners of her mouth and for an instant Sosi was sure Nell intended to kiss her. Instead, she rocked back on her heels and let out her breath. "I have a fiancée," she admitted, her voice husky as she dashed away a wayward tear. "Tasha. We're business partners. Going to get married."

"You love her?"

"Very much." Nell nodded, no doubt visible in her eyes.

"Then?"

"I don't know. I won't lie. I wanted to see you again," Nell admitted. "I felt like we left things unsaid, not finished, and I was curious. No, it was more than that." Her gaze was troubled. "Sosi, I love you."

"But . . . Tasha?"

"I love her, too. It's different, you know?" She actually rolled her eyes as she cleared her throat. "She's my future, I know that, and it's not that I want to sneak around behind her back . . . Well, that's a lie. Never with anyone else. Uh-uh. But . . . maybe with you for tonight . . ." Oh, God. She stood suddenly. Blinked rapidly, fighting tears again. "You're right. This is wrong. I was just upset about Monica and . . .

505

and I wanted to see you and I don't know, comfort you, have you comfort me. Dumb, huh?"

Sosi couldn't agree. "Not dumb. Just wrong."

She was backing up. "I'd better go." She'd reached the door. "You're going to be okay, with this Monica thing?"

"No." Sosi shook her head. "But yeah. I have to be. We all have to be. Trust in God."

"In God? You think He had something to do with . . . oh, never mind. I get it. I'll see you tomorrow." Nell slid a quick glance at the bed, then yanked open the door and quickly walked out, the door automatically slamming behind her.

It was all Sosi could do not to call her back. But she didn't. Couldn't. And besides, it wasn't that she was all that unhappy in her marriage, not really, and it wasn't that she wanted to have an affair, not at all. It was just that with Nell . . . it was different and fun and . . . impossible. Taboo. She was married. She couldn't flirt or kiss or touch another man or woman.

Joshua was her husband, she reminded herself. He and the kids were her life.

She'd almost convinced herself that she was happy or could be with Joshua when her phone buzzed, indicating she'd gotten a text.

Nell had been gone less than ten minutes, and Sosi wondered if she'd changed her mind, if Nell had experienced second thoughts and was going to try to sway Sosi into doing something she'd regret later. But the text had come from a number she didn't recognize and the message, all in caps, said simply: **YOU WILL PAY.** A photograph had been attached to the text. With shaking fingers, Sosi held her phone and stared down at the image: a woman, laid to rest, in a coffin.

The dead woman's hair was pale, her eyes closed, and a white rose had been placed in her hands.

Sosi recognized her. "Dear God," Sosi whispered, fear sizzling down her spine.

She was staring at the image of a very dead Eleanor Brady.

Chapter 34

Averille, Oregon
Now
Jo-Beth

This is nuts! Crazy. For God's sake, Jo-Beth, you're not nineteen and single. You're pushing forty and married and have a career to think about! Call Tyler and tell him you changed your mind.

But she didn't pay one iota of attention to that nagging, sane voice inside her head. Instead, she changed her outfit twice, settled on a tight red tunic that hugged her butt and had a deep V neckline, silvery earrings, and black leggings. Gray boots, belt, and she was set.

She eyed herself in the mirror, dabbed on more mascara, blush, and lip gloss, and decided she was as ready as she'd ever be. Though she knew she shouldn't take a risk and see Tyler again, she just couldn't wait. She walked through a thin cloud of perfume just as she heard a quiet tap on her door.

Her stupid heart leapt.

She hadn't seen him since that summer, hadn't returned his phone calls, and refused to talk to him. He'd gone off to Colorado State, just as planned, and she'd headed east to Yale, where she'd met Eric, who fell for her and she for him. She'd been the one to steer Eric toward finance. He'd been a psychology major when she'd met him, for God's sake, and she'd decided if she were to marry him, he needed a high-paying career. The way she figured it, he owed her for getting him interested in Wall Street and all things financial.

And that worked out well, didn't it? Exactly how old is that VW bus he's now driving? You remember, Jo, right? That little two-toned orange and tan job with the faded peace sign in the rear window and the pop-up tent feature, the vehicle for which he traded in his black BMW X6? That one?

"Shut up!"

Another tap, louder this time. Good. Whether she'd intended to or not, she'd made Tyler wait a bit, though she didn't want him hanging out in the hallway, where some security camera might capture his image.

She hurried to the door, paused to straighten her tunic, then opened it and braced herself for an older, balding, potbellied man with a stringy ponytail who reeked of weed.

But she wasn't disappointed. Tyler, damn him, was as good looking now as he had been then: in shape with thick hair, chiseled features, and a half smile playing on razor-thin lips. In beat-up jeans, a T-shirt, and a jacket with a hood that partially obscured his face. Yeah, he was still the cool kid, the football player she'd fallen for in high school, if a little rough around the edges. His beard shadow was darker, his shoulders broader, the twenty pounds he'd added since high school seemed to be all muscle and gave him a more savage, older male look that she liked. A lot.

"Hey," he said, his eyes glinting a bit. "Long time."

"Am I supposed to say 'no see'?"

"Whatever you want." His slow-growing grin suggested all sorts of guilty pleasures. "I've got just the thing to get this party started." He held up a paper bag and glass clinked from within. Bottles. Hmmm. "Or if you want something a little stronger, I know a guy—"

"No, no, booze is fine. Come in." She stepped out of the doorway and let him pass. Was he offering her drugs? Marijuana? Cocaine? Meth? She cringed. No way. She had a career to consider. "Did anyone see you?"

"Like who?" he asked with cavalier disinterest as he set the sack on a small table in the sitting area.

"I don't know, another guest, a housekeeper, a maintenance guy, like anyone?"

"No." He pressed his lips together, gave a quick shake of his head, his brown hair catching the light. He was already pulling out a bottle of wine from the sack. "Why?" He reached in again and came out with a fifth of some kind of whiskey.

"Because maybe it wouldn't be such a good thing if we were seen together."

"Really?"

"You do know that it was Monica O'Neal's body or skull or whatever that was located?"

"Oh. Yeah. That." With a practiced twist of his wrist, he unscrewed the cap of the whiskey, then poured a healthy shot, well actually maybe two or three shots into a glass he found by the coffee-maker.

"Yeah, that."

"Well, it's kinda expected, y'know." He scrounged around the minibar until he located a corkscrew. Then he paused and, using the corkscrew points, indicated the bottle of red. "Pinot? It's from some tiny little winery around Newberg, I think, that's what the clerk said, like it was some kind of big deal, but you know, I think all wine tastes like shit."

"Such a rousing review." His attitude grated on her a little. He didn't seem to take the discovery of the body seriously.

"Well, you can always get down with me and meet my old buddy Jack Daniel's." He twirled the bottle so that she could view the label. "He's wearing black tonight," he added, referring to the color of the label.

Like she wouldn't get it. "The Pinot is fine."

"Suit yourself."

I always do. Always.

Her cell phone chirped and she saw that she not only had one text, but two. Somehow she'd missed another communication from Kinley Marsh asking for an interview.

Delete. And the text vanished.

The second was from Reva and as the cork popped on the wine she read: Dinner? Drink? I'm bored in this stupid place.

Jo-Beth replied: Maybe tomorrow? I'm going to crash.

Reva: It's barely 9.

Jo-Beth: I know. Long day. Trash TV is calling.

Reva: You can watch TV anytime.

Jo-Beth: Sorry—expecting a call from hubby. Ugh.

Reva finally got the message and texted: Your loss.

I don't think so, Jo-Beth thought as she observed Tyler pour some wine into a cheap, but stemmed glass he'd discovered on the shelf above the minibar. She clicked her phone into Do Not Disturb mode, then thought about it and walked to the door to hang a similar privacy sign from the exterior door handle.

"Hey, what're you do—oh, I get it. Good idea," he said as she twisted the dead bolt. A naughty glint appeared in his eyes. He'd discarded his jacket and shoes, as if he intended to stay for a while.

A tiny thrill sang through her blood as he walked toward her. He was holding both drinks and, as he reached her, handed her the stemmed glass.

"Cheers," he said, touching the rim of his glass to hers.

"Cheers," she repeated, and they gazed at each other over the rims as they sipped. The wine, despite Tyler's scathing remark, was surprisingly good, and they sat together on the tiny sofa that Nell and Jayla had shared earlier. Jo-Beth sat on one end, deciding it was best to play a little coy and let him come to her, rather than to always be the instigator. It was her natural instinct, to go

512

after what she wanted, but she'd learned over the years that patience was sometimes a very valuable virtue, or more to the point, a tool to be used appropriately.

As she kicked off her boots and tucked her feet under her, he was already hitting the bottle again and she wondered how she attracted these kinds of drunks. Reva earlier, and now Tyler had a serious affinity, it seemed, for booze. Or maybe it was just that Jo-Beth and/or this situation of being back in this god-awful little town, near Camp Horseshoe, and Monica O'Neal's body being found were putting everyone on edge.

"I've missed you," Tyler said.

"Not too much. You got married."

"So did you."

So he'd checked her out. Good. "Yeah, a mistake, I think. Even now he's questioning everything we worked for, going through some early midlife crisis."

"Let me guess: yellow Ferrari and super-hot twenty-something girlfriend." Another swallow.

"No—"

"Okay, okay, a red BMW—maybe an M6 and a really hot chick." With a knowing smile he took another gulp.

Closer. "No, you've got it wrong—"

"Right, a Lexus then, top of the line, or, no, wait! Wait! He's got a Tesla? Shit! A Tesla

Whatever and a really cute girl. Damn, is she under twenty-one?"

"Are you nuts?" All the inferences about a young, beautiful girlfriend were pissing her off. "No, it's not like that, for God's sake. He's got an old VW van and he's off in the wilderness trying to find world peace or inner peace or some such crap."

Tyler had his nose in the glass again, but was about to say something else when she cut him off before he got started. "And no, there's no other woman involved, not young or old."

"There's always a woman. And she's never old."

She felt her back teeth grind together and her smile was tense, her lips compressed together so hard her jaw ached. "Wrong," she said, and took a drink from her glass. Was Tyler a cretin? Some man who'd never grown out of his high school jock mentality? God, she'd met so many of them over her adult years, but she hadn't expected it from Tyler. Yeah, she'd fantasized that he still *looked* like the younger man she remembered, but she'd assumed he'd matured over the years and had . . . what? The razor-sharp wit of a forty-year-old, a man who could look at life with some knowledge and a little bit of irony? *Forget it. Even Eric let you down. You can't expect any more from your high school crush.*

Almost angrily, she polished off the remains of her wine.

"He sounds like a dick." Another drink and he drained his glass again. He pointed at Jo-Beth. "Make that a stupid dick." He poured himself another couple of fingers of whiskey, then slid closer to her on the couch. "You're smokin' hot."

The compliment shouldn't touch her so deeply, but it did. And she felt tears brush the back of her eyelids. Obviously Eric's rejection of their lifestyle and dreams, their plans, all their goals, in essence his rejection of her, had sliced further into her heart than she'd admitted, even to herself.

"If you were my wife," Tyler said, moving in closer, so close she was certain he was going to kiss her, "I would never have left you."

"Uh-oh," she said suddenly, not allowing herself the chance to fall for any of his lines. "Not so fast. Look at this." She wiggled her wineglass by its stem, indicating that it was empty.

"Can't have that." He reached behind him to the table and found the bottle before filling her goblet nearly to the rim. He nearly slopped some of the wine out of the glass.

"Oops."

She grinned, but worried a little about any kind of spillage. Red wine on her tunic? No way. The long top probably cost more than Tyler made in a week. And that was a problem. Jo-Beth, as she sipped the wine down quickly, realized that she was slumming. She should be having this conversation, this damned seduction, with one of the

515

partners in the law firm, or a senator, or the president of some company. Instead, she was with Tyler and though his good looks did make her heart pound, there was no future with him. She drank down the glass. Tonight, she decided, was a one-night stand, a fling, a chance to get back at him for playing around on her way back when.

Still sipping—dear God, was she actually slurping?—she thought about that time when he'd actually two-timed her and stuck his horny dick in that skank's—

"Hey, babe," he said, breaking into her thoughts, his breath warm and smelling of smoky whiskey as he plucked the glass from her hand. To her surprise it was near empty. As was his. Also, she felt that familiar buzz that was dangerous; she'd drunk just enough to feel loose-tongued and relaxed enough to anticipate sex as he drained his own glass, then dropped it onto the carpet. His pupils were dilated and she saw the tip of his tongue lick the edges of his lips. He'd always been such an eager lover; not as practiced as Eric, but what Tyler had lacked in skill, he'd certainly made up for with enthusiasm.

She could teach him, she thought.

Maybe.

He leaned in closer, kissing her and sliding his tongue into her mouth.

She was already tingling all over, and the pressure of his lips and slickness of his tongue as he touched the roof of her mouth made her want more.

Memories rolled through her mind and oh-so-easily Jo-Beth remembered the taste and feel of him.

As if twenty years had melted away.

Then she had wanted him so badly she'd ached. And she felt that need now.

But she also remembered that he'd fucked another woman while practically being engaged to her. The thought was sobering. "Hey, slow down, cowboy," she said.

His hands were already under her tunic, lifting the hem, cupping her buttocks as he pulled her tight against him, making certain she felt his erection pushing hard against the denim of his jeans.

"God, you're still so wicked sexy." He pinched one cheek, his fingers skimming close to the edge of her vagina, and her heart went into overdrive. Even with the barrier of their clothes.

Suddenly she wanted him to touch her, but she was still pissed: twenty years' worth of pissed. "So did you fuck her that night?"

"What're you talking about?" He didn't stop. He was licking her ear, nuzzling her neck. She was having trouble concentrating, her nerve endings thrumming.

"Did you?" she demanded, breathless. "Did you fuck her? Monica? The night she went missing?"

"What? No. Oh, God, forget her. C'mon, babe, it's just you and me." To her surprise, he rolled off the couch, then picked her up and carried her to the bedroom as if she weighed nothing. They tumbled onto the bed together.

"Wait . . . oh, wait . . ." She nearly shot off the bed. She wasn't going to get down and dirty on the coverlet, where who knew how many others had fucked. She'd watched some of those shows on dirty hotel rooms and she didn't think the Hotel Averille was anywhere near to a five-star.

"For what?"

"Just, not on the covers, okay?"

"Whatever you want," he said, and pulled the bedspread and blanket down, then swept them to the floor. "There." He grabbed her again and yanked her down to kiss her hard. Determined. As if he'd had enough playing around.

She responded, her body thrilling at his touch. A dozen questions flitted through her mind, but she was so anxious, desire drumming through her, that she couldn't ask a single one. Instead she kissed him back. Passionately. Angrily. With all the pent-up energy and resentment of two decades. She stripped off his shirt and he nearly ripped her tunic, yanking it over her head. He dispensed with her bra and scraped his teeth over her bare nipples.

Her flesh pimpled. Her blood ran hot.

Oh. Dear. God.

How long had it been?

Too long.

A needy sigh escaped her lips.

His fingers scratched her skin as he yanked down her leggings, then kissed her inner thighs.

More, she thought desperately. *I want more.*

She let out a broken scream of desire and he ripped off her panties before anxiously kicking off his own jeans. Her throat tightened. He wore no underwear and his cock stood erect. He teased it near her lips, the tip brushing her cheeks.

No way.

Not yet.

She wanted her own needs met and pulled hard on his hips, pushing him down as she bucked upward, showing him that she wanted him. Now. In her. Thrusting hard.

"Later," he growled, catching her rhythm. "We'll go slower next time and trust me, babe, then you'll suck me. Like you've never sucked anyone in your life."

Blind with desire, she arched again. "Just do it!"

"Okay, okay, I gotcha." Deftly, with a strength that surprised her, he flipped her over. He mounted her quickly, thrusting deep, bracing himself with his hands on her back and gathering steam, going faster and faster, harder and harder, nearly pummeling her as she responded in kind, desire pounding through her brain.

Hot. Wet. Wanting more.

He complied.

Harder and harder until they were both gasping in short, rapid breaths.

Her body convulsed in pleasure. She let out a high-pitched moan and he answered in kind. Stiffening and grunting, falling against her before she even thought about a damned condom. She'd been on the pill for years, of course, but . . . she'd only been with Eric, and Tyler, she knew, had never been monogamous.

Oh, hell, who cared?

For a few seconds she was content to close her eyes, shut off her brain, and let the ripples of pleasure roll over her.

Only when her breathing had slowed and he rolled to one side did the enormity of what she'd done hit her. She'd fucked him. Without protection and, worse yet, without gaining the information she'd wanted for all these years. "Tyler?" she whispered into his ear.

"Wha—?" Levering himself up on one elbow, he looked at her, then growled and buried his face in the cleft of her breasts. "God, I love your boobs."

"But not enough to keep you faithful."

"What?"

"You didn't love them, or me, enough to keep you from screwing Monica."

He stared at her dumbfounded. "Hell, are you never going to get over it? I mean, here we are, babe, like, in bed, just having done it and I'll be ready to go again soon. Goddamn, you're good."

She almost warmed under the compliment.

Almost.

"And besides," he went on, touching one of her nipples with a finger that swirled lazily around the tip, "she's dead. What the hell does it matter?"

But it did. She pushed his hand away. "I just never understood."

"I know. I get it." He was getting angry. "But again? She's dead," he repeated. "There is no Monica, there is no baby. Right? Like, 'poof.' " He smiled then, a cruel little grin that seemed off.

"Poof?" she repeated. She didn't like the sound of that.

"I got rid of the problem."

And there it was. "What?" she said, hoping she misunderstood, but knowing deep in her heart that all of her suspicions had just been confirmed. Fear slipped through the chambers of her heart, but she had to be certain. "Wait a second."

"What?"

"You *killed* her?"

He hesitated, sized her up. "You knew that, right?" he said almost casually, but something in his eyes gave him away, as if he realized he'd tripped up.

"You told me that the killer, the guy who attacked you, somehow got the knife away, the knife Reva stole so you could 'scare the shit out of' Monica. Those were your exact words, 'scare the shit out of' her. Not kill her or harm her."

He didn't respond, just stared at her. But didn't try to seduce her again.

"So," Jo-Beth persisted. "So now, what? You're saying that the attacker didn't kill her? That you murdered her and your unborn child?" Her heart was jackhammering. That couldn't be right, could it? She'd always wondered, had a niggling doubt, those horrible little suspicions, but had tried to convince herself that Tyler never would have actually hurt Monica. Oh, sure, she'd known he was going to scare the shit out of her so she'd leave. Jo-Beth had been in on that plan, but this? "Oh, Jesus."

"You *knew*. Come on, you and Reva, you both knew. You gave me the goddamned knife."

"But the attacker? I mean, I thought . . ." She swallowed hard, scooted away from him. He was a killer? A stone-cold killer? "It was a prank. And that the guy, the prisoner, Waldo Grimes, that he came upon you in the chapel and some-how got the knife from you and chased Monica and when you tried to save her, he turned the knife on you and you never knew what happened to her. Isn't that what you told the police?"

"Yeah." He was nodding.

"And me? That's what you told me. Now, what? You're saying that was a lie?" She was panicking now, scooting away. Tyler, the ex-boyfriend, the man with whom she'd just made love—no, scratch that—had sex, he was a stone-cold killer? She couldn't believe it. Wouldn't. "What about Elle?" she asked.

"What about her?"

"Did you . . . What happened to her?"

He lifted a shoulder. "How would I know?"

Did she dare ask? Could she not? "Did you 'get rid of the problem' of her, too?"

"No! She wasn't one! Come on, babe," he said, slightly irritated. "What is this? Who cared about Elle? It was Monica. She was the problem. Saying she was pregnant and all. You know that . . . right? You told me she was just trying to trap me. That maybe there wasn't even a baby."

And then she saw it.

An iota of fear in his gaze, but something more, something deadly. Something akin to the juiced-up, adrenaline-fired rage of a cornered animal. Oh. Dear. Jesus.

"You knew," he said again, as if to convince them both. "You had to have known."

"No . . . I . . . I believed you." Oh, crap, she should tell him she was lying, that of course she knew, that she was just teasing and then get the hell out of the room and away from him.

"Jo—"

"Okay. I was just messing with you. I knew that . . ." But he wasn't buying it. Oh, damn. He saw through her lie. Panicking, she tried to scoot away but was too slow.

He pounced.

Pinned her to the bed with his weight.

No!

She opened her mouth to scream, but he shoved a pillow over her face and as she struggled, raw terror settled in. Her heart beat crazily, as if it would shoot out of her body. Her breath was trapped in her lungs!

He pressed harder.

No, no, no! She hit at him with her arms, flailing at him, trying to buck with her legs, doing everything she could, squirming and wriggling, kicking frantically, but he wouldn't budge.

Her lungs were on fire!

He was going to kill her! Right here. Right now. In this awful bed. In this cut-rate hotel. In *this hicksville town.*

God, please—

Her lungs ached so painfully. Her eyes bulged. Her heart was going to explode.

Stop! Please, stop!

She tried to drag in a breath. Couldn't. The world started to go dark and her brain began to shut down.

Stop! Get off me. Let me breathe.

His weight held her fast and her arms dropped to her sides as the blackness overtook her.

Her last conscious thought was a prayer.

Oh, God, please help me. . . .

Chapter 35

How did she know?

Bernadette was reading Kinley Marsh's latest blog post, which Annette had first seen and texted her sister to read. It's unbelievable. And weird. Annette had posted. It's like she's in my head, or was in my head.

Propped up by pillows on the bed, the remains of her dinner, a take-out tuna salad sandwich from a local deli, on the nightstand, her laptop open on her lap, Bernadette had to agree. She read the post, which was all about the finding of Monica O'Neal's remains. However, more than the usual facts and a little speculation in the "news" story, this was written as if Kinley were closer to the crime, practically investigating the case herself because she had a bird's-eye view of what had gone on, had been a camper who had resided at Camp Horseshoe when Monica had disappeared.

All of that was true enough, but it was the details Kinley had supplied in the long post, about the meeting in the cavern, the hint of a cover-up, Jo-Beth leading the group to stay in line with their sworn statements, and the talk of a love triangle. The story sounded more like the teenage girl Annette had been than the prepubescent Kinley, who had been around eleven at the time. Also, some of the information was too personal, so she asked herself again: How did Kinley know?

Was it conjecture?

Or piecing together conversations she'd over-heard or situations she'd witnessed?

Kinley even hinted that Detective Lucas Dalton might be thrown off the case due to a conflict of interest and, Kinley intimated, inappropriate behavior twenty years earlier.

Included in the post were questions about ghost sightings of Eleanor Brady and if some-how a recent sighting was tied to the discovery of Monica O'Neal's body. Kinley hadn't come up with many answers, the blog was meant as a tease, to lead the readers into the next edition of the *NewzZone*, where Kinley promised more details of the ongoing investigation and what had really happened twenty years before at Camp Horseshoe. She encouraged reader comments and questions, and asked them to weigh in with their opinions.

The post was getting a lot of attention and comments, readers speculating and conversing about the discovery of Monica's body and the ensuing cold case being reopened.

Sick of the conjecture, Bernadette threw the remains of her dinner into the trash, peeled off her clothes, and stepped into a hot shower. She needed to clear her mind, but that, of course, proved impossible. As the warm water cascaded over her body, her thoughts turned to Lucas and how passionately he'd kissed her today. Had there been desperation in his touch?

Longing?

Don't read too much into it.

She dunked her head under the stream and used the hotel shampoo to lather her hair. Why was she focusing on Lucas and a stupid kiss when they knew now that Monica was dead, when Jo-Beth was trying to manipulate them all, when she just needed to make a statement to the police and go back to Seattle?

And return to what?

An empty condo?

A job that wasn't as fulfilling as she'd hoped?

"Stop it," she muttered. She was making more of a kiss than it was. For the love of God, was she really second-guessing her whole life because of one innocent kiss?

Innocent?

Oh, come on.

You felt it, Bernadette: The heat. The need. The wanting.

And you were as into it as he was, you're just not admitting it.

"No way," she said aloud, but knew she was lying.

Angry with herself, she rinsed her hair, used the minuscule bottle of cream rinse, then rinsed again, all the time refusing to think about Lucas and what a ninny she became around him. What was wrong with her? Acting like an obsessed teenage girl with her first boyfriend? She was a grown woman, an adult who'd been married, divorced, and miscarried and . . . Oh, no, she couldn't think of the baby now, the lost dreams, the painful way she and Jake hadn't been able to get past it, had somehow blamed each other.

She sagged against the plastic enclosure. So that was it. Somehow in all of this, Lucas represented hope. "You are a fool," she said, and turned her face to the spray, letting the water rinse her scalp and body. She had a home, a townhouse in Seattle, and a job teaching little ones; her life was full. She didn't need a man to complete it. That idea certainly hadn't worked with Jake, and she knew full well, from past experience, it wouldn't work with Luke.

"Get over it," she said, and twisted off the tap, then stepped onto a thin bath mat before belatedly switching on the fan and toweling off. Refusing to think of the feel of Lucas's lips on hers, the scrape of his stubble against her face, or the smell of him, so earthy and male, she used a dry towel to clear the mirror, combed the tangles from her hair, and pulled on her pajamas.

She'd catch the news, read for a while, go to sleep, and then, in the morning, talk to Detective Dobbs and leave Averille, Lucas Dalton, and the ghost of Camp Horseshoe forever.

She'd just started brushing her teeth when she heard a door slam against a wall with a bang; then Annette's screaming practically shook the walls.

"Oh, my God, oh, my God, oh my God!" Annette screamed.

What in the world? Bernadette rinsed her mouth, then entering her bedroom nearly ran into her sister. "I can't believe it!" Annette cried, her face drained of all blood and contorted into a mask of horror. Dressed only in panties and her bra, she was holding her cell phone in one hand. "Have you seen this?" she screamed, shaking the phone. "Have you? Oh, dear God."

"Seen what? No—why would I?"

Annette twisted the phone in her hand and shoved it toward Bernadette's face. On the small screen was the image of a woman dressed in white, lying in a coffin, a white rose folded in her hands, her eyes closed. Elle Brady.

"What is this?" Bernadette whispered, disbelieving.

"It's Elle!" Annette screeched. "And see what the sender wrote? Look at the damned text."

YOU WILL PAY had been typed in bold caps.

"Dear God."

"What the fuck is that all about? And why is there a picture of Elle?" Annette demanded, freaked out of her mind. "What?"

"I . . . I don't know." Stunned, Bernadette stared at the picture. "This . . . This could be a fake. Someone's sick idea of a joke or—"

Her own cell phone pinged. She snagged it from the nightstand and saw the image of Elle in the coffin. She, too, had received a copy of the gruesome message. Someone knew their cell phone numbers.

"You too?" Annette asked, her eyes rounding. "For the love of God, what's going on?"

"I don't know, but panicking won't help. You need to calm down."

"Oh, right. Look, I can't! This is no joke," she said, holding the phone up and shaking it as if in so doing, she would make Bernadette understand the gravity of the situation, which was pointless. Bernadette got it. "What does that mean, anyway? 'You will pay'? Pay for what? Why? Because of frickin' Elle? This is insane! What the hell's going on?" Annette was yelling, practically hyperventilating.

Bernadette dropped her phone on the bed and grabbed her sister by the shoulders. "Stop it!" Her fingers dug into Annette's skin. "Pull yourself together."

"Are you kidding? Do you see what someone sent us?"

Dragging her sister toward the bathroom, Bernadette pushed her face so close to Annette's she could almost smell her sister's panic, saw the raw fear registering in her eyes. "Stop it! Right now. Or, I swear, I'll slap you. We have to figure this out!"

"But, but, but—"

Bernadette shoved her sister into the shower and as Annette gasped, she yanked the phone from her hand, then turned on the faucet full blast. Icy water sprayed the tiny enclosure, immediately drenching all of Annette and half of Bernadette.

"Whaaaat! No! No! You bitch!" Annette sputtered, blinking and coughing. "God. Damn. It!" Outraged, she shrieked, "Are you out of your freaking mind?"

"Not me. You." Bernadette released her, then backed away from the shower.

Annette, dripping and glaring daggers at her older sister, scurried out of the small enclosure to drip on the bath mat and floor.

"For the love of God!" Gasping and shivering, Annette looked like she might tear her older sibling limb from limb.

Bernadette tossed her a fresh towel. "Go change," she said, already thinking ahead. "We need to talk to the others, see if anyone else got the message." Still holding her sibling's phone as Annette, fuming, but at least no longer frantic,

531

toweled her face and shoulders, Bernadette studied the message again and checked the menu of people to whom the text was sent. "Yeah—it looks like everyone got one."

"Why?" Annette was starting to calm down as she dabbed at her face with the towel, her hair hanging wet and lank to her shoulders.

"Don't know."

"To scare us?"

"Obviously."

Annette met her sister's gaze in the mirror. "Well, then: Mission accomplished." She took in a deep breath and snatched her phone from Bernadette's hand just as another text came in. This time Bernadette's pinged and she scooped it up from the bed to read a new series of messages:

Who is this? Reva demanded of the mystery number who had sent the text.

Nell chimed in: ID yourself.

Sosi: OMG this is so sick. Who are you?

Jayla wrote on a separate thread that didn't include the unknown number, or the person who sent the text: I'm so freaked out! Can't believe this! Who would do this? Is it really Elle? Meet in Jo-Beth's room? Accompanying the text was a nervous-looking happy face, teeth clenched along with six praying hands.

Bernadette typed a response. Yes. 5 min.

"Okay, we're meeting on the third floor," she

said, stripping out of her pajamas and finding her jeans, bra, and long-sleeved tee.

"I see." Annette's gaze was still glued to the screen.

Snapping her hair into a still-damp ponytail, she said, "Let's move it."

"I'm going!" Annette was already out of the bathroom and hurrying through the door connecting the two rooms.

From the corner of her eye, Bernadette saw her sister change into a dry bra, underwear, and yoga pants. Annette towel-dried her hair to the point that it stuck out crazily. "Who sent that damned text?"

"Don't know." Bernadette stared at the screen of the phone. "But it's weird, y'know. The only person who hasn't checked in is Jo-Beth. I mean, it doesn't look like I did because I answered on your phone, but everyone else is freaking out. Not Jo-Beth."

"What does that mean?"

"Maybe her phone is off. Or out of battery life."

"I guess." Annette yanked on a cowl-necked sweater. "Ugh, I'm still wet."

"You're fine. Let's go." Grabbing her purse from the bed, she started for Annette's room, then checked to make certain her door was locked. It was supposed to lock automatically, of course, but the hotel was old, the doors not seeming all that secure. As she passed into Annette's room, she found Lucas's name in her contact list, then hit the call button.

Annette applied some controlling gel to her hair and then gave up to follow Bernadette into the hallway. She spied the phone in Bernadette's hand. "Who are you calling?"

"Lucas."

For once her sister didn't argue, roll her eyes, or make some stupid remark as they climbed the stairs to the third floor, where they found Sosi, Nell, and Jayla gathered around the door of room 302. Bernadette hung back and when Lucas's phone went to voice mail, she left a brief message: "It's Bernadette. Call me. It's urgent." Then she hung up and joined the others.

"She's not answering," Jayla said, pounding on the door. "Jo-Beth!" she called. "Hey!"

"She's obviously not here," Sosi said.

Across the hall, the old elevator rumbled to a stop. The second the doors rolled open, Kinley and another woman strode into the hallway.

"Get back, please," the woman ordered. Dressed in a navy suit with a name tag reading JACQUI SIMMONS, MANAGER, she was holding a passkey in one hand and looked scared to death. Grimly she headed straight to the door of Jo-Beth's room, while next to her, Kinley was ashen-faced, appearing shell-shocked.

"What's going on?" Nell demanded.

"I said stand back," Jacqui ordered again. "Security's on their way."

"Security?" Sosi whispered, her eyes rounding. "Why?"

Bernadette said, "What the hell is happening? Is something wrong with Jo-Beth?" She thought of the text they'd all received with its ominous message: **YOU WILL PAY**.

"Just open the door!" Kinley said, seeming to tamp down her fear as footsteps pounded in the staircase and the door at the end of the hall was shoved open to bang against the wall.

A heavy-set African-American man dressed in a white shirt and dark pants jogged toward them.

"Everyone back up," he ordered, dark eyes flashing. "Clear this hallway."

As Jacqui slid her passkey into the lock, the man pushed through the group that had collected and the minute he heard a buzz that indicated the door was unlocked, he shoved it open and stepped into the suite.

Jacqui stood blocking the entrance as Kinley leaned against the hall. From inside the room, the security guard yelled, "Call nine-one-one! Get an ambulance."

Bernadette's heart sank.

"What the hell happened?" Reva yelled. She struggled to get past Jacqui, but the hotel manager, cell to her ear, stood fast.

"Back up!" Jacqui warned.

"Is it Jo-Beth? What's going on?" Reva was wild-eyed and appeared desperate. "What happened? Where is Jo-Beth? Oh, God, what the fuck is wrong?"

The guard reappeared. "Everyone, out. Now!" His bulk blocked the doorway. "You heard me, this is a crime scene."

"What?" Sosi whispered. "A crime scene?" she said, as Jacqui connected to the emergency dispatcher and was shaking and demanding help.

"Oh, dear Lord." Jayla's hands flew to her mouth. Her eyes rounded and she began mumbling a prayer.

Kinley's chin was wobbling and she was sliding down the wall opposite Jo-Beth's door. "I saw it," she said almost woodenly as if she were saying the words to everyone, but no one. "I have it all on tape."

"Have what on tape?" Bernadette asked.

"She was murdered." Tears in her eyes, Kinley had sunk to the floor and was rubbing her arms.

"Murdered?" Annette whispered.

"No, you can't be serious. No. No." Reva was backing up, shaking her head. Then she stopped. "I want to see her."

"Yes, yes, I'll stay on the line," Jacqui was saying into her cell phone, her free hand over her opposing ear as she listened to instructions. "Please, just hurry. We need that ambulance."

"It's too late," Kinley said tonelessly, as if she were in a trance. "He killed her. Dear Jesus, I watched as Tyler Quade killed her."

Chapter 36

Camp Horseshoe
Then
Tyler

The bitch is going to ruin everything! Everything! You can't let it happen, Ty! You've got too much going for you, and it's all over if Monica tells anyone she's pregnant. Jo-Beth is right, Monica will stop at nothing to tie you down and ruin your damned life. So, do it. Do it now! You're running out of time. She'll be here any second. Fucking do it!

Sweating, his heart jackhammering, his adrenaline rushing through his veins in the creaky chapel, Tyler knew what he was doing was dangerous, but it had to be done. He had to screw up his courage and stab himself. Not only that, it had to look good, as if he'd been attacked.

In the dark he adjusted the butcher knife, the hilt wedged into a niche he'd carved in the sofa's frame, the blade protruding from the cushions in exactly the right spot. There was no room for error. Not tonight. He didn't want to risk nicking an artery, or vital organ, or his damned spinal cord. What would be the point to survive but not be able to walk or maybe even fuck?

He listened for the sound of approaching footsteps, quick patter of footfalls indicating that Monica was nearby, but all he could discern was the scratch of tiny claws. Mice? Rats? He didn't care.

There wasn't much time. He would have to work fast. Quickly he stripped off his clothes, didn't want any evidence of blood spatter to mess them up. Then he threw his shorts and T-shirt into a pile on a dirty pew.

Jo-Beth had done her part and supplied him with the weapon, sharp enough to slice easily into his skin and muscle and embed in the backside of one of his ribs. Careful not to cut himself, he readjusted the hilt to ensure that the blade would hold steady until he flung his body against it with enough force that it would stick into his bone and muscle so that when he straightened, the knife would protrude from his back.

You can do this.

Once the knife was set into his back, he would stumble his way back to the pews and lie down to wait. He had already stashed the smaller, folding knife on the floor beneath one of the benches, pushed into the rotting pages of an old hymnal, right where he could reach it easily. He would make certain his fingerprints weren't on it and then hoist it into the woods or ocean. If it happened to be found, it couldn't be traced to him.

Tyler had swiped the jackknife from Dustin Peters, after he'd seen Peters playing mumblety-peg, tossing the blade into the dirt behind a tool shed over and over again. But when Dustin had left the jackknife on the fence post when he'd gone into the stable to check on a horse, Tyler had pocketed the blade.

Jo-Beth thought he just wanted to scare Monica, but that was just Tyler's cover story. He intended to snuff her tonight. No more seduction, no more teasing, no more sex, and no more crying jags. Most of all, no more coercion. And, for the love of frickin' God, no more threat of a baby. Real or not. Hell, no!

Now, the butcher knife was finally in position.

He tested it. Sitting where he needed to on the edge of the couch, he leaned back and felt the prick of the blade. Perfect. At least according to that incredible video he'd gotten from a friend and watched over and over again, enough times to make certain he wouldn't permanently harm himself.

He knew he could hold his breath several minutes if he had to. His pulse would be a problem, but he'd slow it as best he could, Zen out as much as possible, force himself not to blink, and hope that she would be freaked enough to not check, or misread the signs. Hopefully there would be enough blood to panic her.

Everything else was set. He'd even positioned a tree branch on the other side of the stained glass window. Inside, in the near dark, the branch's murky silhouette looked enough like a person that, again, if Monica were as frantic as he suspected she would be, she'd think someone was around and then he'd take off after her.

And he'd kill her.

Hunt her down and twist her neck, then slit her throat with the smaller knife. He kept telling himself it was just like killing a deer or maybe a bear. He'd hunted all his life and he'd just dehumanize her, make her the prey.

And your own baby, the one she says is growing in her womb? You're willing to snuff out that life, too?

Yes. If it even existed. She'd probably lied about that. And it didn't matter. Even if she was pregnant, it had been a mistake and she couldn't be more than four weeks along, right?

He counted backward slowly from ten. Calming himself. Readying himself. He leaned back once more, felt the prick of the tip of the knife again, just to be certain the position of the blade was perfect. Then locating that area of his brain he used when hunting, the place where his patience and concentration were so intent nothing else existed, he centered himself. The darkness faded, the smells of rot and decay were no more, the scurrying of rodents' feet and the sigh of the wind disappeared. All he thought about was the knife entering his skin. He set his jaw—couldn't afford to let out a sound—took in three deep breaths.

Now!

With a Herculean effort, he propelled himself backward.

Zzzt!

The knife pierced his skin, the hot sting of the blade centered just an inch from his spine. The cushions gave to the force of his body weight, but the butcher knife held fast. Fixed. Searing pain radiated from the spot. He sucked in his breath. Refused to let out the tiniest sound. He didn't wait for the pain to start throbbing, but knowing the knife was secure, pushed himself upright. His legs felt a little wobbly from the shock, but came back, and he quickly felt his way to the pews.

Then he lay down.

He slowed his breathing, straining to hear.

Two minutes passed.

Blood oozed from the wound.

Three more minutes.

What was taking her so long?

What if she didn't show up?

What if this whole charade was for nothing?

What if he'd gone to all this trouble and pain, nearly killed himself and—

He heard footsteps.

She was here!

A final movement, to make sure the old hymnal and its hidden weapon were within reach and then he relaxed every muscle, every fiber in his body, and drew in a deep breath. He would wait until the last moment to twist his body so the knife could be seen, then stare upward at the decaying ceiling and feign death.

Footsteps on the porch.

A door creaking and then her voice. "Tyler?" she whispered, and he had to force his heart to keep from pumping wildly at the thought of what was to come. Could he do it? Could he chase her down and kill her and throw her body into the sea?

Of course he could.

He'd just had the balls to thrust himself against a razor-sharp knife, hadn't he? He almost grinned. He might even enjoy it.

A few beats. She was entering. He heard her. Felt the slight vibration of her feet moving on the floorboards. "Ty?" Her voice quavered, barely audible over the rush of the wind. More foot-steps and he thought he could sense her fear. Good. Then she called out to him, "If this is a game, it isn't funny."

You're right about that, baby.

It's definitely not funny.

Not funny at all.

Chapter 37

Averille, Oregon
Now
Lucas

"It's Bernadette," she said across the wireless connection, her voice sounding tight. Strident. "Lucas, you have to come here. To the hotel! I think . . . I think Jo-Beth may be dead!"

"Dead?" Lucas repeated. He was holding the cell phone to his ear as he hauled his stakeout equipment bag down the stairs from his loft. He stopped on the third step, thought maybe he'd heard wrong.

"Probably. I mean, I think so. Oh, God, I don't know what to think. Some of us had gotten this weird text and we wanted to talk to Jo-Beth, but her room's been cordoned off." She was talking fast, breathlessly. "The manager came and a security officer has put a call in to nine-one-one. Kinley Marsh swears that she saw Tyler Quade kill Jo-Beth, right there in her room. I can't believe it. I just can't believe it. This is awful!" she said, and he heard other voices in the background, maybe someone crying, someone else praying, and another, more serious voice telling everyone to calm down.

"Wait a second. Slow down. Take a deep breath," he advised, unable to keep up with her disjointed story. "How does Kinley know that Quade killed Jo-Beth? She was there? She escaped?" On the move again, he snagged his keys from a hook near the front door. Roscoe was waiting, whining to be let out. "Sure. Fine," he said to the shepherd as he opened the door. Roscoe shot through.

"What?" Bernadette said.

"Nothing. I was talking to the dog. You were telling me about Kinley . . . ?" He locked the door behind him while the dog streaked across the wet grass to dance and spin at the side of his Jeep.

"Yes, oh, yes. I mean, no, Kinley wasn't actually there in the room when Jo-Beth was . . . was attacked. Believe it or not, Kinley was spying on us. Electronically. Somehow she'd gotten into Jo-Beth's room and had set up equipment. You know, microphones and cameras and that sort of thing. She says she was just trying to get information for the series of stories she's writing about what happened to Elle and Monica, to find out what we all knew. Anyway, so while she was watching, she witnessed the whole awful thing as it happened." Bernadette's voice was tight, as if she were trying to maintain control. "Can you imagine? Lucas, she saw it!"

"I'm on my way." Opening the driver's door, he watched Roscoe sail inside to claim the passenger seat. "Stay on the line."

"I don't think I can. They're making us leave, herding us to some conference room or dining room, somewhere downstairs. They won't let us leave or go back to our rooms."

"The cops are there?"

"Yes, a couple of deputies." She was still breathless but sounded a little less frantic. "So far. I think, I think more are coming."

At that second, he heard a short series of beeps indicating he had another call coming in. Maggie Dobbs's number flashed onto his screen. "Just do what they say," he told Bernadette. "I'll be there in ten, maybe fifteen minutes. Sooner if I can." He fired up the Jeep and was already speeding down his lane as he clicked over to the incoming call.

"Hey."

Without preamble, Maggie said, "I'm on my way to the Hotel Averille. There's trouble."

"I heard. I just got off the phone with Bernadette Al—Warden. I'm heading that way, so don't give me any bull about not being assigned to the case."

"I won't. You deal with Locklear yourself about all that," she said, surprising him as he cut a corner a little too close and his back wheels hit gravel. "I actually want you there. I think you could help. You know these people. You could be a calming effect."

"Then I'm not a suspect?"

She paused and his jaw tightened.

"No," she finally said, "not a suspect. Come on, Lucas, you know I don't think you're a criminal."

"Comforting," he said tautly.

"But Locklear's right, you could be perceived as having a major conflict of interest, so just be cool. Don't talk to anyone without me or a deputy present. We need to cover our asses. And whatever you do, don't get in my way or make me regret not banning you from the scene."

"Got it," he said. Not liking the terms, but understanding, he slowed for the ess curves, still taking them ten miles over the posted limit. The cops were already at the scene, he had no reason to hit the panic button, but he couldn't stop himself from worrying.

"Okay. Good. So here's what I know—" She told him about Kinley spying on Jo-Beth and the others, hoping to come up with a news-worthy story. Through hidden cameras placed in Jo-Beth's room, Kinley had watched and listened as Tyler Quade had entered room 302; the couple had drinks, then sex that had turned violent immediately afterward. "The way Kinley tells it, Jo-Beth asked him if he'd murdered Monica O'Neal, and he'd gotten upset. Acted as if she knew he'd killed her."

"He admitted it?"

"Basically, according to Kinley Marsh. We'll find out. She taped it and we've already got the digital copies."

"Jesus," Lucas muttered.

"Some people will go to any lengths for their career."

"All of this is highly illegal, you know. Bugging the room. Could be a snag when we're taking Quade to court. His attorney—"

"Hold on a sec. That's really getting the cart before the horse. And tell me something I don't already know. Kinley Marsh is already worried about it, her part in the illegal bugging. She was stunned, kind of out of it just after the attack, but she's pulled herself together and figures she could be in serious legal trouble. She's already talking about working some kind of deal. But, you know, we've got bigger problems."

"Like Quade. Where is he?"

"Don't know. He and his truck are gone. I've already set up a BOLO for it. We'll get him, though. He can't be far. This all went down less than a half hour ago."

"Okay. I'll meet you there. I'm three minutes out," Lucas said.

He reached the hotel in two. Maggie, already at the inn, met him on the first floor, where she told him Bernadette was with the others, all of the women being questioned.

"I need to see her," he insisted.

"You will."

Irritated, he decided not to argue. Maggie filled him in on a few more details, then, despite the fact that Locklear might hit the roof, she even allowed him onto the third floor, which had been cordoned off to anyone but the police. He peeked into the hotel suite, where in the bedroom attached to a living area Jo-Beth Chancellor Leroy lay naked and very dead, someone from the ME's office examining her, pictures of the room being taken, a thin layer of fingerprint dust every-where.

After viewing the crime scene, Maggie walked him to the next room, 304, registered to Kinley Marsh. An open suitcase, laptop, and various other pieces of equipment were being gathered by a deputy.

"You've seen the tape of what happened?"

"Part of it," Maggie said as they headed downstairs. "The important part, where he practically admits to Jo-Beth that he killed Monica O'Neal. When she seems surprised and he thinks maybe that she's going to rat him out, he puts a pillow over Jo-Beth's head and murders her, not ten minutes after screwing the living daylights out of her."

"Premeditated?"

She thought. Shook her head as they reached the first floor. "More of an act of passion or self-protection. This time. With O'Neal, definitely premeditated."

"Kinley March couldn't have prevented this?"

"She claims she was watching on a bit of a delay. Maybe two minutes, but she might just be covering her ass. Again. She's pretty into that. Anyway, who knows?" Maggie thought about it a sec as they passed through a hallway on the first floor. "Kinley says that when the attack on Jo-Beth went down, well, when she was witnessing it, delayed by a hundred and twenty seconds, she flew into action. She ran downstairs and got the hotel manager, but by the time they returned to the room, via elevator, he was gone, the tape shows him leaving through the French doors that lead to a long deck out back, staircase at the end near the parking lot."

"Damn."

"Garcia has already looked through security footage of the hotel. Sure enough, Quade climbed into his pickup and drove toward Main Street less than five minutes before the security guard gained access to Jo-Beth's room. The footage on the camera shows that he headed south."

"He lives in Roseburg? That's south."

She was nodding. "I don't think he'd go home. Too suspicious. He's supposed to give a statement tomorrow. And all of his things are here. We've been in his room. He didn't clear out."

"Weapons?"

"No, no drugs either."

"I figure he left because he's trying to pull together some kind of alibi." They reached the reception area, where several other cops were gathered. "You know, Tyler Quade skated on Monica O'Neal's murder. Possibly Eleanor Brady's. We don't know about that, yet. So he has a history of getting away with murder. Literally. Maybe he thinks he can here, too."

"That'll be tough. To come up with a logical alibi."

"But he doesn't know about the room being bugged." She smiled coldly as they reached the first floor. "We got him. We just have to find him."

"We will," he said, and meant it. "But right now I need to see Bernadette," he said. They were walking through the foyer of the old inn.

"In a second. They've all gathered in the dining room."

"No," he said, "Not in a second. She called me. Was freaked," he reminded Maggie. "I want to see her now."

"Fine, Romeo. We're on our way." She shot him a cool-your-jets glance and before he could respond, as he passed by the glass doors that opened to the back side of the hotel, he noticed, out of the corner of his eye, a truck rolling into the parking lot. The big rig slid to a stop in the slot next to his Jeep. And behind the steering wheel? None other than the man in question.

Tyler Quade, as if he hadn't a worry in the world, parked his rig and, holding two white sacks, hopped to the ground. What the hell? Why would he return?

"Looks like we got lucky," Lucas said under his breath, then made a beeline for the door. If Quade didn't realize he'd been filmed, he would probably try to lie about his whereabouts and assume that if anyone had seen him with Jo-Beth earlier, it wasn't a big deal. Even if his DNA was found on the bed, his sperm inside Jo-Beth, he could claim they hooked up earlier, and so what?

In the vaporous light from one security lamp, Quade glanced around the area and seemed slightly nervous at the sight of cop cars, their lights flashing, pulsing red and blue on the sides of the old inn. No doubt he hadn't expected Jo-Beth's body to be discovered so quickly. He'd probably thought no one would suspect her dead until the next morning and by that time, he could have either paid for alibis or been in and out of the hotel and different local establishments often enough to muddy the waters of his whereabouts.

Surely he would expect to be the primary suspect, but Maggie could be right. Quade might just be arrogant enough to think he could pull a fast one on the cops. After all, he'd done it before.

Not this time!

Lucas burst through the doorway.

"Lucas!" Maggie yelled behind him as he sprinted to the lot. "Detective Dalton! Don't! Do not approach the suspect!"

Tyler Quade froze, hesitating between his truck and Lucas's rig. "What the fuck?"

"Tyler Quade," Lucas yelled at the moment he realized his service weapon was still locked in his vehicle.

Stupid!

But he couldn't let the suspect get away.

Lucas ordered, "Police! Freeze!"

"What? Why?" A mask of innocence. *Yeah, right.* The lying prick!

"Drop the bags and put your hands in the air." Lucas kept walking toward him, eyes locked with Quade's gaze, and silently prayed the bastard didn't have a gun. If he made a move, Lucas would have to leap out of the way.

"Are you crazy?" Quade yelled back at him. "Dalton, what is this?" Now a nervous tic had started just under his eye and his muscles were tensing. "What's going on?"

"Just do it!"

"Hey, man, I just went for takeout for me and Jo-Beth," he said, and there it was, the alibi, a bald-faced lie coming into play.

Like hell! "I said drop the bags! Raise your damned hands! Do it. Now!"

"What the fuck's going on around here?" Quade asked, but seeing the expression on Lucas's face, he did let the bags fall to the ground. One sack exploded as the soft drinks inside hit hard pavement. Dark liquid splashed and foamed upward, soaking the paper. "All the cop cars . . . holy shit. What happened?" To credit Quade's acting skills, his face did change expression, as if it had just dawned on him that somehow he could be a suspect in some horrendous crime. "Hey—wait. What're you doing?"

Still the tic continued to throb.

From behind him, Maggie's voice, low and loud. "Tyler Quade, put your hands in the air."

"I don't understand," Tyler said uneasily.

"Don't say another word," Lucas warned. "Just do as Officer Dobbs commanded. And do it now."

Quade was shaking his head, still acting confused. "But I—"

"I've got this!" Maggie was suddenly beside Lucas, weapon drawn, aiming straight at Quade. "Police," she yelled at Quade as Lucas reached his Jeep. He reached into his pocket, found his remote key, and pushed the button to release the door lock. Maggie ordered, "I said put your hands in the air and then drop to your knees."

"I don't know what's going on here," Quade argued, backpedaling a bit and easing closer to his truck. "But you've got it all wrong."

"Now!" she screamed. "Do it!"

Quade was cool. Aside from that telling little twitch. "Okay, okay, but I'm tellin' ya, whatever the hell this is, it has *nothing* to do with me. You got it all wrong." As he raised his hands and fell to his knees, he sent a look in Lucas's direction that silently spoke volumes. The hairs on the back of Lucas's neck raised. No way was Tyler Quade giving up so easily.

Lucas opened the door to his truck to grab his gun.

Maggie stepped behind Quade to cuff him.

In that second, when her weapon wasn't trained on him, Quade reared up and threw her against his truck.

Bam!

The side of her head hit the steel door. Quade jumped forward and rolled to the front of the truck just as Maggie, stunned, raised her gun and fired. The shot went wild.

Somewhere nearby a woman screamed. Other voices shouted. Quade, bent low, started scrambling through the parking lot as pandemonium ensued.

As Quade started to run, Lucas took off after him, rounding the front of the truck. Voices shouted around him as Quade ducked behind a minivan.

"Give it up!" Lucas ordered. "Freeze!"

But the other man ran, dodging and hiding

between the cars as other cops took up the chase and onlookers watched in horror.

No way, with all the people around, could the officers risk a shot.

As Quade cut to a hedgerow, Lucas sprang.

He tackled Quade on the fly.

"Ooof!"

Together they fell, skidding over the thin gravel and hard pavement.

The side of Lucas's face scraped over the uneven asphalt. Pain screamed through his jaw. Still he wrestled with the muscular man. Cursing and spitting, rolling and kicking, Quade tried to wriggle free and escape. "Get the fuck off me!"

Blood ran down Lucas's face, but he had his arms around Quade. "You're done, Quade. It's over! We got you."

"Bullshit!" Quade yelled, rolling and bucking, trying to get free. "Let me go!"

"Not a chance," he said, breathing hard.

"You fucker!" Quade kicked upward, breaking Lucas's grip. Rounding, Quade swung wildly at Lucas's head.

Crack! Quade's fist pounded into Lucas's nose and he heard cartilage crunch. Blood spurted. Pain exploded through his head, and Lucas swung hard enough that his fist smashed into Quade's jaw so hard he felt the bone give.

Quade howled and rolled away, scrabbling,

trying to find purchase. "You broke my goddamned jaw! You fuckin' cocksucker!"

In his peripheral vision, Lucas saw a streak of black and brown, a growling mass that leaped, white teeth snapping, black gums pulled back as Roscoe clamped down on Quade's arm.

He squealed in pain. "Get off, you fucker!" he yelled at the dog, but Roscoe held on. "Get him off me!"

"Stop!" a voice yelled, and Lucas spied Maggie, her gun trained on Quade. "Lucas, call off your dog! I got this." Then to the suspect, "If you move one muscle, Tyler Quade, so much as roll your eyeballs," she swore, "I'll blast your sorry ass to hell." Her eyes were hard, her lips flat, a bruise already visible under one eye.

"Roscoe! Release!" Lucas ordered and, breathing heavily, pulled himself to his feet.

The dog immediately slackened his jaw and backed up, his gaze still trained on Quade.

"Cuff him," Maggie said, her set of handcuffs dangling from her free hand as the muzzle of her pistol never wavered, was trained directly on the suspect. She tossed the cuffs to Lucas. "Tyler Quade," she said, "you're under arrest for the murders of Monica O'Neal and Jo-Beth Leroy. You have the right to remain silent . . ."

As she continued to repeat the Miranda warning, Lucas, still bleeding, doomed for at least one, and more likely two, black eyes, yanked Quade's arms behind his back and snapped on the cuffs. It felt good. Because he knew, without a doubt, this time Quade was going down.

Chapter 38

Averille, Oregon
Now
Lucas

Lying in a hospital bed despite being hyped up from the investigation and fight, Lucas waited impatiently to be released. He had work to do and couldn't be bothered with biding his time while doctors, nurses, and aides tended to other people. He was contemplating just leaving when in this night of bad karma, his luck just got worse.

The last person Lucas wanted to deal with was his father.

But here Jeremiah Dalton was, striding into the ER of the small hospital in Seaside and acting as if he owned the place.

"What in God's good name is going on?" he demanded when he found his son on a bed separated by the other patients in the ER by thin curtains. "By the way, you look like hell."

"Nice to see you, too," Lucas mocked. "Don't

try to cheer me up." But he knew Jeremiah wasn't exaggerating. He looked worse than he felt and he felt pretty damned bad. Though Lucas hadn't sustained any life-threatening injuries, he was more than beat-up with two black eyes, split knuckles, and a face scraped raw in places. But Quade had it worse with a broken jaw and more than a few abrasions, nothing that would keep him out of court for the charges that were being filed against him.

That was the good news.

The bad? That the old man had shown up. Lucas couldn't help but wonder why. He'd never been a doting father, and there had never been much love lost between father and son, so why the hell had he shown up at Grace Memorial Hospital?

"Sir, you'll have to leave," a nurse said, scurrying over from a central hub, where other nurses and aides gathered and a series of monitors provided information on the patients. In blue scrubs, she was tall and thin, with a straight black ponytail and a no-nonsense attitude.

"This is my son," Jeremiah stated, and she glanced over to Lucas, who gave a short nod. He was feeling rough, cotton wadding still jammed up one nostril, an ice pack pressed to the right side of his face, a massive headache pounding behind his eyes. He'd put two calls in to Bernadette; both had gone straight to voice mail, where he'd left a couple of messages. She hadn't called him back.

"I'm leaving," Lucas said, and the nurse frowned.

"A doctor needs to release you."

"I'll sign myself out," he said, rolling off the bed. "It's a broken nose. I'll live."

She was undeterred. "Hospital policy—"

"Be damned," he said as his feet hit the floor and he found his wallet, keys, and phone. Except that his car was back at the hotel. He'd arrived at the hospital, under protest, by ambulance. His father's vehicle was obviously the fastest means of transportation back to Averille.

"Let's go," he said to the old man as he pulled on his boots. "I need a ride."

"Mr. Dalton," the nurse cut in, "Detective, I strongly advise—"

"Duly noted." He knew he'd survive. He'd only come to the hospital because of department policy.

"There's paperwork," she said, and stepped away from the bed as if to find the proper forms. He didn't wait, just headed for the exit.

His father kept up with him. "What was that all about, the commotion at the inn?" Jeremiah wanted to know as they walked out of the ER to the night, where a thin drizzle was beginning to fall.

Once they were in the Caddy, Jeremiah fired up

the engine. "So what happened?" he asked as he drove south through the town.

So that was what this was all about. Of course. "I can't tell you anything that might compromise the investigation."

"I'm not asking for that." He drove out of town and Lucas watched as the lights of Seaside faded behind them.

"A woman was murdered," he said. "ID isn't being given out until next of kin is notified."

Jeremiah nodded. He'd probably gleaned that much already. "And?"

"And it looks like we might finally have Monica O'Neal's killer behind bars." While his head pounded and his father drove ever south, the windshield wipers slapping at the rain, he sketched out what he could of the story, giving out the same details that the PIO would offer in a press release, including the fact that Quade was the suspect.

"So you think Tyler Quade killed the O'Neal girl?" Jeremiah frowned.

"That surprises you?"

"Oh, I've learned not to let anything surprise me much," he said. "But I am hoping that the sheriff's department will keep Camp Horseshoe out of this as much as possible."

"Kinda hard to do as both victims and the alleged killer were counselors at the time."

"I know, but the more I can distance any of this

560

nasty business from the camp, the better. I've got serious buyers interested. We're talking real money here, son." He nodded to himself and Lucas bit back a sharp retort. The only time his father ever referred to him as his son was when he wanted something.

"You don't think that money should go to Naomi?"

"What? No." Jeremiah's face turned sour. "Her father left that property to the church. Specifically. The gift was by the book, all on the up-and-up. We've been through the legalities during the divorce. She contested the gift, but it was a done deal." His lips twisted a bit and he slid a sly look in Lucas's direction. "Of course she wasn't happy about it, no way. The phrase 'mad as a wet hen' comes to mind. But," he said, nodding to himself, "it was a done deal. Fair and square."

They drove in silence, the old man's hands clenched around the wheel, his knuckles showing white. "So, I just want all this commotion to go away, you know, the stink of any scandal to dissipate so I can sell the property."

"Why is it so important?"

"Finally got interested buyers." He stared straight ahead.

"So you said. But there's more to it, isn't there?" The old man was holding back; Lucas could sense it.

"I just want to pull up stakes," he said. "Start fresh. Reorganize the church, maybe start a new camp."

That sounded suspicious. Why now? Why not here, where he already had the property? "Where would you go?"

"I was thinkin' Montana. Pretty country there. God's country." He squinted as a car going the opposite direction drove past, its headlights washing the interior for a second and, in that spray of light, Lucas saw the set of his father's jaw, the little downturn of his mouth. He wanted something. Bad. And somehow showing up at the hospital and demanding that Lucas, as a cop and out of some sense of misaligned duty to the old man, could help.

"Where in Montana?" he asked as they rounded the curve of the road as it swept around the cliff face of Neahkahnie Mountain. "It's a big state."

Jeremiah shrugged. "Not sure. Helena, maybe. Lots of land available."

"And something else," Lucas guessed, starting to understand. His father wanted three things in life: a church where he could be the spokesman of God, enough money to have a decent life-style, and, of course, a woman. He'd been long without all three. Selling the property and moving would satisfy his first two needs but didn't explain the third. "Who is she?" Lucas asked.

"What?"

"The woman in Montana. Your girlfriend, if that's what you call it when you're on the north side of sixty."

"I don't have—" He started to argue, then slid a glance at his son. For once, he didn't try to bullshit Lucas.

"She got a name?"

His father hesitated and must've decided lying wouldn't work. Lucas was, after all, a detective, and Jeremiah Dalton hadn't been known for his discretion when it came to the ladies. "Fine. Winona."

"How old is she?"

"What does it matter?"

"How old?"

He didn't respond and Lucas got a sick feeling in his gut.

"I'm gonna find out."

"Twenty-five."

Lucas let out a long whistle. "Let me guess, her family wants to invest in the church. Jesus, Dad, she's younger than Leah."

"Do not use the Lord's name in vain with me."

"*That's* what you're worried about?" Lucas charged. "Blasphemy? When you're contemplating what? Marrying a woman little more than a third your age and starting a new life, creating a church out of the money you made from your latest ex? You're unbelievable!"

"She loves me."

"Of course she does," he mocked. "Don't they all? Man, you've gone through them and they just keep getting younger all the time."

"At least they're not married when I get involved with them."

Lucas felt the bite of that one. He deserved it, but his affair with Naomi was long over, past history. He wasn't going to be dragged into a fight about it all over again. He itched to get out of Jeremiah's SUV and almost told his father to pull over, that he'd walk the remaining miles to Averille, but he needed to return as quickly as possible. Unfortunately Jeremiah's Caddy was the fastest means of transportation. "How the hell did you meet her?" he asked. "This Winona?"

"Online."

"Man, this just gets better and better." He was shaking his head, turning his attention to the passenger side window, where beyond the rain-streaked glass he saw the Pacific, stretching far into the darkness, shining with the little bit of moonlight piercing the clouds.

"Look, Lucas, all I need from you is to wrap up this investigation, keep it out of the press so that the old camp sells quickly and for a good price."

"And so you don't spook your new in-laws? Tell me, Dad, how does Naomi feel about that?"

"I don't see her much," he admitted as the road turned inland and the city lights of Averille came into view.

"So, Jeremiah," he finally said. "Just so you know. I'm going to want to talk to you officially, or at least Detective Dobbs or Garcia will. I'm off the case."

"What?"

"Yeah." He glared at the man who had sired him and thought he saw his father actually starting to sweat. Maybe this was the time to put the screws to him. Why not? His face was throbbing, he'd been thrown off the case, and he had no respect for the man anyway. "Sheriff Locklear isn't going to rest until every aspect of this case is solved, so I wouldn't be planning on heading to Montana anytime soon. She's got four missing people to locate and so far has only found one."

"Four?" he said. "Eleanor Brady and Monica O'Neal, right? That's two."

"And Dustin Peters, you remember him, right? You hired him? And then there's the con who vanished about the same time: Waldo Grimes. I'm telling you, Locklear's gonna leave no stone unturned and you're a big one. Owning the camp where everything went down. She's going to dig deep."

His father took one hand off the wheel to scratch his chin, a nervous gesture.

Lucas couldn't believe it, but felt the old man might actually crack and give something up. "If I were you," he pressed, "and I was hell-bent to go to Montana or anywhere, I'd come clean. If you had anything to do with the deaths of—"

"Oh, whoa, whoa, whoa," Jeremiah cut in. "I've never been involved in murder of any sort."

Lucas snorted, felt something give in his nose again and a trickle of blood start to flow. "So you avoided one deadly sin."

"Still an insolent pup." They passed the WELCOME TO AVERILLE sign and a mini-market gas station, not open, the neon lights surrounding the canopy glowing red and yellow.

"Locklear's going to find out all your secrets," Lucas said, "and they'll be made public. Nothing I can do about that. You'd better sell that land quick."

"I haven't done anything wrong."

"Sure."

"I mean it . . . I . . ." He guided the SUV through a couple of side streets to turn a corner. The hotel came into view. A cop car was still positioned at each end of the street and a news van, satellite cocked, was parked at the barrier. The Hotel Averille itself was lit like a Christmas tree, all the exterior and interior windows of the third floor glowing in the night, the first floor, too, illuminated, people visible inside as the crime scene team searched for evidence, and workers of the hotel, along with a few guests, were still up and about. Only a few of the guest rooms on the second and first floors were dark, either unoccupied or their inhabitants turning in for the night despite all the commotion that had occurred.

"The press is still here," Lucas said, hitching his chin toward the news van. "They'll be all over you, Jeremiah. Whatever it is you're doing, including this planned move to Montana, will be explored. Kinley Marsh, you know her, she was a camper, works for some Astoria online newspaper or something. She's hoping to make the story go viral and national. Camp Horseshoe will be at the center of it."

"No."

"Looks that way."

The Cadillac was slowing as his father thought. Even in the dark, Lucas could see by the way Jeremiah's eyes narrowed that the wheels were turning frantically in the old man's brain. As the Caddy got close to a barrier, a cop in rain gear waved Jeremiah off.

"This can't happen," Jeremiah said, pulling his SUV into an empty parking spot near the barrier, the inn only a hundred feet away. He shoved the gear shift into park but let the engine idle, the wipers swiping at the rain collecting on the windshield.

"Oh, it's happening."

"No."

"Look, if you know something, anything at all about the case," Lucas said, gambling and playing to his father's false sense of pride, "and you want to look good, you know. Like you were helping the police rather than hindering them? That you as a responsible citizen and pillar of the community wanted to set things right, you'd be smart to spill it, right now."

"I don't—"

Lucas snapped. Was sick of the game-playing. He was on his old man in an instant, springing across the interior and grabbing Jeremiah by the front of his shirt. Fingers twisting in the soft fabric, he snarled. "I've had it. I'm beat-up and tired and pissed as hell. I don't need any more of your bullshit lies, okay? What the fuck do you know, Jeremiah? It's going to come out one way or another, and it's best if you confess."

"I have nothing to—"

"Enough!" he growled, his headache pounding, his rage exploding. "Enough lies." He shoved his face to within an inch of his old man's. "You know something. What the fuck is it? Tell me, or I'll have you arrested and then you can explain that to the investors and your new little bride-to-be in wherever-the-hell fucking Montana!" His fingers were wound so tight in the fabric of his father's shirt that they ached.

"Let go of me," Jeremiah finally said, a forced calm in his voice.

Lucas backed off. Released his grip. Reached for the door handle. "Fine."

"Wait!"

"What?"

Jeremiah cleared his throat. Smoothed the wrinkles from his shirt with a big hand. "There is . . . there is one thing."

"Tell me."

"It's about Dustin Peters."

"What about him?" Lucas, his blood still up, eyed the old man in the reflection of the dash lights. In the weird illumination, Jeremiah appeared older than he had been, his eyes more sunken, his cheekbones more prominent, his entire face taking on the likeness of a fleshless skull.

"I paid Peters five thousand dollars, cash money, to disappear."

"You did what?" Lucas couldn't believe it.

"It was a mistake," Jeremiah admitted. "But Naomi told me about the fight you two had and I saw for myself the way that no-good was looking at your little sister. Damn, but Leah was only eleven at the time, not quite twelve, and that piece of garbage was looking at her like a starving wolf stares at a wounded lamb. It was no good, so I told him to get lost."

"And paid him to do it? You thought that would solve the problem?"

"I hoped."

"For the love of God, Dad! Didn't it occur to you that he'd go after some other underage girl?"

"Not my problem. My daughter would be safe. And . . . I hoped he'd learned his lesson."

"Where did he go?"

"Didn't say and I didn't ask. He disappeared and I was satisfied." Then, as if he thought God might be listening in, added, "But David thought he saw him once, riding the rodeo circuit, well, not the big leagues, but on the B or C circuit. David wasn't sure, mind you, but he nearly ran into a cowboy who looked like Peters. The guy caught sight of him and headed in the other direction, got lost in the crowd before David could say anything. According to the program for the rodeo, that cowboy's name was Pete Denver, from somewhere in Colorado. As I said, small-time."

"You never checked if Denver was Peters?"

"Nope. That was about five years ago, I think, and all of this mess was long behind us. Or so I'd thought."

Jeremiah was unbelievable. Lucas wanted to throttle the old man. "Did you even think once that he might have had something to do with Monica's disappearance?"

"I just wanted him gone." A self-centered non-answer.

"What about Elle? What if Dustin had an inkling as to what happened to her?"

Jeremiah flinched a little at the mention of Elle, as if Lucas had hit a nerve. Geez, how many secrets had the old man buried? "What?" he demanded, intent on finding out. "You know something about Elle? About what happened to her?" The pain throbbing through his head started to recede as he focused on this piece of shit who was his father.

"I don't know anything about her. Not really!" Jeremiah said with more vehemence than was warranted. Another nervous scratch of his finger-nails under his chin. "I just know that there have been people who claim to have seen her."

"And that's it?" No way. He was lying straight through his porcelain-capped teeth.

Jeremiah hitched his chin to the parking lot. Again, the tell-tale avoidance. "There's your truck."

"What the hell do you know?"

His father leveled his gaze at his son. "Let her go, Lucas. As you did for twenty years. Before all this trouble started. Just let her go."

"Wait a minute. Do you know where she is? What happened to her?"

"Nope."

"You're lying! You bastard, you know what happened." He was across the cab again in a shot, his nose inches from his father's, his fists clenched. "What happened, Jeremiah? What the hell happened?"

The skeletal face studied him. "I don't know," he said. "But whatever it is, it's best left alone."

"You son of a bitch!"

"Get out."

"Listen to me, if you're lying or covering up something—"

"Hey!" There was a tap on the driver's side window and Lucas noticed the cop who had stopped them from driving closer to the hotel on the other side of the water-spattered glass.

Jeremiah rolled down the window.

"Is there a problem here?" the cop asked, peering inside.

"I was just bringing Detective Dalton to his truck." Jeremiah added, "I'm his father."

"Yeah, we're good," Lucas lied and, releasing the old man, reached for the door handle. As he stepped into the drizzle, he looked inside. "We're not done, Jeremiah," he promised, and slammed the door. "Not by a long shot."

Chapter 39

Averille, Oregon
Now
Lucas

To Lucas's surprise, Bernadette was still up, waiting in the lobby of the hotel. A hotel clerk was at the desk, a couple of cops still working with the crime scene as the techs finished processing the hotel.

"Thank God you're all right," Bernadette said, her face a mask of worry as she approached him. "I was . . . I mean, I saw part of the fight from here, but they wouldn't let us go near, then I heard shots and the ambulance came and took you away. Detective Dobbs said you were okay, but they kept us here and confiscated our phones and I couldn't come to the hospital and . . ." As if she realized she was rambling, she cleared her throat and flung herself into his arms.

He held her tight for a moment and kissed the top of her head before he realized others were watching them.

". . . and I have your dog," she finished.

Lucas released her. "Roscoe? Where is he?"

"In your Jeep, waiting, so technically I don't have him, but I've snuck out and given him a treat . . . well, possibly two or three. Are you okay?" she asked, eyeing him. "Geez, you look like hell."

"So I've heard." And he couldn't argue the fact. He'd caught his reflection in the glass of the front doors as he'd walked in, seen evidence of his black eyes, and suspected that there was probably blood crusting his nostrils. "It's been a long day," he admitted.

She smiled and her eyes sparked a little. "Amen to that." To his surprise, she hugged him again and kissed his temple in a very un-Bernadette display of affection. "Okay, you do look like hell, but you're still sexy." Then, as if realizing she might have crossed a line, explained, "I'm just glad you're okay."

"Me too."

"There's been a lot of weird stuff going on."

"That's the understatement of the year, or maybe the decade," he agreed. "But at least we know what happened to Monica O'Neal and who killed her and Jo-Beth." Scowling at the thought, he rubbed the back of his neck and was royally pissed that he and the department hadn't figured out the twenty-year-old crime earlier and pre-vented another death.

The elevator door opened and Maggie Dobbs appeared. Spying Lucas, she crossed in front of the reception desk and shook her head as she stared at his face. "You look like—"

"So I've heard," he said.

"Shouldn't you be home recuperating or something? Seriously. Your face—"

"I'm fine! It's not that bad."

"If you say so." She arched a disbelieving brow and glanced at Bernadette. "Did you show him the text?"

"What text?" he asked as Bernadette shook her head.

Maggie said, "The one that was sent to all of the ex-counselors including Jo-Beth."

She was already retrieving her own phone. "I've got it. Nell Pachis forwarded it to me and

I've got the lab and cell phone company already working on it." She found the text and handed her cell to Lucas, who caught sight of the image on the screen and froze.

"What is this?" he whispered, and felt bile climb up his throat as he stared at the picture of a woman, dressed in white, in a casket, the words "YOU WILL PAY" written as the message. "Elle in a coffin?"

"That's what we think, or what it's supposed to look like. We don't know yet," Maggie said.

"You all got this?" he asked Bernadette.

"Yes."

"Even Jo-Beth Leroy. We checked," Maggie said as he automatically sent the picture to his own cell phone. "They came in at the same time, group text, all the counselors, but not Kinley Marsh."

"She wasn't a counselor," he said.

"Precisely. Come over here and sit down before you fall down and I'll fill you in. I don't know about you, but I'm dead, despite the buzz from the hotel's complimentary coffee." To Bernadette, she said, "You too. In case I forget anything. This is, of course, off the record."

"As I'm not on the case," Lucas said.

"Exactly," Maggie responded, and they exchanged a look. He knew she was going out on a limb, including him in part of the investigation, but Maggie was smart and would hold just enough back that she could deny involving him as a cop. They sat in a grouping of chairs positioned around a fireplace stacked with ceramic logs, gas flames visible.

Maggie told him about Kinley Marsh's equipment and recordings, how they had Tyler Quade's confession on tape, then explained that all of the counselors had gotten the same text. As she'd said, the phone company had already been contacted and was searching records to see what was the origination of the original text while the image was being enhanced at the lab, searching for clues as to its authenticity.

Lucas brought up his conversation with Jeremiah, how the old man had bribed Dustin Peters to leave the camp twenty years earlier and how David Tremaine had told his ex-stepfather that he'd seen a two-bit rodeo rider named Pete Denver who might be one and the same. "Jeremiah claims he doesn't know where Dustin Peters went, but he did say the cowboy hailed from Boulder, Colorado. Maybe that's how he came up with the name Denver."

"I'll check it out. We're wrapping things up here," Maggie said. "The crime scene unit is about finished and so I'm going to call it a night. We've asked the women who had come down here to make statements to stay on at least overnight in case we have any more questions tomorrow, er"—she looked at her watch—"later today as it turns out, but, understandably, they weren't that crazy about staying here in the hotel."

Lucas couldn't blame them. "So what's the plan, then?"

"We offered to post deputies here, and they all agreed."

"Reluctantly," Bernadette said.

Maggie continued. "They're all in one wing of the second floor, deputies on watch at both ends of the hallway, everyone's room door to be dead-bolted. The second floor doesn't have balconies, so we're only concerned with securing the interior corridor."

"You're okay with that?" he asked Bernadette.

"Yeah, Annette and I share connecting rooms; we'll leave the door open between."

He wasn't convinced. "I could stay," he offered when he knew that he shouldn't as he had a lot more work to do. But the thought of spending the rest of the night with Bernadette was tempting. In a quick-silver flash of memory, he remembered the nights he'd lain with her all those years ago.

Her smile was slow-spreading, as if she'd read his mind and even may have had the same thoughts. "I'll see you tomorrow," she promised, and he let her go, watching as she rose to her feet and walked to the elevator, her butt as firm as ever in tight jeans.

"Man," Maggie said, observing the exchange.

"You've got it bad." Her eyebrows arched knowingly. "That's the trouble with a teenage crush, you know, the feelings you experienced as an adolescent never go away. They're always there, just below the surface."

"Sounds like the voice of experience talking."

"Maybe, but even so, I might remind you that you don't know her, have barely reconnected, and there's been a lot of emotional water flowing beneath the bridge. Not that it's any of my business."

"Exactly," he said, "it's not." Though she was echoing his own inner monologue of all the reasons not to get involved or re-involved with Bernadette. And yet . . . "Look, I have something I've got to do," he said. "I'll call you in the morning."

"Make that the later morning." Maggie glanced at her watch as he headed for the exit. "It's almost two."

And probably too late for a stakeout, he thought, and let it go, returning home with an excited Roscoe and thinking about Bernadette for most of the drive. At his cabin, he cleaned up a little, then sent the picture of Eleanor Brady in the casket to himself so that he could blow it up on his computer. When he did, he studied the image.

The woman sure as hell looked like Elle, or what he remembered of her . . . and yet he felt there was something not quite right. Since it had been nearly two decades since he'd seen her, he couldn't place what was off about the picture, but there was something. He spent forty minutes searching the attic space adjacent to the loft, sorted through some dusty boxes, and discovered his old yearbook, which he dragged to his desk. Leaning back in his desk chair, he sifted through the pages and found several with pictures of a teenage Eleanor Brady.

As he studied the slightly yellowed pages, he remembered the time he'd been with her, the innocence, the desire. And the guilt. It was during the time when he'd been dating Elle that he'd gotten involved with Naomi, the only time in his life that he'd been sexually involved with two women at once. It had been exhilarating and terrifying, a horny teenager's fantasy that had quickly become a nightmare.

When he'd taken up with Bernadette on the heels of the Elle/Naomi debacle, he'd been loyal to her, never once looking at another woman, including Elle and Naomi.

"Honorable of you," he scoffed, unhappy with his younger self.

He wondered about his relationship with Bernadette. If things had worked out differently, if there hadn't been the horror and chaos of the missing girls, would he and Bernadette have stuck it out? Eventually married? In the back of his mind he had a niggling suspicion that Bernadette Alsace could have been "the one."

Well, if you believed in those kinds of fantasies. Deep down, he didn't.

He compared all of the pictures of Elle in the yearbook to the girl in the casket. Yes, the woman in the casket was blond, with a straight nose and blue, blue eyes, but her lips didn't seem as full and the dimple in her chin was less pronounced. Was it his imagination, a trick of light, or was she a different woman, posed to appear to be Elle? Of course, she would have to be someone else, someone much younger than Elle if the picture of the woman in the casket was recent. Elle would be close to forty now. And the girl in the picture couldn't be older than twenty.

Zooming to enlarge the photo, he studied every detail of the woman in the coffin.

Of course the picture could have been altered or Photoshopped; the lab would be able to figure that out.

He felt as if he were missing something, something important. What was it? With no answer, he walked downstairs, found a beer in the fridge, and returned to the loft. His face ached, so he popped a couple of ibuprofen, then with Roscoe snoring at his feet, he studied the woman's face once more and wondered why all of the women had received the picture. YOU WILL PAY. What the hell did that mean? Pay for what? Monica's death? The camp being closed? It had to be something to do with Elle, right? But what? Nothing was making any sense, and he even tried throwing Tyler Quade's confession into the mix and that didn't help. Yes, Tyler had killed Monica, but what did that have to do with Elle?

"You will pay," he repeated. All of the female counselors? For what? What kind of threat was that, and from whom? He sipped his beer, his eyes narrowing on the photograph. The dress, white, almost like a wedding dress, the white rose in her hands, the coffin . . . wait. He studied the rose again and his stomach tightened.

He'd seen white roses recently.

In Jeanette Brady's living room, a bit of white in an otherwise gloomy room.

A coincidence? He didn't think so.

His pulse quickened, though he told himself it could be nothing, the flowers were a thin connection at best.

But it was the only connection he had.

And he thought, draining his bottle, he was damned well going to check it out.

Maggie was beat. It was long after three in the morning by the time she'd showered and crashed in bed, Mr. Bones curled up on a pillow next to her. Still, despite the lateness of the hour and her body being exhausted, her mind was racing, her brain far from shutting down.

581

She'd spent most of the night at the hotel, then another hour at the station, which had been a madhouse, officers called to duty, the press arriving en masse and demanding answers at the hotel and again at the Neahkahnie Sheriff's Department. Somehow news of Kinley Marsh's recording of the homicide had leaked, possibly from the reporter herself, and the story of Jo-Beth Leroy's murder and arrest of her lover/killer was going viral.

Kinley Marsh had wanted fame.

Well, she'd found it.

The ex-counselors had each opened up, including Reva Mercado, who had admitted to stealing the butcher knife for the prank to be played upon Monica O'Neal. The idea was to scare her, either by Tyler feigning being stabbed by the homicidal maniac Waldo Grimes, the escaped prisoner, or by threatening Monica with the weapon, but never, Reva had sworn, was anyone supposed to really get hurt or die. "That was all Tyler," she'd insisted, sucking on a cigarette on the front porch of the hotel. "Jo-Beth and I, we had no idea. None. He's crazy and he went rogue on us."

Which, of course, confirmed what Kinley had taped, Jo-Beth seeming upset and surprised that he'd actually killed Monica. And Tyler Quade had as much as admitted to the crime in the seconds before he killed Jo-Beth, both the confession and the homicide caught on Kinley's hidden camera.

There was no doubt in Maggie's mind that Tyler Quade was going to spend the rest of his life behind bars.

Good.

One less bit of homicidal vermin on the streets, the homicide cases of Monica O'Neal and Jo-Beth Leroy buttoned up. She was even certain that when she reinterviewed Reva Mercado, she would confess to another crime, that of being behind the wheel in the accident that had happened years before. Mercado would be looking at serious charges: Negligent Homicide was just for starters. Then there was the cover-up and lying to the authorities. Yeah, Mercado was going to need a good lawyer. Maggie wasn't letting that one go. She thought she could, because of recent events and Mercado's change of heart, convince her to come clean.

Maybe.

Time would tell.

As the cat purred Maggie plumped her pillow, then rolled over, trying to fall asleep, but too many questions nagged at her.

But what about Eleanor Brady and her disappearance? How did that fit in with Monica O'Neal's murder? Or was it all coincidental? During the interviews, each of the women had shown Maggie texts that they'd received, pictures of what appeared to be a dead woman in a coffin, a woman who was a dead ringer for Eleanor. The images could have been Photoshopped, an old picture of Elle's face superimposed on the body in the coffin. But why? And why would all the women receive the same picture—including Jo-Beth—along with the warning: YOU WILL PAY.

It was troubling, to say the least.

And what about all the sightings of Eleanor? Sosi Gavin, no, Gaffney now—she said she'd seen Eleanor the night on the beach and again recently when she'd arrived in Averille. Caleb Carter had sworn, though he'd been drunk, that he'd seen her. Annette Alsace had seen the "ghost" on the beach, too, years ago. Now, her sister, Bernadette, had sworn someone who looked like the missing woman had followed her in a blue Ford.

Really?

So now "ghosts" had driver's licenses? And showed up in pictures? It all didn't make sense, but then, tonight, Maggie's brain was on overload. Tomorrow morning, if she could just sleep a few hours tonight, she'd look at all the facts and testimony with fresh eyes.

Once they heard back from the phone company and the lab, maybe they could find answers. Yawning, she yanked the covers to her neck, exhaustion starting to overtake her just as Mr.

Bones was waking up, doing his own stretching, and no doubt would want to go outside. Three a.m. seemed the time he chose to stir.

He stretched lazily, then came closer to paw her face. "Not a chance," she whispered, and burrowed deeper under the blankets. She knew he would settle down. Eventually. Until then, she'd ignore him and sleep; a clear mind would help her sort out fact from fiction, and maybe by then the department would discover the source of the pictures of a supposedly dead Eleanor Brady and finally learn what had happened to her.

Somehow, some way, Maggie thought, her brain finally shutting down, sleep tugging at her mind, the disappearance of the woman kept circling back to Lucas Dalton, her ex-lover and the last person to have admitted to seeing Eleanor alive.

Dawn was still over an hour away when Lucas parked on a side street a quarter of a mile from the Bradys' house. Once his Jeep was hidden behind a hedge, he grabbed his stake-out bag and jogged through the night to the lane, where he positioned himself on the far side of a fence, his cover being a patch of Scotch broom. Equipped with night-vision goggles, he saw a doe and two fawns leap across a small creek before disappearing into the surrounding brush. Nearby he spied a handful of rabbits hopping through the skeletal berry vines and bracken that were encroaching on the Brady property.

The rain had slackened, a mist rising as the night wore on.

The Brady house was dark, no signs of life until nearly six when a light appeared in the window of Elle's room, a patch of illumination in the dormer, the same window where he'd observed the blond woman the night before. The shades were drawn and he couldn't make out an image, even with magnifying binoculars, but he was certain he'd seen a woman. Less than a minute later, a smaller window on a side of the house, a bathroom window, glowed bright as a light was snapped on.

"Bingo," he whispered to himself, though, of course, this could be nothing, a relative or friend of Jeanette's she didn't want to name—nothing more.

But the little zing firing his blood, that gut instinct that he was on to something, suggested otherwise.

And someone other than Jeanette, whose bedroom, the one she'd shared with Darryl, was on the first floor. The guest was definitely up very early.

He considered knocking on the door, but believed whoever was in the house would hide, and he doubted he could obtain a search warrant to flush the visitor out. Jeanette would balk at letting him inside, so he had to wait.

See what was up.

Also, if it turned out to be nothing, if the visitor was just some shy friend, no one besides him would be the wiser.

Either way, he'd find out.

It didn't take long.

Under the cover of darkness he spied a woman emerge from the back door of the house. She walked quickly to a shed at the edge of the yard and unlocked a sliding barn door, then wheeled out a motorcycle.

In a second, she was astride and kicking the bike to life.

Lucas didn't wait. He was on his feet in an instant and running to his SUV. Rather than confront her, he decided to follow her and even if it turned out to be a wild goose chase, he would have at the very least satisfied his curiosity. He couldn't help but think that because she'd been hidden in Elle's room there was some thread of connection to Elle, but he couldn't for the life of him figure out what it was.

Yet.

He reached his Jeep and threw himself inside.

Half a minute later, he was giving chase.

To God-only-knew-where.

Chapter 40

Averille, Oregon
Now
Bernadette

Another text came in and Bernadette, having just fallen asleep in the hotel room bed, mentally kicked herself for not turning off her phone. She groaned, trying to rouse.

After being interviewed by the police, she'd eventually been given back her phone; then it had come alive with text after text from the other women who had, too, given their statements.

Reva had wanted to go to a bar and talk it out, Jayla was opting for a church service, Sosi complained about not being home, and Nell had just said she was "done with this," whatever that meant. Bernadette figured they never would be done, not as long as they could remember Jo-Beth and Monica. Bernadette had waited for Lucas to return and after seeing that he was all right, she'd finally come up to the bedroom and checked in on Annette. Wearing an oversize T-shirt and pajama bottoms, Annette had lain on top of the covers and used the bed's oversize pillows to prop her back against the headboard.

"She stole my diary, you know," Annette had said, looking up from her novel. "Kinley. She was the one. What a little bitch." She'd tossed the book onto the foot of the bed. "Now it's going to be out there, you know? On the Internet fo God's sake, the musings of a seventeen-year-old. It's so embarrassing. It could go viral or even worse, it could become like . . . like a movie of the week!"

"Don't you think you're jumping to conclusions?"

Annette had rolled her eyes. "Maybe. But I don't like it."

"Neither do I. And here's the thing, Kinley's taking all of the credit for it, so even if she uses the stuff in your diary, it'll look like it was all hers, I think. She loves to be the center of attention. Good or bad."

"Ugh." Annette had gotten out of the bed and stalked to the window. "I can't sleep. My mind is going round and round in circles," she'd admitted, staring out at the night that was finally dark, the strobing of police lights having stopped an hour before. Leaning her head on the glass, she sighed, causing a bit of condensation on the panes.

"I just can't stop thinking about Jo-Beth and Monica and Tyler and that damned Kinley." She'd obviously been wound up. On edge. "Did you talk to Lucas?"

"Yeah, he's pretty beat-up."

"I thought maybe you'd, you know, be with

him tonight?" She'd looked over her shoulder. "You two are kinda picking up where you left off, aren't you?"

"Maybe," she'd said, hopeful.

"I don't blame you." Annette had sighed.

"Don't tell me you still have a crush on him."

One side of Annette's mouth had lifted. "Nah, that was a puppy love thing, but you?"

"Who knows?"

"I just wish this was all over, you know? Behind us."

"It will be. Try to relax. Get some sleep."

"Oh, sure. Like that's going to happen." She'd turned to face her sister and had rolled her eyes. "I guess . . . I guess I can be glad that at least the diary is in the police's hands," she'd said, then frowned. "Maybe I should get a lawyer. You know, try to get it back legally. Then, at least, I'd have control." She'd looked at her sister. "So irritating." And then, as if a new thought had hit her, she started rubbing her temples. "What am I thinking? So what if the police have it? I'll bet you dollars to doughnuts that Kinley made at least one copy." Annette had sat down on the foot of the bed and hung her head. "This is horrible. All of it. The murders. The fight. Tyler . . . Lucas." She'd shivered violently.

"Can't you Zen it out, do some yoga or meditation or something?"

"Like I haven't tried that," she'd spat out, seemingly angry at the world and especially at Bernadette.

"Think on it. Right now I'm going to bed."

"Just don't say *Namaste*, okay? Cuz you don't mean it."

"Wouldn't dream of it," Bernadette had lied as the word had been on the tip of her tongue.

And so she'd retired and fallen asleep almost immediately, but now her phone was practically leaping off the bed it was vibrating so loudly.

This text was from Annette. It just said: Can't sleep. Going for a drive.

What? After two in the morning? That seemed sketchy. And how could she do it? She had no wheels, not of her own, not here in Averille. They'd driven from Seattle in Bernadette's car. Groggily, Bernadette threw back the covers and padded to the window to look out at the parking lot.

Her car was there, where she'd parked it, in a far corner of the parking area, partially obscured from view by an outbuilding and a low fog oozing through the town's streets. The night was quieter than it had been, though, the news vans and crime scene vehicle having left the area, just the flapping yellow warning tape and a single cruiser from the sheriff's department indicating that there had been any trouble.

So what was Annette talking about?

Bernadette peered through the open connecting door and stepped into Annette's darkened room. "Hey?" she called, looking at the bed. "Annette?" When she didn't get a response, she fumbled for a light switch and snapped it on.

The room was empty.

Annette wasn't in the bed, though the covers were wrinkled, the book she'd been reading on the bedside table near a half-full glass of water. "Annette?" she said, and stepped into the bathroom, reached for the light switch, and snapped it on.

Nothing.

What the devil?

A frisson of fear slid down her spine. She found her phone and typed in, **Where are you?** before sending the text. Something was wrong. She could feel it. She considered calling Lucas, then decided it was silly to wake him at three in the morning. He'd already been through the trauma of a fight and a stint in the ER, so she'd wait. For now.

A text came in: **In the car. I took your keys.**

What? No! She ran to the window of her sister's room, where she had a better view of the spot where she'd parked and sure enough, through the thickening mist, she spied Annette behind the wheel. Her mind was starting to clear a bit as she flew back to her own bedroom and checked the bureau where she'd left her key for the room next to her car keys. Sure enough, they were missing. Her fingers flew over the keys of her phone as she sent another message.

Wait. You shouldn't go anywhere.

What was Annette thinking? Bernadette threw on her jeans and a sweatshirt, then snagged her hotel key and phone, stuffing them into her back pocket as she ran out of her room. This was nuts. They needed to stay in place. Even though the danger had passed as Tyler Quade, the murderer, was behind bars, there were still the weird texts with the picture of Elle in a coffin.

Tyler hadn't sent that message, at least she didn't think so. She saw the deputy at the end of the hall, his eyes glued to the screen of his iPad. He heard her coming and looked up quickly. "You leaving?"

"Just going to find my sister."

He nodded. "She said she was going out for a while."

"And you didn't stop her?"

One eyebrow raised. "I'm here to keep the hotel secure, but I can't keep anyone from leaving if they want to. My job is to keep the bad guys out, not the good guys in."

"But it's the middle of the night."

"My exact words, but Annette was determined. And an adult," he said as Bernadette decided arguing with him would get her nowhere. She took the stairs down to the first floor, then finding a door that wasn't locked, she ran outside to the damp night. Fog lay in patches, a breeze moving the mist ghostlike across the lawn.

As Bernadette reached the yard, she saw Annette starting to back out of the parking slot.

"No! Wait!" For the love of God. That was the trouble with Annette: outwardly calm, inwardly a mess. "Annette!" Bernadette sprinted across the wet grass of the back lawn, then hurried across the parking lot, gravel crunching under her feet, puddles splashing as she ran. She raced to the Honda and as Annette braked, grabbed the passenger side door. "What the hell are you doing?" she asked as she yanked open the door just as the car jostled to a stop.

"Go-going for a drive. Seaside. All-night restaurant." Annette was pale as death.

"That's crazy," Bernadette said, and thought something was off, something more than her sister driving thirty miles for a burger.

"It's . . . It's what I'm doing." She stared at Bernadette with round, worried eyes.

"Are you all right?"

"Yes," she squeaked out, but she looked as if she might pass out.

That's when Bernadette realized what was wrong. No interior light had flooded the car when she'd opened the door. No alarm bell indicating that a door was opening while the car was in gear had dinged.

"Annette—?" The hairs on the back of her neck stood on end.

"Get into the car," a voice ordered from the darkened back seat, and for the first time Bernadette realized someone was huddled behind her sister, hidden in the darkness by the head rests and tinted back windows. "Get in now, or I swear I'll shoot your sister right here and now."

Bernadette stared at Annette, then as she looked behind the front seat, she saw the gun, muzzle pressed to the back of the driver's seat, aimed straight at Annette's back. Obviously the assailant had somehow forced her sister through the hotel, past any security and into the car at gunpoint, probably threatening her life.

"I'm sorry," Annette said, and tears began to slide from her eyes. "I'm so sorry."

"Get in," the familiar voice ordered. "Now."

Bernadette wanted to run, to scream for help, but she believed that the assailant would easily squeeze the trigger and shoot Annette. But she had her phone in her pocket. If she could just slide it out. Cautiously, she slid into the passenger seat.

"Close the door."

She yanked the door shut, though she knew it was a mistake.

"Now drive," the assailant commanded.

"Where?" Annette squeaked out.

"To the camp," was the even response. "Where else?"

Chapter 41

Following the motorcycle wasn't difficult. The roads were nearly deserted, the bike's taillight a red beacon. Lucas hung back, sometimes turning off on a side road only to return to 101, just in case the woman on the bike was paying attention.

He tailed her through Tillamook, where there was more traffic, early risers driving, on their way to work, or conversely, those who were on their way home from a night of partying. The town stretched along the highway, the smell of cattle manure from the surrounding dairy farms noticeable, neon lights of businesses and street lamps offering some illumination, headlights flashing past. He lagged behind a semi as they reached the center of town, where the buildings were older and taller, pushed together in city blocks and the road split into one-way streets.

Lucas kept the bike in his sights and watched as she headed east, toward the surrounding hills, where dawn was just beginning to send fingers of light through the low-hanging mist.

The fog was a blessing and a curse, providing

him cover, but also creating a blanket that sometimes hid the motorcycle speeding toward the mountains.

Who the hell was she?

What was she doing?

Why had she been hiding upstairs when he'd visited Jeanette Brady?

He nearly got caught behind a tractor-trailer rig and was forced to pass as the town gave way to suburbs and then rural countryside. The taillight of the bike glowed bright for seconds, only to become obscured as the fog became thicker.

Lucas stepped on it. He couldn't afford to lose her. The road curved up through the mountains, trees rising on either side. Eventually this road would lead to the Willamette Valley and beyond, and he wondered how far he would follow her before either giving up or calling for backup.

And say what? That he had a gut feeling about a woman who'd spent the night with Jeanette Brady? That he'd chased her for miles with nothing more than instinct that "something was off" about her? Maybe he was making a big mistake. "Mine to make," he said aloud, and saw the bike turn off the main road. His pulse leaped. This would be the tricky part. Until now if she'd spotted him, she could tell herself that he wasn't following her, that his headlights were just part of the normal flow of early-morning traffic. But from the looks of the narrow gravel road onto which she'd turned, she would have more difficulty rationalizing that any vehicle behind her wasn't tailing her.

He drove past the spot where she'd turned onto the smaller road, glanced to see her taillight disappearing around a bend, then kept driving. Only when he rounded another corner did he initiate a quick U-turn, doubling back.

This time he didn't pass by the gravel road, but slowed and eased onto it. A sign reflected in his headlights: NO TRESPASSING. GUARD DOG ON DUTY.

Rolling down his window, he heard the whine of the bike's engine, lugging down it seemed, slowing. He couldn't risk keeping to the road, which was little more than twin ruts winding through thickets of fir and pine.

The sky was lightening enough that he could cut his lights as he continued driving slowly, all the while straining to listen. Soon enough the motorcycle's engine was cut. Immediately he eased off the gas and parked in the middle of the lane as there was no shoulder. Stealthily he opened the door, grabbed his stake-out bag and service weapon, then started jogging, following the road, wondering what the hell he would find. Running through drifts of fog and slippery puddles with the canopy of branches above him, he moved quickly, around several turns until he spied a cabin, not much larger than his own, set in a clearing and ringed by mossy-barked trees. A motorcycle was parked on the front porch. No dog in sight.

Still, he surveyed the area.

Two windows were patches of light that shone bright in the gloom of the forest. Whoever was home was up, and he saw no reason now not to walk up to the door and knock. At least he'd know what he was dealing with. He took the two steps in one stride and pounded loudly on the front door.

Nothing.

The house seemed to go incredibly still. No sound, not so much as a footstep from within could be heard.

No warning growl or scrape of paws on the floor.

Lucas waited.

He strained to hear even the slightest sound, but the only noise was the sigh of a soft breeze rustling the fir needles overhead and the soft murmur of wings—bats on a final forage before daylight settled in. Sweating a little, he knocked again, more loudly this time, and when the door wasn't immediately opened, he yelled, "Police. Open up." Pistol in hand he flattened himself against the side of the house just in case whoever was inside came out blasting a shotgun. Obviously whoever lived here didn't want to be disturbed.

Muffled voices reached his ears, but he couldn't make out the words.

Still no sound of a dog.

The voices stopped.

Footsteps approached.

Jarringly, the door opened.

His heart clutched and for a second he was thrown back in time. Elle Brady, or her damned doppelganger, stood backlit, in the doorway.

Bernadette sat in the passenger seat and wished to high heaven that she had a gun or some kind of weapon. Her little Honda, Annette at the wheel, was speeding down 101, closing in on the access road to the camp, the woman in the back seat never flinching but holding the gun steady in her gloved hand, ready to fire point-blank at Annette's back.

"What do you want?" Bernadette asked, and snuck a peek at Naomi Dalton. She'd aged in twenty years, her beauty having faded with time and, Annette suspected, her own bitterness.

"It's not what I want," Naomi said, "it's necessary. Payback."

"You're the one who sent the texts?"

"See, you are clever. Not just a pretty face after all."

"You will pay? What's that mean? I don't understand."

"Nor do you have to," she said, and to Annette, who had eased off the gas, "Keep driving."

"What are you going to do?" Annette asked,

and her voice shook, tears drizzling from her eyes.

"Just take care of business. Okay. The turnout's up ahead. Slow down."

Annette did as she was told, driving into the lane leading to Camp Horseshoe.

"The police will be here," Bernadette said, hoping to waylay whatever plans Naomi had in mind. "They're going to search the beach. To look for more bodies."

"I don't think so." A tone of satisfaction had entered her voice. "They're busy at the hotel, with that nasty business of Jo-Beth Chancellor and Tyler Quade."

"Leroy," Annette said. "Her name was Leroy."

Naomi muttered, "Whatever."

The Honda bottomed out on the hump between the ruts and Naomi said sharply, "Be careful. Unless you want to be shot right now!"

Annette threw her sister a panicked look. She'd driven to the camp without incident, but she was frantic, biting her lower lip, sweat beading on her brow, blinking against the tears that collected in her eyes.

Bernadette, too, was fighting panic, wondering how to stop this madwoman. Her heart was racing, fear in the form of adrenaline fueling her pulse. Somehow, someway, she had to fight back, to turn the tables on Naomi. God, was the woman homicidal? Bernadette had seen her anger before, had noticed a cold calm she was able to force upon herself, but this? Kidnapping? Possible murder?

They rolled into the parking area in front of Columbia Hall and, as Naomi had predicted, there were no other cars around. The camp was deserted, the broken and boarded windows, sagging roof, and general sense of despair of the decrepit buildings heightened in the fog.

"It's too bad about this place," Naomi said as if she'd sensed the grinding dreariness of the area. "It used to be so beautiful, you know. It once held so much promise." Her voice was almost wistful before she cleared her throat. "But that was a long time ago. A very long time ago. Before you all showed up and the trouble began. You know, if you"—she turned her attention to Bernadette—"if you wouldn't have come here, Lucas would never have ended it with me."

What? This was about Lucas? No. "What're you saying, that you were in love with Lucas?"

"What I said was you coming here was the start. The start of the end. For me." From the back seat, she poked the muzzle of the gun against Annette's shoulder. Annette visibly started. Naomi ordered, "Hand me the keys. And both of your purses."

Annette reached for the ignition switch but hesitated. "Just let us go."

"Can't do it."

"Why?" Bernadette asked.

"What are you going to do?" Annette was shaking. "Kill us?"

"What do you think?" she said. "All of us, we're going to have a big campfire, kind of just like the old times, remember?" She gave a little laugh. "But trust me, no one's going to be singing 'Kumbaya.'"

Bernadette's blood turned to ice.

Annette screeched now in a full-blown panic, "What? You're going to what? Start a fire. Oh, Jesus, burn us?"

Naomi hit her with the pistol. "Shut up! Give me the keys and your purses."

"No! Annette! Get out! Run!" Bernadette yelled as she yanked the keys from the ignition and Annette opened the car door. Bernadette hurled the keys hard, straight at Naomi's face, then in one swift motion opened her door. The keys struck Naomi in the eyes and she howled, screeching to the heavens. "Aaaauyyyrrrh!"

Annette was already out of the Honda. "Run! Just run!" Bernadette screamed.

Shrieking in pain, Naomi fired.

Blam!

A blast shattered the back of the seat, the bullet screaming past Bernadette's ear as she threw herself out of the car, rolled to her feet, and took off at a sprint.

She heard another blast and prayed that Annette was okay as she dived around the corner of the rec center and hoped to put distance between herself and the deranged woman who'd kidnapped them. What the hell did Naomi want?

To kill you. And Annette. And possibly the others. Run, Bernadette! Run like you've never run before.

She dove into a copse of saplings before she remembered her phone. Still in her back pocket! Fumbling, still running in the half-light of breaking dawn, she stumbled through the trees and prayed she had a signal.

Within two seconds she was able to punch out the numbers for 9-1-1. As the operator answered, she yelled, "This is Bernadette Warden. I'm at Camp Horseshoe south of Averille and a woman, Naomi Dalton, is trying to kill me and my sister, Annette Alsace! Send help! Now!"

"Do you have the address?"

"No!"

"Stay on the line—"

"I can't. She'll hear me! Just send someone to the camp south of Cape Horseshoe! That old church camp off of Highway 101! Tell Detective Lucas Dalton!" she said, and spied a shadow darting through the trees.

Naomi!

"Dear God, send someone now!" She clicked off and ran headlong down the path that led to the old chapel. The roar of the ocean was in her ears and the smell of salt spray filled her nostrils, raw fear propelling her. The trail was overgrown, vines and brambles cutting into her skin, cobwebs brushing her face. She thought she saw Naomi in every shadow of the forest, around each tree trunk. And Annette, where the hell was Annette?

Breathing hard, she doubled back, hoping that she'd drawn Naomi away from her sister.

Why? Why was this happening? Why did Naomi hate them enough to want them dead? It wasn't just about losing Lucas to Bernadette years ago. No, no . . . that didn't make sense.

It doesn't have to be logical. You're dealing with a homicidal maniac!

Heart in her throat, Bernadette turned onto an overgrown side trail, stubbed her toe on a rock, and paused, gathering her wits, trying to slow her breathing, hoping to figure out a way to save them. The sun was starting to rise over the eastern hills. A good thing, or bad? How much time did they have before the police arrived? Good Lord, where were they?

Barely daring to breathe, she poked her head around the bole of an old-growth Douglas fir and froze when she spied a figure slinking through the forest. A woman's silhouette in the rising mist. Friend or foe? Annette or Naomi?

Bernadette couldn't take a chance. Heart hammering, she slowly crouched and silently reached around her, fingers scrabbling through the dirt and weeds, brushing against something slimy before she felt the jagged outline of a rock, the only weapon she could find.

It wasn't much against a gun.

Nothing in fact.

But she clung to it as if it were a lifeline and straightened just in time to see the figure heading in her direction. Her heart pumped crazily, beating so hard she was certain whoever was nearby could hear.

Heart in her throat, nerves strung tight as piano wire, she poked her head around the edge of the trunk and squinted into the sunrise.

Nothing.

Just plays of shadow and light in the thick woods.

Where did she go?

Dear God, where?

She peered around the other side of the bole and thought she spied the woman again, this time hiding behind a huge, jagged stump.

Annette!

Her sister spied her as well and then, to Bernadette's horror, gathered herself to run away from her cover.

"No!" Bernadette mouthed, shaking her head violently, then screamed, "No! Stay back!"

Blam!

A shot blasted through the forest.

Annette's body bucked and she squealed in pain. In horror, Bernadette saw her sister fall to the damp forest floor.

Chapter 42

The Coast Range Mountains
Elle
Now

"Elle?" Lucas said, even though he knew in his heart this young woman couldn't be Eleanor Brady.

Glowering at him, she shook her head, platinum hair fanning around her face. "No." Light spilled onto the porch and she eyed him suspiciously, her gaze taking stock of his battered face. "Man, you look like shit."

"And that's about how I feel."

"Let him in," a weak voice called from within.

The girl turned her head and yelled over her shoulder. "Are you sure, Mom?"

"Yes." The faint voice was so damned familiar. *Elle.*

Giving Lucas a once-over, the girl said petulantly, "I don't think it's a good idea."

"For God's sake! It's over, Rebecca! Let him in."

Rebecca?

"Ooookay." Reluctantly, the girl, the spitting image of Elle, opened the door wide enough so that Lucas was able to step into a rustic cabin not much larger than his own. A kitchen ran along one wall, a battered table separating it from the living area that was dwarfed by a massive fireplace. A fire burned within the blackened grate and a long couch stretched along one wall. Upon the cushions, covered with a mound of blankets, lay a woman.

Elle.

Not dead.

Not a ghost.

Very real and very sick.

"I can't believe it," he said. "After all this time, you're alive?"

"Barely." Her mouth twisted at the irony of it.

"But what happened to you? Why'd you disappear? Where did you go?" He was astounded that he was really seeing her again. Had she been here all the time, in this cabin not twenty miles away from the town where she'd grown up?

"This may take a while," she admitted.

"That's okay," he said, though he did feel the pressure of time. "Jeannette? She knows? She had to. You"—he looked at the girl—"you were there, that's where I saw you."

"So you followed me here," she said as if she'd already figured it out. "Shit!"

"Rebecca!" Elle reprimanded. She was propped up by pillows and in front of her was a coffee table strewn with magazines, an array of pill bottles, a water bottle, and several boxes of tissues. Pale and thin, her face drawn and showing wrinkles, age taking its toll, though obviously some kind of illness added to her frail state, she forced a sad smile.

"Hello, Lucas," she said, barely moving. "I figured you'd be showing up." She pushed herself a little more upright and winced with the effort. "What with all the commotion, you were bound to find us out."

"Us?" he repeated, looking at the girl again. "And by commotion, you mean the murders? Of Monica and now . . ."

She looked up at him. "One of the counselors, I'm guessing."

"Jo-Beth," he said, though he probably should have waited until the department released the information, even though enough people knew because of Kinley Marsh and the rest of the ex-counselors being involved.

"This is your daughter?" he asked.

"Oh, yes." She said it as if she expected him to know. "Rebecca."

His eyes thinned as he studied the younger woman. "The girl in the coffin."

"What? Oh, yes." Elle sighed and rubbed the fingers of one bony hand with the pads of her other. "That."

"Yeah. 'That.' Why? Why did you send out the text?"

"That wasn't me."

He believed it. The place looked like a time warp to 1970. Aside from one portable bubble-faced television with rabbit ears, the place showed no signs of technology. No wireless router, no satellite dish, no cable connection that he'd seen, not so much as a digital clock glowing in a corner. Elle, and whoever lived with her, was one of those people who survived pretty much "off the grid," though she did have some electricity. But not so Rebecca, he suspected. "You?" he asked. "Why?"

"Not me either."

Obviously there was at least one piece he was missing in this puzzle.

"What happened to you, Elle?" he asked, feeling the heat from the fire.

"First of all, that's not my name." She sighed with an effort. "I go by Caroline now. Caroline Brown. Don't ask me why, it just sounded good to me at the time that I needed to come up with a new identity, which I did after I left Averille. It's amazing what you can buy in Portland if you need it."

"That's where you got it?"

"A friend of a friend of a friend. That kind of thing. Once I had my new ID, I moved to Oakland, wanted to be in the Bay Area and San Francisco." She fluttered her fingers. "*Way* too pricey."

"But why?"

"Because of Rebecca, of course."

Her daughter snorted.

"And you came back because?"

"She got sick, A-hole," Rebecca cut in. "Why do you think?"

"Shhh! We don't need that kind of language."

"But he is. He's the guy who dumped you, right?" With a surly snort, she stared at Lucas as if he were the worst kind of snake. "You dumped Mom when she was pregnant and took up with that skank Bernadette Alsace!"

"Pregnant? Then?" he said, and mentally did the math. "Wait a second, how old are you?"

"Almost nineteen. That's right, Sherlock. I could be your fuckin' daughter."

"Rebecca, stop that!" Elle dissolved into a coughing fit, and Rebecca, who had been standing near the door, was at her side in an instant, offering water and tissues and swearing under her breath. "You need to be in a hospital." She looked over her shoulder at Lucas. "Maybe you can talk some sense into her."

"They'll just put me in some kind of nursing facility." To Lucas she said, "Stage four. Terminal. Nothing they can do, and I don't want to be trapped in a room that isn't my own, probably with some terminal roommate." The coughing subsided and she dabbed at her lips with a tissue. "I'm fine here," she assured him. "And it's where I want to be."

"Stubborn old thing," Rebecca muttered, but she said it with fondness. To Lucas, her attitude was still bristly. "I said, you 'could' be my father. I know all the history, but you're lucky. You're off the hook. You're not my daddy. Just my fuckin' brother."

"Your what?" The girl had to be yanking his chain, but she looked dead serious and satisfied to have delivered the news to him. "Brother, but . . ." The dawning was like being thrown into a frigid cave, a jolt so severe, every muscle in his body tensed.

"Oh, Lord," Elle said.

"What's she talking about? Her brother?" But he guessed the truth and felt sick inside. "Jeremiah? You were—?"

"It was payback. To Naomi. For being with you." YOU WILL PAY.

The message cut through his brain.

Rebecca said, "This is one fucked-up family. Literally."

"But you . . ." Lucas said, staring at Elle. "You went along with it? Or did he—?"

"What? Rape me? Oh, no!" She was vehement in her denial, her head scratching against the pillow as she shook her head. "No, no, it was nothing like that. Believe it or not, Lucas, your father, he always liked me. He was nice to me. Kind. Told me I was beautiful and that you were a fool. It was what I wanted to hear."

Sighing loudly, she stared at the fire. "I guess I thought I would get a little payback myself, against you, but it didn't turn out that way. And then . . . As I was thinking I'd made a horrendous mistake, that my life was over anyway and I might as well end it, I went up to Suicide Ridge."

"You jumped into the ocean and survived?"

"Not quite," she admitted. "I wasn't alone on that ridge." She shivered. "I was pushed off, by the very man to whom I'd turned. The man who had been so kind, so nice."

"Jeremiah?" he whispered, and nearly threw up.

She closed her eyes. "He . . . He wasn't thrilled at the prospect of being a father again, the scandal and all, you know. And things weren't great with Naomi; he couldn't give her any reason that would make her appear the victim if they divorced. So I ended up in the ocean and when I didn't die, when I didn't drown and hypothermia didn't get me, I washed up near Arch Cape." She stared into the fire, as if reliving those harrowing moments, as if she were in another place and another time. "I stole some dry clothes from a dryer on a back porch and tried to figure out my life. The next night I thought I'd return to the camp to confront Jeremiah and you, to tell everyone the truth."

"And that's when you were seen," he said.

"I guess. I didn't know it at the time, but I heard about it later." She brushed a strand of wheat-blond hair from her eyes. "I thought better of the idea, decided I needed to start a new life. My father . . . he would have killed Jeremiah and probably shunned me if he'd found out. The situation would have been intolerable." She frowned slightly. "I guess I was a coward." She coughed again, then cleared her throat. "I hitchhiked to Portland, hooked up with some people who knew how to keep their mouths shut, and decided to keep my baby. It's been Rebecca and me ever since."

"But your mother knows?" he said.

"Now." She turned away from the fire to look at him, her eyes pained. "Because I got sick. I had to come back and she promised she'd keep my secret because of the life insurance she and Dad had taken out on me. The benefit had been paid long ago, and it seemed impossible for her to return it. The money was long gone."

"But still . . ."

"It's what we all decided."

"So what's with the haunting?"

"Naomi's idea," Elle said.

He tried to put the pieces together in his mind. "Naomi?"

"She saw Rebecca one day, noticed the resemblance, and got suspicious. Like you did today, she followed Rebecca here. She'd been pissed at me when she'd found out that her husband and I had been involved in an affair, but over time, she'd let it go. Probably because she was divorcing Jeremiah anyway. It wasn't like I was the first person he screwed around with, and I certainly wasn't the last. Naomi herself knew all about that," Elle added. "Right? I mean, she knew from the other side of the coin what it was like to be the other woman. Wasn't she involved with your father while he was still married to Isabelle?"

"Yes," he said, remembering his mother.

Elle nodded. "Anyway, it was Naomi's idea to have Rebecca 'haunt' the town and especially Jeremiah. You know, to mess with him. With his head. By that time they were split, and she thought he was screwing her over in the divorce by holding on to the property her father had owned."

"He was."

"Rebecca agreed. Thought it was fitting, I guess. Maybe it was her way of getting some of his attention, the daughter he never wanted." She sighed, the flames of the fire reflecting on her even features. "So, she was in."

"Served the old bastard right," Rebecca said, her mouth pinching at the thought of her old man. His old man. "I need a smoke."

"Don't! Honey—" But the girl was out the door before Elle could put up any kind of argument. Through a window facing the porch, Lucas watched as she lit up and drew deeply. Another half sister, he thought, like Leah. All of them were fathered by the same son of a bitch.

Leah.

He cringed inwardly at the thought of how his sister was going to react to the news of her parents' involvement in the scandal. Then again, she was used to it, had suffered through their divorce and heard the ugly accusations and heated arguments between Jeremiah and Naomi for most of her adolescence and all of her adult life.

"You have to testify, Elle," Lucas said, turning back to the woman he'd once thought he'd loved. "About Jeremiah trying to kill you."

"Too late." She shook her head and glanced up at him. "What good would it do?"

"It's the truth. Justice."

Her smile was weak. "I wouldn't make it to the trial. The doctors are giving me weeks, Lucas. Not months and certainly not years." Clearing her throat, she said, "No, Jeremiah will have to deal with his Maker when his own time comes. God will be his judge."

"But you can't let him get away with it!"

"Nothing I can do. Really. You have to accept that."

The fire popped and hissed, the smell of wood smoke heavy in the air, and Lucas wanted to rant and rail, to shake her, to somehow convince her to stand up and fight, but as he saw the pain in her eyes, noticed how gaunt she was, he couldn't do anything more than apologize.

"I'm sorry," he said. "For my part in this."

She waved him away. "You were a teenage boy. You fell in love with me, until Bernadette came along. As for Naomi, that . . . well, I won't lie. That's messed up, Lucas. Really messed up. Your own stepmother? Because she was hot? Sexy? Or to get back at your dad?"

"I don't know."

Her lips twisted a little. "I suggest deep psychological counseling." Then she laughed and the laughter turned into a coughing fit. She doubled over and scrabbled for a tissue. He handed her the box and felt like hell.

"You need to see a doctor."

"Trust me, I've seen more than any person should," she said, finally taking a deep breath. "Just do one thing for me, okay?" she asked, and he was already nodding, guilt for how he'd treated her and guilt for surviving and being healthy while she was so obviously ill, convincing him not to ask what she wanted. She continued. "Tell me you'll help look after Rebecca when I'm gone. Mom's agreed, but she's older and . . ." She started coughing again, doubling over in spasms.

That was it! She was too ill to make any decisions on her own. "You're going to a hospital. Right now."

"What? Oh, no, no, no! Lucas, please don't . . ."

But he was already dialing 9-1-1 when Rebecca, smelling of tobacco smoke, returned.

"What's the address here?" he demanded as his call connected, and Rebecca rattled it off automatically, her anger dissolving as she saw her mother struggling to breathe.

"Are you okay?" she asked anxiously, kneeling at her mother's side, taking hold of one bony hand. "Mom?"

"Of course she's not okay! Look at her." He hung up. "An ambulance is on its way. Ten, maybe twelve minutes." He wished it would arrive faster.

Rebecca was still rubbing the back of her mother's hand with her thumb. "She'll just discharge herself. She's done it before."

"Fine, but she's going. Now." He'd had it with pussyfooting around. "And you," he said, changing the subject abruptly. "You want to tell me why you dressed up and laid in a coffin for Naomi to take a picture?"

"She paid me a thousand bucks," Rebecca said, her eyes flashing as she straightened and let go of her mother's hand. "I thought it would be fun. Y'know? A kick."

"A kick?" Lucas repeated, and shook his head as he kept one eye on Elle, who had settled back against her pillows, some of the fight knocked out of her. "And you've been 'haunting' the area, right? Tore your dress at Crown Creek?" He was anxious, needed answers. Wished to high heaven the ambulance would appear.

"Stepped on a damned berry vine, ripped the dress, and cut my ankle. How'd you know?"

"Honed powers of detection," he said sarcastically. She was starting to piss him off.

"Yeah, sure."

Maybe he should cut her a break, but he couldn't stand the thought of Elle lying here, dying by inches, while her daughter at Naomi's prodding was getting her jollies by scaring the townspeople and visitors. For what? So that Naomi could exact some sort of revenge against Jeremiah? So that Elle could? Hell, so that Rebecca herself could?

Where the hell was the ambulance? Elle was lying peacefully now, her eyes closed, her breathing regular, but she needed medical attention and a clean environment, not this smoky, drafty cabin.

His phone chirped and he saw the number for the station appear on his screen. "Just a sec," he said, and stepped away from the couch as he answered. "This is Detective Dalton."

"We've got a situation," a dispatcher told him. "Nine-one-one just took a call from Bernadette Warden, who claims she's at a local camp near Cape Horseshoe. She says a woman identified as Naomi Dalton is shooting at her and her sister, Annette Alsace. Deputies are responding."

Shooting? His heart nose-dived. Bernadette? Naomi? "I'm on my way!" he said, fear galvanizing him. He spun on his heel and ordered, "Stay with your mother."

"Why? What's going on?" Rebecca demanded as he flew through the door. "Lucas!" she said, following him. "What is it?"

"All hell's breaking loose!"

He took off at a dead run down the lane and through the trees to his Jeep. Once behind the wheel, he flipped on the ignition and hit the gas, reversing until he found a spot wide enough to turn around. He cranked on the wheel and floored it. Tires spinning in the mud, the Jeep fishtailed, then straightened.

Daylight was stealing through the forest, seconds ticking off. What the hell were Bernadette and Annette doing at the camp? Why was Naomi shooting at them? Nothing was making sense, no matter how he analyzed it.

He was twenty minutes away, maybe thirty.

Too long for any kind of gun play.

"Son of a bitch," he growled, punching the accelerator and driving like a madman. He had to get there. Fast. But deep in his heart he feared that he was already too late.

Chapter 43

Camp Horseshoe
Now
Bernadette

Noooo!

Through the trees Bernadette watched Annette fall, her body convulse as she hit the ground.

Naomi was stalking her, pistol trained on Annette's unmoving body, ready to kill her if the first bullet hadn't taken her life.

No, no, no!

Bernadette couldn't let the monster murder her sister! Annette could already be dead, but there was a chance she was still alive.

"Stop!" Bernadette yelled, showing herself, her fingers clenched around the wet stone. Naomi's head snapped to attention and, spying the older Alsace sister, she turned the gun on a new target.

A slow, wicked smile crept across her face, changing what had once been a beautiful visage to something evil and sick. "So there you are. Willing to give yourself up for your sister?" She kept walking toward Annette's body, though she kept the gun trained on Bernadette, who was twenty yards away. As she passed Annette, she gave the unmoving body a kick in the ribs and there was no scream of protest, no response whatsoever. "Such heroics."

Bernadette's heart sank. Her sister was probably dead. She blinked against an onslaught of tears. How had it come to this?

"You know, I should shoot you right now and then finish off your sister if she isn't already trying to break past Saint Peter at the pearly gates." With a quick glance at Annette's body, she frowned. "Probably a waste of a good bullet, though." Emotionless, she said, "But I don't think I can carry you both back to the hall." As if that were her largest problem right now. Not Annette's life-or-death situation, not whether or not to kill Bernadette, but how to pack out a body. "So you"—she waggled her gun at Bernadette— "you do the work for me. And drop that pathetic rock. You're not going to hit me with it."

Bernadette hesitated, so Naomi pointed the nose of the pistol at Annette's unmoving form again, as if she really were going to shoot her in the back of the head.

"Okay, okay! Just don't. Okay? I'll . . . I'll do it." She was panicking inside, all of her senses on alert, her muscles tense, her mind screaming that the madwoman was going to kill both Annette and her.

Unless Bernadette could somehow outsmart her until the damned cops arrived. Where the hell were they?

"Let's go, then." Naomi pointed the gun at Annette again. "Pick her up."

Steeling herself, forcing her brain to remain calm and functioning while expecting a bullet to hit her square in the face, Bernadette obeyed, but she kept her eyes focused on Naomi as she made her way to Annette's side.

Remarkably, her sister was still breathing, though the spreading stain on the back of her shirt was more than worrisome. "She needs a doctor!"

Naomi snorted a laugh. "I think it's a little too late for that."

"No, you have to give yourself up. She's alive. You haven't committed murder yet . . ." But she didn't know that. What about Elle? Or someone else? "It . . . It will go easier on you if you turn yourself in."

"Oh, sure. Like maybe to Lucas?" she said, her smile twisting into an ugly snarl, blood smeared from her eye where the keys had hit her. "You think he'd help his ex-stepmother out? The woman he dumped for you?" And there it was: the hatred. Aimed straight at Bernadette. "Give me a break."

Oh, God. Annette, I'm so sorry. So, so sorry.

"Haul her to the rec center," Naomi ordered. "Now."

Wondering if she were causing Annette more harm than good, still trying frantically to come

623

up with a scheme to save them, Bernadette leaned down and pulled her sister to her feet. Unconscious, Annette collapsed, and with an effort Bernadette caught her and carried her fireman-style through the forest. Sunlight was piercing the shadows now, chasing away any lingering patches of fog that still lay near the ground. Morning birds were starting to chirp, the rush of the sea ever present, but Bernadette barely heard anything other than the wild beat of her own heart and the footsteps walking steadily behind her, snapping twigs and scuffing at gravel as they crossed the parking lot to Columbia Hall, a place they'd gathered a lifetime ago, a warm building where they'd sung songs, told stories, gossiped, and listened to sermons . . . and a place where she would catch a glimpse of Lucas, feel his gaze on her back, catch him looking at her. God, how she'd loved him.

Now, she had to push any sense of nostalgia aside. She had to concentrate. Couldn't let Naomi win. Staggering under Annette's weight, she played up how difficult the task was, gasping for breath, stopping every once in a while, stalling for time.

Where are the police?

Where is Lucas?

God, how long had it been since she'd made the call?

Isn't anyone coming?

No! Bernadette, you're on your own. It's up to you to save Annette and save yourself.

How? Oh, God, how can I get us out of this horror?

She nearly tripped with the immensity of the burden.

Think, Bernadette, think. You can't let this bitch kill you and Annette in cold blood. You can't. There has to be a way out.

"Up. On the porch," Naomi yelled.

Bernadette pushed herself. Up the first step, then the second, the rotting boards giving a little as she carried her sister toward the main door of Columbia Hall. She was on the porch when she smelled it: the distinctive scent of gasoline.

Her heart nearly stopped and she fell against the building, the terrifying odor filling her nostrils. "What have you done?" she asked, but the question was rhetorical. Obviously Naomi had doused the old rec center with gas.

Dear God, this monster meant to burn them. Alive? Dead? Either way, Naomi was going to torch the place with the Alsace sisters trapped inside.

As if she'd read Bernadette's mind, Naomi said, "You see the beauty of this is that I used Jeremiah's gas can, his fingerprints are all over it. And I'll hide it, but not too well, so the police will find it."

"This is crazy! Naomi, you can't do this!" She turned to face the woman holding the gun. There had to be a way to wrench it from her, to save them. "The police," she said, stalling for time, hoping beyond hope to reason with her, to get through to her sense of decency or at least self-preservation. "They'll figure it out and you'll go to prison for the rest of your life."

"Oh, no, no, no." She was shaking her head, so damned sure of herself. "All they'll know is the fire was set by arson, and it will make sense that he set it as his investors, thanks to my scheme, have backed off and the place is heavily insured. And then there'll be the murder charges when two bodies are found in the rubble. As for this gun?" She held it up in her gloved hand. "Registered to Reverend Jeremiah Dalton." She laughed. "Such a man of God. Did you know that he knocked up Eleanor Brady, then tried to kill her? That's why she jumped off the ridge."

What? Elle pregnant? With Jeremiah's baby? And dead . . . No, wait, she'd said 'tried' to kill her. His attempt was unsuccessful?

Bernadette's head was spinning, her legs threatening to give out.

Naomi, waving the gun, prattled on. "But Jeremiah didn't count on the fact that Eleanor survived. Not only that, but she came back here with her daughter to haunt him. Such good payback," she said, while Bernadette listened and tried to find a means of escape, the scent of gas nauseating. "Karma. What goes around comes around and all that . . . Okay. Enough. We're wasting time." She opened the door of the rec center, a door she must've unlocked when she'd poured the gasoline over the porch. "Inside!"

At that second, Bernadette thought she heard the distant scream of sirens. Faint, but distinctive.

Naomi froze. "What's that?" And a bit of panic appeared in her eyes. "Sirens?" Sure enough, high and reedy, the sirens were getting louder. "But it's too soon . . . Maybe there was an accident." But she was starting to get nervous. "On the highway, it happens all the time . . ."

Bernadette shifted while Naomi's attention was split.

"Oh, God . . . how do they know?" she asked.

As if she suddenly understood, Naomi's eyes widened and she glared at Bernadette. "You called? But how? Your purse and your phone . . . in the car." She glanced at the Honda. "I saw it!" Agitated, she stepped behind Bernadette and shoved the muzzle of the gun into her back. "Inside. Now!" Naomi pushed hard and with the added force and the weight of her sister, Bernadette stumbled forward, landing on the old wood floors, Annette moaning as she fell.

With a horrifying click, the lock was engaged.

She and Annette were alone.

Move! Get out of here.

She scrambled to her feet just as she heard another sickening snap.

Oh, God. A lighter? Oh, God, please, no!

"Annette, get up!" she screamed, terror riddling her body. Her sister groaned.

Whoosh!

The sound seemed to echo to the rafters as the gasoline caught fire.

Oh, dear Jesus. "Come on!" Bernadette cried, as if her sister could hear her. She raced to the door and twisted the handle. Nothing! The deadbolt! But its handle had been removed. Couldn't be twisted. "Damn!" They were locked inside!

No way! She couldn't give up. Just let them burn to death.

Flames crackled as the old wood ignited.

No, no, no!

The smell of smoke seeped through the cracks and she witnessed flames licking hungrily at the walls.

Frantically she dragged Annette across the dusty floor, past the old conversation pit and soaring fireplace, toward a back entrance. Maybe Naomi had forgotten one of the locks. If only!

The first door, the one that opened to a hall-way leading to the dining area, was locked fast.

More fire. More smoke.

The room was getting hotter and hotter. Darker

and darker. Bernadette was coughing, sweating, praying to find an exit. She checked the French doors leading to the back of the building, facing the stables, but they'd been boarded over years before and now flames were burning through the plywood.

Annette moaned and coughed.

She was still alive!

"God help me," Bernadette said, and crawled along the floor, smoke filling the cavity of the hot rec center. Over the growing roar of the fire she thought she heard sirens screaming, closer now. If only.

Please, please, please.

But even if the fire department was on its way, it could be minutes before they arrived and broke through the walls and . . . no, no, no. She had to save them both. Somehow! Through the smoke she spied a window that was broken, but not completely boarded, a small window on the side of the building. Reeling, blinking through the smoke, unable to draw in a breath without coughing, she found a café chair near the old fireplace. Leaving Annette, she used all of her remaining strength to pick up the chair, then as fast as she could, she ran with the back of the chair pointed in front of her and charged at the window.

Bam!

Craack!

The glass splintered, jagged pieces still sticking to the frame. She fell backward with the force; then, using one of the chair's legs, she kicked out as many of the remaining shards as possible, though the fresh air only seemed to feed the fire. More flames surrounded the window! Licking, roaring, eager to burn.

Barely able to see through the smoke, her eyes running with tears, she found her way back to Annette and started dragging her sister. Her legs threatened to give out and her lungs burned. Annette groaned as Bernadette, fighting smoke inhalation and the urge to pass out, hauled her sister closer to the window, their only chance of escape.

"Come on," she ground out. "A little help here, Annette."

But her sister was dead weight and the temperature in the room was searing, her skin seeming to curdle as she reached the window.

Rather than risk Annette being cut, Bernadette propped her up and flung herself through the opening. Feeling the scrape of glass, shards penetrating her flesh, flames singeing her skin, she landed on the porch, felt it tremble. Fire climbed up the posts to the roof.

Still she reached back through. "Come on, Annette," she said, leaning against the searing window ledge, grabbing Annette beneath her arms with both of her own hands and dragging her sister through the window, tugging her body across the porch and onto the gravel parking lot. Her nose was filled with smoke and she was still coughing, but she forced her legs to move toward the woods, faster and faster, away from the raging inferno as it roared and rushed, threatening the surrounding woods.

All the while she expected to see Naomi, pistol raised, ready to shoot her dead.

Instead she noticed headlights cutting through the forest. She went weak in the knees. At last! The police! Thank God! She wilted against the side of a tree only to see through her tears and coughing fit that it was not a vehicle from the sheriff's department arriving. It was a huge silver SUV speeding into the lot, spraying gravel.

"No!" she whispered aloud as she recognized Reverend Jeremiah Dalton behind the wheel. "Oh, please, God, no."

"What the hell's going on here?" he roared, staring in horror at the growing conflagration. The rec center was totally engulfed, heat radiating from it in waves, flames climbing through the charred roof, black smoke billowing to the morning sky. "Oh, dear God, no! No!" Frantically he looked around, as if he could find some hose or fire extinguisher to futilely battle the blaze. His gaze landed on his ex-wife, who stood only steps away from the inferno. She was staring at the blaze as if mesmerized, appearing unafraid of the heat, unconcerned about the smoke.

"For the love of God, Naomi, what have you done?" he yelled over the crackle of flames, roar of the fire, and scream of ever-approaching sirens. "What the hell have you done?"

"Just giving you what you deserve," Naomi said, turning to face him, as if she'd known he would arrive. The blood on her face had dried, but her eye was swelling shut as she raised her arm to show the pistol in her grip.

"Are you insane?" he cried, and started to turn away from her just as she fired.

Pop! Pop! Pop! Shooting in rapid succession, she managed a cruel smile that widened as his body jerked with each bullet's hit. "Go to hell, Jeremiah," she said, the flames behind her shooting to the sky while a cop car skidded, siren blasting, lights flashing, and ground to a stop, spraying the thin gravel. "Go straight to hell!"

Behind the cruiser Lucas's Jeep slid to nearly plow into Bernadette's Honda. He was out of his SUV in a second, waving wildly at her. "Get back—get back!"

Two deputies, weapons drawn, opened the doors of the cruiser and, using the doors as shields, yelled at Naomi. "Police! Drop your weapon! Ma'am, put the gun down!" a burly, red-haired deputy ordered.

As Lucas made his way to Bernadette, Naomi, still in whatever weird trance had overtaken her, stared at the cops, the fire growing and shifting like a great crackling curtain behind her.

"Drop your weapon!" the deputy ordered again.

"What?" she said as something inside the old building exploded. The earth shuddered, smoke and debris spit from the rec center, and with the crack of ancient timbers, the roof collapsed. Naomi was knocked off her feet by the blast. She flew through the air screaming.

Craaack!

She landed on the parking lot, her head hitting with a sickening thud, her body crumpling not five feet from her dead ex-husband.

As fire trucks roared through the trees, rumbling, deep sirens bleeping, the timbers of Columbia Hall gave way. One heavy, charred beam tumbled from the building and landed hard, pinning the bodies of both Jeremiah and Naomi Dalton.

Lucas reached Bernadette. Shielding the sisters with his body, he wrapped one arm around Bernadette. "It's all right," he said. "Everything's going to be all right."

"Never," Bernadette whispered, watching the shallow rise and fall of her sister's chest. "It'll never be right again."

"Trust me," he whispered, and kissed her temple. She melted inside, wanting to believe him, to think that this terror would somehow be banished.

"Get back!" a fireman yelled, screaming at them and waving an arm frantically.

"Come on." Lucas picked up Annette with one arm and led Bernadette quickly away from the inferno, down the lane, past emergency vehicles. Other trucks and ambulances arrived, the firemen fighting the blaze, the wounded carried off by EMTs.

Bernadette's last image of Camp Horseshoe before she, along with her sister, was hauled into an ambulance was of the blackened, skeletal frame of Columbia Hall, flames reaching skyward being doused by geysers of water, and she realized that the nightmare, should she and Annette survive, was finally over.

Epilogue

Averille, Oregon
Now
Bernadette

Bernadette was at a crossroads.

As she stood on the porch of the Hotel Averille with Lucas at her side and watched the women she'd become reacquainted with pack up and leave, she wasn't certain which path she would take.

Thankfully Annette had survived, the bullet

from Naomi's gun miraculously missing her spine and every vital organ. She would be laid up in a Seaside hospital for a few more days, but Bernadette, treated for superficial burns and abrasions, had been released and had decided to stay in Oregon until she could haul her sister home.

Both Naomi and Jeremiah had perished, which was no surprise and, Bernadette thought, well deserved. They had been miserable people who had been hell-bent on destroying each other. None of Jeremiah's children—Lucas, Leah, or Rebecca—seemed too torn up at his passing, though Leah, according to Lucas, was struggling with reconciling her mother as a cold-blooded killer. Her sons, David and Ryan Tremaine, appeared unfazed as to Naomi's homicidal tendencies and were already checking into the legalities of regaining the title to what was left of Camp Horseshoe.

But Bernadette felt her own future was uncertain. As she observed Jayla pile into her car to drive back to her family in Portland and Nell head out in her Subaru to Bend, where her fiancée, Tasha, was waiting, Bernadette saw no reason to hurry back to Seattle and her empty town home. Her job was waiting of course, and she had responsibilities. Still, she lingered.

Because of Lucas?

Absolutely.

Sosi had already taken off and was reuniting with her husband and kids. Reva, too, had left, though there were rumblings that a case involving a car accident from years before, where a woman died, was being reopened, and Reva might be charged with some kind of manslaughter.

Kinley Marsh had recovered. Fully. And no way was she surrendering any of her footage or Annette's diary. "Try a court order," she'd advised Bernadette when she'd broached the subject on Annette's behalf.

"It's my sister's diary," Bernadette had reminded her. She'd run into the reporter while Kinley was simultaneously checking out of the Hotel Averille while reading some text on her phone.

"Since when?" She'd looked up and her smug smile had said it all: Kinley Marsh, *NewzZone* reporter with more prospects in the wings, was back. Big-fucking-time. Her blog and stories had gone viral, and she wasn't about to let go of the fame she'd chased all of her adult life.

Now, Kinley, too, had driven off and Bernadette was finally alone with Lucas. "I was thinking," he said, taking her hand, "that you might want to stick around a while."

"Until Annette's released?"

"No, longer."

She glanced up at him and arched an eyebrow, but before she could respond, another car wheeled into the lot, a cruiser from the sheriff's department with Maggie Dobbs at the wheel. Spotting Lucas, she parked and headed up the flagstone walk to the porch.

"Figured I'd find you here," she said. "I wanted you to know that the DA won't be pressing any charges against Rebecca Brown for her part in the scam concerning Elle Brady. Nor her mother. Jeanette will have to deal with the insurance company that paid out a settlement on Elle's death, but nothing criminal is being considered at this point. And Elle . . . well."

"Yeah."

Bernadette understood. Elle was currently in Seaside, in a home where hospice was seeing to her final days.

"Tyler Quade isn't getting off quite so easy, though. The DA is going to throw the book at him."

"Good."

"Oh, and more news. It turns out that Pete Denver and Dustin Peters are one and the same. He's giving his statement in Boulder as we speak."

"So that just leaves Waldo Grimes as unaccounted for," Lucas said as a breeze rattled through the trees near the street.

"Yeah, still MIA. I think he made it to Astoria and with the help of some unknowns sailed out of the country. As easy as it seems to be to come up with a new identity, I'm guessing that Waldo did just that."

"Or he died."

"Better yet," Maggie said. "Some things in life have to remain a mystery, I guess." She eyed Lucas. "So you coming back in, or what? The case you were thrown off of is essentially solved, but that doesn't mean the Neahkahnie Sheriff's Department is no longer. The last I heard, you were still on the payroll."

"Just taking a couple personal days," he said, and she nodded, her gaze sliding to Bernadette. "The sheriff knows."

"Okay, good. Just, please, come back, okay? Garcia's fine, but . . . he kind of cramps my style. Too 'by the book' if ya know what I mean."

"I do."

"Figured." Maggie took her leave then, crossing back to her car and driving off.

Bernadette glanced up at him. "Personal days?"

"Uh-huh."

She couldn't help but grin a little. "Just how personal?"

"Well, that's an interesting question," he said, glancing at the sky before returning his gaze to hers. "One I thought you might just be able to answer."

"Maybe I can." She nodded and then, surprising him, she wrapped her arms around his neck and kissed him. Hard. Her lips molding to his, her body pressed along the length of his. When she lifted her head and saw the surprised look on his battered face, she winked at him.

"Whoa! What was that all about?" he asked.

"Payback, I guess." She smiled. "I thought maybe we should just get that out of the way."

Center Point Large Print
600 Brooks Road / PO Box 1
Thorndike, ME 04986-0001 USA

(207) 568-3717

US & Canada:
1 800 929-9108
www.centerpointlargeprint.com